June 6, 1997

Happy Birthday Monica

Many More

Mail

THE
SYSTEM

D0368789

GEORGI
ARBATOV

TIMES 𝕿 BOOKS

RANDOM HOUSE

An Insider's
Life in Soviet
Politics

THE

SYSTEM

Library of Congress Cataloging-in-Publication Data

Arbatov, G. A.
    The system : an insider's life in Soviet politics / Georgi Arbatov.—1. ed.
        p.   cm.
    Translated from the Russian manuscript.
    Includes index.
    ISBN 0-8129-2274-3
    1. Arbatov, G. A. 2. Soviet Union—Politics and government—1985–
3. TSK KPSS. Politburo—Biography. 4. Soviet Union—Officials and
employees—Biography. 5. Soviet Union—Politics and
government—1953–1985. 6. Soviet Union—Foreign
relations—1975–1985. 7. Soviet Union—Foreign relations—1985–
I. Title.
DK290.3.A73A3 1992
947.085'092—dc20
[B]   91-51034

Manufactured in the United States of America

9 8 7 6 5 4 3 2

First U.S. Paperback Edition

FOREWORD TO THE AMERICAN PAPERBACK EDITION

This book, published in Moscow in 1991, was first published in America in 1992 with extensive changes and additional commentary to clarify for an American reader what may have been evident to a Russian one, and to take into account some of the events in my country's volatile political evolution.

The stormy events of the past year have not altered the book's main theses and conclusions or my views of the system itself—the reasons for its self-destruction and the possibilities of creating a more or less normal society. I have updated a number of passages and the book's final chapter to reflect the most recent changes.

For me 1992 was a year rich in emotions, new hopes, and new disappointments as I participated in the debates and struggles that raged over Russia's economic and political future. The process of political and societal changes that began in the first post-Stalin years is still unfolding, and the future remains uncertain. But I do hope that before too long we will get out of the deepening crisis and move faster and more forcefully along the path of democratic reforms. If this hope is not realized, it will be a tragedy for my countrymen and myself and a crisis for the whole world. But while there is life, there is hope.

Translation and editing have involved considerable time and effort—and not only on my part. Thus I would like to begin with deep thanks to those who did so much to make this edition possible: to Peter Osnos and Ruth Fecych at Times Books. I have known Peter for many years, but only good fortune brought us together again at the right moment and at the right place. I often felt guilty at having made Ruth work too hard, but she never lost her temper or her dedication to the book and contributed a lot to it. To Vladimir Pechatnov and Sergei Plekhanov, who helped me a lot both on the Russian original and the American version. To the translators, John Glad and Oleg Volkonsky. I am deeply indebted to Strobe Talbott for his friendly advice and ruthless criticism—both were tremendously helpful. And, of course, my sincere gratitude to Esther Newberg of International Creative Management, who took the risk to try to sell this book, having given me a few lessons in this high art.

I hope American readers find that this book provides them with a description of the Soviet system, of the political establishment, of some of the most dramatic events and struggles in my country. This insider's view belongs not to a dissident or an enemy of the system, but to someone who has lived and willingly worked within it, however critical of its many tenets he may have been. Why should it be of interest to Americans? Simply because, beginning from the 1940s, our two countries were as entangled with each other as Dr. Jekyll and Mr. Hyde (although we may have had different opinions of who was who), or as the hero of that great storyteller E.T.A. Hoffmann's famous tale of the man who became miserable when he lost his shadow.

Through these years we were first gallant allies and friends, then bitter rivals. The Soviet Union became the "evil empire" before changes overtook our confrontation. In 1987 I warned Americans that the worst thing we could do to them would be to deprive them of their enemy. I didn't add something that I understood all along: that by doing so we would be depriving *ourselves* of an enemy as well.

Life without an enemy is a totally new experience for societies and states that went through the Cold War. We are now in the process of adjusting to this new life and new frame of reference. The adjustment will be easier if we get to know and understand each other better, and I hope that this book will make a small contribution to that critical enterprise.

The System covers a long period—from the days of my youth under Stalin to the aftermath of the August 1991 coup attempt, which finally destroyed the Communist political structure and led to the state's demise, and the first very dramatic years of reforms, which have led to even deeper crises. But its main focus is on political developments in the hard years, from the death of Stalin to the rise of Gorbachev, when our society was striving to recover from the grim legacy of Stalinist totalitarianism. I think this was an important and instructive period, which if appreciated may help readers to better understand the possible options for my country in the future.

In the course of my career, I worked with six top Soviet leaders: closely with Brezhnev, Andropov, Gorbachev, and Yeltsin, at some distance with Khrushchev and Chernenko. It was these associations which on the eve of the August coup attempt became the focus of attacks on me from the extreme right and some military circles which charged me with, among other things, "opportunism." My answer to the accusation that I was culpable because I had been an adviser to six leaders is simple: I didn't choose them, they chose me. I tried my best to be helpful—tried because to be called upon to work with the leadership was a temptation to which mortals are susceptible and because I wanted to help my long-suffering country.

Judging by the fact that the former Soviet Union is today in the midst of disintegration and reorganization, my colleagues and I did not succeed in many things we tried to do. I can be held responsible only for my own advice and not for the total policies of any particular leader. Still, I will not run from responsibility for whatever I did. Though I recognize certain mistakes, I hope that I have not lived and worked in vain; but on this point, readers must judge for themselves.

For more than a quarter of a century I have been the director of an institute (a think tank, in American terms) set up to study the United States and Canada. Having been to both countries dozens of times, I have acquired many friends and—as you might expect—some enemies. This book is an attempt to explain not only myself but also my country so that Americans and Russians can understand each other better and find it possible to live together on this small and fragile planet, which is our common home, the only home granted to us by God or good fortune—whichever one chooses to believe in.

INTRODUCTION
by Strobe Talbott

Now that the Union of Soviet Socialist Republics no longer exists, a question nags: What was it, really, this extraordinary political concoction that sprawled across eleven time zones, occupied a sixth of the earth's surface, devoured or starved to death tens of millions of its own citizens, yet also launched the first man into space, earned a reputation as a superpower, and preoccupied the United States and much of the rest of the world for over forty years?

In retrospect, it appears that the U.S.S.R. was never really a viable country. Its 280 million people spoke too many languages, nurtured too many grievances against one another, and strained too hard against the ties that bound them to the "all-union" capital, Moscow. Nor did the U.S.S.R. really qualify as a empire, even though that's what it was often called, most famously by Ronald Reagan. Its supposed metropole, Russia, turned out to be just one more sullen inmate in the prison of nations, one more would-be independent state that wanted out when the doors were finally thrown open.

So if the Soviet Union was neither a country nor an empire, what was it? The best word, I think, is the one that Georgi Arbatov uses as the title of this book: the U.S.S.R. was a *system*, which my dictionary defines as "a complex unity formed of many, often diverse parts subject to a common plan or serving a common purpose."

In the strange case of the U.S.S.R., the plan in all its dimensions—Five-Year Plans, Gosplan, and so on—was no good. It turned out to be monstrously inefficient, incapable of providing sufficiently for the material needs of the people. It was also destructive of the human factors, notably individual initiative and self-esteem, necessary for the successful functioning of a society and a state.

We all knew that. Yet most of us who tried to understand the U.S.S.R. were profoundly wrong about it in one crucial respect. We believed that, bad as it was in so many ways, the system was good at one thing—its own preservation; that was the common purpose the diverse parts of the system served. Therefore the system would surely last for a very long time.

Then, on Christmas Day, 1991, the whole thing collapsed. In the end, contrary to what many of us assumed, the system proved inadequate even to the task of assuring its own survival. That was partly because some of its own custodians had chipped away over the years at the assumptions on which "Soviet power" was based. They reprogrammed the software of the system in myriad small ways, with the result that the hardware melted down spectacularly in 1991.

Hence the importance of Georgi Arbatov's memoir. He was a member of the Academy of Sciences, the Central Committee of the Communist Party, and the Supreme Soviet of the U.S.S.R.; he was an adviser to six leaders in succession, from Nikita Khrushchev to Boris Yeltsin. Yet his career illustrates that the system was never as monolithic as it seemed from the outside. Behind the façade of uniformity, there were different currents of thinking, competing schools of opinion, and what he calls "oases of creative thinking."

Arbatov depicts his career as a journey from one such oasis to another, with long, often difficult, stretches of desert in between. The first oasis was a think tank where he worked in the late fifties for the Politburo ideologue Otto Kuusinen. Arbatov found him willing to let his subordinates question Marxist-Leninst dogma and its utility in the real world. Under Kuusinen, Arbatov also had more access than before to information about the outside world. "It was probably then," he writes, "that I first understood how backward we all were."

In the mid-sixties he found another mentor in Yuri Andropov, who was in charge of a department in the Central Committee that advised the Politburo on foreign-policy issues. Arbatov's account of their dealings is especially intriguing, since Andropov, who went on to head the KGB and then to succeed Leonid Brezhnev as general secretary of the Party, played a key part in the rise of Mikhail Gorbachev.

Arbatov vividly conjures up the atmosphere of those years, the so-called era of stagnation. However, the portrait he paints of Brezhnev does not quite match the puffy, doltish, slack-jawed image that lingers in our minds. Brezhnev, says Arbatov, initially impressed his subordinates as a reasonably skillful manager, less inclined to bullying and out-right cruelty than his predecessor, Khrushchev, and "endowed with common sense, not prone to take extreme or hasty decisions."

However, as Brezhnev's health deteriorated—in addition to the usual troubles brought on by age, he was addicted to sleeping pills and often showed the effects on the job—he fell increasingly under the influence of hard-liners who were, among other things, furious at "deviations" in Czechoslovakia. They prevailed in what he calls the "battle for Brezhnev's soul," with the result that the Warsaw Pact crushed the Prague Spring in 1968. Arbatov remembers being "overcome by a burning shame" over the invasion, but he acknowledges the limits of how far he and others in the Party were willing to go: "Even the bravest of us did not have enough fortitude to raise the issue of complete freedom of choice for the 'satellites.' "

Since soon after the first Russian Revolution of 1917, academic experts on politics and economics had always been on shaky ground. Marxism, after all, was the only recognized approach to both political science and economics. The Academy of Sciences did its share over the years to enforce orthodoxy and stifle free thinking. Its members were not immune from persecution in the worst of times or from subtle pressures in the best of times. They all conformed and compromised to one degree or another.

In 1968, Arbatov established an "oasis" of his own: the Institute for the Study of the USA and Canada, under the umbrella of the Academy of Sciences, but he was no less immune from the pressure to conform than the others. Still, members of the academy had more freedom of maneuver than most other citizens, for the obvious reason that their expertise was deemed useful to the state. Arbatov makes the case in this book that he and a few others used that freedom, especially in the seventies and early eighties, to engage in cautiously critical inquiry and to nudge the U.S.S.R.'s leadership toward more constructive policies.

Among the others who carved out similar niches for themselves and played similar roles were Oleg Bogomolov, the director of the Institute for the Study of the Economics of the World Socialist System; Alexander Yakovlev, the director of the Institute of World Economics and International Relations from 1983 to 1985; and Nikolai Petrakov, an economist at the Central Economics and Mathematics Institute. There are also "hard scientists," like Roald Sagdeyev, the director of the Space Research Institute, and Yevgeny Velikhov, a physicist and vice president of the Academy of Sciences.

Bogomolov encouraged Communist reform in Eastern Europe, partly in hopes that it might set off sympathetic vibrations within the U.S.S.R. itself. Yakovlev argued for a policy of greater openness that became known as glasnost. Petrakov pressed for an end to the centralized command economy. Sagdeyev and Velikhov questioned some of the more dubious and dangerous tenets of Soviet military strategy.

As for Arbatov's own role, he recounts how he and his allies in the Party and government had to contend with conservative opponents who accused them of "leniency toward imperialism" and "bourgeois pacifism."

Cyrus Vance and other American officials who have dealt with Arbatov over the years give him credit for helping to lay the ground for East-West détente in general and, more specifically, for the Soviet Union's engagement in strategic nuclear arms control negotiations with the United States.

"I know from my own experience," says Vance, "that Dr. Arbatov was one of those who, in the depths of the Cold War, was always looking for ways to diminish the danger of a military confrontation."

On other issues that arose in the seventies and early eighties, Arbatov recalls having lost numerous intramural struggles. For instance, he remembers trying, unsuccessfully, to convince Brezhnev that the U.S.S.R. should not be drawn into the postcolonial civil war in Angola. That conflict between proxies of the two superpowers became an intense point of U.S.-Soviet contention. It accelerated the demise of détente in the seventies and fanned support for the Reagan defense buildup of the eighties.

During the Brezhnev years, it often seemed on the surface that virtually nothing was changing in the U.S.S.R. But Arbatov makes the case that reform-minded academicians were preparing the way for eventual reform: "The level of thought developed in these 'oases' improved, enlivened, and modernized the intellectual atmosphere of our society and—this is the main thing—sowed seeds that sprouted only many years later" in the form of glasnost, perestroika, democratization, and new political thinking.

No wonder, then, that after he rose to the pinnacle of power in 1985,

Gorbachev brought Yakovlev on to the Politburo; Bogomolov, Petrakov, Sagdeyev, and Velikhov all became important Kremlin advisers.

So did Arbatov. He accompanied Gorbachev to his first meeting with
Reagan in Geneva in 1985. During the next summit, in Reykjavík, Ice-
land, in October 1986, Arbatov was a member of the Soviet arms-control delegation. At the Washington summit in December 1987, Arbatov
was the Kremlin's principal traveling "spin doctor," responsible for trying to put the best face on Soviet policy. A year later, he was part of the
official entourage when Gorbachev gave a landmark speech at the
United Nations, and again in December 1989, when Gorbachev met
George Bush aboard a ship off Malta. Arbatov briefed Gorbachev for
each of these meetings.

Even when he made his debut as a presidential adviser, he was already
a familiar figure in the West. From the late sixties until the mid-eight-
ies, Arbatov was the insider whom many of us outsiders knew best. He
traveled frequently to the West and presided over a kind of clearing-
house for Westerners visiting Moscow. His institute's headquarters in a
converted eighteenth-century mansion on Khlebny Pereulok ("Bread
Lane"), just behind Kalinin Prospect, was, for many of us, our home
away from home. It was there that we checked in the morning after our
arrival at Moscow's Sheremetyevo airport; it was there that we sat in
dark offices and conference rooms, sipping tea from glass tumblers in
metal holders, nibbling cookies, and probing for hints about what was
going on in Soviet society and government.

I dubbed our hosts the *institutchiki*. My friend and colleague Michael
Mandelbaum, the director of East-West studies for the Council on Foreign Relations, called them the Boys from Bread Lane. As those nick-
names suggested, we felt something other than total reverence for Arbatov and his colleagues and something less than total pleasure in their
company. They were, on the whole, gracious and helpful, but they were
also our sparring partners in what were often rather tedious and exas-
perating debates.

American visitors to the institute, particularly those inclined to voice
disagreements with their own government back in Washington, would
try to break the ice with evenhanded little speeches about how U.S.-
Soviet relations were in a dreadful state and both sides were to blame.
The Soviets would reply, in effect and often in so many words, "Well,
you're half right: your side is to blame."

Once, in 1983—when the Reagan administration and the Kremlin leadership, then under Arbatov's longtime mentor, Yuri Andropov, were almost literally not speaking to each other—my patience with this dreary pattern gave way, and I threw down a challenge: "All right, let's see if one of you can name so much as a single thing that your side may have done wrong in the past seven years that has contributed to the problem."

There was a long, awkward pause. Finally, one of the *institutchiki* spoke up: "To be frank, our side probably has made a mistake in underestimating the capacity of the United States to shift course erratically and to plunge into periods of hysteria. Or, to put it differently, we overestimated the stability and continuity of the American political system."

I recall this exchange here because it captures one aspect of the way the institute interacted with its guests—that is, with a mixture of accessibility and stonewalling.*

Arbatov himself often seemed to personify those qualities in his guise as a spokesman for the Soviet point of view. He relished engaging in old-fashioned polemics and scoring debating points off the American administration of the time. His pugnacity, combined with his command of English, made for lively television, so he became something of a regular on the evening news and the weekend talk shows in the U.S. The White House, particularly in the first Reagan term, considered him the worst sort of apologist for the evil empire and therefore a public menace on the airwaves.

In 1981, during one of his many visits to the U.S., the State Department cut short his visa in order to prevent him from being interviewed by Bill Moyers. The following spring, he was granted permission to return to the United States on the condition that he promise not to meet with "representatives of the mass media."

Throughout this period—the bad old days of United States–Soviet relations—Arbatov's institute, both in opening its doors to visitors from the West and in sending abroad its flying squads, gave American students of the Soviet Union far more exposure to the logic, such as it was, of Kremlin policy than we would otherwise have had. For their part, Arbatov and the other Boys from Bread Lane had a chance to test their

---

*Indeed, I've recounted it before—in *The Russians and Reagan* (New York: Vintage, 1984), pp. 13–14.

government's positions on skeptical foreigners as well as an opportunity to hear about U.S. policy, and politics, from Americans.

And it was a good thing that they did. I sensed that even though our hosts at the institute were sticking fairly close to the official line during those debates, they were also listening. They ended up absorbing a good deal about Western political institutions and values, which they later put to use once perestroika was under way. Furthermore, we visitors had to keep in mind that the *institutchiki* were running genuine risks in even carefully qualified and supposedly confidential expressions of disagreement with their government's policy. More than once Arbatov was called on the carpet for telling Americans things that found their way back to the KGB or the Central Committee.

During the years I was in and out of the house on Bread Lane I heard numerous stories about how Arbatov had shielded colleagues from the wrath of the system. In 1966, the lawyer Boris Nikiforov refused to sit on the puppet jury that was supposed to deliver a guilty verdict against the persecuted writers Andrei Sinyavsky and Yuli Daniel. The KGB and the judicial authorities mounted a campaign to disredit Nikiforov, including trying to frame him with compromising documents. Arbatov rescued him from further trouble and brought him onto the staff of the institute as its principal expert on American law.

In 1968, Vladimir Lukin was a young journalist in Prague when Soviet tanks crushed the reformist government there. Lukin protested the invasion and probably would have paid with his career, perhaps his freedom, if Arbatov had not brought him into the institute. Arbatov protected him on several other occasions as well.

In 1982, Igor Kokorev, a senior research fellow at the institute, wrote a play commemorating the iconoclastic poet and folksinger Vladimir Vysotsky for his son's school. Someone in the audience reported him to the authorities. Arbatov intervened and prevented Kokorev's expulsion from the Party and from his job at the institute.

When the hard-liners within the Party and the KGB attempted a coup d'état against Gorbachev in August 1991, Arbatov was out of the country, but he was immediately in close touch by phone with his colleagues, who were among the first members of the Moscow establishment to rush to Yeltsin's barricaded headquarters in the Russian parliament. Arbatov, meanwhile, worked to mobilize foreign opposition to the coup.

Since then several alumni of the Arbatov institute have emerged as important figures among the powers that be in the post-Soviet period. Among them are Georgi Mamedov, the deputy foreign minister of Russia responsible for the U.S. and Canada, and Yuri Matyukhin, the head of the Russian Central Bank. Others went on to establish oases of their own or to hold influential positions at existing ones. In 1987 Arbatov's longtime deputy Vitali Zhurkin founded the Institute for the Study of Europe. Boris Milner became deputy director of the Institute of Economics; and Alexander Kislov, deputy director of the Institute of World Economics and International Relations.

Lukin, meanwhile, had already risen to the position of senior policy planner in the Soviet Foreign Ministry, then became an important member of the Russian parliament and a key adviser to Yeltsin. In early 1992, Yeltsin named him Russian ambassador to Washington. I saw Lukin in Moscow on February 7, 1992, shortly before he left to take up his new post. He called his political and diplomatic career "a temporary abnormality" and said that "basically I'm still from the [Arbatov] institute."

Over the years, the institute performed three important services: it made available to the leadership analysis and advice that were often better than what it received from the Party apparatus and the ministries; it kept open a channel to the West that was especially useful when government-to-government relations were strained; and it offered sanctuary to a number of intellectuals who had run afoul of the authorities and who were later able, thanks in part to Arbatov's protection, to emerge as constructive figures in the reforms of the eighties.

That is why when Peter Osnos, the editor of this project, asked me to write an introduction, I agreed. However, I wanted to check my own impressions and judgments against those of someone who had known Arbatov even longer than I had, so I called Marshall Shulman, a renowned scholar of the U.S.S.R. and, on several occasions in his distinguished career, a counselor to U.S. secretaries of state, including Cyrus Vance.

"Arbatov," said Shulman, "is a leading example of what I call the within-system modernizers who made the Second Russian Revolution possible. In any study of how all these extraordinary transformations came about, we'll have to pay attention to the part of people who, in different ways and to different degrees, went about their business [while] all the time pressing for a more modern political culture. Some became dissidents and suffered accordingly. Others, like Georgi Arbatov, worked from within. That's not to diminish the heroism of the ones, like Andrei Sakharov, who chose a more courageous path. But there was an osmotic relationship between the two groups—those who broke openly with the system, and those, like Arbatov, who, when it was not popular to do so, advocated a more rational foreign policy and a more enlightened society."

Shulman's assessment resonates with something that Arbatov writes about the Second Russian Revolution: "I pay tribute to the courage and fearlessness of those who, like Andrei Sakharov, risked taking an uncompromising stand. These people were heroes, even martyrs. And if they had not done what they did, I think the changes in our country would not have gone forward so quickly. But had it not been for the many hundreds and thousands who in their daily work inside the system, in routine skirmishes, tried to stop the pressure of Stalinist conservatism and defended and promoted the ideas of democracy and peaceful economic reform, the process of revitalization would not have been possible at all."

None of this is to suggest that Arbatov or any of the other Boys from Bread Lane foresaw where the small changes for which they were personally responsible would lead. Nor is it to suggest that they intended to contribute, however incrementally, to the disintegration of the Soviet Union. Quite the contrary: as he states repeatedly in this book, Arbatov wanted to help the Soviet Union enter the twenty-first century as a strong, prosperous country as well as a "civil society."

In precisely that way, Arbatov's biography is very much of a piece with those of the men who brought about the big changes of 1985–1991: Yeltsin, Eduard Shevardnadze, and Gorbachev himself. All three, like Arbatov, were products, functionaries, and beneficiaries of the system. Yeltsin, it should be remembered, had been the Communist boss first of Sverdlovsk, later of Moscow. He did not resign from the Party until July 1990, when he was fifty-nine years old. Shevardnadze, long the Kremlin's proconsul in Georgia, remained in the Party until July 1991, when he was sixty-three. Gorbachev will go to his grave believing that his version of socialism, and the Soviet Union, were both good ideas.

None of these three aspired to being remembered as a liberator of

Eastern Europe, to say nothing of the Baltic republics—and certainly not to mention Ukraine. Their intention, until very late in the game (and, in Gorbachev's case, even after the game was over), was to improve and thus save the U.S.S.R., not to bury it.

Yet they set in motion forces that brought the system down. Yeltsin rode those forces back into power, sweeping Gorbachev aside. But they were essentially on the same side.

Arbatov was there with them, an ally in the system. He does not try to present himself as having been a closet capitalist or a sleeper agent for Jeffersonian democracy. Nor does he claim to have experienced a Saul-on-the-road-to-Damascus conversion from a believer in the Soviet system to an advocate of the Western one. Quite the contrary: as he makes clear in several passages, particularly in the postscript, he is sorry the system did not yield to reform and that it collapsed; he wishes that what he regards as its positive features, and parts of its basic structure, had been maintained, though in a radically changed and improved form. I suspect Arbatov himself is not sure whether this was actually possible.

Nonetheless, the pages that follow reflect a genuine intellectual odyssey, the evolution of a member of the *nomenklatura,* or ruling class, who "for a long time . . . did not give much thought to the monstrous absurdity" of the system, but who came to recognize many of its flaws and tried to make a difference for the better. "It is no accident," Arbatov writes, "that Gorbachev and his comrades-in-arms who started de-Stalinization and perestroika came from inside, and not from outside, the system. These also were people burdened with their past sins and with limitations imposed by that very system."

Clearly, Arbatov is referring here not just to Gorbachev but to himself. His story is an important part of the record of our time.

Washington, D.C.
April 23, 1992

CONTENTS

THE SYSTEM

1 Why I Have Written This Book

My life in politics, journalism, and scholarship coincided with a crucial and fascinating but extremely difficult period of my country's history. There were considerable hidden risks and dangers for those who took part in the tumultuous political events of the time. Everything that befell the Soviet Union in the past fifty or sixty years affected my generation: those born at the beginning of the 1920s, who are now at the biblical threescore and ten.

We remember the 1930s, years of oft-repeated hymns of praise to the heroics of building a new existence. My contemporaries and I knew of the "triumphs" from newspapers, books, films, and politicians' speeches, but also (and there's no point in denying this) from eyewitnesses, including our relatives and their friends. We also remember the dark side of the 1930s, one of the grimmest decades in the history of our long-suffering nation: the liquidation of the Kulaks, the campaign to eliminate the country's most populous class, the peasants, through collectivization, and the famine that followed. And of course, we remember the mass repressions of, in the end, tens of millions of people. Most of my contemporaries were witnesses to this, and it is an era they will never forget. I can judge from my own experience—the repressions were not something distant or abstract for me. They mowed down the parents of my friends, and the friends of my parents, including my relatives and, eventually, my father. But, by the standards of the times, my father was extremely lucky. He did "only" one year (while the investigation went on and then expecting a retrial) under the infamous Article 58 of the Criminal Code (concerning treason and counterrevolution), and was then released, as noted in the tribunal's findings, for "lack of a committed crime." Nevertheless, right up until Stalin's death, my father—and I, to a certain extent—were consequently frequently mistrusted as politically unreliable.

Then, as the decade turned, World War II scored a direct hit on my generation. I went into uniform on June 21, 1941, literally on the eve of the German invasion of Russia. I was then eighteen, and soon became commander of a Katyusha rocket battery, but the war came to an end for me in 1944. By then I was a captain—and a second-category invalid of what we called the Great Patriotic War. I was discharged after I contracted severe tuberculosis, which before the discovery of today's medicines was almost always fatal. I was among the relatively few lucky people helped by contemporary medical techniques and surgery.

Next, as a student, then as an editor and journalist, I lived through the postwar ideological pogroms and the new outbreaks of political repression. By this time I understood much of what was going on: the lies, stupidities, and perversions of the state system ostensibly working for our benefit.

Finally an adult, formed by my past, I worked as an editor and journalist for the Central Committee of the Communist Party, then as an official of the élite Central Committee apparat, and still later as the director of an academic institute for political research. In these years I observed and experienced at the closest possible quarters the "recovery" from Stalinism. These were years of hope for the future, a time when the Party seemed at its most secure. In the difficult, controversial, and often agonizing process of "de-Stalinization," the nation moved toward what was intended to be normal life in normal conditions.

It is still difficult to write about all this in the past tense. Especially now, as the country is gripped by upheaval, I feel the social challenge, the pressure of responsibility. The feeling is physical as well as emotional, not only because of my official posts but, above all, because I am human, with my own personal characteristics and beliefs, and because I am a product of my times.

My proximity to so many important events, and the fact that I met and often worked with the most prominent political and social figures* of my time has led me to write down these observations and recollections. This long-standing urge became irresistible during the years of perestroika, when, at last, taboos were lifted and many of us had the opportunity to speak the truth however bitter, as we really saw it, and to deal with subjects that were previously forbidden. The writing proved more difficult than I had expected, and not only because it was hard to find the time. The social changes have come so thick and fast in recent years that we have been forced to reassess the past and the present, our notions of what is right, our values and judgments—and all of this has put greater demands on us and on what we write. Amid this continuous upheaval it was almost impossible to keep from inserting new additions and corrections.

My first drafts were written in 1987, but each time I went back to them, I had to rewrite almost everything from scratch. If you are a captive of habitual perceptions, opinions, and circumstances, this is a long, painful, and complex process. Not to mention the fact that I, like every other memoirist, was faced with two temptations: to settle old scores and in retrospect to make myself appear wiser and more honest and brave than I was. I hope that I have managed to avoid sacrificing truth to these temptations as much as possible. So, there did come a point when I finally got up the courage and did dot the last "i."

This is not because I now understand everything at last. I doubt that I do. But I do think it is extremely important that people like me—of my generation and experience—should start writing, compiling, and publishing a substantial history of the post-Stalin era.

Not that the subject of Stalinism or Joseph Stalin himself has been exhausted. That is certainly not the case. We sometimes forget that Stalin was in power for thirty years. And over forty years have passed since his death. I am convinced that our main historical mission over these

---

*Among them Yuri Andropov, Leonid Brezhnev, Mikhail Gorbachev, and Boris Yeltsin, as well as dozens of members of the Soviet leadership from the 1960s to the 1980s, and many well-known foreign political and civic leaders.

latter decades has been the recuperation and resurrection of society from the dreadful deformities inevitably bred by totalitarian dictatorship, starting at society's very foundations—economic, political, intellectual, and moral.

The recovery proceeded slowly until the dramatic era of perestroika. But that is not necessarily surprising.

History shows that totalitarian and despotic dictatorships always leave scorched earth in their wake. There are many examples of a long period in limbo or even of a collapse of state and society following such dictatorships. Indeed, it was not the so-called Eastern European satellites but our own country itself that may have been the ultimate victim of Stalinism.

The post-Stalin decades provided us with the experience on which we could build perestroika, fundamentally reorganizing a static society. So far, however, the attempts to describe, let alone understand, all that went on in those years have been pitifully scarce—just a few publications in journals and newspapers, read only by a relative handful of our people. Perhaps the only exceptions are Nikita Khrushchev's memoirs and the memoirs of his son.*

Naturally, even the publications that describe events of the post-Stalin era differ in their degrees of credibility, depth of thought, and literary merit. This is not the place for a critique, but the point is that despite their merits and faults, such publications are far too few. This particularly applies to the quarter-century after Khrushchev's ouster in 1964. Reports—mainly available abroad—about court proceedings and political intimidation of dissidents are interesting, but still they do not replace a fuller work of history. There is a great deal to be done on that score.

I don't know why publications concerning this very recent period of our history are still so scarce. I hope there will be more—and soon. My concern is that when the archives are opened, we may find that the number of documents will not be all that great. As far as we know, no detailed minutes were taken of debates and discussions in the Politburo in recent decades. Some of the most important decisions were apparently not even made at a meeting of the whole Politburo, but simply at an informal gathering of a few members of the leadership.

*Nikita Khrushchev, *Khrushchev Remembers* (Boston: Little, Brown, 1970); Sergey Khrushchev, *Khrushchev on Khrushchev* (Boston: Little, Brown, 1990).

And what has been said publicly or written was all too often far from the truth. During and even after the harsh Stalin era, people very seldom turned to letters, diaries, or journals (priceless sources of information in the past). Ubiquitous fear was the greatest obstacle to the keeping of such records, but the turbulent tempo of the time, its particular style, its frenetic way of life and thinking, did not create the right atmosphere for writing lengthy letters and diaries. In many ways, my people lost the habit of keeping accurate accounts of their lives.

For this reason, I believe that the remaining witnesses to the events of that watershed period, especially those who participated, should speak out, however humble their role may have been. I have often applied these arguments to myself to overcome not only natural inertia but also some inner psychological barriers erected throughout a lifetime of caution. I want to add right away that I do not have great pretensions. This book is, above all, my personal account of some important episodes in our agonizing journey toward the liberation of our political life since the death of Stalin, especially following the Twentieth Party Congress of 1956, when Stalin was openly denounced. But this is far from the whole story.

The fine Kirghizian writer Chingiz Aitmatov told of a legend (perhaps he created it himself) about the "Mankurts," people who from early childhood were deprived of the capacity for thought. Their skulls were tightly squeezed in strips of raw leather. This made them silent and obedient slaves. One of the most dangerous manifestations of Stalinism lay in the forceful, consistent efforts to castrate our people mentally and spiritually through merciless repression and total propaganda, to turn them into unthinking cogs of the totalitarian machine.

It proved impossible to implement this plan fully. Otherwise, neither the Twentieth Party Congress nor perestroika itself would have ever occurred to complete the transformation of society. But Stalin and his entourage managed to achieve a great deal in their years of domination, and this weighed heavily—not only on our culture and art, and on our social and natural sciences, but on the whole mentality and political behavior of our people to this very day.

If any more symbolic proof of Stalin's impact were needed, it was provided by the death of the "Great Leader" in March 1953. Our majority found itself transfixed by what soon turned out to be a deeply erroneous feeling of universal grief and by a completely irrational fear of the future.

Even some of our best writers were so overwhelmed by this feeling that
they proclaimed as their main task the glorification of the departed
leader so he would stay in the minds and hearts of people for many centuries to come.

The days when Stalin was lying in state witnessed a horrifying manifestation of mass hysteria. (I won't deny that this is not the way it
seemed to me then. I grieved like everyone else around me, with very few
exceptions.) The emotion turned into a real orgy of blood when hundreds, if not thousands, of people in Moscow were crushed to death by
the crazed crowd rushing toward the Hall of Columns to say farewell to
the dictator's embalmed corpse.

But the real mental and spiritual state of society was worse than any
symbols. Its inner impoverishment, a dangerous undermining of its intellectual potential, manifested itself quite vividly in the deterioration of
sociopolitical thought. In a word, the service record of theoretical creativity during the seventy postrevolutionary years was miserable, even if
the point at issue is only Marxism, which was reduced to the empty dogmas of Stalinism.

As to non-Marxist sociopolitical theory from abroad, its development
came to an end with the victory of the Bolsheviks in 1918. Everything
written outside the U.S.S.R. thereafter was portrayed as part of a conspiracy against Marxism-Leninism. Whole schools of philosophy, political theory, and economy became known to us only by the criticisms
leveled against them. Foreign literature disappeared into the depths of
the "special departments" of the libraries, where it was labeled as "classified." (The censor would stamp the document with a single hexagon,
with his personal serial number inside; this was known as a "screw" in
slang, or "double screw" for "top secret.") Even for specialists, access to
this literature was difficult. The rest of the population became familiar
with foreign thought only through the works of our critics. As a rule, it
was difficult to find anything on the bookshelves apart from denunciation, vicious epithets, and pure fabrications.

Soviet specialists, scholars, scientists, and students missed several important decades of world sociopolitical thought. I think that the consequences of this gap will continue to be felt for a long time to come unless
urgent steps are taken, including the publication of the works, teachings,
and concepts of the leading Western philosophers, economists, sociologists, psychologists, and political scientists of the twentieth century. The

people of this land need to be reeducated in all these areas. In the years since Marx's death, a Russian revolution has taken place (in fact, twice); the Austro-Hungarian Empire and the Hohenzollern monarchy have fallen. The Weimar Republic and the Nazi regime have come and gone. The destructive storm of World War II swept over Europe and Asia. Revolutions triumphed in China and a host of other countries. Colonialism crumbled. Nuclear weapons appeared. At least two scientific and technological revolutions have taken place. All social structures have changed, as have the political map of the world and the way of life of most people. At this very moment, the process is continuing apace.

But for more than seven decades none of these events had any practical impact on our sociopolitical thinking, with catastrophic results. We cannot avoid asking: How could this have happened?

I think it would be wrong to put the blame on Marxism itself. For many years before the Bolshevik revolution, Marxism developed as a flexible theory open to change, unafraid of forsaking old ideas and absorbing new ones. (In rereading the works of the "founding fathers," you are more inclined to take them to task for an excessive zeal for what was "new" than for their dogmatism.) It was Joseph Stalin who turned Marxism first into dogma and then into a religion. In addition, the old testament and then the new testament were taken away from the believers. By that I mean the true message of Marx's and Engels's works, and then those of Lenin. We were left with just one prayer book: Stalin's *A Short Course in the History of the Communist Party,* and a collection of articles and speeches of the "Great Leader."

Indeed, we have lived through a great tragedy, one of the greatest in history. In these pages I want to talk about some of Soviet society's first attempts to overcome the consequences of this tragedy, to free itself intellectually and morally. I want to describe the system that governed our society and shaped our thinking. This is my responsibility to myself and to the future of Russia. But I want to begin with some early personal history to help the reader understand who I am and what my family, my childhood, and my youth, including my wartime coming of age, were like.

2 My Family, My Youth, and My War

Beyond my grandparents, I know nothing about my genealogy. Genealogy in general is a privilege of the noble and the rich. I was descended from very common folk, and they usually do not show great interest in their distant ancestors. Besides, to keep track of them in the turmoil of constant change and movement so typical of my country during the last century would have been difficult. And not always safe. Who knows whom you might find among your ancestors? Maybe a counterrevolutionary or a priest, or somebody else who, by Stalinist standards, could spoil your career, maybe even your life—forever?

I will begin with a description of my family. My father died in 1954, a few days before his fifty-fourth birthday. I was a grown man of thirty, but I did not then understand how young my father was, and what a full and complicated life he had lived. I only realized this much later, as I began to overtake him in years. But from the time of his death and for a long while after, I could not get over a feeling of sharp regret, even guilt, that I had not talked everything over with him.

This feeling is probably common to everyone who has lost a loved one. Only after such a death do we suddenly realize how important the person was and regret each missed moment of his company.

My father was born in 1900 into a poor Jewish family in one of the outlying rural regions of what was then Yekaterinoslav Province (now it is called Dnepropetrovsk Region). His was a somewhat unusual family of Jewish peasants, people of the land and, as far as I can tell, not very successful ones. They were so poor that it was a joy when they managed to get my father into a vocational school in Odessa, where he began independent life at the age of seven. That was his "university." He talked little about his years there. After graduation, my father started as a metalworker at a foundry in Odessa. In February 1918, at the age of seventeen, he joined the Communist Party. (Like many of his contemporaries in those turbulent times, he began his political activity at a very young age.) Then he took part in the Civil War. When it was over, he lived the usual life of a Communist of those years: first he was transferred to Party work, then to administration, then back again. For some time he worked in a village; then fate took him to Kherson, where he married and where I was born in May 1923. A few years later my father was made director of a canning factory in Odessa, and in 1930, as was the practice those days, he was chosen, on the strength of a recommendation by a recruiting commission sent down from Moscow, to work at the Soviet trade mission in Germany.

In 1935, our family returned to Moscow, and my father started working for the People's Commissariat (as ministries were called at that time) for Foreign Trade. In 1938 he was removed, along with most of those Communists still not arrested who had entered the Party in the pre-Stalin years (he told me about this much later). He managed to find himself a job as administrative assistant director of the Lenin Public Library, the biggest library in the country. Then he drank of the bitter cup of the era—in one of the Stalinist purges he was arrested, accused of "counterrevolutionary sabotage," and imprisoned for one year. After his release from prison and right up to his death he worked in modest administrative jobs (his last one was director of a small construction company in the Forestry Ministry of the Russian Republic).

The fact that my father and I never had a chance to talk everything over was in no way due to an estranged relationship. Not at all. In spirit we were close and we spent as much time together as possible. I respected him deeply, sought his advice, and listened to his opinion. I sensed then, as I do now, that despite his lack of formal education, my father was a man of great knowledge, unusual intellect, and enviable talent. I remember from childhood how, to my surprise, he learned German within a few months, and later French with equal speed. (In 1935 we lived in Paris for four months.) He could also read English, and worked on translations of Friedrich Engels's correspondence.

All this notwithstanding, there were many subjects that my father categorically did not wish to discuss with me. One, of course, was Stalin. Others were the intra-Party struggles of the 1920s and 1930s, the mass repressions, the collectivization. He would say that he was sure that so-and-so of his friends or acquaintances, who had been arrested, was innocent, or that so-and-so had turned out to be a denouncer and had betrayed his friend. But he would never generalize or say anything about his own arrest except for intimate details about life in prison. Above all, he never made any comment about Soviet leaders.

Later, I often thought about the reasons for such caution. You could understand his circumspection while I was still a child. He kept information from me so that I wouldn't blurt out something to my friends, who might then pass it on. But by the time I became an adult and came back from the war, I was sure that he would trust me, and he did so implicitly. Nevertheless, for a long time he kept silent.

Only after the death of Stalin and after Lavrenti Beria's arrest did we start our heart-to-heart talks, though unfortunately they didn't last long—he died a few months later. Once, I asked him why we hadn't been able to talk like this before. He answered that with his long and hard political experience, he had found it tremendously difficult to keep his political and moral integrity. "I knew too much and have seen and witnessed too much," he told me. He did not want to shift the same burden to my shoulders in such difficult and dangerous times. It was getting harder and harder to combine everything you knew and understood with faith in some kind of ideal and to maintain a moral and spiritual balance. "I was afraid for you," my father said to me, "and of course for the whole family. If you had made a blunder somewhere, that could have been disastrous for all of us." That is why he preferred to remain silent. Or, as my mother put it on those occasions when she would let her thoughts and feelings show, he would "screw up his pellets." (My father had a habit of screwing up whatever he happened to be holding— pieces of paper, bread crumbs, and so on—into little pellets.)

To a great extent, intuition saved us both. He did not speak about

certain subjects and, without even fully realizing the cause of my restraint, I did not ask any awkward or dangerous questions. You developed a sort of political sixth sense. If you didn't have it, you were
doomed. Even by the age of fourteen or fifteen I understood perfectly
well that the authorities arrested and destroyed completely innocent
people who were loyal to their country. These were my parents' comrades and my father's friends. I thought it quite conceivable that they
could also arrest my father. Each night in 1937 and 1938 I went to bed
anxious. I even muttered a kind of secular prayer to myself: "Just don't
let them arrest my father!" We lived at that time in an apartment house
for employees of the People's Commissariats for Foreign Affairs and
Trade, and a few people were "taken away" almost daily. The parents of
at least half my classmates at school had been arrested, and the children
had to go through the disgusting and humiliating ritual of denying their
fathers or mothers. Two or three of my friends and schoolmates were
also arrested and convicted, although they were minors. A few others, as
I later found out, were recruited as informers.

When the heavy stone of danger was rolled back a bit after Stalin's
death, and with the first signs of change—the rehabilitation of the "doc-
tor-assassins," Beria's arrest, and the first mention in the papers of what
was still then an anonymous "personality cult"—my father began to talk
frankly for the first time. He spoke about the years that had left a very
deep imprint on his life, and through him, on me. I did not find out
from him anything beyond what everyone knows today. Probably there
were many things then that he himself did not know. People got out of
the habit not only of speaking about forbidden subjects, but even of
thinking about them. Maybe this was the instinct of self-preservation at
work. But you cannot hide all your thoughts all the time. When a person
is being constantly and professionally watched, sooner or later almost
anyone will reveal himself. I think George Orwell is right about this.

My father divided his contemporaries, members of the Party, people
who had taken part in the revolution and in what followed, into four
strict categories. The first were the fanatics. Such people, he used to say,
can probably belong to any movement, espouse any idea; this was not so
much a matter of convictions, but rather a state of the mind. Such people will be blind true believers no matter what. My father numbered
some of these among his friends, and I met some of them in our home.

My father told me that once he asked one, an official with Glavsevmor-put,* Pyotr G. Kulikov, a comrade since Civil War days, what was going on. How was it that people they both knew very well, who were bound-lessly loyal to the Party and the country, had suddenly become "enemies of the people"? He named a few names. In reply he got an angry tirade: "Arkadi, how can you, as an honest Communist, even think of things like that? You have to put your trust entirely in the Party and Stalin." That very same night Kulikov was arrested. By some miracle he sur-vived. By the time he came back from the camps my father was dead. Kulikov was rehabilitated, his rights were returned to him, and he retired as a respected "special pensioner." I often met and talked with him. In memory of my father I kept up good relations with him until his death. What amazed me was that despite everything he had been through he remained, if not quite a fanatic, then a blind believer to the end. And although he no longer deified Stalin, he rabidly defended the regime Stalin had created. Once, after a heated argument, I said to him, "Pyotr Grigoryevich, it was a mistake to put people like you inside a prison, but it was also a mistake to let you out. If you had the power, you would turn everything back to the 'good old days.'" He wasn't even of-fended.

The second category, according to Father's classification, was re-served for the ruthless and unprincipled careerists. They can adapt to any regime, and the harsher the regime, the greater their career oppor-tunities. There were such people in the Bolshevik old guard, who even had a long record of prerevolutionary Bolshevik activities, and plenty of them among those who joined the Party later. My father mentioned a few names. They are not worth repeating. They were not people who occupied any important positions. But a great number of those cynical careerists—such as Andrei Vyshinsky and some KGB bosses of the thir-ties—held responsible positions; quite a lot of them were elevated to top posts in the wake of the mass repressions, lies, and denunciations of the thirties.

The third group consisted of the "nonvicious cynics." They did not believe in anything, but pretended to be believers for the sake of their positions and careers. And career was their obsession. At the same time

*The Main Northern Sea Route Inspectorate, in effect a ministry that handled shipping and military matters.

they avoided dirty deeds as much as possible and were unprepared to forge ahead and tread on corpses. My father knew such people, but however tolerant, sometimes even friendly, he was toward them, he did not treat them with respect. When I asked about a specific friend of his, my father replied: "Most of them are neither heroes nor villains. They just want to live a better life, and we shouldn't despise those who try to do that without getting their hands dirty and destroying others."

Finally, in the fourth category were the "moderate believers," people whose beliefs were tempered with reason, who were loyal to the essential socialist ideas and were honestly prepared to devote their efforts to what they believed in. But they were not willing to trust whatever nonsense they were told by the leaders, and even less willing to betray others or to build a career on their bones. They were neither fanatics nor cynics. My father belonged to this group of people.

During the Stalin years one could, of course, encounter some real heroes, but they were few and far between. In answer to my question— Did my father and his friends believe in the hysterical campaign against the "enemies of the people," including the widely publicized trials of 1936–1938?—he said that in his heart he and, he was sure, many of his friends, did not. But they would talk about this only among their very closest friends. They soon realized, he said, that prisoners were being tortured, although at first they could not believe that not only confessions but false accusations against others were being extracted this way. Once, I asked: "Well, hasn't anybody ever protested, even some of the Old Bolsheviks who had been, one would have thought, through hellfire in tsarist times?" He said that very few of those said anything openly. At first, people were fooled into thinking that a great cause justifies any sacrifice, and by the time they woke up, it was too late to protest.

He told me (once again I kick myself for not having written down the name) about a Soviet trade representative to Japan who had just returned and came to a Party meeting at Narkomvneshtorg.* On the agenda was the expulsion from the Party of an "enemy of the people" and those who had not shown enough vigilance concerning him—that is, had not denounced him, betrayed him, or exposed him. The trade representative was witnessing this ugly procedure for the first time and sat and listened. Then he went up to the podium and made an emotional

*People's Commissariat for Foreign Trade, later renamed the Ministry of Foreign Trade.

and angry speech: "What's going on here? How low we've sunk! We're all cowards! Don't we know these men as honest Communists and our comrades? Won't anyone say a word for them? Disgrace and shame on us all! We can't go on living like this." After he finished his speech, there was a deadly silence, then a burst of applause, which, my father said, was astonishing in such an atmosphere of ubiquitous fear and psychosis. The speaker was, of course, arrested without delay as he left the Narkomvneshtorg building.

I know from our family friends and acquaintances that my father was regarded as a good and tolerant man. He was liked by many, including his cellmates in prison. He discussed this tragic year of his life only after Stalin's death. And I think he kept silent not because he was afraid that someone might find out that he had committed a breach of his signed statement of "nondisclosure" (demanded of everyone who was released from prison) but because, until 1953, he was simply not sure whether he (or perhaps I) might have to make the trip to Stalin's Golgotha again, and so he cast ugly memories of the past and premonitions about the future from his mind.

He was arrested at the end of 1941. Perhaps someone had suddenly remembered that he had worked in Germany (although only the sick imagination of the investigators of those days could have led them to suspect that he, a Jew, could have collaborated with the Nazis). The charge was counterrevolutionary sabotage and the tribunal* sentenced him to eight years. (Before the trial, father had already spent seven months in prison.) As my father recalled, the chairman of the tribunal (both my father and my mother remembered his name with reverence until their deaths, but I have forgotten it), having pronounced the sentence, immediately murmured under his breath: "Appeal immediately." In his confusion, my father asked: "What did you say?" Without saying another word, the chairman walked out of the courtroom. Of course, an appeal was made. The chairman reversed the sentence he had passed and ordered a new investigation. A few months later the case was retried, and in October 1942 my father was acquitted by the same judge for lack of evidence. (So even there, in the immediate vicinity of the gulag, one could come across a decent man!)

---

*I think it was the military tribunal of the Interior Ministry troops of the Volga Military District. During the investigation my father was brought to a prison in Ulyanovsk.

Father used to tell me about that year in prison without any bitterness, even with a sense of humor. There were about forty people in his cell. Among them were an Estonian former admiral, several generals and officers of the Soviet army, and some transplanted Muscovites.

We kept some of my father's souvenirs from prison: for example, a tobacco pouch, which one of his cellmates had embroidered on my father's twentieth wedding anniversary, using colored threads pulled out of a mattress; and a medallion with my father's profile made by some artistic convict out of moist rye bread. The medallion has been preserved to this day. It has virtually petrified, which says something about the quality of the bread.

Even after such an ordeal, my father did not lose his faith in the ideals to which he had devoted his life. I think that what helped him was the fact that he was a very active person, phenomenally devoted to his work. Even toward the end of his life he took each failure in his work to heart, and rejoiced in each success; living so intensely probably shortened his life. As far as I can tell, he was motivated by a sincere desire for justice and freedom, the absence of which he felt almost daily from his youth. He knew on what thin ice he and many others were treading and how quickly everything could end in irreversible tragedy.

My mother, Anna Vasilyevna, was a year younger than my father, but outlived him by twenty-three years. She was an intelligent woman, with a very strong, even harsh, character. Being the opposite of my father proved an invaluable asset.

Her parents were peasants. My grandmother was a hired laborer at Aksania Nova, on the estate of the famous German pioneers and landowners the Pfaltz-Feins. My grandfather was born in Grodno Province and, after serving as a soldier, went off to the southern Ukraine, where my grandparents met. Then they moved to Kherson and lived in a peasant cottage on its outskirts. They lived very humbly and were illiterate all their lives, but they saw to it that all their children received a high school education. My mother became a primary-school teacher, and for some years worked with homeless children.

The hardest year of my mother's life was 1942. I was at the front; my father was in prison. She and my three-year-old brother rented a room in a little house in Ulyanovsk during the evacuation. They stayed there for almost a year. She went to the local villages to barter clothing and other personal belongings for food to feed my brother and gather enough of the permitted allotment of food and tobacco to bring to my father. During one of the worst winters of the decade she carried the packages across the frozen Volga in bone-chilling cold and then climbed the long staircase up the steep bank on the opposite side of the river to the prison.

From her accounts I could vividly imagine the tremendous hardships of her life at that time. Although I had never been to Ulyanovsk, I instantly recognized it in Andrei Sakharov's memoirs. Not far from where my mother and brother had lived was a cartridge factory, where the outstanding scientist and great citizen worked and made his first discoveries and inventions. Again a paradox of life: the future winner of the Nobel Peace Prize started his career by making and inventing weapons. We owe him a debt of gratitude for both; he helped to win the war. And later he became the conscience of the best part of our society, and a symbol of honesty and courage. I had great respect for him for many years. But only now do I understand just how significant his role in our history was. One of the things I have to repent is that I was not more active and vocal in defending this great man during the difficult years of his life.

My mother loved my father very much. She took his death very badly, but it did not break her spirit. She focused her energy on raising my younger brother. I was very close to her until her death in 1977; nonetheless, my conscience troubles me to this day. I could have paid more attention to her, helped her more. I do think that this feeling is normal; we are all left with a sense of debt unpaid to our parents.

From 1930 to 1935 my family lived in Germany, where we experienced the Great Depression, Hitler's coming to power, and the victory of fascism. I arrived at the age of seven and left at twelve and a half, but I understood a great deal. My father and his friends talked mainly about politics. I already knew German, so I read about political events, heard about them on the radio, saw what happened on the streets. During my last year at a German school, in Hamburg, I witnessed dramatic developments right there in the classroom, where children of the most different backgrounds—from Communist to fascist—were studying (and often fighting).

Those early years abroad at such a critical juncture gave me a sober view of the West and of capitalism. For the rest of my life I was immunized against two extremes. The first was a profoundly negative view of capitalism and Western society, as it was dished out by our propaganda. In particular, "impoverishment" of the proletariat, contempt for humanitarian ideals and human spirituality, inherent aggressiveness in foreign policy, and so on. The second was an idyllic concept of the West as a kingdom of ubiquitous well-being, with unlimited freedom and justice. And of course I still carry with me today unforgettable impressions of the advent of fascism. By my early years I had seen the realities, in the mood and attitudes of my father's German acquaintances and in their subsequent fates, their growing fear and confusion in the face of inexorably advancing misfortune. I encountered an animal hatred on the streets and in the schoolroom simply because I was a Russian. A couple of times while I was out walking with a friend and talking loudly in Russian, we were roundly cursed in the vilest language; once we encountered a group of White Russian émigré children, who really laid into us. I saw the brutal militarism and the fascist rallies, meetings, and torchlight processions of hundreds of thousands of people who had lost their human faces and turned into a herd. I saw the anti-Semitic boycotts and then the pogroms against Jewish shops—and much more.

There were two incidents. The first took place across the street from the building we lived in (I even remember our address: Augsburgerstraße 1, Berlin). I had been a regular customer and visitor at the tiny office- and school-supply shop. I knew the owner well, though I had never given any particular thought to his nationality. Or at least I didn't think about it until I set out for school one morning and saw six-pointed stars painted on his display window and the humpbacked profile of a sort of monster intended to depict a Jew. Two stormtroopers stood before the shopkeeper's locked doors carrying posters that read DON'T BUY FROM JEWS. Coming back from school that day and on the following days, I found the store closed. A week later a new owner appeared, but one who was evidently a hundred percent Aryan. At that point it became simply impossible for me to enter that store.

The second incident took place in 1933–1934, when we were renting two rooms in the home of a Mr. Sinsheimer. We became friends with his entire family. Mr. Sinsheimer was a highly decorated hero and invalid of World War I who held a modest position in a local bank. He and my father quickly developed a close relationship. Mr. Sinsheimer was a

Jew married to a devout Catholic woman; their daughter, Suzanne, shared her mother's piety (at the time she and I were ten years old, going on eleven).

The political situation created very complex problems for the family; on the one hand, as an invalid and war hero, Mr. Sinsheimer enjoyed certain privileges (even under Hitler's legislation of 1933–1934). On the other hand, no one had any idea how long they could hang on. In the meantime, the persecution of the Jews was taking on a frightening dimension. The mother and daughter were under constant pressure for having violated the new laws on racial purity. To emigrate meant to abandon all their savings, Mr. Sinsheimer's job, their home, their pension. And where could they go?

As Germany's anti-Semitic policies reached new heights in the years that followed, we often wondered about the Sinsheimers and what had happened to them. In 1969 I made my first trip to the United States; I spoke on television, and there were a number of articles on me and the U.S.A. Institute in the press, including one in *Time* with my photograph. Upon returning home, I found a number of letters waiting for me that had been forwarded by *Time*'s editorial office. Among them was a letter from Kansas City, written by Mr. Sinsheimer's wife and daughter. Despite enormous difficulties, the entire family managed to leave Germany in 1938 and thus escaped the fate of so many others. Mr. Sinsheimer, however, had died not long after they arrived in the United States.

I have carried these personal experiences of German fascism through my life. They have, in many ways, determined my view of much that has occurred in the world and in my own country.

When we returned home, in the autumn of 1935,* the famine of the collectivization years was over. Food rationing had recently been lifted, and living conditions had improved. But the political atmosphere had just started to become ominous, for though repressions had begun fol-

---

*The return was a hasty one. My mother had been denounced for being a member of the nobility. Fortunately, we were easily able to counter that accusation when she found her birth certificate (I still have it today). Later my father said that the denunciation had been no less a stroke of luck than our having uncovered the birth certificate. Thanks to the denunciation we returned to Moscow from abroad in late 1935. If we had come back later, during the arrests of 1937, my father, and maybe my mother, would automatically have been packed off to prison and destroyed.

lowing the assassination of Stalin's aide Sergei Kirov in December 1934, in the fall of 1935 the situation was not yet too bad. There was even some euphoria because we were approaching serious democratization; soon the public debate started on the draft of a new constitution.

It was a joy to return to my country, but despite hopes for a better future, returning also meant coming home to a rather meager and primitive life.

In Moscow, we at first lived in one or two small rooms in the apartments of my father's colleagues who were out of the country on foreign-trade business. Only in 1938 did we receive *our own* two rooms, and there were four of us by then, thanks to the arrival of my little brother. Life consisted of only the bare essentials. What was worse, bit by bit I started to discover the extent of the hypocrisy and political cruelty; this was a bitter experience, especially for my friends and me, who were patriotic by conviction, not only about the country, but about our society and our socialist ideal as we understood it.

But youth is a great conqueror. Despite the worsening political situation, I, like most of my schoolmates, studied, went to parties, played sports, and made friends, some of whom I have kept to this day. But we could not avoid responding to the events going on around us. The political and ideological strain of the late thirties was a growing burden upon each of us. Some broke down and retreated within themselves, others became vicious and started to participate in the political games initiated by the leadership. Still others began to fear everything, became conformists, and lost the capacity for independent thought. And some allowed themselves to be exploited, and in that atmosphere became paid informers. Americans experienced something similar, although in an incomparably milder version, with McCarthyism and its witch-hunts. But in my country this movement was massive, prolonged, and terribly cruel.

Looking back, I try to assess how it has affected me. No doubt I have become more cautious and had to adjust by adopting appropriate patterns of behavior and political instincts. But I did not break. In general I shared the values of my society, but did not lose the capacity for independent thought (though this did not develop properly until much later, and in my early life existed only in a latent form). Of course I could not escape being stultified to some degree. But somehow I did not become an idiot. I did not allow anyone to stuff my head completely with ideological trash, but could not avoid some degree of indoctrination either.

And most important, though I hope the reader won't regard this statement as immodest, I preserved my honor. Not in the sense that I rejected the system or defied it. I would not have survived if I had. And not in the sense that I did not make compromises. This was not only a matter of personal survival and well-being. If you felt that you had an opportunity to make an important contribution in foreign policy or regarding internal political and economic problems, you had to comply with the rules of the game and be ready to compromise on some other issues. I have observed that this is also true of American politics, and so is not unique to a totalitarian system. The final judgment can be made only when you weigh the achievement against the compromises you had to make.

This does not mean that even if the balance was generally positive you can escape responsibility for your mistakes and wrongdoings. No, I for one am ready to bear this responsibility. Though I was not altogether silent I bear a particular responsibility for not having been resolute enough in protesting the wrongs and defending the rights.

But one thing I can say for sure: I have never betrayed anyone, never denounced anyone, never taken part in any campaigns to hunt people down and "work them over." This, of course, is not an achievement to boast about. But at least it's something. And I can assure you that in a totalitarian state, it was not easy. I succeeded not just because of my virtues, but also because of good luck. I mean that I was never pressured by the KGB into betraying or denouncing someone. Of course, in a totalitarian state there is, as a rule, a high reward for betrayal and denunciation. But to withstand such a temptation does not take high heroism.

A lively debate is taking place in our political literature about the difference between totalitarianism and authoritarianism. I agree with those who regard totalitarianism as a system which demands that each individual participate in fulfilling the ruler's aims and in the suppression and stultification of all the people, including oneself. This is precisely what happened under Stalin. Authoritarianism does not demand your participation—only your full submission. But this is bad and dangerous enough. Therefore I do not agree with those who believe that authoritarianism is a necessity in the transition to a market economy and democracy. Authoritarianism is the absolute opposite of democracy; it forces people to submit to the will of the ruler and does not allow them to participate in politics or to have any influence on it.

To assess post-Stalinist history correctly, it is important to be aware of the burden from which we had to free ourselves, including that of distorted morality. Is it an act of courage simply to refrain from participating in something evil even if it is expected or demanded of you? In a democratic society—no. In a totalitarian one—yes. Sometimes even very much so.

My youth ended abruptly on June 22, 1941, when Hitler's army attacked the Soviet Union. My military career was brief, but it left an imprint on the rest of my life in the sense that I matured more quickly and acquired an independence, even a boldness in my judgments and decisions, that I would not have had otherwise.

I must say that courage in battle is not equivalent to civil courage. Many times, men who were heroes in battle turned out to be pitiful cowards and conformists when confronted by their superiors. During the war there was an army joke to that effect:

"Are you afraid of the Germans, soldier?"

"No."

"Then who are you afraid of?"

"My sergeant."

After all, your daily well-being depends on him: an extra ration of bread or a portion of kasha, new leggings, or, if you're really lucky, a new pair of boots. In the end, the "sergeant's" attitude to you in a society like ours could mean your survival. I reached maturity at a horrible period in our history. The fact that I was at war helped me to grow up with more dignity and a feeling of a duty fulfilled, without an inferiority complex; it added some self-confidence, which was important and helped to preserve my identity.

Quite frankly, I was lucky during the war years, and not only because I survived. I faced fewer risks and physical hardships because I was fighting in the more or less elite regiment handling rocket artillery—the famous Katyusha multiple-rocket launchers.* We certainly had an easier life than in the infantry. Among my comrades I was regarded as quite brave and willing to take risks—mainly because I spent most of my ser-

---

*This strange name comes from that of a popular contemporary song about a beautiful girl called Katya, or Katyusha, waiting for her beloved who is serving in the army; the rocket artillery made a lot of noise, but it was music to our soldiers' ears. By the way, the Germans called our Katyushas Stalinorgeln—"Stalin's church organs."

vice at the front in reconnaissance, which meant I had to be close to the infantry battle positions, sometimes even in advance of them. Nonetheless, life in the Katyusha units was less dangerous, less arduous; as a result, more people survived. On top of all this, to serve in a regiment using new, powerful, and top-secret weapons was very exciting, even romantic, especially for a young officer.

In addition, I did not see combat at the very worst time for the Soviet army. I did not have to live through the tragic retreats, the panic, the encirclements, and the crushing defeats. Under those circumstances, many of my fellow officers who started their service a few months earlier broke down and were seriously traumatized psychologically. I am thankful that fate spared me the agonies of the first months of the war. At the same time, I saw the war at critical stages—Moscow in the autumn of 1941, through the very harsh, risk-filled period from 1941 to 1943, when we began our counteroffensive and the whole course of the war changed, though we still suffered awful and often unjustifiable losses.

But how did I become an officer? By instinct, I think—I sensed somehow that war was approaching and I would have to join the ranks. By the beginning of 1941, in my last year at high school, I had made up my mind to join a military college. I was initially attracted to the College of Communications, in what was then Leningrad. I even wrote to them. But then my uncle, my father's brother, came to visit us. In 1941 he was a major, the artillery commander of a tank brigade stationed at Brest-Litovsk. An extramural student of the Frunze Military Academy, he had come to take his exams, and he talked me into going into the artillery.

I submitted my documents to the First Moscow Artillery College. I enlisted a day before the war started. We had to complete a six-month crash course, instead of one lasting the usual two years.

We started our training with the heavy artillery, which was soon converted to rocket artillery. We saw these new weapons on the college grounds in June, but thought that they were pontoons. We noticed that there were an extraordinarily large number of them and they were always coming and going—going, as we learned later, to the front.

In the middle of October 1941, the situation in Moscow grew very tense. One gloomy day in October our whole battery was told to fall in outside HQ, and one by one we were ordered to report to the commander's office. There a commission of three military men and two civilians interviewed each of us. Each interview lasted for quite some time. My turn came. "Comrade Cadet, if secret technology is entrusted to you and there's a threat that it might fall into enemy hands, could you blow it up, even sacrificing your life?" "Of course I could," I said. Today, such a conversation would seem artificial, even pompously insincere, if not idiotic. But in those days it seemed perfectly normal.

I was dismissed and, together with seven other cadets, I was led to a corner of the wide yard of the college. There, behind a small fence, was something we always called a "pontoon." I was told that I had been appointed commander of this piece of equipment and the other seven men were my squad. A hood was removed from the "pontoon." Underneath, I saw something that looked like eight rails, or rather, double beams, on a frame that moved up-and-down and left-and-right on its mounting.

They showed us the projectile—actually a rocket, about four feet long and weighing forty-three kilos—and demonstrated how to fire it from inside the cabin. You lowered a plate of armor over the windshield and then started one rocket after another by turning a specially designed handle. There were two boxes of tolite explosive (twenty-five kilos each), placed on the mounting, which you had to blow up in the event of danger. Later, at the front, I thought: Why should I sit on top of these and show off my heroism? One could use an electronic detonator or set off a Bickford fuse at some distance from the trench, without having to commit suicide. But to the minds of our superiors, the times demanded self-sacrifice—or did the commanders want to destroy our secret technology along with those who knew about it?

The next day we went along the Volokolamsk Highway and turned off. At some point we opened fire. I never did find out whether we were firing at the enemy or whether this was a demonstration. But I will never forget the volley from the sixteen rockets on each truck—the deafening noise, the fire, the smoke, the dust, the truck shuddering with each launch.

The following day they took us back to our college, took our Katyushas away, issued us rifles, and made us do arms drill from dawn to dusk: "One-two! One-two!" "Right-left-right!" "Attention!" and so forth and so on. We couldn't understand what on earth they wanted from us. Other troops were fighting just outside Moscow. New military units were being formed from untrained civilians on our military school's grounds and hastily marched off in columns to the front, about forty or fifty kilometers away. And here we were indulging in nonsense! It never entered anyone's head that they were getting us ready for a military parade.

We got up early on November 7—a national holiday. We went to a festive breakfast—they even gave us white bread and butter—despite the fact that the Germans were at the gates of Moscow. We had hardly had time to raise the food to our mouths when the alarm sounded. We fell in and marched straight to Red Square, with our college at the head of the parade. Only then did we understand that we were to proceed with the traditional military parade, even at the risk of being under enemy fire. The idea was business as usual, and in such a desperate situation we went through with it. It was a tremendous boost to the morale of the army and the whole country.

I remember the low cloud cover (that's probably why it was decided to go ahead with the parade) and snow. Most of the marchers went directly to the front, forty kilometers from the city. Those who remained in Moscow were given 100 grams of vodka—quite a lot, I thought—by special order of the minister of defense, that is, Stalin. That was the first time I drank half a glass of vodka.

Then the college was forced to move to Mias, in the Urals; there, just before the new year, I graduated, with the rank of lieutenant. I continued my training, first in Tataria, near Arsk, and then in Moscow. Finally, we boarded the train to the front. The train was bombed twice on the way.

At this point I want to shift the scene to May 1990. For half a year I had been waging a very tough public battle, first in the newly constituted parliament of the Soviet Union, then in the press, against some of our generals (and even one marshal),* demanding much deeper cuts in military spending and arms and advocating far-reaching military reforms. The generals were mad as hell at me. Suddenly, on the evening of May 17, while I was in my office with one of my deputies and a guest who had dropped by, the *vertushka*—the government telephone line—rang. I picked up the phone and heard someone's voice.

"Georgi Arkadyevich?"

---

*The marshal, Sergei Akhromeyev, a former chief of the General Staff and a military adviser to President Gorbachev, came to a tragic end when, after the coup attempt of August 1991, he hanged himself in his office. He left a note saying, "Everything I believed in is lost."

"Yes."

"I know it's your birthday tomorrow. I would like to congratulate you, and wish you health and success." A pause.

"Pardon me, but I don't recognize you."

"This is Dmitri Timofeyevich Yazov [the minister of defense]. I have a present for you. I have a book before me. The central archive of our ministry has collected the documents relating to your personal service and combat record and the history of your regiment. How shall I get it to you?"

I gave him my address, saying it wasn't too far from the Defense Ministry.

Yazov answered: "Well, in that case, maybe I'll bring it around myself tomorrow."

He brought it very early in the morning. I wasn't in yet, so the secretary took the gift. It was, indeed, valuable. The book contained copies of documents related to my regiment and me, and even some photos. The documents—I had never seen them before—were very flattering; I had had no idea that my war record was so good. My deputy and I tried to guess what this gesture could mean. I thought that this might have been one of reconciliation. My suspicious deputy put it in another way: Why should our military bosses start digging in the archive on Arbatov's behalf? In order to find some "compromising" material to discredit him? These questions remain unanswered.

I have related all this to explain where and how I got the documents from which I am about to quote: from the "Military Operations Log" of the 221st Guards Artillery Battalion (that is where I began my service as officer in charge of reconnaissance).

> March 13, 1942. Sector 65 of the Kalinin railway. Killed—engine driver and Sergeant Vladimirov of the 2nd Battery; they were buried nearby. Wounded—Master Sergeant of the 2nd Battery Frolov and Guardsman Dovgolyuk, who were transferred to the hospital in Ostashkov.
>
> March 15, 1942. Sector 84. Bombardment. No dead or wounded. One armored car destroyed.

The one person killed and two wounded in this first air attack on our train to the front were simply unlucky. They were doing what all of us were doing: throwing the small unexploded bombs, not much larger than hand grenades, off the railway flatbed cars. One of the bombs exploded while being handled. My war could just as easily have ended the same way.

Then came a long, hard year of defensive, diversionary, and offensive operations in Smolensk Region, the offensive to the Dniepr after the Battle of Kursk, the crossing of the Dniepr south of Kanev, and then north of Cherkassy. (In 1985, as one of its "liberators," I was made an honorary citizen of that town.) In Cherkassy I fell seriously ill with tuberculosis and was sent to the rear. I was saved by a doctor (who by sheer chance turned out to be the mother of a schoolmate of mine who was also at the front) and by my mother's care. I was demobilized in the summer of 1944.

How did I fight? As well as I could. And, judging from the documents given to me by Yazov, my superiors did not think I did too badly. It may seem immodest, but I would like to quote a few extracts from my combat record.

From the "Combat Service Record" issued by the Battalion Command on August 25, 1942:

> The battery commanded by Comrade Arbatov has performed well. There has not been a time when the fascist slime has been able to escape the fire of the battery. Comrade Arbatov dealt with organization, command, and leadership while fulfilling combat missions in a knowledgeable and expert manner. On August 6, his battery destroyed more than an infantry company of the enemy, and one mortar battery. He set an example for his subordinates by displaying personal courage in battle.

From the "Combat Service Record" of October 22, 1942:

> During the time of his service with the battalion, Comrade Arbatov has shown himself to be a brave, steady, disciplined, orderly, and cultured commander. In the battles against the fascist invaders, he has shown examples of courage during the battalion's fulfillment of combat missions aimed at destroying the Hitlerites, and personally took charge of the battalion's fire. As an artillery commander, he is knowledgeable, possesses a complete grasp of his task, and is demanding of

himself and his subordinates. He enjoys the respect of all battalion personnel. Comrade Arbatov is recommended for battalion command.

This was a flattering report for a nineteen-year-old! But I did not receive this appointment; as I found out later, that was because my father was in prison as an "enemy of the people." But in 1943 I was not aware of the recommendation, so I had no cause to feel offended or even disappointed.

From the "Combat Service Record," April 14, 1943:

He copes well with his work in fulfilling combat reconnaissance missions [at that time I was the officer in charge of reconnaissance for our regiment] and supplies valuable data, as a result of which we opened fire several times, destroying several hundred fascists.

And then, alongside all this:

. . . insufficiently disciplined, makes little effort at self-improvement.

But in conclusion:

Enjoys the respect of his subordinates, ideologically correct, morally stable.

I tried hard to recall why I had received that sole reprimand. Finally, with the aid of a comrade from my old regiment, I remembered: One evening, when we were reorganizing (we were taking delivery of some new equipment) there was nothing to do, and we—three or four young officers—were playing cards. The regimental commissar, who had signed the above-mentioned Combat Service Record, walked in. He was a crusty type with an "Old Bolshevik" passion for denouncing his subordinates and colleagues. This time he depicted us as incorrigible "gamblers." And, as it turned out, he couldn't resist old habits, so he wrote a couple of nasty sentences in my service report.

One last word. Half a year later I was recommended for a decoration (this was signed by the regimental commander, not by the commissar). From the "Decoration Presentation List," dated September 10, 1943:

An energetic, brave, and fearless reconnaissance man. During his time of service in that capacity, he provided much valuable intelligence about the enemy, which was gathered under regimental fire. On September 4, while at the forward observation position, he established the basic areas of enemy concentration in the villages of Gusan and Pilipenki, at which the regiment fired two salvos each. After the salvos our troops advanced forward successfully and took those two objectives. On September 5, Arbatov, while under heavy enemy fire and in an exposed location, displaying a contempt for death and despite the danger, precisely located the enemy's first line of defense, after which a salvo was fired. Following the salvo, our units captured the high ground and continued their advance.

My short military service made a deep impression on my life and my views. Naturally, I sometimes recall my wartime experiences with a sense of a nostalgia for duty, for camaraderie in battle, and the knowledge that you are prepared to fight as long as you have any strength left. But what I went through also demystified the army and the Great Patriotic War and stripped them of that super-romantic aura that was nurtured in us for years. I discovered for myself the great opportunities that exist for petty tyranny, for a superior to humiliate a subordinate, for bullying, for mediocre and untalented people to flourish and succeed, for nepotism. I also learned how the operations of our army were managed: how many mistakes were made and at what tremendous cost! This made me quite skeptical toward the top brass, and allergic to all kinds of militarism.

Our whole postwar development and its crowning success, the "stagnation" period, brought about many ugly developments in the army and its leadership; at the same time, the military became a political sacred cow. I could not restrain myself from voicing criticism, particularly when the interests of the military-industrial complex began to clash so glaringly with the interests of the country and the people.

This led to the conflict I mentioned with some of our generals, in which my opponents have been extremely aggressive; some of them employed classic Stalinist methods, such as political denunciation and stigmatization, against anyone who dared to be critical. I was prepared for this reaction when I launched into my heated debates with the generals, and I am glad that I decided to go ahead. The whole episode helped to launch the first public debate in my country about military and political-military affairs in many years, and may have contributed in a modest way to the defeat of the military coup d'état in August 1991. The ensuing debate also helped to reveal well before the coup that our military-industrial complex had become a real threat, not only to reforms, but to our vital national interests.

I am convinced that today the demilitarization of our society and of international relations is a most important precondition not only for progress, but for survival. I think that my position on this subject, which I adopted as a result of some of my war experiences, reflects a reality that is of utmost importance. Demilitarization of Soviet society has become a prerequisite for success in economic reforms and democratization, and for my country's political stability. That's why critical analysis of militarism has been my favorite subject from my first days in journalism and my work as a scholar. As I remember, I started to write about it in 1955—after Stalin's death, when you could write a little more boldly, but still (and I am proud of this) before the Twentieth Party Congress, when certain taboos on this subject were officially lifted. My major points were that militarism was doomed historically, and had to be done away with.

In July 1944 I was released from the military hospital and became a war invalid, Category 2. This was the penultimate in terms of severity: you were not obliged to work, but you could care for yourself. I received food stamps and a pension of about ninety rubles per month. (At that time ninety rubles was enough to buy what you were entitled to with the food stamps, but was not enough to buy a single bottle of vodka at market prices.) Then the question arose: What shall I do next? My family lived humbly but was in a position to help me out financially for the years of schooling, so I decided to take up my studies.

Actually, I had been thinking about this for a long time. I had even selected an institute. In the autumn of 1943, while still at the front, I read an announcement in *Izvestia* that a department of international affairs was going to open at Moscow University; I remember saying aloud in the presence of my comrades: "That's where I'm going after the war." They laughed at me good-naturedly. At the time, the end of the war and the idea of going to a university seemed very far away—how could you know whether you would live that long?

A year later I submitted my application to this department at the university* and was accepted. My student years began, and they provide some of my happiest memories. My classmates and I were young and studying at a prestigious institute, but the years were lean and hungry, and disappointed everyone who hoped that after the war, which had sorely tested the nation's loyalty and faith, Stalin would agree to some sort of loosening-up in economic, political, and cultural life. Nothing of the sort. Very soon after the great victory new persecution and repression compaigns began.

This atmosphere was palpable at our institute. We students were being groomed for careers in foreign political affairs and for work abroad. Therefore, the scrutiny was savage. We had to fill out the longest and most meticulous *anketa*. This was a form about ten pages long, with all sorts of nasty questions about you and members of your family: "Were you or any member of your family in other [i.e., non-Communist] parties?" "Were you or any member of your family on territories occupied by the German army, or prisoners of war?" "Have you any relatives abroad? If you have, who? Where? What are they doing? Are you corresponding with them?" And so on. And this form had to be completed each year at the institute—and God help you if there was any difference between this year's and last year's. What was much worse, practically every year a group of students was arrested. When you look for something really hard, you will almost always find it, particularly when, as the standards of the day allowed, you do not have to find much: so-called unhealthy conversations on political themes; or a diary that might have been too frank, discovered by an informer in the dormitory; or even a chance contact and conversation with a foreigner started by a careless student wanting to practice his foreign-language skills—any of these was quite enough to get you arrested and convicted.

Why did Stalin behave like this after the war? My guess is that he was dogmatic and he remembered that large numbers of Russian officers and soldiers who found themselves abroad after the victory over Napoleon became prone to free thinking and displayed a discontent with life in Russia. The probing spirit of these officers provided fertile soil, first for the opposition movement and then for the attempt to bring about the

---

*A few months later it became a separate institute, under the Ministry of Foreign Affairs of the U.S.S.R.

first revolutionary uprising (aside from the peasant revolts) in Russian history: the Decembrist revolt. As far as I can judge, there were no such mutinous sentiments among the military returning home from abroad after World War II. But the fact that these people had seen another and more prosperous way of life could have helped to foster a desire to improve conditions in their own country. Such a train of thought was deeply alien to Stalin.

In general, the same old ugly and bloodthirsty Stalinism continued after the war, but with new criminal horrors: entire nationalities were repressed; the prisoners of war returning from Hitler's concentration camps went straight into ours; Stalin's anti-Semitism was elevated to the level of government policy. There were efforts to stultify the people, to deprive them of knowledge about society and politics (never before had our social sciences reached such a pitifully low level), and to start a campaign against many natural sciences (genetics, cybernetics, and others). Equally apparent were efforts to defile the culture of a great nation by squeezing it into a tight and ugly frame. And all this took place against the background of noticeable improvements in the educational level of the population. After the revolution, 80 percent of our people were illiterate. Since World War II we have become the most industriously well-read nation in the world, and millions have seen life abroad. A new generation was coming up—literate, curious, and not as scared as its parents.

Such was the complex environment in which my generation was formed. Despite the repressions, the education we received was quite good, especially at the institute where I studied. Our professors were the best of what was left of the brilliant galaxy of Russian scholars of the old school, many of whom were soon to be hunted down.

It was then, in the autumn of 1944, that I decided to study English and specialize in the United States. This was a voluntary decision, and I made it without hesitation. My American friends have often asked me why. I think the choice was the natural result of a number of straightforward considerations. The war was on. The United States was our main ally. The attitude among most of my contemporaries toward America was warm and friendly. Even first-year students understood that the United States and the Soviet Union would play a special role in the postwar world. And the country itself was undoubtedly very interesting.

When the time came to be assigned to a job upon my graduation, I had serious problems. Although I was one of the best students in my year and graduated cum laude, and though I had been a decorated officer at the front, I was simply not proposed for any job. The chairman of the commission (one Silin, who was the head of personnel at the Ministry of Foreign Affairs) put it to me bluntly: my father had an arrest record. In reaction to my incredulous response that he had been falsely accused and therefore rehabilitated, he simply shrugged his shoulders. He did not mention that my father was Jewish—but this, of course, was another fact that was used against me.

Nevertheless, I was lucky. To supplement my meager income during my last year and a half or two at the institute, I made a little part-time money by writing book reviews and doing translations for Foreign Literature Publishing House, which had just opened. Evidently, the editors liked what I did for them, for they wrote to the institute asking that I be sent to work under their authority.

My main responsibilities were to read American, English, and German political, economic, and philosophical literature and select the most interesting books and articles for translation and reference use for the classified publications (set aside for the leadership). I never read so many political books in my whole life as I did in those four years. The job was also a way of storing knowledge for my subsequent career in journalism and scholarly research.

The publishing house, incidentally, was a rather unusual institution. It was created in 1946, on Stalin's initiative of the previous year. Its main purpose was to open up a door in the Soviet Union to the knowledge and culture of the world at large. (This, by the way, is one of the grounds for my thinking that Stalin was not planning a confrontation with the West at the end of the war or immediately after it, but hoped to preserve relations based on some degree of cooperation.)

The plan was for an enormous publishing house. There were fourteen editorial departments, comprising all fields of learning—from physics and mathematics to economics, international relations, and belles lettres. The employees' salaries were two to three times higher than in other publishing houses, including the prestigious Politizdat,* which was directly under the authority of the Central Committee of the CPSU. Foreign Literature Publishing House received generous alloca-

*Specializes in political publications.

tions of convertible currency, and we subscribed to more periodicals and bought more books than anyone else in the Soviet Union.

Boris Suchkov, a high-ranking functionary in the Central Committee apparat, was appointed as the first director. He was quite well known at the time and was regarded as a rising "ideological star."

By the end of 1947 or early 1948, I was doing free-lance work for the publishing house and knew its employees. (I had to receive security clearance for access to the "secrets" of the foreign press and literature.) At this time Foreign Literature Publishing House was already in a stage of faded glory. It became clear that the initial plans were not being put into effect, at least not in their original form. The international and internal political situations had changed. The witch-hunts had begun and censorship was becoming increasingly harsh. It became more and more difficult to publish any foreign sociopolitical literature. Instead of an open door we got a keyhole, at least in these fields.

To top it all off, Suchkov was arrested (later, of course, he was exonerated), and so was his deputy, Semyon Lianders.* Thus, the publishing house became an institution like any other, except that it contained more foreign literature and the salaries were higher.

I worked at the publishing house until 1953. I celebrated my thirtieth birthday that year, but the most important event of 1953 was Stalin's death. In recalling who and what I was at that time in my life and at such a historic juncture in Soviet history, I must say that I was neither a fanatic nor a careerist. Nor did I become a cynic. (Perhaps I simply did not have the time to become cynical: Stalin's death and the approach of a new era got in the way, although I do not think I am inclined to such a personality.) I confess without hesitation that I was not a secret "progressive" and "reformer," hiding my views in a closet and masquerading as a loyal Communist in front of others.

I was, like the majority, a "rational believer," to use my late father's classification. I had inherited my faith from my family. It had flourished on very good soil, on the fine ideals of socialism, the roots of which go back to early Christianity. I must note the words of the late Friedrich von Hayek, the prominent Austrian economist and Nobel laureate: "Ev-

---

*Lianders was the father of the writer Julian Semyonov, who became well known much later as the author of popular detective novels, mostly about the glorious exploits of our spies.

eryone who believes in social justice is already halfway to being a social-ist." (The attraction of the socialist idea may have turned out to be its greatest threat, for it has allowed power seekers and tyrants to cloak themselves in it.)

At the same time, my critical attitude toward Stalinism was stronger than the average, because of my family experience and inquisitive mind. In addition, I had fewer false notions and prejudices about both the West and my own country, and fewer illusions. I also had the opportu-nity, later, to work with interesting and innovative people, and from 1957 on, I had access to some of the leaders of the Soviet Union.

3 | Stalin's Death: Between Hope and Disappointment

When Stalin died, I was still working at Foreign Literature Publishing House as head of the group of "special" publications. Meanwhile, I was literally waiting for the end to come. In January 1953, the KGB arrested one of my subordinates, and I was severely reprimanded by the Party for "absence of political vigilance"—one of the most ominous accusations of the time. The case rapidly assumed larger proportions as new allegations were added on at each level of the investigation. What began as a mere notification and warning was transformed into a "severe reprimand and warning" by the time it got to a Party meeting of the publishing house, which included some morbidly silent representatives of the Moscow City Party Committee and the Central Committee of the CPSU (the latter represented by a certain woman called Mrachkovskaya, whose colorful name—*"mrak"* means "darkness" or "gloom" in Russian—I remember to this day). As I later learned, the Regional Party Committee was planning to expel me from the Party, and the management of the publishing house was about to fire me. Had it not been for the sharp turn in the political situation the worst* might have

---

*When the fellow toward whom I did not manifest proper "political vigilance," Vadim Ligsky, did not appear in the morning at his job, I phoned his mother and asked what

happened—being accused of "absence of vigilance" toward the "enemies of the people" could easily become an introduction to criminal prosecution. It seemed that 1953 would be the beginning of a new 1937, a date which for my country was the symbol of merciless mass repressions, witch-hunts, and the destruction of millions of completely innocent people.

Experienced people (including my father, who died a year later) could not help but notice, aside from all else, the atmosphere of the Nineteenth Party Congress, which took place in the autumn of 1952, and the wording of the political report presented by Georgi Malenkov. They were remarkably similar to the rhetoric of 1937, when the strengthening of Party discipline, the improvement of cadre politics, and the heightening of criticism and self-criticism (repression and witch-hunt campaigns were implied) all were stressed. The creation of the "Inner Office" alongside the broad Presidium of the Central Committee also signaled that some important reshuffling was about to take place at the highest levels of the leadership.

At the end of 1952 and the beginning of 1953, the press—particularly the lead articles in *Pravda,* which played a kind of first violin to all Soviet propaganda—began to bristle with the terminology of 1937. Making their reappearance were invectives about "capitalist encirclement" (at a time when many European countries and China had become our allies) and about the "law" by which the class struggle intensifies as the successes of socialism increase and the enemy becomes ever more sophisticated.

After the January 1953 publication of the editorial on the "Doctors' Plot"* and the articles in praise of Lydia Timashuk, who had secretly denounced and "exposed" these villains, the media launched a veritable hysteria campaign that poisoned the political and moral atmosphere and whipped up the same brand of mass psychosis that had accompanied the

---

happened. "Oh, it is awful," she said. "Is he sick?" "No, much worse." "Is he alive?" "Yes, but it is much worse." "So what is it?" "He was arrested by the KGB last night."

*A group of physicians at the privileged Kremlin hospital had been arrested for supposedly having murdered or conspired to murder their high-ranking patients. They were said to have acted on the orders of foreign intelligence agencies and a Jewish sabotage agency (actually it was a charitable organization called the Joint Distribution Committee). The overwhelming majority of the physicians were Jewish, and their arrest and subsequent news items served to launch a raucous campaign of anti-Semitic propaganda.

sweeping repressions of the 1930s. Later I learned from my colleagues at the publishing house who were invited to work for the state security forces after Stalin's death that preparations were being made for a sweeping new wave of repressions.*

I had never seen such a campaign of hate and hysteria before, although in my work at the publishing house and during my student years my contemporaries and I received a multitude of impressions and ideas about the methods of the moral rape, enslavement, and even murder of the mind. Right before our eyes we saw how postwar ideological campaigns were unleashed one after the other against "obsequiousness" vis-à-vis the West and against "deviationists" in literature, the cinema, music, genetics, linguistic theory, and other areas. We witnessed the cruel perfection with which absolutely innocent people were being victimized and beaten down. Many of us were deeply disturbed by this, but few dared to protest openly—that would have been tantamount to suicide. Just as many people realized that what was being touted as scientific truth was, in fact, nonsense. People were equally aware that anyone who questioned the guilt of the accused or the truth of such nonsense risked merciless reprisals. All this was amply supplemented by increasingly harsh secrecy, censorship, and denunciations that ate away at our minds and souls like sulfuric acid.

At that time I did not devote much thought either to the meaning of life or to the meaning of governmental politics. Only later did it occur to me that my thoughtlessness was due not only to my youth, but to the

---

*One of these colleagues, my partner in crime, so to speak, who was involved in the same Party case as I, was Boris Manoilovich Afanasyev, a Bulgarian revolutionary and Soviet intelligence agent. Afanasyev was fired from the intelligence service in 1948 and ended up at our publishing house. When Stalin died he was invited back to his previous job. True, he retired soon afterward, and worked for many years as the assistant editor of the journal *Soviet Literature*. In 1954 he told me that because of his second, short stint with the KGB he knew for a fact that at the beginning of 1953, instructions were received to increase the holding capacity of prisons and camps in connection with the expected flood of new prisoners, and to prepare more railway rolling stock for the transportation of prisoners. According to Afanasyev, permission to beat and torture people under investigation, which had been mainly a monopoly of the KGB headquarters for many years after 1937, was now granted to everyone. In a word: during the last months of Stalin's life, the punitive machinery was getting ready for a new wave of mass repressions. The Doctors' Plot would probably have served as a pretext for its beginning. What Afanasyev told me was later confirmed by others.

instinct for self-preservation that the system fostered and developed in people. The rule was: Do not be too curious. (Those who would not submit simply did not survive.) As I have already written, one of the primary aims of this campaign was to instill in all of us the main code of behavior that subjects of a dictatorship have to follow: to be afraid of your *own* thoughts. Each one could be dangerous (after all, the powers that be would not only systematically lock up those who thought conspiratorially, but who thought without due caution). The whole structure of life, beginning with one's seemingly free student years, taught our future politicians, theoreticians, and journalists to write, say, and even think someone else's thoughts: those of the "classics" of Marxism-Leninism (carefully, and very, very selectively—otherwise you might end up in a very unpleasant situation; of Stalin (you were supposed to quote him two or three times more than Lenin, and five or six times more than Marx or Engels*); of the other accepted "leaders" of the day; those of the past (although they would quickly become dated); and the lead articles in *Pravda*. We all found out from experience how an enslaved consciousness is formed.

I would like to digress briefly. In 1961 I read George Orwell's *1984* for the first time. I read it with a feeling of depression, but also with a sense of relief that it never happened, that Big Brother's totalitarian empire turned out to be as mortal as Big Brother himself. Had the book fallen into my hands ten years earlier, I would have been devastated.

But let us return to March 1953. The first signs of change did not come from the world of thought, but from the world of politics. As it later became known, the press ceased its general moaning and groaning about the departed leader's death on orders from the leadership. Not long after came a real sensation: the whole campaign about the Doctors' Plot was exposed as fallacious and criminal, and those who had been its victims and were still alive were released. In June, Lavrenti P. Beria, the ominous boss of the secret police, was arrested, and by the end of the year he and his associates had been executed. Even in Beria's case, the

---

*Later, an interesting analysis was done of the official *Short Philosophical Dictionary*, edited by M. Rozental and P. Yudin, which was published in 1951. Fifteen columns were devoted to Stalin and three columns each to Lenin, Marx, Hegel, and Aristotle; but on the other hand, a whole six columns were given over to Andrei Zhdanov, the chief Party ideologue at the time.

leadership still could not proceed without using some of its traditional methods. The fact that Beria killed, tortured, and persecuted thousands upon thousands of Soviet people seemed an insufficient accusation for the leadership to bring against him. In order to make the crimes of this Stalinist henchman and pervert appear worthy of capital punishment, the authorities tacked on the traditional charges of spying for (as far as I remember) British intelligence.*

The September 1953 plenum of the Central Committee issued a very unusual, though indirect, piece of criticism aimed at the accepted order of things and the previous leadership, although no names, and certainly not Stalin's, were mentioned. Eventually, a new term started to show up here and there (again without mention of Stalin's name): "personality cult." Bit by bit, the atmosphere of fear began to lessen.

Even more important, news came with increasing frequency, not that someone else had been arrested, but that someone had been released from prison or had been posthumously rehabilitated.

There were also some very important changes in foreign policy. At first, our leadership did not show any new initiatives in international affairs. This is understandable, in that Stalin's death represented much too radical a change, and the situation inside the Soviet leadership at the time was also far too complex. In general the situation was such that any initiative, even a purely symbolic one, had to come from the West, and especially from the United States. In my opinion, this was so not only because of the situation in the U.S.S.R., but because of the state of Soviet-American politics.

In 1952 and at the beginning of 1953 the Cold War was at a particularly critical stage. In the United States and, as far as one can judge, in

---

*Just recently it occurred to me that, without this version, the arrest, conviction, and execution of Beria would not have looked good, from the point of view not only of the leadership, but of the people. I remember how I learned of his arrest. I was traveling with my wife and two-year-old son to my birthplace, Kherson. We stopped for a couple of days at my aunt's dacha, not far from Odessa. Early one morning we were awakened by the plaintive voice of the mail- and paper-boy: "Beria's been exposed as an enemy of the people! Beria is a spy!" I think the people were simply not conditioned to think that one of the "leaders" whose portraits were an obligator decorations of almost every official room or office could be judged as assassins, thugs, and criminals. "Spies," "traitors," "terrorists"—that was something different. That was something acceptable. Our people were conditioned in this way. Stalin had seen to that.

the U.S.S.R. as well, the two countries were considered to be on the brink of war. A sharp debate about political doctrine arose in the United States, and the doctrine of "containment" was adopted at the beginning of the Cold War. This doctrine is legitimately associated with George Kennan, the noted American diplomat and historian, and the patriarch of Sovietology. But some of the more conservative and militant American politicians put forward another doctrine, that of liberation. This meant freeing Eastern Europe and part of the U.S.S.R.—or even, perhaps, the whole of the Soviet Union—from Communism (the borders here were purposefully hazy). I remember this vividly, for in 1953 I was editing the translation of James Burnham's book *Containment or Liberation* for "secret" publication, that is, for the Soviet leadership.

During the U.S. election campaign of 1952, a number of political leaders close to Eisenhower (including John Foster Dulles, who later became secretary of state), and even the future President himself, expressed their preference for the idea of liberation. We knew about this in Moscow. Eisenhower's electoral victory, his Cabinet appointments, and the prominent political role of the Dulles brothers—John Foster and Allen, the director of the CIA—convinced the Soviet leaders that American policy was going to harden even further.

President Eisenhower's speech to the American Association of Editors on April 16, 1953, in which the President not only rejected the policy of liberation but also implied that if the Soviet Union offered such an opportunity the United States would be prepared to proceed with the normalization and improvement of American-Soviet relations, came as a complete surprise both for Soviet society and for many of its specialists and politicians. (I want to make this qualification: I cannot speak for everyone, since at that time I was rather far removed from those who shaped policy.)

What was for most of us no less of a surprise was the fact that *Izvestia* reprinted the speech. This was a signal to the Americans that we had noticed the speech, and to our own citizens that we had to take the words of the American leader seriously, even though *Pravda* printed a critical commentary on the speech at the same time.

I would like to digress here. Our leaders' serious response to Eisenhower's speech, whether they knew it then or not, was fully justified. Just recently, I learned some details of the debates in the Eisenhower administration from George Kennan and from American participants at a

seminar in Moscow in November 1990 on the centenary of Eisenhower's birth. Kennan, the U.S. ambassador to the Soviet Union until
1952, was declared persona non grata (obviously with Stalin's knowledge—or, more likely, on Stalin's instructions*) and forced to return
home. Soon after Eisenhower's inauguration and after John Foster
Dulles's appointment as Secretary of State at the beginning of 1953,
Dulles received Kennan. The conversation was a harsh one: "I won't
have a place for you. I'm giving you three months to find a new job."
Kennan spoke about Dulles as a bright man, but believed he was frightened by the extreme right, which was then in ascendancy.

*Professor Kennan told me about one version of his expulsion from Moscow. Not long
before it, a young Soviet came to the U.S. Embassy, saying he was from the Soviet Ministry of Foreign Affairs, and demanded a meeting with the ambassador on what, he said,
was a very important matter. The ambassador was informed, and received him. He told
Kennan that he was the son of a high-ranking Soviet functionary who had been arrested
or executed (Kennan took this to mean that he was the son of the chairman of the KGB,
or perhaps that he was saying that he was a friend of the chairman), that he represented
many sons and daughters of high-ranking persons who had been persecuted and wanted
revenge and was now asking for American help. Kennan decided this was a provocation;
he answered that the U.S. Embassy would have no part in such affairs, and asked the
young man to leave immediately. The visitor said, "Fine, but let me leave in such a way
that the KGB doesn't see me." Kennan answered: "You managed to get in somehow, so
getting out is your problem, which you should have thought about before." The visitor
asked if it would be possible to take him out in the trunk of an embassy car. When this
was refused, the young man left. And shortly after this apparent provocation fell through,
Kennan was declared persona non grata. Andrei Gromyko, as the professor noted, told
him later that he had nothing to do with his expulsion from the country.

A remarkable coincidence: it turned out that I knew about this whole affair—and not
only that, I had suffered as a result of it. Kennan's visitor was N. N. Yakovlev, the son of
the marshal of artillery, who had been arrested at the time. After his visit to the embassy
the younger Yakovlev was also arrested (although this does not prove that the visit was
not a provocation). During interrogation, Yakovlev willingly collaborated with the KGB
and denounced a dozen people, including Vadim Ligsky, who worked for me, and whose
arrest got me into serious trouble. All of those denounced were arrested shortly thereafter.

After his release from prison Yakovlev became an Americanist. He wrote a few books,
but was primarily known for his pasquinades—his denunciations of Alexander Solzhenitsyn and Andrei Sakharov (it was he who appeared at Sakharov's in Gorky and got a slap
in the face from him). He has attacked me slanderously many times. And, finally, I would
like to add that he is one of the authors of the new version of the "Judeo-Masonic Conspiracy," which has been circulating in the Soviet Union of late and which the foulest
reactionaries have latched onto.

"A few days later," Kennan concluded, "I was invited to the White House. And there I received an assignment to head one of three teams, each of which would give an assessment from its own perspective of the prospects for future American-Soviet relations." Shortly thereafter, Eisenhower heard each team out, and it was Kennan who presented the most moderate, optimistic, and constructive scenario—the one that the President eventually supported. The President's speech came soon after that; apparently, it was a first, experimental step. (Nonetheless, Kennan soon had to leave the State Department.*)

Why do I think that Eisenhower's acceptance of Kennan's position was so important, and had a direct bearing on the first stages of the thaw that began after Stalin's death? First because an exterior foe, a state of international tension, and an outside danger (regardless of whether any of these things actually exist, or are provoked, or are simply invented) all are important preconditions for an internally repressive regime to exist. At minimum, they provide the most fertile ground for such a regime. And conversely, a healthy international situation and a relaxation of international tension always lead to a weakening of repression and to a normalization and moderation of internal politics.

Thus, step by step, the preconditions for political changes and spiritual awakening in the Soviet Union were being created. They began as they always had, with literature and publications. Our writers and journalists reacted more quickly and decisively to changes, and spurred those changes along. The new works of Valentin Ovechkin and his followers describing the tragic conditions in rural Russia were published and had a strong impact upon the public consciousness. Ilya Ehrenburg's novel *The Thaw* was a more vivid precursor of the coming changes, giving its name to the whole period; it was greeted with fierce opposition and attacks from the establishment. These books were soon followed by Pomerantsev's "On Sincerity in Literature" and Vladimir Dudintsev's *Not by Bread Alone*. Similar works followed. Freedom of thought was being reborn particularly quickly in poetry, and it was during those years that Yevgeni Yevtushenko, Andrei Voznesensky, and Robert Rozhdestvensky were publicly acclaimed.

---

*Kennan also mentioned in our conversation that he would never forget the courage and kindness of Robert Oppenheimer, who invited him to Princeton University, where his second career began.

All this was extremely important for the intellectual, moral, and political health of the country. Without this preparation, the truth about the
past and the subsequent statements from the podium at the Twentieth
Party Congress would probably have been accepted with even greater
reluctance and pain. This new writing became the axis on which the
spiritual life of the thinking segment of the population turned. Historians, journalists, poets became symbols and barometers of change and
contributed to the fact that the number of people who were learning to
think for themselves was constantly growing.

Similar works would probably have been created earlier—to the extent, of course, that the reigning cruelty of fear did not freeze the minds
of even the bravest people. Only a very few wrote "for the desk drawer,"
that is, for future generations, without any hope of seeing their works in
print during their lifetimes. This was also a dangerous thing to do in
Stalin's time—but to a certain extent in Khrushchev's and Brezhnev's,
too.

At first, it was not necessary even to mention Stalin's name publicly to
give society the signal that the criticism, and perhaps even the overturn-
ing, of Stalinism had begun. The end of mass arrests, the "rehabilitation" of innocent people, the arrest and execution of Beria and others
signaled that the past would not be repeated. And who could say—perhaps even life itself would start to change radically. Hopes were being
born that inspired bold thoughts, and bold publications as well.

At the same time it became clear that our society had ceased to be
monolithic. The thaw revealed undercurrents of contradictions and conflicts. A polarization began. At first, it was quite an elementary one, with
just two positions: for change or against it, for the rejection of the Stalinist legacy or for its retention. Both sides appealed to the leadership
and pinned their hopes on its answer. And as for our leaders, their position on Stalin was precisely the one subject they chose to keep mum
about, mainly because they had not yet made up their minds. It became
clear later that they were also silent because they were deeply divided.
Stalinism remained the most important issue throughout the post-
Stalin era, including the years of perestroika: there is no doubt that
today's ideological landscape is much more varied, multifaceted, and
complex, but this split has remained and in some ways has become more
clearly defined, despite the fact that the supporters of Stalinism, for the
most part, prefer not to declare themselves.

Debates along this great divide started in politics and literature; they spilled over into the social and the natural sciences, and then went further: into history, psychology, genetics, physiology, physics, mathematics, and chemistry. In time each of these became an ideological battleground and had to be depoliticized after the Twentieth Party Congress. The first unorthodox and critical articles began to appear, people started to speak more freely, and like-minded people soon learned to recognize each other almost through symbols: by their attitudes toward the theory of relativity, toward cybernetics, toward Trofim Lysenko or Vyacheslav Kochetov, Nikolai Gribachev, and Anatoli Sofronov, toward Ehrenburg's *The Thaw* or the poetry of Yevtushenko. For the first time in many years, unusually vivid and independent people appeared, and the world noticed them.

As a rule, the lives of these people later became difficult. Almost all of them experienced fierce attacks and witch-hunts; at times, long periods of disgrace; and sometimes repression. The fateful irony was that the places where they could express themselves least freely were those that ought by nature to have been the freest—the academic institutions of the social sciences and the institutions of higher learning. There, Stalinist dogmatism was as dominant as before.

I had the chance to witness both the conservatism of official social science and the first attempts by scientists to shake off the old patterns and the theoretical perversions that were imposed by force and fear.

I remember all this vividly because in the autumn of 1953 I was forced out of Foreign Literature Publishing House. Soon after, I was invited to work for the academic journal *Problems of Philosophy*. This unique publication was created at the beginning of the postwar ideological campaigns to replace the journal *Under the Banner of Marxism*, which had been closed down in 1944. Its clear mission was to act as an ideological watchdog over philosophy and other disciplines. This reflected, to a great extent, the function of philosophy in Stalin's time.

After Stalin's death the winds of change reached the realm of philosophical studies, but these disciplines proved to be quite capable of resistance, having entrenched themselves in the bunkers of Stalinism. And such was their position when, in the autumn of 1953, I went to work for *Problems of Philosophy*. The conservative management of the Institute of Philosophy (the director, Pyotr N. Fedoseyev, and the journal's editors, Fyodor V. Konstantinov and, later, Mikhail D. Kamari) toed the line at all costs, relying on the support of corresponding departments in the Central Committee. But it was becoming increasingly difficult to do this.

Naturally, the journal had to play a significant role in the first stirrings on the philosophical front. Books require a longer production time, so it was easier to stop them. The journal was fortunate to have some good people on its editorial board, and this helped it play its part. Many younger editors were ready to search for new ideas and approaches. If anyone is curious enough to leaf through back issues of the journal—say, from mid-1954 on—he will find the first sprouts of these efforts. There was, for instance, a series of articles criticizing the works of the "official" philosopher G. F. Alexandrov, who portrayed most philosophers of the past and present as ideologues of the exploiting classes.

In 1955, the discussion on the problems of philosophy ended with the complete victory of those who decisively rejected the efforts by some of our philosophers to proclaim the theory of relativity incompatible with Marxism and to repeat in physics what Lysenko had done in genetics.* In 1956, cybernetics, which had previously been labeled a bourgeois pseudo-science, was rehabilitated. The journal printed the first attacks on Lysenkoism (soon, unfortunately, any criticism of Lysenko was again banned) and the earliest attempts to legalize and legitimize sociology. New names began to appear in the journal, among them Yevgeni U. Plimak, Yuri F. Karyakin, Ewald V. Ilyenkov, and Alexander A. Zinovyev.

A similar situation prevailed, albeit less quickly, in other social sciences. A discussion, an exchange of opinion, was initiated. Philosophy, history, political economics, and the study of government and law were fated to remain static for quite a long time to come. Three years of superficial and piecemeal liberalization could not plow up a field and make it fertile after almost thirty years of being downtrodden by the

---

*Trofim Lysenko, director of the Institute of Genetics and president of the Academy of Agricultural Sciences under Stalin, was the leading advocate of a doctrine of heredity based on the inheritance of environmentally induced characteristics. He was a vehement opponent of Mendelian genetics as a basis for practical plant breeding, and wielded his influence as a member of the Supreme Soviet to prohibit the teaching or practice of non-Soviet genetic principles in Soviet educational and experimental institutions. In addition, he did not hesitate to denounce and physically destroy his opponents, among them the famous scientist Nikolai Vavilov.

power of government and Party authority and the heavy steamrollers of arrogant, ignorant careerists and fanatical semiliterates indulging their base passions.

I would venture the conclusion, however, that by the mid-1950s our society had become more aware of its situation, saw itself in a more sober light, and had freed itself of a number of illusions. People began to think for themselves. The feeling was increasing that changes were necessary and that they were coming. At the same time, the old patterns of thought formed such a thick layer that the Twentieth Party Congress and Khrushchev's speech on Stalin's personality cult came like a bolt out of the blue, shaking the Party and our whole society to their roots.

In the evening after Khrushchev's speech I spoke to Yuri Frantsev, who had been at the Congress. He was the assistant chief editor of *Pravda,* responsible for foreign affairs, and an editor at *Problems of Philosophy,* supervising the department of foreign philosophy and ideology, where I worked. He invited me over for a talk.

I had known him since my student days at the Institute of Foreign Relations, when he was director. Frantsev was an almost legendary figure. He was sophisticated and intellectual, increasingly rare traits among people of his rank. He was a prominent Egyptologist and an historian of philosophy. Because he was a refined intellectual, for a long time he was kept away from politics. Only in 1940 was he admitted to the Party, and not until 1946 was he invited to Moscow. Among students he had a reputation as a democrat, and among the teaching staff that of a strict and meticulous boss, known for his sharp and sometimes vicious tongue.

Describing Khrushchev's speech that evening, Frantsev, despite his well-deserved reputation as a skeptic and even a cynic, was genuinely flabbergasted. I remember his words: "I could have thought that one day this could happen, should happen, but I never thought I would live to see the day." I remember that during our conversation, he nearly whispered, such was the fear that had been instilled in him when discussing the truth about Stalin.

Next day, the whole of Moscow was talking about how Khrushchev had "exposed Stalin," and a few days later the whole country was discussing the event. It is a shock to hear what you may have guessed at, or even known well and discussed in a circle of close friends, read aloud from the podium of a Party meeting. (Khrushchev's speech soon was being read at all local Party organizations.)

Looking back, one can probably say that the Twentieth Congress, having officially revealed the truth about many things, did not so much provide our society with answers as pose crucial questions. This was quite an achievement. But in order to make society aware of those questions, it was necessary to speak the hard truth about the past, about what had happened to our country and how Stalin had deceived it. To this end, the exposure of Stalin and his crimes was the most effective thing Khrushchev could have done. The fact that after Khrushchev's speech many efforts were made in the wrong direction is another matter. There are many reasons for this; one of them is obvious.

The Stalin period and its legacy could be overcome, as everyone later found out, only through a long, hard struggle embracing various aspects of our social life. The most far-reaching decision of the Congress could not replace the huge task of reshaping people and society which lay ahead.

Second, there were also subjective factors at play. The situation among the leadership was such that in the three preceding years it had failed to prepare the Party and the people sufficiently for the monumental step undertaken by the Twentieth Party Congress: the break with the Stalinist past and the sharp turn in political direction. The congress's criticism of Stalin was rejected by many members of the Politburo, in particular by the Stalinist old guard. For the same reason, apparently, the congress was unable to put forward a positive program, even a short-term one, for overcoming the legacy of Stalinism.

The conflicts in the leadership were exacerbated by the inconsistency of Khrushchev's own position. There are several possible explanations. One of them is that Khrushchev, like all the other leaders of the time, could not have refrained from participating in Stalin's repressions, and therefore could not go too far in his rejection of Stalinism. In addition, Khrushchev carried the heavy burden of Stalinist convictions, morals, methods, and attitudes. That was only natural; he had not experienced any alternatives.

I personally also see a third reason for Khrushchev's inconsistency and the absence of a positive program. It is connected to the main motives of his "mutiny" against Stalin. I have no doubt that Stalin's cruelty, perfidy, and despotism were repugnant to Khrushchev, who had been personally humiliated by Stalin more than once and had suffered the crushing loss of human dignity that comes from constant fear. Khrushchev also found that his criticism of Stalin was a weapon in his power struggle with the Stalinist old guard, mainly Molotov, Malenkov, Kaganovich, and Beria. The latter's fate is testimony to how desperate that struggle was.

I am sure criticism of Stalin helped Khrushchev to repulse the first attempt to oust him, undertaken in June 1957 by the so-called anti-Party group—Molotov, Malenkov, Kaganovich, and other hard-liners. (The ouster was actually attempted by the majority of the Politburo. Their decision was overturned by a plenary meeting of the Central Committee, supported by the army.)

At the Twenty-second Party Congress, Khrushchev's use of the Stalin personality cult in the struggle against his political opponents came out especially loud and clear. The emphasis placed in the keynote address and in virtually all the speeches, for no apparent reason, on the criticism of Stalin and his comrades in arms who were still alive surprised many people (including myself, and I won't hide the fact). It would seem that enough had been said about Stalin's personality cult at the Twentieth Party Congress. Why make it the most important subject of the congress now? There could be only one explanation: Khrushchev was aware of the danger (perhaps even had information to that effect) that the anti-Party group, in revenge for the June plenum, might appeal to the congress. The hard-liners had, in fact, petitioned the congress to reinstate them in the Party. This could have provoked Khrushchev into turning the debates at the congress into an anti-Stalinist channel. In the continuing uncertainty over the Stalin question, this proved useful, and, I think, hindered the attempts at open re-Stalinization of the country that were undertaken by conservative party leaders after Khrushchev's ouster.

The struggle for power played a large part in Khrushchev's exposure of what was called the personality cult; but in fact his efforts were limited to his denunciation of Stalin's crimes. Khrushchev's criticism of Stalinism was inconsistent; he swung between exposing crimes and ruminating about the achievements of the departed leader. And among the achievements he named were Stalin's successes in his "struggle against the enemies of the Party"—that is, in the very sphere where Stalin's crimes assumed fantastic proportions and turned into mass repressions and terror against his own Party and against his own people.

Khrushchev's vacillation on this subject was blatant. And the first evidence of it was his lack of a clear ideological and political stand, even immediately following the Twentieth Congress. The congress had given him great power and authority. But it became apparent at Party meetings where the decisions of the Twentieth Party Congress were discussed (and at which the Secret Speech was read) that, after some initial confusion in their ranks, the old leading cadres of the Party quickly pulled themselves together and made a concerted effort to minimize the damage caused by the ideas expressed at the Twentieth Congress and to punish those who had taken the congress seriously and wanted to go further. While the entire country, and soon the world, was debating his speech, when many questions were being asked and no official answers were being given, Khrushchev kept mum, and during passing exchanges with foreign journalists made calculatedly ambiguous remarks.

Despite these assessments, I do not want to diminish Khrushchev's achievements. Khrushchev could not help being a true product of the Stalin era, an era that nurtured an abnormal fear in politicians and made them follow rigid rules of self-preservation. Those who did not possess such qualities simply perished on the first rungs of their political careers.

Nor can I ignore the conviction of people who knew Khrushchev well that he was sincere in his criticism and personal dislike of Stalin and really wanted to dismantle the oppressive system the tyrant created. Some of these people think that this was the real goal of Khrushchev's very bold, albeit disorganized, attempt to create two (though both Communist) parties in our country, one "urban" and one "rural." And even his unsuccessful and risky attempt to divide the "rural" Party into further independent units can also be regarded not just as an amateurish piece of improvisation, but as a deliberate attempt to undermine the monopoly of the all-powerful bureaucratic machinery. I concede that all this was so.

I had another suspicion at the time: did Khrushchev suddenly get frightened and lose his calm after the Twentieth Party Congress, having seen what ghosts he had awakened and what genies he had let out of the bottle? I am now convinced of this, and I think this failure of nerve is one of the greatest mistakes Khrushchev ever made.* In the Party (I do

---

*Looking back, I came to another conclusion. Most probably it was not even a failure of nerve. Deep in his heart Khrushchev was afraid of appearing too liberal—not less afraid, and maybe even more so, than his old buddies the Stalinists. He showed it later, initiating a vicious campaign against Boris Pasternak and an attack against liberal writers and art-

not mean in the apparat at the top, but among the millions of rank-and-file members who formed a very important part of the politically active strata of society) and in the nation, a spark of hope had been ignited, an awakening of faith, even a genuine eagerness to cleanse society and to strive for truly humanistic ideals. For a while, the Twentieth Party Congress had put fear into the Stalinist bureaucracy and undermined the position of the conservatives. In this unique situation it would have been possible to make use of the awakening social energy and to go much further than we actually did. And, worst of all, there was even an element of provocation in all this: thanks to the de-Stalinization movement he started, people began to think and talk independently, to write what they thought, but within a few months they were being forced back into the narrow confines (even if these confines were somewhat less narrow than before) of what was prescribed from above. Those who had been particularly active were punished and publicly humiliated. And by the end of 1956 everything seemed to be back in the same old rut.

Characteristically, Khrushchev did not venture (or perhaps he was unable) to have his Twentieth Party Congress speech published in the U.S.S.R.; this had to wait until the years of perestroika. One version of events is that he was not allowed to do so by the other members of the Central Committee Presidium. Through an emissary, Kostya Orlov, in all probability a former KGB agent,* he even handed over a detailed version to the Reuters correspondent, John Retti, for publication in the West. But surely later—after the June 1957 plenum, which expelled Molotov, Malenkov, Kaganovich, and a number of others from the leadership (and subsequently from the Party itself)—Khrushchev could have had the Secret Speech published within the country, and no one could have prevented him from doing it. He did not do it because, most likely, he was afraid and could not bring himself to take this important step.

Besides the domestic causes of Khrushchev's inconsistency and vacillation, a very serious role was played by developments abroad. The international Communist movement reacted dramatically to the Twentieth

---

ists. My conclusion, however, is also prompted by later events, in particular the behavior of Mikhail Gorbachev at the end of the eighties and the beginning of the nineties. According to the old Bolshevik tradition, liberalism was regarded as a mortal sin.
*See Moscow News, July 11, 1990.

Party Congress. Khrushchev had, in essence, confirmed much of what the enemies of Communism had been saying about the U.S.S.R. and socialism, but which foreign Communists had disputed. As a result, many Communists, particularly those in the radical leftist intelligentsia, became disillusioned and left the Party. In some parties, criticism of the CPSU and the Soviet Union was growing, as was the call for ideological and political independence—all of which was previously unheard of. Others experienced internal crises, factional splintering, or an altered political line. Plenty of people both outside and inside the Soviet Union laid the entire blame for this crisis in the movement on Khrushchev and the Twentieth Party Congress.

When the political leadership accepts responsibility for correcting past mistakes and exposing past crimes, conservatives attempt to put the blame not on those who committed the crimes and mistakes, but on those who try to expose and correct them. This is what happened after the Twentieth Party Congress as well, although here the essence of the matter was the inevitable accounting for Stalin's evil deeds and for the fact that foreign Communist activists had so stubbornly refused to notice them, or had even justified or denied them, thinking (many were genuinely deceived, and others were not) that all the accusations made against the Soviet Union for years were propagandistic fabrications of the anti-Communists.

The matter was complicated by the fact that such fabrications had indeed been created ever since 1917. This explains why some of the foreign friends of the Soviet Union disbelieved the events of the 1930s, including those that were indisputable, like the infamous political trials, which were a criminal forgery. In addition, many of the foreign Communists possessed an almost fanatical faith in the Soviet Union and in Stalin.

This faith was embedded in thousands of honest and intelligent people. History had its own reasons for this, of course: the First World War, then the Second, the horrors of fascism, the hardships of the Great Depression of 1929–1933. These catastrophes produced a passionate desire among the left-wing community and the labor movement abroad for a bright future. For many the future seemed to have arrived in the Soviet Union, and that led, imperceptibly, to the next step: hope was pinned to Stalin personally. If one is to be objective, this hope was not just an illusion or a deceit. The U.S.S.R. in its early years had breathed new life into some democratic ideals and later became the main force in the defeat of Nazism.

Undoubtedly, there were historical reasons for the blind faith of the foreign Communists—especially as fascism became a mortal danger to Europe. But this blind faith and unconditional support of Stalin was destructive not only for Communists and their Party. It damaged the Soviet Union and the whole experiment undertaken, for better or for worse, after the revolution. In the twenties and even in the early thirties, the opinion of foreign Communists could, to some degree, still restrain Stalin.

This under no circumstances changes the fact that the full weight of responsibility for the crimes lies with those who committed them. Stalin and his entourage bear a tremendous burden of guilt not only before the world Communist movement, but before all leftist movements—labor, radicals, social democrats, and others. They compromised the very ideals of socialism and crudely disdained their international responsibility as the leaders of a government that called itself socialist.

I have known quite a number of foreign Communists, I have friends among them, and I understand the difficulties and problems they faced after the Twentieth Party Congress, and later, during the perestroika years.* That is why I dwell upon these problems in some detail.

But let us return to 1956. The growing criticism of the CPSU abroad and the repression of the debate over the CPSU's policy at home left Khrushchev with two choices. One was to go boldly forward, acknowledging the complete sovereignty of each foreign Party and making all of them independently able to find their own way out of problems, while he concentrated on bold reforms within the Soviet Union that would enhance the reputation of the CPSU and the country. The second was to sound a hasty retreat and confine himself to a few concessions to the new international realities. Khrushchev chose the second option. In its documents, the Twentieth Party Congress made concessions on a number of issues, including the possibility of averting war and the possibility of a peaceful transition to socialism and the acceptance of various ways of building it. At the same time care was taken to restrain the non-

---

*This is not a contrived analogy. If you get to the essence of the arguments that critics of perestroika make, you will find the same logic in many of them.

Soviet parties as much as possible from making deeper revisions in ideological problems, politics, and tactics, and to retain some form of organization of the international Communist movement, some instruments that could discipline it. Unfortunately, the second choice could not, and did not, solve problems, which was to be expected. But it was a much easier option for Khrushchev.

Of course, even if you regard the first choice as preferable, you cannot discount some positive elements in the first international meetings of the Communist and workers' parties that followed the disbanding of Cominform (a Moscow-based information agency for the international Communist movement), in particular, attempts to overcome some old political dogmas and to bring the theory closer to new realities of life. But all such attempts to stop the mounting difficulties in the Communist parties failed. One of the reasons was our inability to overcome our imperious attitude toward other Communist parties and our dogmatic approach to their problems.

Perhaps the most damaging consequence of Khrushchev's policy was that the difficulties in the Communist movement made him more inclined to slow down rather than accelerate de-Stalinization, reform, and democratization in the Soviet Union. This became even clearer in Krushchev's and the leadership's policy on the political crises in several Eastern European countries, particularly Hungary and Poland.

The turbulent developments in these countries had a very painful effect on the situation inside the U.S.S.R. True, at first they enlivened political discussion, but ultimately they hastened its suppression, giving the conservatives and Stalinists not only an excuse but an effective weapon to fight against those who had accepted the Twentieth Party Congress at face value. The ghosts of "counterrevolution" and "anti-Soviet activity," which for many years had been used to suppress not only dissent but elementary freedom of thought, became flesh and blood.

I soon learned through my own experience how quickly this weapon could be brought into play. In 1956, *Problems of Philosophy* had published several daring articles, including the one in issue 5 by B. A. Nazarov and O. V. Gridneva entitled "On the Question of the Backwardness of Drama and the Theater," which attracted wide attention. (It is an old tradition in Russia, created by severe censorship, to discuss political issues in the guise of a debate about literature, drama, or art.) The journal was worked over immediately in the wake of the events in Poland and Hungary in 1956. Many articles were banned, including one I wrote toward the end of 1956.

The complex interrelationship between events in Eastern and Central European countries, which were later to be called the socialist community, and developments within the U.S.S.R. is apparent. Unfortunately this interdependence has had, more often than not, negative consequences for the Soviet Union as well as the other countries of the community. I will touch on this question later, in connection with the events in Czechoslovakia in 1968 and the developments in China in the 1960s and then in the 1980s. Why did things, as a rule, go against us, against our reforms? I think that to a great extent we have ourselves to blame.

From the Stalinist years through the Brezhnev era, the official point of view in the U.S.S.R. and in the other socialist countries was that there was only one true, or at least correct, form of socialism, and it was embodied in what the Soviet Union had created. This also ensured us a position in the Vanguard and gave us the right to be the real leader. The other countries, apart from their humble right to take national characteristics into account when fine-tuning their economic and political structures, were required to reproduce our experience. Any departure from the Soviet model was regarded as heresy. Such a universalization of our model unwittingly forced our people to measure everything that went on in the other socialist countries according to our own yardstick: Was it better than what we had here? Or was it worse? Under such conditions, events in other countries did indeed affect the internal struggle in our country and helped to polarize opinions and attitudes. And, of course, changes in one country caused sharp reactions in its neighbors, sometimes throwing them off track like the last car of a long train that has taken too sharp a turn.

Mutually dangerous situations arose that constantly egged us on in our desire to influence events in neighboring countries or even to meddle in their affairs. Certain factors like political developments, economic reforms, or even cultural events could be interpreted not only as undesirable but as threats to our own internal stability. Only toward the end of the 1980s did we finally abandon our monopoly on the "only true socialism," when we stopped interfering in the internal affairs of our friends and allies. As a result, many complications, even political tragedies, were avoided.

In the first years of perestroika these changes were sometimes perceived with too great a degree of sensitivity by representatives of democratic circles. I heard accusations from old friends in Czechoslovakia that "when you wanted to crush the Prague Spring and reestablish Stalinism in our country you sent tanks; and now you're playing the game of 'noninterference,' leaving us at the mercies of the very Stalinists you put in power." What could I say? Only one thing: I understand your feelings, but at some point we have to stop intruding in our neighbors' affairs. I regret that we did not do that sooner, but if Gorbachev had intervened, he would simply have made something very bad permanent, even if it was for a good cause.

The dramatic changes that engulfed the Eastern and Central European countries in 1989 became a hot political issue in the U.S.S.R. From the podiums at the Party plenums and congresses, and in parliament, an attack was launched against Gorbachev and Foreign Minister Eduard Shevardnadze, who were blamed for causing a "collapse of the socialist system," losing a "buffer zone," and undermining the security of the country. I do not think these accusations deserve serious attention.

The ideals of socialism, which I consider legitimate and sound, form a part of human civilization. We can find them in early Christianity, in the works of the great thinkers of the past, and in the democratic movements of the last several centuries. But socialism cannot exist, no matter where, contrary to the will of the people. We tried to go against this truth (which, incidentally, is to be found in classical Marxism) by imposing certain policies and institutions, which we considered to be socialist, upon a number of European countries. Events took their inevitable course as soon as we gave up this policy of coercing other countries into "socialism." In most of those countries the model of society we planted had not grown deep roots of its own and had not acquired any vitality.

That is the social side of the problem. As far as its foreign-policy aspects are concerned, some of the accusations leveled by critics of Gorbachev and Shevardnadze (for example, about the loss of a "buffer zone") are imbued with an unacceptable imperial thinking that simply does not conform to today's realities. And the accusations that their policy undermined our security are wrong and contradict the new realities of international relations.

On June 15, 1990, I spoke about some of these problems at a session of the Commission of the Central Committee of the CPSU on Foreign Affairs. I noted that our security has not suffered from the fact that we have ceased to regard as allies people who sold secret Soviet military technology to NATO (according to the press, Ceauşescu and several former Polish leaders used to do this systematically). More important: countries that were kept in the alliance by force cannot now be counted on as reliable allies. In fact, shedding our illusions about the alliance has only increased our security.

What is more, in order to maintain our pseudo-alliance—I have in mind the Warsaw Pact—not only did we have to pay a high price, but, time after time, we had to resort to armed intervention: in the German Democratic Republic in 1953; in Hungary in 1956; in Czechoslovakia in 1968. We also found ourselves on the verge of such an act in Poland. Each time this led to an increase in tension, a worsening of relations with the West, and an escalating arms race. And so long as an "alliance" existed that was based on coercion, the possibility of new interventions and all their consequences, including armed conflict in Europe, also existed. Was this a contribution toward security? I am sure not all present at this meeting were persuaded by my speech. Nobody likes to preside over the dissolution of his empire, to paraphrase the famous words of Winston Churchill. But it is even worse and much more dangerous to try to preserve it when its time has expired.

A graphic illustration is the armed intervention in Hungary. (I would like to state one reservation: our actions were to a great extent linked to the Cold War, which was fueled also by the propaganda and the clandestine activities of the United States.) Hungary paid a heavy price for these events. But we, too, paid. Brakes were applied at home to the policy of de-Stalinization and of reform. Our interventions in Hungary aggravated international tensions and complicated the situation within our leadership. This compounded Khrushchev's difficulties in pursuing his anti-Stalinist policy.

But I would not like to reduce everything to a matter of external affairs. There cannot be any doubt that the sharp criticism of Stalin undertaken by Khrushchev at the Twentieth Party Congress was a desperately bold step into the unknown, and into problems, many of which he could not have foreseen.

The congress awakened the conscience of the people. Of course there were individual heroes who did not allow themselves to be intimidated or silenced—though, tragically, you can count on your fingers the ones who survived. For years we were obedient and fearful subjects of a totalitarian state. After the congress we started to become citizens and rebels. A new vitality of thought blossomed that was not quashed even during the frequent lapses into neo-Stalinism. I am convinced that this was one of the essential sources for perestroika and glasnost. Here, at last, the sixties generation had a real chance to speak its word.

The old dogmas, however, continued to reign in many spheres of social thought, and the same old people continued to rule. They obstructed, stifled, and, whenever the opportunity arose, pitilessly crushed individuals whom the Twentieth Party Congress had formed intellectually and morally and who had waited for their day to come. Khrushchev presented many such opportunities to them, and his successor gave them many more.

So the picture was very contradictory. Awakening, vibrant life at one pole—and unshaken dogmas, mummified ideas and perceptions at the other. The reforming energy looked for outlets, but most of these were closed or very narrow.

Despite conditions of general stagnation in the development of theory and social and political thought, oases of open thinking sprang up here and there. As a rule, this could happen when people of sufficient courage and authority appeared who were prepared to think differently and were capable of doing so.

4 Oases of Open Thinking

I have been particularly lucky in my professional life to have worked in several posts where the open exchange of ideas was practiced. Moreover, I did so while I was in my late thirties and early forties—the most productive period of life.

Otto Kuusinen's Think Tank and the Textbook Fundamentals of Marxism-Leninism

After I left the journal *Problems of Philosophy* I went to work at the weekly *New Times (Novoye Vremya)*. There I met Otto Wilhelmovich Kuusinen, who had been one of the editors of *New Times* since its inception, though this fact was never publicized.

A man of Finnish ancestry, Kuusinen was a distinguished politician and theoretician and a prominent figure in the international labor and Communist movements. When I started work at the magazine, he was almost seventy-five years old and practically in retirement. He was an honorary member of the Presidium of the Supreme Soviet. But at the June 1957 plenum of the Central Committee, after he passionately spoke out against Molotov, Malenkov, and Kaganovich, and helped to save Khrushchev from being ousted, he was elected secretary and member of the committee's Presidium.

The leadership had taken note of Kuusinen earlier. Apparently, just after the Twentieth Party Congress in 1956, the Central Committee had decided to produce a few works—textbooks and guidelines—on the main social disciplines: political economy, Party history, and the fundamentals of Marxism-Leninism. The work on this last subject was to embrace philosophy, political economics, and so-called scientific socialism—that is, everything else. In addition, the book was to be understandable to the widest possible audience in the Soviet Union and abroad. Kuusinen was appointed head of the authorial team for the "fundamentals" book.

The decision to prepare all these works as quickly as possible was reached because of the desire to fill the vacuum created after the "dismantling" of Stalinist theoretical and ideological ideas and perceptions and the discrediting of Stalin's *Short Course in the History of the Communist Party*. But, as often happens, a good idea got distorted and emasculated by the time it was put into practice. All the more so in this case because those who were entrusted with producing the new books were, for the most part, the same ideological high priests and their acolytes who had been working long and hard to strengthen Stalinist propaganda in the various spheres of learning.

These were precisely the people the Propaganda Department of the Central Committee recruited to fill the slots of Kuusinen's creative task force, taking advantage, perhaps, of the fact that he was not well acquainted with people in the social sciences and journalism. At the beginning of 1957, when Kuusinen read the first draft of the manuscript written by the authors foisted upon him, he fell at first into a deep depression, as he later told us, and then started frantically looking around for other people. He managed to do this only after he became secretary of the Central Committee. Up to that point, some of the apparat functionaries were bitterly opposed to the idea of any more people coming to join the writers' team, and nobody was accepted for work. Four months after I joined the staff of *New Times* I received an offer to join Kuusinen's new team.

I remember quite well how all this came about. In mid-April of 1957 I received a telephone call. A woman (a secretary, as it turned out) asked if it was Arbatov on the line and said: "Otto Wilhelmovich Kuusinen will speak to you; I am connecting you." I then heard Kuusinen's voice, which was familiar to me, since I had seen and heard him speak at meetings of the editorial board from time to time: "Hello, Georgi Arkadyevich, I need your help. Could we meet?" Of course I said yes, and he invited me to drop by his home that evening. It was the famous Government House—the "House on the Embankment" described in the novel of the same title by the fine writer Yuri Trifonov.

Constructed in the style of the 1920s and 1930s, just opposite the Kremlin on the island between the Moscow River and the canal, the building was gloomy, enormous, and gray. Only prominent politicians, Party and government bosses, famous military figures, veterans of the revolution, and writers who were close to the country's political leaders were given apartments there. In 1937–1938 many of them fell victim to Stalin's repressions. Their families followed them either to prison or into exile or, at the very least, were evicted to make room for the new bosses.

That evening I came to Kuusinen's modestly furnished apartment; it had three or four rooms, of which the largest was his study. I was surprised to see gymnastic rings hanging from the ceiling, next to the desk. (Later I noticed a gymnast's rack on the opposite wall.) Catching my perplexed gaze, my host pulled himself up on the rings several times— and quite vigorously for his seventy-five years. As he did so, he said, "You have to stay in shape, otherwise you grow old quickly."

We switched to business, and Kuusinen proposed that I become a member of the writing group. He said I would receive a telephone call from the Central Committee. A few days later I was invited to visit the vice chairman of the Propaganda Department, V. Snastin, who grilled me on my acquaintance with Kuusinen. Snastin said that he would include me in the group and that I would be instructed by phone as to where and when I was to appear. After that the Central Committee "forgot" about me; the Party ideologues were very loath to include new, "unsuitable" persons on important projects. But everything changed when only two months later fate carried Kuusinen to the pinnacle of the Party hierarchy. Snastin phoned me and asked in an exasperated voice: "Why haven't you gone to Nagorny [the Central Committee's resort area just outside Moscow, where the group was working] yet? I'm giving you two hours to get packed; you can call for a car on this number."

Awhile later I learned how Kuusinen had come to notice me. After

my arrival at *New Times* I began to write a great deal and since I had
come from an academic journal, which was in a different league from a
political weekly, my articles attracted his attention. He asked another
member of the editorial staff, Lev Maximovich Sheidin, about me. Sheidin, who used to write under the pen name "L. Sedin," was a first-rate
journalist specializing in international affairs and very much underrated
in his lifetime. Kuusinen had a deep respect and a strong personal affec-
tion for him. Apparently, I received good recommendations. From that
moment on, Sheidin, Alexei Stepanovich Belyakov, and I had the good
fortune of helping Kuusinen in his activities till the end of his days.
Belyakov was an employee of the Central Committee apparat who later
became Kuusinen's assistant and then deputy director of the International Department of the Central Committee.*

Among other newcomers who came to work with us, I would like to
mention the philosophers Yu. A. Melvil and A. A. Makarovsky. Professor Valentin Asmus, one of the foremost philosophers of the old school,
was also recruited to work on various philosophical chapters. Professor
Asmus also loved astronomy. When he arrived at the Central Committee dacha where our writers' group worked, he brought with him a large
telescope.

Kuusinen was a very unusual man, especially by the prevailing standards. All of us had to start our work through serious self-education—or
rather, reeducation—by sloughing off dogmas that had become almost
second nature. We had to learn how to question our preconceived ideas
and the habitual quotations from official sources of what was the truth.

It was probably then that I first understood how backward we all
were. Kuusinen was a wonderful teacher. Despite his age he had a very
flexible mind, and was open and receptive to new ideas. I can honestly
say that he was the first person I knew who could be described, without
any exaggeration, as always thinking.

You could almost feel Kuusinen's mind working when you were with
him. You felt that each word was carefully thought out and that each of
your questions and answers was also seriously appraised. You always felt

---

*When Kuusinen died we prepared the drafts for his eulogy and the oration at his funeral,
which was delivered by Nikolai Podgorny. Khrushchev, who had a great respect for Kuusinen and most probably would have given the speech himself, was away in Egypt at the
time.

under pressure because you did not want to say something stupid or dull. But in the presence of his intellect we all got a little wiser and, as we dealt with him, we drew upon our hidden reserves and potential.

Everyone working with Kuusinen made another discovery: a new perception of politics—especially new for us, whose minds had been polluted and blunted by the many years of Stalinism. We evolved an understanding of politics as a complicated creative process combined with a search for new methods. Some things that we had read about and did not absorb, or absorbed only as theoretical abstractions, came to life in our conversations with Otto Kuusinen.

Kuusinen was an incarnation of the best traditions of the European labor movement, which by that time seemed frightfully distant: the social-democratic ideas of the old left, mature Leninism, and the more enlightened pages of the history of the Comintern, which unfortunately were few. (Kuusinen had been one of the leaders of the Comintern.)

All in all, work on *Fundamentals* was a concentrated university experience for the whole team. The year and a half of study not only gave us new insights into Marxism and Leninism, but demystified understanding of the subject of politics itself. The textbook did not go far enough, and much of what it contains has not withstood the test of time, but by contemporary standards we managed to create a truly singular work. The textbook was a vivid testimony to the changes in Soviet political thought that took place after the Twentieth Party Congress. It managed to eliminate the Party gobbledygook that had dominated our political literature for years and translated political ideas and theory into simple, clear, and occasionally vivid language.

It was unequivocally stern in its analysis of Stalin's despotism, of its character and consequences, and refused to dress up these facts with references to "historical necessity" and the harsh demands of the period. This was in accordance with Kuusinen's own outlook—although at that time he could not publicly say everything he thought.

The textbook *The Fundamentals of Marxism-Leninism* could have become a real event in our ideological life. But by 1959, when it appeared, the conservative opposition to the Twentieth Party Congress had grown to considerable proportions, and of course conservatives disliked the book.

My friends who worked in the Party apparat told me that inside the tight circle of his department the Central Committee's then secretary for ideology, Leonid F. Ilyichev, used to call the Kuusinen textbook social-democratic.

Nonetheless, I think that the work was a watershed in the evolution of our political thought. The ideas generated by Kuusinen, his writing team, and others who worked with him found their way into the political process despite everything. That was a serious blow to many Stalinist ideas, and an even stronger attack on the awful dogmatism that permeated our minds.

In this connection I would like to quote Belyakov, who collaborated closely with Kuusinen. "Kuusinen was an implacable foe of dogmatism and sectarian narrow-mindedness. As a result of long hours of thought based on immense experience, he came to understand perfectly well what was going on in our country and in the world Communist movement. His ardent desire was to make the greatest contribution possible toward the resolution of Communism's mounting problems. But he was extremely cautious—his whole past had forced him to be so. Within the CPSU he was still regarded as a 'foreigner,' and moreover, as a 'former social democrat.' And, in addition to that, his wife and a son had been arrested as 'enemies of the people.'* This made him triply vulnerable in Stalin's time and not one hundred percent one of the boys even after Stalin.

"I think that Otto Kuusinen saw his role and his mission as a bridge between Lenin and Leninism on the one hand, and the post-Stalin leadership of the Soviet Union on the other. But here you must take into

---

*In this respect, Kuusinen shared the fate of many of the officials of Stalin's period. Perhaps this was some sort of tribute to an ancient Oriental tradition, or perhaps Stalin simply wanted to turn his cohorts into hostages as well; most among them, including the top leaders and members of the Politburo, had close relatives who had been arrested and convicted. Molotov's and Kalinin's wives were in prison. One of Kaganovich's brothers was shot, and another preferred to shoot himself. They tried to arrest Marshal Voroshilov's wife, but he supposedly defended her with his pistol in a rare act of bravery. He saved the parents of his son's wife, as well. Shvernik's only daughter's husband was arrested and shot—and so on and so forth. Incidentally, Stalin did not spare his own family. All the close relatives of his former wife, who had committed suicide—her sisters, her nieces, and so on—were sent off to the camps, and her brother shot himself under mysterious circumstances. And at the beginning of the war, in execution of his own fanatical command that each one of our prisoners of war was a traitor whose family was subject to repression, he ordered the arrest of his son Yakov's wife and their daughter, who was still a child, because Yakov had been taken prisoner by the Germans.

account the difference in the eras in which Lenin and Kuusinen lived. The main danger in Lenin's view was the 'revisionism from the right,' that is, the Second International. Subsequently, it was the struggle against 'leftist deviationism' that came to the forefront. Lenin saw its danger too, but expressed the hope that one could 'easily heal' 'leftist communism' because it was an 'infantile disease.'* This hope was never fulfilled, even in those two enormous states where revolution triumphed—the Soviet Union and China.

"It is important, however, that Kuusinen took up the crusade against the leftist threat where Lenin left off, and carried it further. In difficult circumstances he did the best he could to debunk 'leftism,' the pseudo-Marxist phraseology of some Communists who were capable of destroying the movement."

I think that Belyakov has described Kuusinen very correctly and I would like to add just a few words of my own.

One of my observations was that Kuusinen avoided any conversations about the past. Evidently, he could not come to terms with it. Here are some purely speculative guesses: he could not, and did not, come to the defense of members of his family and friends who fell into the meat grinder of Stalinist repressions, and he did not wish to recall these events. There were some exceptions, however. Yuri Andropov told me that Kuusinen saved him from some very serious and unpleasant consequences during their work together in Karelia at the time of the Leningrad Affair—a big purge in Leningrad, which started soon after the end of the war. The same may apply to the events of late 1939 and early 1940, when Kuusinen headed the "Terioki government" of Finland, set up by Stalin. Kuusinen was even less willing to discuss that. Several times I overcame a strong temptation to ask him about that period. He never spoke of it, perhaps because he suffered from a sense of guilt, although he could hardly have done anything to avoid the shocking course of events.

Later I thought that Kuusinen must have suffered much humiliation and fear under Stalin. And this was one of the reasons for his special, almost blind loyalty to Khrushchev. I remember the only argument I ever had with Kuusinen: Sheidin and I expressed our indignation at the

*V. I. Lenin, *Complete Works,* vol. 41, p. 88.

fact that the book of impressions about Khrushchev's visit to the United States—*Face to Face with America*—which flattered Khrushchev, had received the Lenin Prize. Kuusinen really chewed us out.

On a more serious point, if you look at the makeup of the Politburo (then called the Presidium) of the Central Committee in post-Stalin times, you will find that with all the now-forgotten Kozlovs, Kirichenkos, Furtsevas, Mukhitdinovs, and Podgornys who surrounded Khrushchev, very few people were progressive influences who would give their honest opinion on any difficult political problem. I know of only two such people. One of them was Kuusinen. The other was Anastas Mikoyan. At the beginning of 1989 I had the pleasure of hearing this confirmed at an international seminar devoted to the Cuban missile crisis of 1962, by Khrushchev's son, Sergei, who read a passage from his father's memoirs stating that only these two men warned him about the possible dangerous consequences of deploying missiles in Cuba. Of course, the warning was given in extremely cautious terms, appropriate to the norms of behavior in the Politburo at the time, but it was clear enough for Khrushchev to understand. Kuusinen and Mikoyan warned Khrushchev that though they would vote for his proposal, that would be only because they trusted him. Khrushchev clearly interpreted this as follows: "His [Kuusinen's] reply placed all the responsibility on me. I greatly respected Comrade Kuusinen and knew his honesty and sincerity and, therefore, I took what he was saying in the right way."*

In his memoirs, Khrushchev writes: "I even said that this step [the deployment of Soviet missiles in Cuba], if you put it bluntly, verged on adventurism. Adventurism in the sense that we, in our desire to save Cuba, could get involved in a nuclear war of the gravest kind and the like of which had never been seen."

The incident involving Kuusinen is very revealing. First of all, it speaks of Kuusinen's political insight in realizing the dangers of the proposed action. It also reveals that long after Stalin, the system was still intact. No one could openly question the decision of the leader. One could express one's doubts only with such subtlety that nobody except the leader would understand. On the one hand, Kuusinen found a way of letting Khrushchev know about his fear. But on the other, he was, in

---

*I quote this with the permission of Sergei Khrushchev.

my judgment, too reticent, because he trusted Khrushchev too much and could not overcome his timidity even in a situation fraught with the most serious possible consequences.

The Institute of World Economics and International Relations (IMEMO)

The creation of the Institute of World Economics and International Relations* was also a direct result of the Twentieth Party Congress. An absurd situation existed in the mid-1950s: despite the numerous research institutes and centers that had been set up in the country, not a single one dealt with international studies, foreign policy, and international economic and political affairs. The only exception was the ancient Institute of Oriental Studies, in existence long before the revolution but limited almost entirely to the study of "exotic" languages, culture, and history.

This had not always been the case. In addition to the research institutes and centers of the Comintern and various organizations connected with it (apparently, they all ceased to exist along with the Comintern), there was also the Institute of World Economics and Politics (IMK), which was part of the so-called Communist Academy (an institution of study and research in social sciences and politics). In the 1930s the IMK was converted to an institute of the Academy of Sciences, and operated from 1924 to 1947. It employed 120 persons. At that time it may have been the largest humanities institute of the Academy of Sciences. It was headed by Academician Yevgeni S. Varga, who was for a long time a trusted consultant to Stalin. This position gave Varga a certain independence of judgment unusual for that time. It also permitted him, along with some other Hungarian émigrés who worked with him, to escape the purges of the 1930s, and gave him the opportunity to embark on serious research on current economic projections and the history and theory of economic cycles and crises in the West. For a long time, apparently because crises were associated with upsurges in revolutionary movements, this subject attracted the greatest attention of the Soviet leadership and, therefore, of Soviet specialists in world economics. The

*An arm of the Academy of Sciences of the U.S.S.R.

institute also studied international relations, but mostly in the context of disagreements and conflicts, and war-threatening situations.

After World War II, Stalin apparently lost much of his interest in Varga and his analyses. In the meantime, the Institute of World Economics and Politics acquired a mighty enemy—the chairman of Gosplan (the State Planning Committee), a member of the Politburo and a man who felt himself to be the dictator of practical economics and economic sciences: Nikolai Voznesensky.*

He unleashed a crushing critical attack against Varga for his "embellishment" of capitalism, and for his concept of the existence of an "organized capitalism." Soon, the institute was closed; a number of the institute's employees were arrested and many others were fired.

Varga tried to resist. He wrote to Stalin protesting the closing of the institute. Stalin forwarded the letter to Andrei Zhdanov. Zhdanov told Varga that the Central Committee was chiefly interested in comparisons that would help solve the problem of how to "catch up with and overtake" the West as rapidly as possible. Such comparisons, according to Zhdanov, were possible only if specialists in Soviet and foreign economics worked together.

Here I would like to refer to the testimony of one of the veterans of IMK, Dr. Ya. A. Pevzner, who has written his notes on the history of the institute for my personal research: "The question arises: Why did Stalin now [Varga and IMK were attacked before the war, but Stalin came to their defense] abandon IMK and close it? Voznesensky's personal motives could hardly have played a decisive role. I assume that this nonsensical decision was the result of Stalin's postwar foreign-policy line; supposedly capitalism had suffered a crushing defeat, its general crisis continued to deepen, we had to get ready to deal it the final, fatal blow. Under the circumstances, an institution like IMK was superfluous. Its very existence injected an element of uncertainty about the swift and inexorable death of capitalism."

So that there will be no misunderstanding, I would like to note that

---

*Soon after, Voznesensky was arrested and executed. Later he was posthumously rehabilitated; of course, he was neither a spy nor a traitor, but I think that along with reestablishing justice, we should not avoid revealing the unbecoming truth about those people who were martyred.

when Pevzner refers to "the final, fatal blow" he has in mind not a military strike or a "revolutionary war" by the U.S.S.R. and its allies, but a worldwide class uprising and national-liberation struggle. I am not sure about the hundred-percent accuracy of this analysis. At the end of the war, Stalin advised Palmiro Togliatti and Maurice Thorez* to refrain from efforts to speed up revolution, although the situation in Italy and France did seem revolutionary; he also agreed to end the civil war in Iranian Azerbaijan, showed a willingness to compromise in a number of other places (including the cease-fire in Korea in 1951), and made special efforts to gain the sympathies of Western intellectuals, taking advantage of their "ban the Bomb" attitudes. I interpret that caution as an indication that he was not at all sure that capitalism was in its death throes or that the final and decisive battle was at hand. At the same time, his policies and political declarations showed no real willingness to find mutually acceptable solutions (though he did this during the war years), let alone to come up with realistic proposals and initiatives. Meanwhile, our propaganda was becoming more and more warlike and hostile, and further and further from an accurate evaluation of capitalism.

Monstrous absurdities were being promoted not only by regular journalists and official propagandists, but by leaders of the Party and government. In *Economic Problems of Socialism in the U.S.S.R.* (1952), his last theoretical work, Stalin wrote that the old Marxist conclusion about "the inevitability of war between capitalist states remained in force"— while, in fact, the advent of the Cold War united the capitalist countries against the U.S.S.R. and its allies! As far as prospects for the economic development of the United States, England, and France were concerned, Stalin categorically insisted that "the increase in production of these countries will take place on a more limited basis, since [their] volume of production . . . will continue to decline." And this was written on the eve of capitalism's twenty-year-long economic expansion—the greatest ever in its history.

Stalin, with all his mistrust and hostility, pursued two different policies toward capitalism. One was a very cautious, even no-win, policy that did not pursue any practical objectives, though maybe the idea was to wait until capitalism collapsed under the weight of its own sins and conflicts. The other "policy" was raucous, boastful, and very militant

---

*The leaders, respectively, of the Italian and French Communist parties.

anticapitalist propaganda. Whether Stalin believed this propaganda is another matter. Therefore, Professor Pevzner's opinion about the real reasons for closing down IMK deserves to be taken quite seriously.

I have dwelt on this story in detail to reveal yet another aspect of the steep decline in our sociopolitical thinking during the last years of Stalin's life: the extremely primitive notions cultivated in these years about the rest of the world and the world economy, about capitalism and international relations. For a long time, we did not want to abandon these notions. They were drummed into the heads of a whole generation of our experts, and became sacrosanct dogma.

I think the significance of the Institute of World Economics and International Relations (IMEMO) and the difficulties that it was to encounter in its development become clear when viewed against this backdrop. They started with the very important question of who would be chosen as director. The head of the Economic Science Section of the Science Department of the Central Committee, Klavdia Kuznetsova (who played a nefarious role in everything she could touch and influence), demanded that Ivan I. Kuzminov be appointed. Kuzminov, who held the chair of the Central Committee's Academy of Social Sciences, was known to one and all in the field of international studies as the most dyed-in-the-wool Stalinist and militant dogmatic in economics.

Fortunately for the newly forming institute and for the world of learning in general, there appeared a very strong rival to Kuzminov. This was Anushavan Agafonovich Arzumanyan, who had arrived in Moscow in 1953 and had become the deputy director of the Economics Institute at the Soviet Academy of Sciences. At the time the director of IMEMO was being chosen, Arzumanyan was virtually unknown in the academic world, but he had a strong ace up his sleeve: he was a close friend (and the husband of the sister-in-law) of Anastas Mikoyan. This apparently sealed his appointment, although officially Mikoyan had nothing to do with the question. I say this not as a rebuke to Arzumanyan or Mikoyan. Nepotism, it seems, is not always a bad thing. And the fact that Mikoyan, who was one of the brightest people in the government in those years, used his influence to reject the arch-conservative candidate and appoint the more progressive one (even if he was a relative) can only be regarded as an achievement. Now Arzumanyan had to deliver, which was by no means easy.

One of the legacies of Stalinism was that the social sciences could not be perceived outside the framework of propaganda. They were reduced to functioning solely as servants of policy, intended in Marxist terms to justify each new political escapade of the leadership.

First of all, the director of the new institute had to overcome several fundamental obstacles.

One of these was the extremely dogmatic and propagandistic view of capitalist economics held by most Soviet experts. Even those who might have been skeptical of the perception that the ship of capitalism was foundering nonetheless found it normal and necessary to feed the public this version of events. Such were the rules of the game for many years. The Twentieth Party Congress somewhat improved the situation, but the standards of what was permissible in the press and even in academic publications remained very strict and were maintained by a host of watchful defenders of the faith.

Naturally, such an atmosphere made Arzumanyan's task of turning the institute into a new type of research center extremely difficult. In the early 1960s he told me frankly about some of the tricks of the trade, in particular how he managed to cope with ideological censorship while creating a serious research institute. The institute maintained the necessary orthodoxy in its journal and the books it published, he said. And this is true. Just read these books and the journal *World Economics and International Relations* in the first years of its publication: they continued to pour out doomsday predictions about the "shakiness and instability" of the capitalist economy, about the new "upheavals" and "crises" that were awaiting it, and promised soon to "catch up with and overtake the most developed capitalist countries" in all the most important sectors of industrial and agricultural per-capita production. However, a far more realistic picture was being presented in the analytical and informational papers sent to the government leadership. In preparing these papers—which were usually labeled CLASSIFIED or TOP SECRET—people were bit by bit freeing themselves of dogmatism and learning to write more freely—a development that later also became evident in various publications.

I must say that later, at the end of the 1960s, I would often recall this conversation when, as newly appointed director, I had to solve the problems connected with establishing the Institute for the Study of the U.S.A.* at the Academy of Sciences. And I had to travel the same road.

---

*From 1975 onward, it was the Institute for the Study of the U.S.A. and Canada.

Arzumanyan's second difficult hurdle was the problem of personnel. The longtime lack of demand had limited the supply of scholars. Of course, there were still some people left over from IMK. But from the small number of those who were not too old and sick it was impossible to fill all the posts at a large institution (IMEMO was assigned three hundred staff positions). Here, Arzumanyan displayed unusual courage. First, he took on board a group of experts who had returned from Stalin's prisons (Semyon A. Dalin, Yevgeni A. Gromov, Vera V. Zubchaninova) and also some people who had long been ostracized and who because of one political accusation or another had been thrown out of the academic community. And at the same time, he was not afraid to invite a large group of young scholars. Two of them, Nikolai Inozemtsev and Vladlen Martynov, were to succeed him.

Here I would like to digress briefly. Inozemtsev will figure numerous times in the course of this book, and I would like to say a few words about him. A close friend, he played a considerable role in the development of Soviet social sciences and, to some extent, in the intellectualization of Soviet politics. I met him while we were still students. He had had a very good career—deputy director of IMEMO, then assistant editor of *Pravda* (in my country a very high position for a *young* man of forty); finally, he became director of IMEMO. There was something solid about him that set him apart from others, and politically we were in very close agreement.

Sometimes I thought that he was too cautious in his positions, especially while dealing with the country's leaders. But he was a very shrewd tactician. On some occasions, he acted boldly and courageously. At one of the Central Committee plenums he made a speech proposing radical reforms in our foreign economic policy and the abandonment of entrenched dogmas in this sphere. This earned him many new enemies. (Incidentally, it was also the only pre-perestroika occasion I remember when someone spoke without a written text at a plenum—and this in itself was taken as an affront by the conservative majority of the Central Committee.) Inozemtsev had every chance of making an even more brilliant career. But the conservatives soon recognized him as an "alien." Among other things, they looked upon his institute as a source of "pernicious" Western influence on the government. (He had direct access to many of its leaders at the time.)

But now let me go back to Arzumanyan.

The third obstacle he faced was the administer-by-command system in the world of science, which had been hardening for many years and had attained the strength of reinforced concrete. And with this came its twin—the fear of fresh and unorthodox thinking. Here Arzumanyan's personal qualities played an enormous role—his human decency, his intolerance toward attempts to victimize people, and his willingness to hear different opinions, including some quite bold ones, provided they were expressed in the appropriate form and within a sufficiently narrow circle. All this helped to build up an interesting institute.

And what real effects did the new institute have in the first years following the Twentieth Party Congress? How did it help to liberate creative thought, and how did it help in the evolution of politics itself?

If one is to judge Arzumanyan by the standards of his day and take into account the whole blemished theoretical legacy that he and his colleagues inherited, one can give him rather high marks. He managed to loosen old dogmas, clearing the way for a more realistic view of the world, of Western economics and international relations. As I have mentioned, this did not show in IMEMO's open publications for quite some time—particularly because many of the old specialists who were offered positions at the institute were victims of their own traditional—I would say honest—"Comintern"-style dogmatism.

But very soon there formed at the institute a relatively small group of social scientists who enjoyed Arzumanyan's personal trust and were allowed a relatively large measure of freedom. Not only that, they were encouraged, up to a point, to be unorthodox. For example, a paper sent up to the top about the appearance in the West of a study comparing the economic development of capitalist and socialist countries produced some impact. Soon research in the same direction appeared in the U.S.S.R. as well, although it was not always entirely objective. The same can be said about papers on Western European economic integration that accepted this process as a reality. Previously, our experts and our journalists had uniformly attacked such an idea as a reactionary invention, propaganda, and a conspiracy by someone or other. (The orthodox view was that in the capitalist world antagonisms and contradictions prevail.) These papers often displeased the conservatives, who wanted to cut off, or at least impose stringent controls on, this new channel of information to the leadership.

One typical episode concerned a note that criticized the forms of Soviet economic aid to developing nations.* Arzumanyan circulated the paper in the form of a flier—that is, he ran off fifty copies for "interested agencies." The administration of one of these agencies complained to the almighty ideological boss of the past, Mikhail S. Suslov, who called in Arzumanyan and, as the latter recalled, told him more or less the following: "Arzumanyan, we are both old Party members; you haven't forgotten how the opposition used to operate, have you? They used to write position papers and send them around as they saw fit. You won't get away with it. If you're going to write a paper, send it to us first, one copy, and we'll decide whom to send it on to."

Arzumanyan had enough courage, navigational skill, and political "buoyancy" to ignore this instruction, and he continued to prepare and send out papers as he saw fit.†

Arzumanyan and IMEMO had another quite important channel of influence in political thought and policy—the preparation of Party documents and speeches for members of the leadership. During the heated discussions in the course of this work (I had occasion to participate in these quite frequently during 1962–1964, when I worked at the institute), interesting ideas would often emerge. Some of these were included in the texts. Arzumanyan found ways of getting some of the others through to the leadership.

Even if all of this was still a long, long way from the new political thinking, it was helping to thaw out social and political thought. Dogmas about the stagnation of capitalist economy, the absolute impoverishment of the working class in the West, and so on, were being rejected, and new concepts were being confirmed and put into political

*Georgi Ye. Skorov, at this time a young scholar, was the author; later he was my deputy for a while.

†Typically, during the last years of Leonid Brezhnev's life it was officially forbidden (perhaps on Suslov's initiative again) to send papers and other material directly to members of the leadership and the Central Committee apparat. Everything had to be sent to the Central Committee of the CPSU—this meant that it just went to the General Department, headed by Konstantin Chernenko. It was there that anonymous officials decided the fate of the material received. Much of it went into the trash can. Some of it went to a couple of departments of the Central Committee; only in a few isolated cases did the fruits of our social scientists' labor get through to the leadership. Naturally, the think tanks soon began to feel this; and scholars were deprived of even a moral incentive to work, to write papers, or even to think. Why work when no one is interested in what you think?

circulation (for example, about the reality of Western European integration and the many different ways in which Third World countries could
develop). It was at this time that the book *Economics* by the well-known
American scholar Robert Samuelson was published—albeit after considerable resistance—with a long introduction by Arzumanyan. (Even
this was very important for the development of our science of economics.)

Naturally, the institute also made some serious mistakes. Arzumanyan and, as far as I know, part of his staff succumbed to the post–
Twentieth Party Congress euphoria of the second half of the fifties and
the beginning of the sixties; they not only made no attempt to bring the
government back down to earth, but supported its illusion that the
U.S.S.R. would soon catch up with and overtake the United States
economically, by 1980 building a prosperous and free Communist society. These illusions were later incorporated into the new CPSU program
(accepted in 1961) and, as 1980 approached, became the objects of sharp
criticism and the butt of caustic jokes.

Nevertheless, IMEMO played a very important role as an incubator
for the new generation of international economists and foreign-policy
specialists. In time, the people who went through the institute came to
figure prominently in our social sciences and, to some extent, in politics.
Moreover, IMEMO became a kind of root from which sprouted a
whole crop of institutes of the Academy of Sciences—the Institutes of
the International Working Class Movement, Africa, Latin America, the
United States and Canada.

The Journal The World Marxist Review *and Its Editor-in-Chief, Alexei M. Rumyantsev*

The World Marxist Review's headquarters were in Prague. The journal
was established as a joint venture of the international Communist movement and was another preparatory school for theoretical and political
professionals who were later to fulfill the thankless but very important
mission of trying to stem the regression of theory, ideology, and politics
in the last years of Khrushchev's rule and all of Leonid Brezhnev's.
These men helped build an intellectual bridge from the Twentieth Party
Congress to perestroika, across the chasm of stagnation. It also served as
a barricade against the counterattacks of Stalinism. Moreover, many of

those who then worked for the journal, and whose ideas and political thinking were formed while on its staff, had the good fortune to make a significant contribution in preparing and laying the theoretical foundations of perestroika.

How did they achieve such success? First, the journal emerged from the general political and moral atmosphere created by the Twentieth Party Congress. And second, there was the personality of its first editor-in-chief, Alexei Matveyevich Rumyantsev. He wanted to attract talented and creative people to his journal, and he was not afraid to defend them. More than that, he was ready to fight the opposition of the conservatives, who had quite different ideas about staffing the Soviet side of the journal, which they saw as an extension of the Party apparat. (Of course they managed to place a number of like-minded people on the editorial staff.)

Among Rumyantsev's staff members were Anatoli S. Chernyayev and Georgi H. Shakhnazarov, who after many years of political and theoretical work became Mikhail Gorbachev's assistants, in positions where they contributed significantly (although our tradition required that they do so anonymously).

Of course, to create an environment where talent could flourish, it was not enough to hire gifted people. You also had to give them intellectual freedom (to the extent that the limits of those difficult times allowed) and to remove fear, which had become second nature over the years. Rumyantsev did a great deal to create a supportive atmosphere, to encourage creativity, and to come to the defense of people who found themselves under attack.*

---

*I myself benefited from his support. When I agreed in early 1960 to work at the journal, F. V. Konstantinov, my boss at the time, tried to get in the way (I was then employed by the journal *Communist,* of which he was editor-in-chief). The method he selected was the usual one for his generation—he made a phone call to a senior employee of the Central Committee and denounced me. He said that I had an unstable political position and had displayed immaturity during the Hungarian and Polish events in 1956, having fallen under the influence of the revisionists. I should not be sent abroad. Rumyantsev learned of the conversation and launched a scandal by demanding that the Central Committee secretaries examine Konstantinov's accusations at a Party meeting of the journal in my presence, and that a transcript be made of the meeting. That was precisely what happened (naturally, Konstantinov did not show up), and I was appointed to a corresponding position on the Prague journal. This started a lifelong personal tie between us, and subsequently I had occasion to help him out.

Previously, Rumyantsev had held responsible positions in the world of social science and in the Party apparat. His work attracted Stalin's attention and he was appointed chairman of the newly created Ideological Commission of the Central Committee. Then he became editor-in-chief of the journal *Communist,* and later was assigned to Prague. Very few members of the older generation of social scientists accepted the ideas of renewal produced by the Twentieth Party Congress as seriously as Rumyantsev did.*

Rumyantsev made a very positive impact at the journal with his personality, his tolerance, and his readiness to trust young people. In relation to the foreigners (the journal staff included members of many foreign Communist parties), he showed diplomatic skill. Even during heated debates (it was a time of troubles between parties) he managed to keep the atmosphere calm and friendly.

Among the Soviet members of the staff, a few of the people holding administrative positions were typical of the Central Committee apparat of Stalinist times. They hated everything that was going on at the journal and did what they could to disrupt the atmosphere. The secretary of the workplace Party organization, Ivan T. Vinogradov, played a key role in this. Over the course of the journal's life, political mistrust began to fester between Vinogradov, together with a small group of his supporters (whose main strength lay in their strong apparat connections back home in Moscow), and the main body of the Soviet editorial staff. This mistrust exploded into open conflict at a Party reelection meeting at which Vinogradov came under some severe criticism and was wiped out in the elections to the Party committee. Rumyantsev supported Vinogradov's critics, and this decided the outcome of the conflict. I expect that back in Moscow Rumyantsev had some unpleasant conversations regarding his position in this conflict.

All in all, the journal could hardly have had a noticeable effect on the country's ideological and political situation, but it helped quite a number of relatively young theoretical and political workers develop a broader,

*After the October 1964 plenum of the Central Committee, Rumyantsev became head of *Pravda* and made his mark there in no uncertain terms. One of his articles, "On the Intelligentsia," was a sensation; it evoked the wrath of his superiors, and he was transferred to the U.S.S.R. Academy of Sciences, becoming its vice president. Shortly thereafter, the conservatives elbowed him out of this post as well as his directorship of the Institute of Sociology, which he had founded.

more open view of the world, of other countries, of international relations, of politics, and even of Marxist theory. After all, we worked in
constant contact with our foreign colleagues, took part in the discussions
and editing of their articles, and learned how to cope not only with our
own problems, but with theirs as well: we learned how to understand
others. The main thing was to understand that one did not have a monopoly on the truth, that other points of view existed with which one
might not necessarily agree, but which had to be taken into account.
This seems elementary and even natural to us today. But one cannot
forget that we were just beginning, painfully, to free ourselves from the
moral chains of Stalinism. To that end, the journal was a very important
training ground; the exposure to many points of view had its effect.
After all, many of the people who worked for the journal were soon appointed to important posts in the Party and government or began theoretical work of their own.

Andropov and His Consultants in the Central Committee

Beginning in the late 1930s, the Central Committee shared the apex of
political power with the KGB, and of course Stalin stood high above
them all. After Stalin's death, the KGB, while retaining some control,
could not compete with the Party. The Central Committee became the
core of the whole power structure.

In the newspaper one could read texts of new laws; decrees concerning some people's receipt of medals and high awards; governmental decisions on agriculture, education, or industry; even reports about political arrests and trials. But only the insiders knew that all such acts were
preceded by a decision of the Politburo or the Secretariat of the Central
Committee and prepared (or very often even initiated) by the almighty
apparat, a couple of thousand anonymous Party bureaucrats in whom
was concentrated tremendous power, though they were not mentioned
in a single law.

By the old rules I could not have dreamed of working at this "holy
place," the Party Central Committee. My father was Jewish and had
been arrested as a "counterrevolutionary." In addition, I had a reputation
as a sort of revisionist, which meant I was not orthodox enough in what
I thought and said, or was not strictly "Party-minded." There may have
been other sins that I was not aware of. When Yuri Andropov proposed

me for a rather important job in his department at the Central Committee, there were some complications with the KGB and the personnel department, but he overcame their objections. I do not think that he could have done so without the assistance of Otto Kuusinen, who was still a secretary of the Central Committee and a member of the Politburo. But why did Andropov's people want me in the Central Committee apparat? I have already mentioned that neither in Stalin's time nor during Khrushchev's first years did the leadership feel any great need for social scientists and intellectuals.

In the late 1950s, this perception changed as a result of the external difficulties in the world Communist movement and the deterioriating relations with the People's Republic of China and the Chinese Communist Party. It became obvious that one could not simply give orders or let the KGB settle all the problems that arose. The leadership realized that far more attention should be paid to preparing positions and arguments, to improving the art of persuasion and discussion, to refining the government's own position so that it could become more attractive to the public—at home and abroad.

The old apparat could not satisfy those needs. It was programmed for completely different times, rules, and functions. At the very beginning of the 1960s, a consultancy for the top Party apparat was created at the International Department and at the Department of Relations with Communist and Workers' Parties of the Socialist Parties of the CPSU Central Committee (known as the Central Committee Department). For the first time in many decades, a considerable number of members of the intelligentsia were invited to join the apparat of the Party Central Committee.

I became a consultant to Yuri Andropov's department in May 1964 and worked there until the end of 1967. I must say that the group he put together was one of the most outstanding oases of creative thought.

Beyond our actual work, this portrait of the apparachiks would not be complete without discussing their life-style at that time. Many people were drawn into the apparat chiefly by the sense of power, of belonging to a select circle. This belonging was embodied in the red identification booklet with the letters CC CPSU ("Central Committee of the Communist Party of the Soviet Union") stamped on the cover. The booklet was called a "jeep," since it could take you almost anywhere, into virtually any government office. It's hard to say what the most prevalent attitude was toward employees of the Central Committee—respect, toadying, or fear. Respect for members of the ruling Party was instilled from one's childhood, for we had been taught to see in them "the honor, the mind, and the conscience of our epoch" (Lenin's words, printed on page one of the membership card). The fear and toadying were just below the surface.

The salary of those in the category of Senior Central Committee Employee was not all that high—at that time it ranged from 270 to 600 rubles per month—but it was only a part of what one really got. My starting salary was 400 rubles per month, which was only slightly more than the pay of a person occupying an analogous position in a less prestigious institution, such as a research institute or a newspaper. But the position came with a lot of perks. There was an extra month's pay once a year when you went on vacation, plus a similar bonus. In addition the government paid 70 percent of the cost of the resort, plus 50 percent for your wife, plus travel expenses. (Altogether, that made up roughly 20 percent of your salary.)

The main perk for higher-level apparatchiks was the Kremlin Dining Room (as a subterfuge it was officially called the "Dining Room of Therapeutic Eating"). A month's voucher for lunch and dinner officially cost 140 rubles, but you paid only half that. Virtually no one ate in the dining room; instead people used their coupons to buy groceries, and had more than enough for the entire family. The dining room sold the most expensive delicacies, including caviar; special fish; sausages vastly superior to those in the stores and produced at special factories; and select sweets and fruits. When I brought home my four-day allotment of groceries for the first time, my mother-in-law, who lived with us, could not believe her eyes. She said she had not seen such food since NEP (the New Economic Policy of the 1920s, when there were foreign concessions and private enterprise). Thus we spent less than 10 percent of our income feeding the family, while ordinary citizens saw 60 or 70 percent disappear. In addition the Central Committee had excellent cafeterias and a number of subsidized buffets.

Apartments were the second major perk. Like those of all members of the Central Committee, my rights were strictly delineated by my position. After having lived for years in one 180-square-foot room with my wife, son, and mother-in-law, sharing one kitchen and two bathrooms with ten other families (thirty-three persons altogether), I got my first apartment, a separate one-bedroom unit. I recall how for a long time my wife and I could not believe our happy circumstances and often woke up during the night and walked around the apartment to convince ourselves that we were not dreaming. Later, when I got a promotion, we moved into a two-bedroom apartment, and then into a three-bedroom unit. All this was simply inaccessible to anyone who was not a Central Committee employee. At best, such an apartment could be purchased only for large sums, and in much more modest co-op buildings.

Medical care was perk number three. Central Committee employees had access to doctors who were better than those in the usual clinics, and their hospitals boasted excellent equipment and medicines and comfortable rooms. There was also an entire network of sanatoria and rest homes in the best parts of the country.

There were numerous other fringe benefits. For example, every weekend you could go to a resort outside Moscow, paying only a nominal amount (at the time it was one ruble per person per day). In the summer you could even rent an entire apartment there for a very small sum. There were a seamstress's shop, a shoe repairman, a special office for plane and train tickets, and many other services.

All the benefits were strictly regulated on the basis of your position—the number of rooms in your apartment or dacha, which apartment building or resort you had access to, which clinic or hospital you used, where you could go for vacation (above a certain level you could travel abroad with your wife, at first to Eastern Europe, and then to certain countries in Western Europe, to Cuba, and so on). Automobile transportation was a particularly complex situation. A department chief, and also, I believe, his first deputy, had a personal car and two drivers. The other deputies (and those "equated" to them—that was the key word—could call for a car from the garage. Employees with a rank lower than deputy could order a car only during working hours and for official purposes. To travel to the Kremlin mess (we used to call it the feeding trough) we had to get two or three people together in a car.

By the time I arrived at the Central Committee apparat, there were two distinct life-styles.

The first was left over from the old days. The low cultural level of senior officials who had been promoted just before or after the war was mixed with remnants of the former ascetic rules of conduct. One example: it was all right to use an official dacha or car, but considered wrong to buy your own dacha or car. This group was characterized by a general drabness, in which people dressed, talked, and thought identically. They all tried to puff themselves up, were very closemouthed, and carefully concealed any appearance of human emotion (not to mention vice). And, of course, they were all up to their elbows in crime or semicriminal activities (denunciation of the innocents, political and moral destruction of those the regime did not like, etc.) and thus had to support each other, no matter how much they might hate each other.

The other style was that of the new employees of the Central Committee. They could be divided into two groups. The majority of the younger people were functionaries who had advanced through the apparat. They began with the Komsomol (the Communist Youth Organization) and climbed the apparat ladder. I very much disliked these persons, who valued only useful contacts (which they made easily) and who, with few exceptions, were cynical, unprincipled careerists. They differed from their older colleagues in that they had had some contact with the West. Though you couldn't call them cultured, they were more educated and openminded than the older group.

When the first intellectuals appeared in the apparat they were perceived as unacceptable, but these odd fellows came to be looked upon as essential.

The appearance of intellectuals and young careerists led to a change in the Central Committee life-style, even at work, where people began to talk about politics, art, and literature in addition to business and soccer. The circle of acquaintances of Central Committee employees was broadened; many established regular contact, albeit cautiously, with representatives of the "free-thinking" intelligentsia. They were dressed differently.

The new generations of apparatchiks made the bosses more tolerant of the employees' personal habits. A divorce or second marriage (or even a denunciation over an extramarital liaison) ceased to lead to automatic dismissal.

I believe that all these changes had a significant impact on the way the entire political situation later developed. First of all, the top of the pyramid—the Central Committee of the CPSU, and the entire apparat—was demystified, and with time, that helped to delegitimize the Party's absolute power.

Given our difficult living conditions, privileges have been an effective instrument for the maintenance of totalitarian rule ever since the revolution. Privileges were not merely a means of bribing the Party, state, and military leadership. The very existence of privileges brought along the fear that they could be lost and that your living standard could decline radically. You could lose not just your status but also your safety net (after all, one of those privileges was a special pension).

I am not sure that people in the West will be able to understand this situation, but privileges are a very effective means for ensuring obedience and conformity at the top. Their weak side is the extremely negative reaction of envy and hatred from those who do not enjoy them. Privileges could exist as long as they were, if not a secret, then at least a little-noticed aspect of life. It was glasnost that put an end to them.

Fyodor Burlatsky was head of the consultants' group at the Central Committee department at the time. He is a very gifted man, though not very lucky in terms of his career (which has been implicated by some of his personal straits). Among the consultants were Alexander Bovin, who later became very well known as a publicist, journalist, and political figure, and Shakhnazarov, who has already been mentioned. Shakhnazarov had a successful career not only in the social sciences and politics, but in literature as well. Because of his writing he sometimes got into trouble. For example, in 1968 or 1969, the proofs of one of his science-fiction works were sent by the editors to the Central Committee for approval and landed on Suslov's desk. Suslov was outraged, and Shakhnazarov was removed from the Central Committee apparat for several years. Three other colleagues of mine were economist Oleg T. Bogomolov, who later became head of the Institute for the Study of the Economics of the World Socialist System at the U.S.S.R. Academy of Sciences and was also a prominent political figure; Nikolai Shishlin, a political scientist and publicist; and Gennadi Gerasimov, later spokesman for the Ministry of Foreign Affairs.

Politically, all of them were united by their anti-Stalinism and their support of democratic reforms, a more liberal policy in culture, and, of course, a desire for better relations with the West. At this time, this political platform had a code name: policy of the Twentieth Party Congress. That reference also legitimized their political attitudes and views—which a short while before had been regarded as an unforgivable heresy, if not an outright crime.

All our consultants were colorful personalities—Alexander Bovin in particular. He was later to become one of my close friends. I first met him in 1958 working at *Communist,* where Bovin, an almost completely unknown postgraduate student of philosophy, had just been invited to work. He was unusual in many ways, beginning with his biography. He was about thirty. He had a law degree from Rostov University and had been nominated for a judgeship in one of the outlying provincial districts in the Rostov region. Later, he was promoted to Party work and became secretary of the district Party committee. A promising Party career was opening up before him, but he decided on the postgraduate study of philosophy in Moscow. And, at the same time, in order to fill the gaps in his knowledge, he enrolled as an external student at one of the famous technical institutes of Leningrad.

Bovin was bright, open, witty, independent, with a lot of ideas that sounded heretical even in those days of Khrushchev's "enlightenment." He also had a rare zest for life. Among other things, he loved good food and plenty of it, which made him grossly overweight. I rarely met a better partner for heart-to-heart conversations over a glass or two. He was always the life of the party.

But behind all this was a very knowledgeable, hardworking, even pedantic person. On occasion Bovin got himself into trouble, sometimes by accident, more often because of his unorthodox views. For example, he was in the doghouse for several years during Brezhnev's time, and one of the reasons was his criticism of our policy in Czechoslovakia in 1968. He was always hated by the conservatives and Stalinists. When he was ousted from the Central Committee apparat, he went to work as a columnist for *Izvestia,* and became a popular television journalist. He was then recalled by Brezhnev and resumed his work for him.

Bovin had the potential to become one of our outstanding political minds, but the system did not want him, could not even tolerate him. That was a loss both for him and for the system.

The fact that Andropov, as secretary of the Central Committee, had gathered such a group of bright and relatively independent-minded people around him was very important. This was one of the first more or less massive breakthroughs by intellectuals into the center of power, through the "iron wall" of the Party apparatchiks, though the intellectuals still served only as advisers or consultants. What did we do in the department? Most of the work was routine. We wrote documents (drafts of Central Committee decisions; memoranda for our leaders; the leaders' speeches, and so on). At the closing stages of a major project, everyone involved would gather in Andropov's office, and an interesting and productive workshop would begin. Lively discussions developed, turning the sessions into stimulating theoretical and political seminars.

This work gave us an understanding of the inner workings of the political process. It was also very interesting to get acquainted with politics through Andropov, who was not just intelligent, but had an extraordinary gift for politics. He was an unusual personality who did not bend to ideology, but was pragmatic; he wanted practical results. In addition, he was not formally educated. He had attended a vocational school (he studied river shipping), but had read widely in history, literature, and philosophy. On the whole, he was much better educated than his colleagues in the leadership, including those who had graduated from institutions of higher learning. He could also write poetry—and to my untutored eye, quite well. He had a reputation for being musical. He had quite a good voice, and played piano and the guitar.

I think Andropov also gained quite a lot from his discussions with his consultants, because in those years the social circle of highly placed Party workers was small and, as a rule, not at all interesting. Basically, it was limited to similar high-ranking Party members and a couple of personal friends. (Frankly, I got the impression that since Stalin's time, not associating with people who did not belong to one's circle had become an unwritten rule of behavior for the elite, and it has outlived its originator by many years.)

In the course of contacts with his consultants Andropov enlarged his knowledge not only of academic subjects but also of new Soviet and foreign books, of cultural events, and of much else. Finally, and this is probably more important than anything else, such daily work and association with other people opened up for him an important new channel of information about ordinary life and served as a source of unorthodox judgments and opinions, providing the urgently needed information that our leaders lacked.

Andropov received this information in full measure, because he set the following rule right from the start and from time to time he would repeat it: "In this room you can come clean and speak absolutely openly—don't hide your opinions. Now, once you get outside the door, that's different. Then you obey the general rules!"

We followed that principle. If we did hide something from Andropov or were not straightforward with him, it was only to a minor extent and for tactical reasons. I think we considered it our duty to talk with him as openly as we could, even about "difficult" subjects: for example, national problems; the complaints of the intelligentsia; external and internal political decisions that from our point of view were erroneous. My colleagues and I regarded Andropov as one of the few channels of communication with the leadership available to us. Yuri Vladimirovich told us a great deal—but, of course, not everything, and we could hardly have expected him to do so. And he would more often than not listen patiently even to those things that in no way could have pleased him. He rarely interrupted anyone who was saying something important simply because he did not like what he heard. The fact that he would often not comment on something, would stay silent, was another matter. And sometimes, for the sake of propriety, he would defend the orthodox line, not really believing it himself. We understood such reactions and imagined that he made these statements because the situation demanded it. Sometimes I even had the feeling that he was concerned that bugs might have been planted in his office, and that he supported the orthodox line just in case he was being overheard.

How did Andropov's efforts and those of the Consultants' Group benefit the evolution of political thinking, and politics itself? In light of the events of 1989, it is difficult to speak of the "benefits" of events in socialist countries from the first half of the 1960s. But I do think that we managed to avoid some problems that were soon to confront us. For example, Andropov and his group of consultants contributed to the loosening of hard-line principles governing our relations with the countries of Eastern and Central Europe. By that I mean the belief that our country had the right to rule the countries of the socialist community by command and to force them to follow our example. This was part of the political philosophy of many of our Party workers, and it remained part of that philosophy even in the mid-1960s, after the Twentieth Party Congress—above all among those who worked in the apparat (including those in the department headed by Andropov). We tried to present an alternative to this way of thinking: a respect for other socialist countries and their experience, a tolerance for their deviations from what prevailed in our country, and an understanding of the need to build relations based on mutual political and economic interests—all within certain limits, of course. Czechoslovakia soon showed us that these limits could be interpreted very narrowly.

What were these limits? How far could the limits be pushed? For quite a time the debate over this question was the major battleground where opposing ideas and politicians clashed. We tried to make the limits imposed by so-called socialist principles as broad as possible. Our primary purpose was very pragmatic. We realized that excessively rigid control would make new explosions more probable, and we understood that loosening the framework of the "principles" would mean more flexibility and freedom of action at home as well.

At the same time, even the bravest of us did not have enough fortitude to raise the issue of complete freedom of choice for each of the satellites. Despite the modesty of our proposals, each step forward cost us a great deal of effort. Nevertheless, I think that we managed to do something in those years. Not as much as we should have done, but more than had been done previously.

We also articulated the need to abandon our autarchic economic attitudes and traditions in favor of economic integration. Unfortunately, we never succeeded in finding a real solution to these issues. Our efforts to make the political élite more tolerant of our allies' aspirations and of the economic, political, and ideological differences between us were only partially successful. One result of our efforts was that in those years the Central Committee Department contributed significantly to the establishment of more realistic and broader views of foreign policy and relations with the West. With our participation a new concept of peaceful coexistence with the West came into being—not as sheer propaganda, but as a real opportunity and even necessity.

Furthermore, during the serious regressions and concessions to Stalinism that began after Khrushchev, we supporters of the Twentieth Party Congress tried to seize every possible opportunity to maintain the congress's course. If we could not stop the reversals in political direction, at least we could slow them down.

Our opportunities were limited. The political battle at this time had entered a stage of trench warfare. Even the mention of certain key words by the leaders in their documents and speeches ("the personality cult," "Twentieth Party Congress," "peaceful coexistence") could decide the outcome of clashes at various levels of society. Sometimes they influenced political decisions, at other times only the fate of books, articles, films, or plays, but they always affected the political and moral climate of the country. Of course, we were also hopeful that Yuri Andropov would be able to bring to the attention of the leadership the ideas and arguments that we had worked out.*

In evaluating the role of the oases, I cannot claim that social and political thought, which had been reduced to a desert under Stalin, blossomed into a flowering garden under their influence. Regrettably, that did not occur, and could not have occurred. On the contrary, the situation began to worsen, and creative thought was subject to still more limitations and to persecution. Nevertheless, the importance of these oases should not be underestimated. It is undeniable that the improved quality of their thinking enlivened and modernized the intellectual atmosphere in our society and, most important, sowed seeds that sprouted many years later and may well have played an essential role in the years of perestroika.

*The Consultants' Group, as well as the International Department, had the opportunity to influence the course of some internal discussions regarding the rapidly deteriorating relations with the Maoist leadership of China.

5 Winds from China

Only in recent years have we begun to talk about interdependence as a new phenomenon in modern societies and states. But interdependence is not all that new. I have already mentioned the events in Hungary and Poland and their impact upon the political processes in the Soviet Union. Less attention has been paid to the effect of the "Chinese factor" on our affairs, although it was often considerable.

When, for example, Mao Zedong, in reaction to the Twentieth Party Congress, proclaimed: "Let a hundred flowers bloom," many of us interpreted this as a call to pluralism, to freedom of expression and opinion in ideology, science, and culture. On the other hand, the Stalinists got their revenge when, having allowed the "hundred flowers" to bloom, the Chinese leadership began mercilessly to mow them down, and the new policy began to look like a provocation.

A sharp political and ideological struggle between the Soviet Communist Party and the Chinese Communist Party ensued in the 1960s and soon jeopardized the relationship between the governments. It became one of the great events in the history of the 1960s and 1970s and deserves particular study. The U.S.S.R. and China were, after all, the largest powers to proclaim themselves socialist. The effect of their relations on the Cold War was enormous. Here I shall analyze only one of this conflict's ramifications: the effect on the Soviet Union's internal political and ideological battles.

In his political struggle against the Soviet leadership, Mao Zedong made the exertion of influence on our internal affairs the highest priority. His was a militant Stalinist platform justifying the most nefarious and repulsive aspects of Stalin's policy as historically legitimate and deifying force, especially military force, as the major instrument of policy. Mao's political platform was an embodiment of brazen sectarianism, intolerance of differing opinions, extreme dogmatism in theory, and primitivization and vulgarization of Marxist political theory.

Even more dangerous politically was Mao's insistence on the inevitability of war, compounded by his monstrous argument that a few hundred million deaths in a war meant only that "the victorious people will very rapidly build on the ruins of destroyed imperialism a civilization a thousand times more beautiful than the one under the capitalist system, and will build their bright future."* And finally, the personality cult of Mao Zedong was taken to the point of absolute absurdity.

Obviously, this was a political platform intended for export to the Soviet Union (although one can imagine that Mao Zedong's main motives were domestic: the desire to strengthen his personal dictatorship, to distract the people from the misery of their lives, to solidify his power, and so on). The Chinese demanded that the Soviet Union abandon the ideas of the Twentieth Party Congress—that it publicly "repent" and return to orthodoxy. To add injury to insult, at the moment when political and ideological passions reached their hottest point, the Chinese leadership approached us with territorial claims and the Red Guards besieged the Soviet Embassy in Beijing. We lived with the fear and danger of a military conflict. From all I know, I can say that we never planned an attack on the People's Republic of China. And I am equally sure that China did not plan an attack on us.

We faced a combination of real political threats and our fear and ignorance of what was going on in China. This pushed our diplomatic crisis onto center stage in the minds of both politicians and the public.

China became an enemy, so the policies it was advocating were auto-

*From the anthology *Long Live Leninism*, published in 1962 by the Chinese Communist Party Central Committee.

matically discredited. From 1962 to 1964 the Chinese factor weakened the position of the Stalinists in the U.S.S.R. As it developed, the conflict with China had positive influences on the policies of Khrushchev, who had been slipping back to Stalinism only too often since 1962. The debate with the Chinese leaders provided the anti-Stalinists with the opportunity, while defending our policies, to speak out on many political and ideological subjects that had lately become taboo. By that time, leaders at every level were starting to quash any appeal for democratic reform and criticism of Stalinism, and encouraging the opposite, and very conservative, line.

The situation created by the discussions with the Chinese opened up new opportunities in art, literature, science, social theory, and politics. One of the outstanding examples, Alexander Solzhenitsyn's story *One Day in the Life of Ivan Denisovich*, was finally published after a long struggle. Debate on political subjects, particularly on Stalin and Stalinism, was resumed and went further than before.

This could only frighten the conservatives. At the end of November 1962, they came up with a real provocation. They used the opening of a modern art exhibition in the main exhibition hall (the Manege) in the center of Moscow for this. The perpetrators (aside from the leaders of the Artists' Union) were Dmitri Polikarpov, who was in charge of culture at the Central Committee's Ideological Department, which he headed, and Leonid Ilyichev, the secretary for ideology of the Central Committee.

On the eve of the opening of the art exhibit, which was very orthodox and conformed to official tastes and standards, a group of artists who had the reputation of being "leftists," "avant-gardists," and even (that forbidden word!) "abstractionists," and had not been invited to participate, were persuaded to part with their paintings by all sorts of tricks and promises. These works were hurriedly collected into a separate exhibit on the second floor of the Manege. The plotters were well aware of Khrushchev's tastes, temperament, and boorishness, and they were hoping for an explosion.

They did not hope in vain. The explosion was thunderous. Was it reasonable for the leader of a great power up to its ears in grave economic and political problems to unleash political wrath on the entire country because he was offended by the political content of a collection of artworks? This episode was the start of a very noticeable shift to the right. I must say, however, that I still have my doubts even today about whether the "leftist" and "avant-gardist" art was what really sent Khrushchev into such a fury for so long. Although he was angered by the exhibition, I think Khrushchev exaggerated his indignation. Very likely he was concerned that he had gone too far to the "left" after the Twenty-second Party Congress and was seeking an excuse to turn back to a much more orthodox policy. That was his favorite way of doing things—to steer politics like a ship sailing against the wind, sharply tacking from port to starboard.

He issued the same kind of invective in foreign policy. On the eve of the summit meeting in Paris in 1960 I was working as a journalist. I asked myself, What will Khrushchev take with him to Paris? How will he fulfill the hopes he raised a few months earlier, during his trip to the United States? And when the famous U-2 spy-plane incident occurred at the beginning of May and the American pilot Gary Powers fell into our hands, Khrushchev let forth a stream of angry speeches. I think he seized upon the incident as a pretext to get out of serious talks; he had not done any real homework for this grand summit, and the following months and years could not have demonstrated this more clearly.

Victimization campaigns began to flare up and were not limited to artists or even to writers. The screw-tightening to which we had grown so accustomed was applied on a very broad ideological and cultural front.

The special Central Committee plenum on ideology scheduled for the summer of 1963 was awaited with fear. Leonid Ilyichev was marked down in advance as the keynote speaker. According to many people in the know, he was hoping to become a member of, or at the very least a candidate for, the Presidium of the Central Committee, bypassing his rivals (among whom Yuri Andropov and Boris Ponomaryov were mentioned most often). The plenum could have only one aim: a serious ideological crackdown. Even before the plenum, the apparat had made efforts to ensure that the problems raised by the Twentieth and even the recent Twenty-second Party Congress were laid aside.

It was in these months and weeks before the plenum that the "Chinese factor" played an important positive role. In many ways it helped to forestall an ideological "palace coup" and to lead the country onto the road of de-Stalinization, if only briefly.

In mid-1963, developments in Sino-Soviet relations unfolded fast and furiously. China was gradually moving toward its Cultural Revolution. On June 14, 1963, virtually on the eve of the Central Committee plenum on ideology, the Chinese published an Open Letter addressed to the Central Committee, attacking Soviet policy on all fronts, as well as the leadership and, of course, the Twentieth and Twenty-second Congresses of the CPSU. The Soviet leadership took this as an open challenge and proof of the irreconcilability of the Chinese leaders to some of our efforts to normalize relations.

The Open Letter appeared on the eve of the long-awaited official talks between representatives of the Communist parties of the Soviet Union and China. When participants in the plenum were informed of the Chinese letter, the Sino-Soviet debate naturally became the focus of the discussion.

I remember those talks very well. They took place between July 5 and July 20, 1963. I was still working for IMEMO, although most of my time was spent on assignments for the Central Committee. I already had an official invitation to join the Central Committee as a consultant and was just marking time in order to finish my Ph.D. thesis. Thus, I was appointed as an adviser to the Soviet delegation at the talks with the Chinese.

Right from the outset, the talks assumed their own unique rhythm and form. They consisted of endless unilateral declarations intended, first, to rip the other side to shreds and, second, to defend one's own case and Marxist orthodoxy. The Soviet representative would get up and read his statement, and the other members of the delegation would add their own statements, which had been orchestrated beforehand. After this, the session would close. As we understood it, the Chinese would then go to their embassy and send the text of our statement by coded telegram (probably with their comments and proposals attached) to Beijing. They then would wait for the reply. We got the impression that this was in the form of a final text of their statement in reply to ours.*

---

*Our delegation joked that the Chinese were waiting for a new "serving of quotes" from Beijing. Amusing ourselves over their style of work we experienced a certain sense of superiority, born of our recently acquired relative freedom. But we were unfair to our Chinese comrades, forgetting, or perhaps not understanding, something we should have remembered: the difficult, dangerous conditions in which our Chinese colleagues lived and worked at the time, under a blatant personality cult and a totalitarian dictatorship.

The next day they would read this out loud and the meeting would break up again; when it was our turn, the members of and advisers to our delegation would prepare our response, which Mikhail Suslov, the head of our delegation, would read the next day.

At the height of these strange talks, our delegation's advisers, myself included, were transferred to another urgent assignment—the preparation of an "Open Letter of the Central Committee of the Communist Party of the Soviet Union." This lengthy document was written in record time. We worked in the Central Committee building for about thirty hours straight and handed in the draft, page by page, to the secretaries of the Central Committee for editing. On July 14 our Open Letter, together with the Chinese Open Letter of June 14, was published in the press.*

I must say that the talks and the Soviet Open Letter provided a very real opportunity to reinforce the course set by the Twentieth Party Congress. And some of the Central Committee secretaries (Andropov above all), the consultants, and the advisers at the talks did everything in their power to take advantage of it. I think we all felt the weight of the moment and understood how important it was to consolidate the counteroffensive that had begun with the Chinese letter. The document contained a number of antiquated, naïve, and simplistic views on the world and international affairs and on the ways in which "the working class and oppressed peoples conducted their revolutionary struggle." However, it does seem to me that the Soviet Open Letter, uneven and sim-

---

Soon thereafter, during the Cultural Revolution, they all (including the head of the delegation, Deng Xiaoping) were subjected to brainwashing, degradation, and repressions.

*One can only guess at the reasons for such haste, or why the letter was published at all at the height of the talks. This gave the Chinese a pretext for breaking off the talks on July 20. I think one of the reasons was Khrushchev's temper, his impulsiveness and impatience. And then, he and some of his colleagues were concerned that the earlier Chinese letter with its accusations against Soviet leadership would become known to our public. The crux of the matter was that one of Khrushchev's weaknesses was, I think, the fear of being accused of having departed from Marxism-Leninism. Most probably for this reason, he at first decided not to publish the Chinese Open Letter in our press at all. The official explanation, however, was different: we were concerned that the letter might spoil the atmosphere on the eve of the meeting of representatives of the two parties. (But right at the height of the talks they published it anyway!)

plistic as it may look now, nevertheless took some significant steps forward. It addressed the people in a new, more human, less official way. In strong contrast with many things written before, it stressed not abstract Marxist or Party concepts, but the very real interests of individuals and the values of civil society. One excerpt:

> The atmosphere of fear, suspicion, and insecurity that poisoned the life of the people during the personality cult has now become a relic of the past. It is impossible to deny the fact that the Soviet person has begun to live better, to make use of the blessings of socialism. [To avoid any ideology was still considered impossible.] Ask the worker who received a new apartment, and there are millions of them! Ask the pensioner who is secure in his old age, ask the farmer who now enjoys a comfortable life, ask the thousands upon thousands of innocent people who suffered from repressions during the personality cult and who regained their freedom and good name, and you will find out what the victory of the Leninist line at the Twentieth Party Congress really means for the Soviet people.
>
> Ask the people whose mothers and fathers were the victims of repression during the personality cult what it means for them to receive an official confirmation that their fathers, mothers, and brothers were honest people and that they themselves are not outcasts in our society, but worthy sons and daughters of our Soviet motherland, enjoying their full rights.*

Even more important, all this was essentially true. The letter cited real achievements of the post-Stalin years—pension reforms, unprecedented housing programs, and stable wages for farmers, not to mention justice—in most cases, alas, posthumous—for millions of innocent people arrested and sentenced under Stalin.

The most important step forward in the Open Letter was its interpretation of the policy of peaceful coexistence, in particular in connection with the threat of nuclear war. The Chinese leaders attacked our policy toward the West as a departure from Marxism-Leninism—which, according to them, demanded from Communists that they focus their attention on the destruction of imperialism. They regarded peaceful co-

---

*"Open Letter of the Central Committee of the Communist Party of the Soviet Union" (hereinafter, "Open Letter"), Moscow, 1963, pp. 34–35.

existence as a piece of utopia, since wars were unavoidable as long as "imperialism" existed.*

The Soviet Open Letter rejected all this, with many fewer caveats and excuses than ever before. And we were frank and clear about the radical changes modern weapons and mass destruction had introduced in the approach to modern war. The letter also rebuffed the fanatical sectarianism contained in the Maoist line on world nuclear war. It faced head-on the fact that there could not be any winners in a nuclear war (later, such statements were banned). It also ended the suppression of facts about the consequences of nuclear war: that truth, which was suppressed for many years, not only in China but in our country as well, and was considered a sign of "bourgeois pacifism"—which allegedly undermined the will of the army and the nation to resort to war if the imperialists attacked us and to resist the West's "blackmail and threats of nuclear war."

The document floated tentative ideas pointing to the conclusion that the interests of humanity's survival and of social development were more important than those of some class or other—that is, were higher than ideological interests. For example, our Open Letter stated that a union of different classes and class interests was possible in the struggle to avert war, since "the atomic bomb does not hold to the class principle, it destroys everyone who falls within its destructive range."† It may be difficult to believe, but we had never before spoken in such terms; if anybody had, he would immediately have been branded as deviationist. And finally, the letter argued more forcefully than before that disarmament was necessary, realistic, and attainable.

Of course, if you read this document today, you can't help noticing the great number of "birthmarks" we still bore from the Stalinist past. Throughout the text you can see patches of doubt in our own ideas.‡

---

*"Imperialism" meant the United States, Western Europe, Japan, and other developed nations.

†"Open Letter," p. xx.

‡To give a typical example, I will quote a maxim that one of the editors squeezed into the section of the letter dealing with the nuclear threat. It defies all logic—to the point that one might think that the words had been copied from one of our opponents and then hastily translated into Russian: "Of course, it is incontestable that if the imperialist madmen should, nonetheless, start a war, the nations will sweep away and bury capitalism" (p. 21). And this came after it had been very clearly proven to the reader that, should we ever reach such a point, there would be no one left to bury the dead.

And in our response to polemics from the Chinese leadership you can see the thinly concealed fear of losing our lead in revolutionary fervor, in our tough opposition to imperialism, in our pronouncements about our readiness to sacrifice everything for the sake of supporting the revolutionary and liberation struggles of our allied nations.

I think the two were interconnected. Precisely because we still had not washed ourselves clean of Stalinism and were still taking the first, very cautious steps toward the new political thinking, it was not all that difficult for Maoist propaganda to intimidate us and force us onto the defensive, causing us to adopt inconsistent or simply erroneous stands. In this light, our leadership's initial decision not to publish the Chinese letter is not all that incomprehensible, nor is Khrushchev's wrath at the Chinese leadership's attempts to disseminate its letter as widely as possible among the Soviet people all that unfounded. The "China factor" also held up to scrutiny the evolution of our social thinking and politics.

This was amply demonstrated after Khrushchev's removal, when it was revealed that, despite the numerous "unanimous votes," the resounding proclamations, and the Party announcements and resolutions supporting the government's new political line, there were many people in the Party, in the government, in the military leadership, in the apparat, and among the general population whose political stance was not all that different from Mao Zedong's. And they were even prepared to renounce some of the reformist lines adopted by the Twentieth Party Congress.

In the meantime, from about the middle of 1963 to the beginning of 1964, the ideological atmosphere improved somewhat. To a great extent this was due to the effects of the arguments with the Chinese Communist leaders—public polemics, which once again permitted the discussion of some topics long barred from the press: criticism of the personality cult; Stalin's repressions; arguments for the democratization of the country, for peaceful coexistence, for the need to pursue an understanding with the West. In 1963 the first disarmament agreement on a partial nuclear test ban treaty was signed by the Soviet Union, the United States, and Great Britain.

Among the important internal ideological and political events that contributed to these developments was the February 1964 Central Committee plenum. The most interesting speech during the debates was made by Otto Kuusinen, three months before he died. He argued that in the absence of democracy, the possibility remained that revolutionary power, which had proclaimed its socialist aims and its loyalty to Communist ideals, could be transformed into a "personal dictatorship."

At first, the press could not summon up the courage to publish this speech (it finally appeared in *Pravda* on the day of Kuusinen's funeral, May 19, 1964). It's easy to understand why: the parallels to Stalinism and warnings about possible developments in the future were too apparent. Kuusinen spoke about the legacy we inherited from Stalin, and about what we had to rid ourselves of, if we really wanted to have a decent future.

Soon, the "China factor" began to play quite a different role in our lives. After Khrushchev was removed from power, we began gradually to push many of the ideas of the Twentieth Party Congress into the background. Even the fiercest attacks on Soviet policy by the Chinese leaders did not annoy the new leadership, because they could be taken for criticism of Khrushchev. First, the conservative wing of the government started showing a readiness for a rapprochement with the Chinese, with whom it shared some common political views. Second, the conflict with China was rapidly becoming an ideological discussion about correct ways to build socialism and make mankind happy. Third, in the chaos of the Cultural Revolution the Chinese leaders were up to their ears in internal squabbles, and soon discovered they had better things to do than to indulge in theoretical debates with the Soviets.

By the end of the 1960s and the beginning of the 1970s we were increasingly concerned with China, not as a participant in a domestic dispute, but as a hostile foreign power. In this period the armed border clashes began, and China acquired considerable nuclear potential and began to normalize its relations with the United States.

The successful reforms in China at the very end of the 1970s and in the 1980s once again made that country's agenda a factor in our internal politics; we were becoming increasingly interested in the problem of reform. And the first people in the U.S.S.R. to speak about the necessity for a radical improvement in Sino-Soviet relations were the same ones who took the most consistent and strongest anti-Maoist stand during the debates of the early 1960s. It was for this reason that the June 1989 repression of the Tiananmen Square protesters for democratic reforms was so emotionally denounced by the true supporters of perestroika.

6 The "Palace Coup" of 1964 and the Struggle for the Soul of Leonid Brezhnev

I regard the removal of Nikita Khrushchev from power in October 1964 as a coup d'état in the truest sense of the term. That his resignation was confirmed by the plenum of the Central Committee does not change this fact. The confirmation was no more than a formality designed to lend the coup an air of legality. The plenum was convened after Khrushchev was recalled from his vacation to face the Central Committee Presidium, which forced him to resign.

I was a rather senior official in the Central Committee apparat at the time. We had been working for quite a while just outside Moscow* on our latest assignment, probably a speech by Khrushchev or some political announcement of the Party; I no longer recall. After several days we noticed that the leadership seemed to have lost interest in our work. New arrivals brought rumors with them. The atmosphere became tense.

*We were at the Gorky dacha, a lovely house on the high bank of the Moscow River. It had been built before the revolution by the wealthy Moscow businessman Savva Morozov, and Stalin had "given" it to Maxim Gorky after Gorky was no longer permitted to travel abroad. For his health—and also, I suspect, for political reasons—Gorky had lived for years on the island of Capri. Stalin and other members of the Politburo frequently visited his Moscow dacha. Although Gorky was used in Moscow for evil purposes such as blessing Stalin's repressions, honors were also constantly heaped upon him, evidently to demonstrate that he was not under house arrest.

Finally Nikolai Inozemtsev left to learn what was happening. A few hours later he called and uttered only one sentence: "They're attacking the very top."

By the evening of October 14 most of the group had slipped away. Two or three of us were sitting in the living room watching television. That day the latest cosmonaut was to return from orbit and old news clips were being shown. Yuri Gagarin was walking down the red carpet at the airport. We must have seen that clip a dozen times, so we knew that next we would see Gagarin walking up to Khrushchev. To our surprise the clip was broken off as Gagarin walked down the carpet.

Next they showed him being greeted at the airport, not by Khrushchev, but by a nervous Anastas Mikoyan, who kept adjusting his false teeth. Realizing that something was wrong, we called the Central Committee, and were told to come in.

As instructed, we went immediately to the office of V. Shaposhnikov, Ponomaryov's assistant. There was a real crush of people from both the International Sections of the Central Committee. You could feel the tension—people were exchanging nervous remarks and drinking tea. When we asked what was happening, we were told that Khrushchev was being ousted. That had to be serious, since no one would have dared crack such a joke aloud. But no one could answer any other questions.

Soon thereafter the telephone rang. Shaposhnikov listened to the caller and asked: "Who's been appointed?" Then he announced to us that Khrushchev had been removed and pensioned off; Leonid I. Brezhnev had been selected first secretary of the Central Committee and Aleksei N. Kosygin was to be chairman of the Council of Ministers.

The lack of reaction to this coup seemed very strange. There was virtually no outcry in the Party or among the public. In fact, the changeover was met with approval, and even joy, almost everywhere. (The fact that it caused concern about the future of the country among many people was another matter: in Khrushchev's place a group of politicians came forward who had no broad support and were not even well known.)

You would have assumed that everything Khrushchev had done for the Soviet people while he was leader of the Party and the nation would have guaranteed him considerable popularity. As it turned out, he had none. The profound deterioration of his public image could not be explained only by his domestic and foreign-policy failures over the previous couple of years, although they were real: the substantial price increases for meat, butter, and milk; the massacre of striking workers in Novocherkassk, the Cuban missile crisis. I think the main cause of disaffection was the public's impression that Khrushchev and his policies had become irrelevant, that he was being tossed around at sea, that he had left one shore (that of traditional Stalinist politics) and could not find the other, however much he tried. He had pursued a policy of doomed half-measures. I think it was Winston Churchill who compared such a policy with an attempt to cross a ravine in two jumps. That is why, when the crucial hour came, he could not count on anyone's support and irritated almost everyone.

Toward the end of his reign even many of those who essentially supported his policies realized that Khrushchev was exposing, criticizing, and trying to bury Stalin—but not Stalinism. Maybe he sincerely believed that by exposing Stalin he had solved all the problems of liberating the society from the deadly grip of its totalitarian past. His memoirs bear this out. He remembers how he tried to persuade the president of Czechoslovakia, Antonin Novotný, to " 'raise the curtain, expose the abuses, if you had any. And you did have some, I know you had some. . . . If you don't do it, others will, and you will end up in a very unenviable situation.' Novotný did not listen to me, and everyone knows what that led to, both for himself and for Czechoslovakia." What follows is a very revealing comment: "If we had not exposed Stalin, then, possibly, we would have had even graver events on our hands than in Czechoslovakia."* And three decades later, we have plenty of them. But for Khrushchev this was beyond understanding. That is why in what he has said and written there is hardly a single word about the need for serious changes, about reform in economics, politics, and the moral life of society.

Herein lies Khrushchev's main misconception. He really believed he had fulfilled his mission by exposing Stalin as an individual. He did practically nothing, however, to remove the deep deformities to which all aspects of life in our society were subjected. I do not think that Khrushchev was entirely blind to these deformities, and I accept the possibility that those people are right who think that the Party reforms Khrushchev undertook were really an attempt to undermine the almighty bureaucracy. But when I read his memoirs I was struck by the fact that he was either absolutely closed-minded to some obvious things or obsti-

*Ogonyok, no. 28, p. 31, 1989.

nately loyal to the old lies, even when his later experience completely exposed them. He asserts, for instance, that in picking out the leader, "the question of which person replaces another can always be put before the Congress or the plenum of the Central Committee." It is as if he has forgotten that the Central Committee rubber-stamped his retirement on the orders of a few conspirators in the leadership. As if he himself, well trained in Stalin's court, did not build his career to a great extent on intrigue—and sometimes on sheer force—when he needed to eliminate rivals. (The case of Beria is an example.)

Khrushchev, in my opinion, quite consciously did not wish to abandon the political system inherited from Stalin's time because, as head of the Party, he saw his own interests directly at stake, and because he could not imagine the alternatives. If you do not strive for far-reaching changes in political and economic institutions—and he did not—staying in power becomes more and more an end in itself. It was much easier and more convenient to govern the Party, and, through the Party, the country, by preserving the old mechanisms inherited from Stalin, which had been created precisely to ensure "personal dictatorship." (Khrushchev uses this expression of Kuusinen's in his memoirs. Apparently, it had stuck in his mind somewhere without his realizing its full meaning.)

His own "little personality cult" was therefore not so ominous and bloody as Stalin's, but it also was harmful and discredited his major achievement—the exposure of Stalin at the Twentieth Party Congress. Khrushchev was most probably simply incapable of achieving greater things in the effort to overcome the legacy of Stalinism. He neither saw nor understood the more fundamental tasks ahead, and, therefore, settled in the end for a policy of marking time.

In the middle of September 1964, my wife succeeded in dragging me out to a cinema not far from home. As usual, there was a newsreel before the film. The lead item—I remember it as clearly as if I had seen it yesterday—was the opening of a new canal somewhere in Central Asia. Khrushchev was there with some other dignitaries. He ran down to the bed of the canal, which was still dry; there he gesticulated and said something. Then he scrambled back up with some difficulty. A ripple of laughter spread through the audience. I nudged my wife with my elbow. Such a show of mass disrespect for the leader was still most unusual. And about two weeks later (maybe ten days before the coup)—we went to the same theater again. Once again, a newsreel was shown, with

Khrushchev appearing in the lead item (the wedding of cosmonauts An-drian Nikolayev and Valentina Tereshkova). This time there was loud and unabashed laughter in the audience. We left the theater with a sense of foreboding.

Such attitudes among the public naturally made the coup easier and maybe even encouraged its organizers to a certain extent, just as Gorba-chev's loss of popularity inspired the organizers of the coup against him in August 1991. But, in sharp contrast, not a single person went out into the streets to defend Khrushchev, while hundreds of thousands rose in support of Gorbachev and Yeltsin, and bare-handed they defeated the largest army and largest secret-police force in the world.

As to plotters, conspirators against Khrushchev, these people were not motivated by any great "ideas," but by the desire for more power or by the fear of losing their big desks and chairs. But who were these people?

Leonid Brezhnev was, of course, one of them, but from all I know about Brezhnev—and later I got to know him rather well—he could hardly have been the brains and the will behind the plot, though he was probably one of the three or four main organizers. From everything I know and remember, I can draw the following conclusions: Nikolai Podgorny, who was more willful and persistent, played a very active part, and Mikhail Suslov could not but have participated. Alexander Shelepin played a very prominent role in organizing the actual takeover itself. He was a man of extreme ambition, strong-willed, and well schooled since youth in apparat intrigues. His main advantage was that he already had his own team, a real shadow government (including a shadow Politburo) at his disposal. Evidently, he had set about forming it while he was still first secretary of the Komsomol.

Not only did Shelepin keep in close touch with a large number of the former Komsomol officials who subsequently were promoted to high positions; he was instrumental in promoting them, especially during the last years and months before the coup when, as a member of the Polit-buro and as one of the secretaries of the Central Committee, he was responsible for personnel appointments. And as the former chairman of the KGB, he saw to it that his men were in key positions there as well. They included his successor, V. Semichastny. I don't know whether Shelepin was the brains behind the conspiracy (I assume that, together with Podgorny, he was), but he was its hands and muscle. That was possible because Shelepin (he had a nickname, "Iron Shurik"—"Shurik" is the diminutive of "Alexander") had the full support of Semichastny and a number of others in the KGB leadership, as well as in the Ministry of Internal Affairs (headed by another close associate of Shelepin's, Vadim Tikunov, who was formerly a high-ranking official in the Komsomol). And a more important figure was Nikolai Mironov. An ex-Komsomol functionary, Mironov became head of the Department of the Administrative Offices of the Central Committee, which oversaw the army, the KGB, the Ministry of Internal Affairs, the courts, and the prosecutor's office. Chief of Staff Marshal Biryuzov was also close to Shelepin's group; he had been informed about the plans to remove Khrushchev and was probably involved in them.* So the strongmen, the "enforcers" of the Soviet system, were all on the side of the conspirators.

It is deplorable, but in our country the military started to participate in such internal affairs after the death of Stalin. This was particularly evident at the moment of Beria's arrest. In addition to the group of generals who made the arrest, troops were brought into Moscow and occupied barracks belonging to KGB units. In another instance—during the June 1957 Central Committee plenum—Marshal Georgi Zhukov and the armed forces behind him helped Khrushchev win over Molotov and his group.

Later Khrushchev repaid Zhukov with ingratitude by firing him as minister of defense and publicly blaming him for "Bonapartism" and political ambitions. All this was done while Zhukov was abroad. I felt pity for him. But here one has to make a choice. If the military wants to take part in internal political rivalries, and if the political leadership wants or agrees to rely on military participation, each side has to consider the consequences; the politicians will fear the military and try to render it ineffective, and must guard against the military's taking complete control by restraining its actions—which is not always pleasant for the generals. But the main issue is that when the military takes a role in expediting political events, society must always fear a dangerous precedent.

It is impossible to make this country really democratic without putting the armed forces under strict political control and excluding them from political power battles. This was confirmed by the coup in August

---

*A few days after the October plenum, Biryuzov and Mironov died in an air crash in Yugoslavia, where they were attending the twenty-fifth anniversary celebration of the liberation of Belgrade.

1991. Sooner or later, the question of the depoliticization of the army arises. We are facing this issue now.

Returning to October 1964, I would point out another characteristic detail that confirms the conspiracy version: just before these events took place, Khrushchev's tight circle of associates was quite cleverly removed from Moscow (in some cases, they were sent abroad on assignments, and this required official permission from the Central Committee Secretariat). This applied, first of all, to the so-called Press Group, which was charged with directing the mass media (Vladimir Satyukov, the editor of *Pravda;* Mikhail Kharlamov, the chairman of Gosteleradio [State TV and Radio]; and others). I doubt that they would have mounted an opposition, but the organizers evidently remembered Lenin's advice to revolutionaries very well: first of all, seize the post office, the telegraph, and the telephone exchange. The conspirators even modernized Lenin's aperçu, giving utmost priority to the mass media.

And indeed, late in the evening before the day of the coup, Nikolai Mesyatsev, who till then had been working as one of Yuri Andropov's deputies in the Central Committee offices, arrived at Gosteleradio with his credentials as chairman in hand. He did not have any journalistic experience, having worked for a long time in the police and the KGB, but he was a friend and trusted comrade of "Iron Shurik."* Still another Komsomol official, Dmitri Goryunov, who at one time was editor of *Komsomolskaya Pravda,* was appointed head of TASS, the official news agency.

By characterizing the removal of Khrushchev as a coup, I am not prepared either to justify or to condemn this act. To make the final judgment about the course of events one needs to know Khrushchev and the internal state of affairs at the time much better than I did. I also don't want to start moralizing: Khrushchev himself often reverted to the old rules of the game, which had evolved in the nether depths of our totalitarian past. I am also not sure that when changes were required in the leadership, means other than a coup existed. This remains one of the weakest aspects of our political system.

---

*Those who witnessed Mesyatsev's arrival at Gosteleradio later told a funny story that throws light on the psychological atmosphere surrounding Khrushchev's ouster and the preparations that were being made for it. Having arrived at Gosteleradio, Mesyatsev asked only one question: "Where's the button?" At first, the assembled management of Gosteleradio did not understand which button the new chairman meant. As it turned out, it was the button to take everything off the air—that is, to make radio and television go dead.

Khrushchev was removed by means of a conspiracy, and whatever the real motives of the plotters, they tried to justify the coup by invoking the interests of socialism, the state, the Party, and the people at the session of the Presidium and the subsequent Central Committee plenum. One or another of the participants might really have believed that he was performing an important deed for the country and the people. Very often in such situations, the human mind and conscience seek a comfortable moral stand in which one's own interests are identified with those of the common good. Bearing in mind the condition of Khrushchev's leadership at that time, this was not all that difficult to do.

After the removal of the leader the next question concerned the policy accompanying this change: What political ideas should now come into force? This question was never answered. Even those high up in the leadership had to guess. The people who came into power did not have a well-defined ideological-political program.

Not everyone, including those who were well informed, realized this at first. I remember how on the first morning after the October plenum, Yuri Andropov briefed the top people in his department, including some of the consultants. He concluded with the following words, which are ingrained in my memory: "Khrushchev was removed not because of his criticism of Stalin's personality cult, and not because of his policy of peaceful coexistence, but because he was inconsistent in this criticism and this policy."

Alas, it soon became increasingly evident that Andropov was deeply mistaken.* (I simply cannot imagine any reason why, if he knew the true

---

*In connection with the television and press interview granted by former Politburo member Gennadi I. Voronov, which appeared at the end of 1969 (and was used by Alexei Adzhubei in one of his articles), I must mention that there are some mistakes in his recollections about Andropov's role in Khrushchev's removal. For example, the episode cited by Voronov in which he describes how he was invited by Brezhnev to go hunting at Zavidovo and there met Andropov, who was supposedly reporting to the future general secretary of the Party about support for Brezhnev against Khrushchev. I do not believe this story, and not merely because Andropov's intense dislike for hunting was so well known. Going to Zavidovo would have meant a flagrant breach of the primary rules of security. More important is the fact that Andropov was not close to Brezhnev; after the October plenum he was in disgrace for almost half a year; and he began to enjoy the trust of the leadership only later—at the end of 1965 or in 1966. Most likely Voronov is confusing Andropov with someone else, and I can already guess with whom. He describes his return together with Brezhnev and, supposedly, Andropov from Zavidovo to Moscow,

situation, he would purposely have misled us.) The first signal came, literally, two weeks later. The November 7 anniversary of the October Revolution was approaching, and Leonid Brezhnev, as the reelected first secretary, had to deliver the traditional address. Andropov and his group of consultants prepared one section of the address. Incidentally, contrary to the usual practice, this was a section dealing with internal policy. We took this as a sign of trust from our chief and enthusiastically set to work. I can't remember the details, but we wrote quite a decent and progressive draft. It was given to Pyotr N. Demichev, who had been assigned to put the pieces together and edit them.

The final product dismayed us. All the parts that contained the most substance and the most politically advanced ideas were gone. Demichev later became quite well known for his ability to spoil any text.* Still, this did not yet prove that our hopes for a better future were groundless—particularly since we were getting more encouraging signals. For example, some of us were assigned the job of writing an editorial for *Pravda* for Constitution Day (at that time it was celebrated on December 5—the day of the "Stalin Constitution"). We stressed criticism of Stalin's misdeeds—the personality cult, and repressions—and pointed out the need for democratic reform. The article appeared in its original form. But a few weeks later we were left in no doubt that Andropov was cruelly mistaken in his first assessments of the changes. It was also proof that he had not taken any active part in the anti-Khrushchev plot.

But first, to maintain the sequence of events, I will recall what happened on November 7. After quite a long break for this holiday, a very

---

when, as a result of the conversation which took place in the car, the role assigned to Andropov in the conspiracy became clear to Voronov: to collect compromising material on Khrushchev about his former activities in Moscow and mainly in Ukraine. Evidently this was connected with illegal repressions. But Andropov had no connection to any such material, or, in general, to the archives of the KGB, the Central Committee, and the other central bodies, and could not have had any, right until May 1967, when he was appointed chairman of the KGB. Therefore, the man Voronov most likely met in Zavidovo in 1964, and with whom he returned to Moscow in the same car, was not Andropov, but Semichastny. In this case, memory has played a nasty trick on Voronov (though that is understandable—a quarter of a century has elapsed since then!): he has forgotten who was chairman of the KGB and when, and who it could have been, therefore, who could have collected "compromising material" on Khrushchev in 1964.

*His nickname was "The Chemist," because Khrushchev had made him secretary in charge of developing the chemical-fertilizer, insecticide, and herbicide industry.

representative Chinese delegation arrived, headed by Zhou Enlai. Everyone understood that this was a feeler, an attempt to find out what made the new Soviet leadership tick. Also, Zhou Enlai had the reputation of being the most moderate member of the Chinese leadership, and his visit to Moscow could have been regarded as an opportunity to reach a sensible solution to the problem of Sino-Soviet relations (or as a clever move calculated to put us in a difficult spot). Therefore, opposing views existed about the visit, at least among us consultants at the Central Committee offices. The growing concern that our new leaders might sacrifice some important political principles was, nonetheless, accompanied by the hope that we would succeed in putting an end to the increasing hostility between the two countries.

On the seventh, I was on duty at our department. Toward evening Andropov's secretary called and asked me to come over. Andropov was sitting at his desk, looking concerned and withdrawn, gazing blankly through the window. He launched into an animated description of what had just occurred.

The traditional holiday reception at the Kremlin had just ended. Rodion Malinovsky (the minister of defense) had drunk too much and proposed a cocky anti-American toast which offended the U.S. ambassador, Foy Kohler. "That," said Andropov, "is the first piece of bad news. In every capital of the world people are carefully scrutinizing each word from Moscow, trying to evaluate what the new leadership's policy is. And this is what you get. . . . But the further you go, the worse it gets. Zhou Enlai and the other Chinese delegates came up to Malinovsky and congratulated him on a 'wonderful anti-imperialist toast.'" (Later I tried to find out what it was that Malinovsky had said; it proved to be nothing out of the ordinary, just our usual propagandistic phraseology, which people simply began using more carefully and more selectively in Khrushchev's time. But there was some saber-rattling, which generals like to do.) "And there I am, standing next to him," Andropov continued, "not knowing what to do with myself, with all our leaders and the whole diplomatic corps watching. And at this point Malinovsky—by this time he really had the bit in his teeth—says to Zhou Enlai: 'Let's drink to Sino-Soviet friendship. Now that we've kicked out our Nikita, why don't you do the same to your Mao Zedong? Then we'll get along just fine.' Zhou Enlai turned pale—he was probably thinking of the denunciations his colleagues would concoct against him on his return—

then said something nasty, turned on his heel, and walked out of the reception. Well, what would you say to that?"

Picturing this scene, I said to Andropov: "Maybe it's not all that bad after all—is it worth getting upset over?" Andropov said nothing, thought for a while, and then started laughing. On that note our conversation ended.

A few days later, the Chinese delegation departed, with no progress made in the talks. During a later meeting with me, Andropov again brought up these November talks with the Chinese: "Mikoyan put the final nail in the coffin. He told the Chinese the Soviet Union wouldn't budge from a single previous political position." And, as if in passing, he remarked: "Not all of our comrades liked what Mikoyan said," making it clear he was not going to answer any more questions on the subject.

As a result of these conversations, I was somewhat prepared for what happened in January 1965. A meeting of the Political Consultative Committee of the Warsaw Pact was about to take place. The Presidium of the Central Committee was discussing the draft for the directives for our delegation, signed by Andropov and Andrei Gromyko. This became the first substantial discussion on foreign policy to take place in the Central Committee Presidium after the October plenum.

Andropov returned from the meeting very upset. In general, I must say, Andropov could get very upset, even lose his head, when he was subjected to criticism by his superiors. I attributed this to the deeply rooted fear syndrome from which many people of his generation suffered when confronted by their superiors—a very typical product of the personality cult period. As we later discovered, a group of the Presidium members—Andropov was then a "mere" secretary of the Central Committee—came down hard on the proposed draft and attacked it fiercely for its insufficient "class position" and "class consciousness." (The expression "class consciousness" remained in vogue for several years and was injected into speeches and documents on foreign policy, whether it belonged there or not.) They accused the authors of the draft of excessive "leniency toward imperialism" and a disregard for measures to improve relations and strengthen unity with our "natural" allies and our "class brothers" (as we understood it, they meant the Chinese, primarily). We discovered from people who were present at the meeting that Shelepin and, to my surprise, Kosygin, played a particularly active part. Brezhnev kept quiet for the most part. When Kosygin started to pressure him, demanding that he pay a visit to China, Brezhnev lost his patience and barked, "If you think it's all that terribly important, why don't you go yourself?"

As a result of the discussion, our proposals and initiatives aimed at improving relations with the United States and the Western European countries were sunk. A side effect was a few months of disgrace for Andropov (he took it very much to heart; he fell sick, and then was hospitalized with a heart condition).*

---

*Andropov was treated at the Kuntsevo Hospital and, when he felt somewhat better, he started to run the department from there, by telephone and through his aides. He celebrated his fifty-first birthday in the hospital. Three of us consultants wrote a humorous birthday greeting in verse, and within a few days we got a reply, also in verse. Since these lines were written by Andropov at a difficult time for him, they provide a certain insight into the personality of this man. I will permit myself to quote from them here.

"To comrades: G. A. Arbatov
A. Ye. Bovin
G. K. Shakhnazarov

Your madrigal, my friends,
Your poem, which you wrote together,
I read, and sighed, and thought all day;
It was quite touching altogether.

Oh, wondrous world! Just look at all the talents
Which we now have, and how they multiply!
And even our consultants try,
Forgetting files and folios in their masses,
To reach the top of Mount Parnassus.

With shaking hand, I took a pen
To answer you right there and then,
With flowing lines, like yours, in rhyme,
And that same Mount Parnassus climb.

Alas, by God's almighty will,
My way ahead seems sad and ill,
The doctors say, "Just take a rest."
In short, it's known as "cardiac arrest."

The way ahead, untrodden and unknown,
With thorns and heartaches own,
Which leads "through trials, to victory!" ahead,
And just for you—to the kingdom of the dead!

I'll tell it like it is,
I'll cross my heart; alas,

But before all that happened, Kosygin did, in fact, visit China, accompanied by Andropov, and this was probably provoked to some extent by the debates in the Presidium that January.

To be more exact, the delegation first flew to Vietnam. It so happened

---

We understand life a lot better
When we land right on our ass!

I warm myself in the balcony sun,
And sometimes I sit on the lavatory "throne"
And though there's nothing new about that,
At least it's a seat of your own.
And you don't have to be Socrates in order to know:
You want to think? Get down on your ass.

But enough is enough, and joking apart,
Feelings, we know, are uncommon these days,
But still, there are moments which touch at the heart,
And mist your eyes over in their little ways,
When something, that something, pulls at the strings,
And you wander around with the look of a fool,
And don't really know what to think about things.

And that's, my friends, the way
I felt the other day.

So, thanks, my friends, that you have found
Amongst life's daily petty tribulation,
That moment, magic and profound,
And filled with inspiration,
To write a sonnet
And spend your time upon it.

It has, you must admit,
A slightly smooth and balmy air,
And is too sweet, a little bit,
But let's be fair:
What's a birthday celebration
Without a bit of glorification?

I'll stop for now.
I dare not read my poem over.
Writing verse
Is so much worse
Than writing speeches,
You might agree, or not, but anyway,
We'll talk about it soon one day.

that the Americans started bombing the northern part of Vietnam precisely when the new head of the Soviet government was there. And this of course led to another increase in mistrust and hostility. I think this was either a very serious mistake by the American government or a calculated provocation aimed at testing the mettle of the new Soviet leaders.

On the way back, Kosygin stopped off in Beijing and had meetings with Mao Zedong and the other leaders. He left with nothing to show for them, which could not have been good news for anyone. But there was one plus: the failure helped to dispel any illusion that we could easily mend our fences with China without unconditional surrender on the main points of domestic and foreign policy. Later, the armed clashes on Damansky Island and a series of other places made us go to the other extreme: it took us too long to shake off our fear of war with China, and we were much too late in normalizing our relations.

But, naturally, the main developments after the October coup were not in foreign but in domestic affairs. This was the battleground, not only of various philosophies and political positions, but primarily of the struggle for power among the victors of the coup. Various reasons made this struggle tough from the very first months.

Brezhnev was regarded by the majority of people in the Central Committee apparat and among the leadership as a weak figure and, by many, a temporary one. The possibility cannot be excluded that this was what united the members of the coup in support of Brezhnev as first secretary of the Central Committee. There were several precedents for this in the past when there was no universally accepted heir to the throne and the leadership was strongly contested. In such cases, there always was a temptation to find someone whom other leaders thought was weak. Possibly this was how Stalin managed to concentrate power in his hands so swiftly after Lenin's death despite the presence of much more popular and charismatic figures like Trotsky or Bukharin. It is also possible that Molotov, Malenkov, and Beria made a similar miscalculation in 1953, when they agreed to transfer Khrushchev from the Moscow Party Committee to the Central Committee, where he had to concentrate his efforts on Central Committee work. "This semiliterate simpleton, who is far removed from the real politics of this world, will never become the leader" was their logic. But it soon became clear that they, too, underestimated the Party apparat as a power base. And that the man who was number one in the Party, whatever his personality* and brain power, almost automatically becomes the "tsar." And that once you got to the top of the Party leadership, there was no further need for legitimization.

In addition, neither Khrushchev nor Brezhnev looked like an heir apparent. Even after they ascended the "throne" they cleverly led others to believe that from now on everything would be different, that now there would be a true collective leadership. Time after time this turned out not to be true. We had very short transitional periods, and each time the collective leadership gave the leader absolute freedom from any responsibility. I think, therefore, that a division of powers and a system of checks and balances are a much better guarantee against arbitrary rule and dictatorship.

Returning to Brezhnev, I must say that those who underestimated his ability to preserve his power and defeat his rivals paid for it later. Some people who had known him for a long time understood that ability very well. Arzumanyan, whom I mentioned above and who served with Brezhnev during the war, said in a confidential conversation soon after Brezhnev became the leader, "You don't have to teach this man anything as far as the struggle for positioning and power is concerned."

Who were the other contenders for the post of Party leader? The most obvious was Alexander Shelepin. He was well known in the apparat. Before the war, he studied at the famous Institute of Philosophy and Literature; according to his former classmates, he had been a mediocre student in academic pursuits, but from his student years was very successful in his political career (he started with the Komsomol). He spent the war in such obscurity that some people claimed that he served at the front, while others believed the opposite. Then he returned to the Komsomol and rose quickly. He became the first secretary of the Komsomol Central Committee. In Khrushchev's time he was made chairman of the KGB, and then became secretary of the Central Committee and a member of the Politburo. Khrushchev apparently trusted Shelepin greatly, giving him the most important and delicate tasks, including supervision of Party cadres. He was quite intelligent and cunning, and took to apparat intrigues like a fish to water. He had a rare gift for surrounding himself with devoted and rather efficient people. By the time

---

*I might mention that both Andropov and Gorbachev underestimated their own sheer power as general secretary of the Party and lost precious time.

of the October plenum and shortly thereafter, these people were, as already mentioned, deployed in the main strategic locations: the KGB, the Ministry of Internal Affairs, the army, the most important Central Committee departments, and the mass media. Another source of strength: Shelepin put great stock in attracting the younger members of the Party and government apparat to his side and, naturally, he knew many of these through his work in the Komsomol.

As far as his political views were concerned, Shelepin was, above all, a proponent of "order." Although he made several anti-Stalinist speeches in Khrushchev's time—which had become a political fashion—this did not in any way prevent him or his followers from launching an aggressive offensive against the anti-Stalinist line after the October 1964 plenum. Both in internal and external politics, Shelepin and his people led the chorus for the restoration of the "class approach" of "class awareness," and rejected the policy of improving relations with the West. In addition, he was known as an ardent proponent of imperial policy and of chauvinism (although the person who was regarded as the main cheerleader in this respect was Dimitri Polyansky, quite an inept fellow).

At first Shelepin's associates did not bother to hide the fact that they considered Brezhnev a transitory figure, soon to be replaced by "Iron Shurik." Shelepin himself confirmed this impression by some of his acts and statements. Perhaps this was his biggest political mistake. Brezhnev, who had a keen instinct for such things, was immediately alerted to Shelepin. All those who feared the appearance of a new dictator and a return to Stalinism gathered around Brezhnev.

Understanding that he had a dangerous opponent, Brezhnev started counterplotting behind the scenes, using some clever maneuvering in the apparat. I don't know how this happened, specifically, but by the autumn of 1965, Shelepin took his first hard political hit on the chin: instead of control over the all-important department of Party cadres, he, as a secretary of the Central Committee, was put in charge of the food and consumer-goods industry. This, by our standards, was tantamount to political disgrace. But something else must have happened, for Shelepin felt it necessary to go out of his way to show his loyalty to Brezhnev, even cutting short one of his foreign trips to meet the general secretary, who was on his way back from Mongolia, at some remote railway station in Siberia.

But although Shelepin suffered a defeat, his political position and his political opinions in the months immediately following the October plenum had a considerable negative impact on the ideological and political situation.

Another potential rival to Brezhnev at the time was Alexei Kosygin. He was undoubtedly more intelligent and better educated than Brezhnev, and an experienced executive, a technocrat who was, moreover, open to some extent to new economic ideas. But in politics, alas, he was a conservative, beginning with his attitude toward Stalin.

There is no doubt in my mind that Kosygin did not support the policy of repression, despotism, and lawlessness. For example, in my first lengthy personal conversation with him, which took place during a stroll in Kislovodsk in December of 1968, I raised the subject of all those executives of bigger industrial enterprises who had suffered as a result of Stalin's bloodletting. (Some of them were personal friends of my father.) Kosygin took up the subject eagerly and began to recall colleagues who had disappeared without a trace. But this did not make him doubt the system. Alexei Kosygin was a product of the totalitarian political society, and he believed in it, perhaps because he simply could not imagine a different one. He had, in addition, a loyal, even warm, personal opinion of Stalin. It was Stalin, after all, who had noticed Kosygin and promoted him, and Kosygin could not but admire the "Great Leader."

Purely sentimental memories also played a role in Kosygin's views. Sometime shortly after the war, Stalin, who always spent his vacations in his native Caucasus, succumbed, for the first time in his life, to advice and went for his holidays to the Crimea. But he did not like it and within a few days decided to move to the Caucasus. Since Stalin had a paranoiac fear of flying, a cruiser was sent from Sevastopol to bring him from the Crimea to the Caucasus. This one-day trip was written into our history as a "visit by Comrade Stalin to our glorious Black Sea Navy." Anyway, Stalin invited Kosygin and his wife, who were also vacationing in the Crimea, to join him aboard. This, it was said, left an indelible impression on the guests; Stalin, when he chose to, could be a gracious, even charming, host.

In a contest with Brezhnev for the leadership, Kosygin, of course, could hardly aspire to victory. He did not have the power of the Party apparat behind him, or the opportunities that the office of first secretary provided. But, more likely than not, he lacked those qualities which make someone the number one man in our country, even among such a poor crop of strong leaders; these were high skill in intrigues and power games within the Party bureaucracy, a special knack for political demagoguery, and ruthlessness.

There was no prolonged conflict between them. Kosygin stayed on as an economics executive, and not a political one. But his views also had a considerable influence on the course of events in the first months and years after the October plenum. In the economy, these were, on the whole, quite positive—at least at the first stages. In internal political and ideological affairs Kosygin was a conservative. In foreign policy the picture was mixed. At first he strongly supported a "class-conscious" foreign policy. But on the whole he was for normal relations and trade with the West.

I do not know whether Nikolai Podgorny had any ambitions to assume the top job, but he was a much more sinister and conservative figure even than Brezhnev. Mikhail Suslov, however, did not seek the role of top man in the Party and the country.* He felt more comfortable in the role of an éminence grise, a behind-the-scenes operator.

With such weak rivals, Brezhnev's positive qualities did acquire some weight. One of these was the fact that people did not see him as an evil or a cruel man. If you compare him with Stalin, and in some instances even to Khrushchev, this was indeed the case. To exile a person as an ambassador or force him into retirement on a big (so-called personal) pension is something quite different from having him executed by a firing squad, sending him to prison, applying torture, or even publicly dishonoring him (sacking him from his job and expelling him scandalously from the Party). That is how Khrushchev handled his enemies.

It is also true that Brezhnev was friendly and democratic in his dealings with other people—at least during his first years in office, before he got out of the habit of listening to people and thanking them for their help, and even admitting publicly that there were many things which he did not know anything about.† Nor is there any doubt that he was en-

---

*I was told how one fine day Khrushchev offered Suslov the position of chairman of the Presidium of the Supreme Soviet (at that time a purely honorary position). Suslov was at a complete loss as to what to do. He talked to the members of the Politburo, trying to convince them that he could not accept such a responsibility. (Apparently, personal responsibility was the thing he feared most of all.)

†Brezhnev did not, at first, build himself up to be "a great man," and he used to tell his aides: "Use simple language, don't pretend I'm a theoretician, because nobody will believe

dowed with common sense and was not likely to take extreme or hasty decisions.

During his first years in power Brezhnev was accessible and unpretentious; he tried not only to win over the people he talked to, but even to help them. If he assigned someone a task, he tried to make the person feel at ease.

I remember my first meeting with Brezhnev, in February of 1965.* The leadership had decided to conduct a new international congress of Communist parties. Moreover, it was decided to send to the leaders of parties that disagreed with our stand or that were creating problems for us, not just a letter from Brezhnev, but people from Central Committee headquarters to hear them out and provide them with explanations.

I was selected to fly to Cuba to meet with Fidel Castro. On the day of my departure Brezhnev was to give me instructions.

There was a guard and a checkpoint on the fifth floor of the main building of the Kremlin, where the leadership had its offices. I went to Brezhnev's reception room and was taken to his assistant, Georgi Tsukanov. We chatted for a few minutes; then the phone rang, and Tsukanov said, "They're calling for us." We entered Brezhnev's office together. Brezhnev was sitting at a small desk at the end of a long table. He gave us a friendly greeting and telephoned Suslov to join us.

I was given a letter to read. It was to be carried by two special couriers in the same plane I was taking. Brezhnev said he would send a present with me for Castro—some Georgian wine, which Castro had taken a liking to, and salmon. Brezhnev asked me a few questions about where I had worked earlier and how long I had been in the Central Committee. He got the impression that I was nervous and began to calm me down: "If Castro doesn't receive you, give it to Raúl [Castro] or to [Osvaldo] Dorticos [the prime minister]. And if you see that everyone is avoiding a meeting, don't let it bother you; just hand

---

I wrote such things anyway and everybody will laugh." And he would edit out the more complicated and high-sounding passages. Sometimes, he would ask for the quotations from the classics to be cut, saying, "And who's going to believe I ever read Marx?"

*I had actually met him formally in 1962, when, as chairman of the Presidium of the Supreme Soviet he bestowed a medal on me. (Incidentally, I first saw Kuusinen under similar circumstances. I received the Order of the Red Star, which I had earned at the front, from him when he was deputy chairman of the Supreme Soviet.)

over the letter through our ambassador. Just keep a level head; we don't know how our request will be received. Fidel is mad at us. After all, this is our first contact after the change in leadership." There were other instructions of a similar nature.

To tell the truth, I was touched that our country's leader was going to such trouble to soothe the nerves of a novice employee of the apparat and was so concerned with helping him in this very important charge. (In the end, everything came off very well; I received an affirmative response to the invitation: Raúl Castro was sent to Moscow. On the third day of my stay Fidel Castro invited me to go snorkeling and we spent the day after that together as well.*)

On several other occasions, I witnessed similar episodes. It was not in Brezhnev's nature to complicate the lives of those who surrounded him. On the contrary, wherever he could, he tried to simplify relations.

Compared with some of our other politicians who had grown up in the lower depths of the apparat, Brezhnev had another advantage: his experience was not limited solely to the apparat. He had served at the front; he took part in the reconstruction of Zaporozhye, which had been devastated in the war; he was one of the organizers of the development of the so-called Virgin Lands beyond the Urals, and then was in charge of the defense industry as second secretary of the Central Committee. But broad exposure did not translate into broad-mindedness or independence. As was the case almost everywhere in those days, being in charge meant being part of the system. One's power was reduced to the mere formality of passing on orders from above; for Party officials, power meant telling others to "get on with it." Independent thinking and initiative were not only unnecessary but unwanted, and could be dangerous to your career.

Many of Brezhnev's faults were also quite apparent right from the start. He had a well-earned reputation as a poorly educated man of limited vision. But those who portray Brezhnev as a fool are wrong. In fact, Brezhnev was capable of showing political savvy, common sense, and know-how. Immediately after the October plenum, he chose to follow a

---

*My mission came off so successfully that even Andropov was jealous. He decided that I had done such a good job that I would be appointed ambassador to Cuba (at that time there was some discussion of replacing the current ambassador). But he and I talked things over and made up.

line of action that proved to be very correct and advantageous; it assured him success.

First, he played up the contrast between himself and Khrushchev. The latter had been put on a pedestal by official propaganda. Brezhnev, at first, was not. Khrushchev had been very much the celebrity and was always appearing in the papers, in newsreels, on TV, whereas Brezhnev, in the beginning, was not.

In contrast to Khrushchev, he was not in the habit of expressing his opinion on each and every subject. In the first years he waited things out, listening and looking. In short, his behavior was cautious, modest, and to a certain degree dignified. (All this is hard to believe if you recall the "late" Brezhnev, but in the beginning it was the case.) And when he did make a statement on something, he made sure he knew what he was talking about.

Of course, all this notwithstanding, scarcely anyone believed that even in his prime, when he was still healthy, relatively young, and not yet corrupted by absolute power, he did possess the qualities of a true leader of a great power.

I do not agree with the simplistic periodization of our postrevolutionary history that is popular nowadays. It divides our history according to the major misfortunes that befell us: the Stalin personality cult, then the period of "voluntarism" (this was the theoretical stamp with which the Party branded Khrushchev's "misdeeds"), then stagnation (Brezhnev). One of the gravest consequences of Stalin's tyranny was that he condemned the future of the country to whole generations of weak leadership. But when you consider that only an accident saved us from Beria or Molotov, from Shelepin or Podgorny, you come to the conclusion that we were even lucky in that.

And herein lies the answer to the question each of us has probably asked himself many times: Why did no one stop Khrushchev, and particularly Brezhnev, when they were making their mistakes? Why were they not replaced—not by a plot, but by a legal transfer of power, as befits a modern state? There are several reasons. But in addition to the absence of democratic institutions, the major one was that the government consisted of weak (at times, extremely weak) people. This situation did not come about by accident; the mechanisms of the personality cult inexorably led to it. Often there was simply no acceptable alternative to tolerating a useless and burned-out leader.

We are condemned to such a condition so long as we do not create new political mechanisms and a new political regime. Only in this way can a nation guarantee an influx of strong leaders into the government. Only the development of democratic institutions can prevent or correct wrong decisions, and if necessary, change the leaders in a legal, peaceful way. And therein lies the historic significance of the reforms that were started in the late 1980s (but up till now not finished).

At the time Khrushchev was ousted I and, I think, the great majority of those who supported the Twentieth Party Congress—were anxious and confused; we were disappointed, then regained hope; we drifted in uncertainty. We still believed that after the coup, Brezhnev was preferable to the other candidates and therefore deserved our support.

It soon became apparent that the country was being pushed to the right by Brezhnev's rivals, as well as some of his close associates. He had behind him a whole train of people picked up in Dnepropetrovsk, Moldavia, and Kazakhstan, and some he acquired in Moscow. Conservative functionaries who were not in competition with Brezhnev but who occupied prominent positions in the leadership (Andrei Kirilenko, Suslov, Shelest, Polyansky, Demichev, and others) were also pushing politics to the right. A real battle for Brezhnev's soul was starting. Many wanted to turn him into the leader of the right-wing agenda, which meant the rehabilitation of Stalin and Stalinism and a return to the old dogmas of domestic and foreign policy.

Of course, my colleagues and I in the Consultants' Group chose our own position in this battle, which was inevitable. But Andropov made it easier for us. He quickly stood in support of Brezhnev. (I will not try to judge what played the greatest role in this: his support, which I think was sincere, for the Twentieth Party Congress line, or the habit of supporting the leader that had become almost second nature to every Party official.) And what was no less important, he joined the battle to shape the political position of the new leader—though he did this cautiously, in accordance with the existing rules of the Central Committee game. This battle was being waged over every document and speech and over many political articles.

The basic question was: What did Brezhnev himself believe? At first, he was very cautious. He did not want to commit himself to anything or make any promises on important issues of domestic or foreign policy. Maybe he did not have a stand at all on many questions. Maybe he hadn't even given much thought to big-time politics before he became first secretary, but had agreed with whatever Stalin said.

This battle for the soul and mind of Brezhnev was fought on different fronts. The main bridgeheads were, of course, the Politburo and the Secretariat of the Central Committee. We very rarely had access to these sanctuaries of power, but from what we felt, we could draw one conclusion: the predominant winds blew from the right. We fought on a lower, though still rather important, level. Here the drafts of decisions, political proposals, and speeches were prepared, as were the leaders' memoirs. At this level the struggle was more open and its outlines easier to discern. Among particularly prominent Stalinists and right-wingers, I should mention Sergei P. Trapeznikov, whom Brezhnev had picked up way back in Moldavia. He was a typical example of a pretentious, semi-literate pseudo-pundit. Later he became a professor at the Senior Party School. When Brezhnev became general secretary, he promoted Trapeznikov to head of the Department of Science and Education at the Central Committee. There his political and personal qualities manifested themselves in their full light: reaction, spite, aggressiveness, dishonesty, and perfidy.

He had an equal match in Viktor A. Golikov, a longtime assistant to Brezhnev, who also regarded himself as a "prominent Marxist" and who was equally illiterate. Like Trapeznikov, Golikov considered himself an expert on the agrarian problem, but whenever he had the chance, he appeared in the press as a theoretician on all possible subjects including culture, ideology, even international affairs. He was a committed Stalinist and outright reactionary.

These two gathered a group of like-minded people around them and went on the offensive, taking skillful advantage of the natural uncertainty and lack of cohesion in government. Of course, they made full use of their close personal ties to Brezhnev. Trying radically to change the Party's ideological and political course, they worked particularly hard on Brezhnev in order to convert him into a personal patron and executor of their view. Also in Brezhnev's kitchen Cabinet were Konstantin Chernenko, Nikolai A. Tikhonov, and Nikolai A. Shchelokov. They, too, were conservatives, but less interested in ideology.

The Stalinists launched their offensive on a broad front. Regarding domestic affairs, they tried to repeal the decisions made at the Twentieth and the Twenty-second Party Congresses concerning Stalin's personality cult, and to declare erroneous and politically harmful new ideas concerning our past and present, our internal and foreign policy. Not only was all this whispered into Brezhnev's ear, but it was obstinately inserted into the drafts of his speeches and Party documents.

This offensive against the Twentieth Party Congress line met with serious opposition despite the absence of any acknowledged leaders of the democratic forces. Apparently the ideas of renewal had already gained serious support, not only among intellectuals and the public, but also in the Party. Also, some members of the Party leadership were against such a sharp turn, including Central Committee secretaries Andropov and Ponomaryov, and, strange as it may seem, even Suslov. The consultants from both the International Departments of the Central Committee took a strong anti-Stalinist position, as did some ranking officials from the Propaganda Department, including, above all, Alexander N. Yakovlev. They tried, as much as they could, to fight off the onslaughts of the Stalinists.

The Twenty-third Party Congress was lusterless and conservative, but the decisions of the Twentieth and Twenty-second Congresses were not reversed, despite the demands of the Stalinists. This can be considered a partial victory for the democrats and moderates. Another victory—although today this may seem incomprehensible and even laughable—was the fact that from time to time references to the Twentieth and Twenty-second Party Congresses would appear in official documents and speeches. But at the time these were symbols, letting the public know that the fort hadn't surrendered. (It was becoming more and more difficult to smuggle direct criticism of Stalin's personality cult into these documents.) The innovations in foreign policy were also preserved, including the concept of peaceful coexistence, although this was bitterly fought over for some time. The vacillation of the leadership was overcome bit by bit at the level of practical policy as well. At the meeting of the Warsaw Pact Political Consultative Committee in the summer of 1966, the idea of talks on security and cooperation in Europe was approved and proposed to the West; in other words, the process was started that nine years later led to the Helsinki Accords.

Given the combination of forces at the time, however, this first battle was not a triumph for democratic ideas. The Stalinists captured some strong positions, and not only in terms of official appointments to important political posts. The tone of official language had changed. The topics, even the ideas and words, that had gained currency after the Twentieth Party Congress were brought up less and less frequently. On the other hand, the key terms became "class consciousness," "Party consciousness," "ideological purity," "irreconcilable struggle against revisionism," and so on—the whole ideological repertoire to which we had grown so accustomed since Stalin's time.

The conservatives, including those in Brezhnev's entourage, had, for all their primitiveness and ignorance, some important resources. For one thing, they had known Brezhnev for a long time, and thus were able to play upon his weaknesses quite skillfully. Brezhnev, who was provincial and had practically never before dealt with people who were reasonably educated and knowledgeable, genuinely believed that his former associates were experts in politics, economics, and Marxism and would shield him from making mistakes.

Nevertheless, these people failed to gain exclusive access to Brezhnev's ear. Here, I think, Brezhnev's innate caution played a decisive role. Although he trusted these people at first, he was not entirely sure of them and was afraid of being misled. He soon began to seek out alternative points of view.

I think another important factor was that Andropov quickly and unequivocally lent Brezhnev his support. Thus, Andropov managed to express his opinions to Brezhnev even within the first months following the October plenum, and although Andropov, as mentioned, was a very cautious man, he was ready to play the part of counterweight to some of the negative pressures on Brezhnev.

Soon, two other aides to Brezhnev, Andrei Alexandrov-Agentov and Georgi Tsukanov, began to play increasing roles. Alexandrov was a career diplomat whom Brezhnev had borrowed from the Ministry of Foreign Affairs on becoming chairman of the Presidium of the Supreme Soviet. Intellectually and in terms of political and human decency, Alexandrov stood head and shoulders above Golikov and Trapeznikov and, at the very least, could neutralize their most outrageous attacks on foreign policy. On some other issues, Alexandrov was, in my opinion, rather conservative.

Tsukanov had been a metallurgical engineer and director of a large plant in Dneprodzerzhinsk. He was plucked from that job by Brezhnev when the latter became second secretary of the Central Committee, to help out in the general management of the defense industry. When

Brezhnev became general secretary, Tsukanov helped Brezhnev in economic and later in political affairs.

I cannot say that in the beginning Tsukanov had any clearly defined ideological and political positions on the issues around which the battle was raging: Stalin and the Twentieth Party Congress line; peaceful coexistence; and so forth. But he soon found a correct point of reference—not least because he knew the people in Brezhnev's close circle very well and had a deep-seated dislike for most of them. This forced him to attract people who were progressive in their thinking to help fulfill Brezhnev's assignments. Very soon, a counterbalance was created to the unbridled Stalinist influence upon Brezhnev.

During the first two or three years following the October plenum, Brezhnev's political views went through a positive evolution. Although he still believed his old advisers, he began to understand that, as general secretary, he could not rely exclusively on them. Among those he began to listen to was Andropov. Prompted by Andropov and Tsukanov, and sometimes on his own personal initiative, he recruited a broader circle of people atypical of the Party apparat of those times.

Through the efforts of a considerable number of people, it proved possible in those first few years to weaken the influence of the most militant Stalinists. Hard-fought struggles were waged at every juncture—during the preparation for the Twenty-third Party Congress, at the congress itself, and even in the drafting of every serious document or speech. But we did win a number of rounds.

A sharp clash erupted over the text of a speech that Brezhnev was to make during his visit to Soviet Georgia at the beginning of November 1966. The first draft was prepared by Trapeznikov, Golikov, and their Georgian friends. It was an utterly unabashed effort to glorify Stalin and proclaim him, once again, the Great Leader. Upon glancing through the text, Brezhnev apparently had doubts about it and forwarded it to Tsukanov for a second opinion. Although Tsukanov was not an authority on the subtleties of ideology, he understood what a scandal such a speech could cause. Wanting to arm himself with arguments for his talk with Brezhnev, he asked me for suggestions and comments. Later that day he told me that Brezhnev had asked to see me at nine o'clock the next morning.

Not wanting to violate my loyalty to my immediate superior, Andropov, I informed him of this development, told him about the content of the speech, and asked his advice. He told me: "Well, since you've got yourself into this affair, do what you think best." I did not catch any displeasure in Andropov's words, or any warning to be careful and avoid a conflict. Indeed, knowing Andropov, I had expected such a reply.

I stayed up late and did my homework. I decided that the most effective way to undermine the draft speech was not to appeal to political decency—How can one praise Stalin, now that he has been exposed as a criminal?—and not to set forth any abstract arguments about the harm done by the personality cult, but to present very concrete arguments about the baneful practical consequences of such a speech for Brezhnev personally and, of course, for the Party and the country.

The first argument boiled down to the idea that the speech would seriously complicate matters in a number of socialist countries (my department was responsible for these areas, so it was natural to begin there). Brezhnev should be reminded that the leaders of two of these countries were people who had been imprisoned by Stalin and had miraculously escaped with their lives: János Kádár in Hungary and Władysław Gomułka in Poland. In the third, Bulgaria, the former leader had been removed by the Central Committee plenum immediately after the Twentieth Party Congress because of abuse of power. What could we do there now—change the leaders again? Certainly, that was what the local Stalinists wanted. Did Brezhnev really need such problems, particularly at a time when the conflict with the Chinese complicated things anyway?

The second argument concerned the reaction of the Western Communist parties. They had digested the Twentieth Party Congress with great difficulty and, in some cases, at considerable political cost. What would they do now: go into opposition against us or make another about-face, confirming the accusation that they did not have a policy of their own and slavishly followed all of Moscow's twists and turns?

The third argument was an internal one. I reread the minutes of the Twenty-second Party Congress and excerpted the most vivid anti-Stalin statements by leaders who were still members and candidate-members of the Politburo and Central Committee secretaries. (These included, among others, Shelepin, Suslov, Podgorny, and even the leader of the Georgian Republic, Mzhavanadze). How would these people look in the eyes of the Party and the public after such a speech by the new general secretary? Just to please Khrushchev they had recently denounced

Stalin, and demanded the removal of his remains from the mausoleum and the construction of a memorial to his victims. Or did Comrade Brezhnev specifically want to discredit them in order to get rid of them later? And finally, wouldn't people ask him: Where were you before? After all, had not Comrade Brezhnev taken part in all the Party Congresses since the Nineteenth? Had he not been a member of the Central Committee for more than a decade?

Everything went as planned. The only surprise was that, when Tsukanov and I entered his office, exchanged greetings, and sat down, Brezhnev proposed: "Why don't we also invite Andropov?"—and called him in right away.

The arguments made an impression. Brezhnev looked increasingly worried, interrupting from time to time with questions for Andropov. Andropov chose a very clever tactic. Each time, with a few insignificant variations in detail, he would say, more or less, the following: "Of course, Georgi Arbatov is too emotional, and perhaps is overdoing it a bit, but, in principle, we can expect damage of the kind he is talking about." And Andropov would add a few arguments of his own, sometimes very substantial ones.

In the end, Brezhnev asked us to write a new version of the speech as quickly as possible. I cannot say that it proved to be profound in thinking or rich in ideas. But the main thing was that Stalin's name appeared only once (I simply could not have done anything more): in the alphabetical list of people who had organized the revolutionary struggle in Georgia.

I got the impression that following this incident Brezhnev was much more cautious about the issue of Stalin's rehabilitation and the annulment of the decisions made at the Twentieth Party Congress.

At that time, from 1965 to 1967, it seemed to me that the chances were growing that national policy might return to the right course, despite the contradictions and uncertainties of the situation.

First of all, the threat of another palace coup, with Shelepin assuming power, was receding. And Iron Shurik was becoming less and less important.* Simultaneously, people close to Shelepin were transferred to

---

*In dealing with his rivals Brezhnev acted very subtly and skillfully, as was typical of the party apparat. He elbowed many people out of the leadership: Shelepin, Polyansky, Gennadi Voronov, Podgorny, and Shelest, and those were members of the Politburo. But he never came out against them publicly, never made any speeches attacking them. One or

posts with no political influence. The coup de grace for Shelepin came
with the removal of Semichastny as chairman of the KGB in May 1967.
As we know, Andropov became his successor. (Judging by Andropov's
words, the appointment came as a complete surprise. I remember how
the morning after the Politburo's decision, Andropov dropped by the
Central Committee and gathered his consultants to say good-bye. He
jokingly told us how, immediately after the session at which the decision
had been made, Suslov and Arvid Pelshe took him to the Lubyanka
Street Prison to introduce him to the KGB top brass. He told us how he
pondered all that had happened within those walls [the building had
been a prison for political "criminals"] in the past, and what an uneasy
feeling he had.*)

In addition to the demise of Shelepin we had other positive developments. The Stalinists, as I mentioned, did not manage to get their way
at the Twenty-third Party Congress. Though the atmosphere in ideology and culture remained unstable and contradictory, it hardly differed
from that of the last years of Khrushchev's leadership. Nor was the hope
lost that the situation could be improved. The fact that things were

---

another decision would simply be made, without any reason given, and that was that. The
same style was applied to people of lower rank. They would be pensioned off or transferred, often as ambassadors to some country or other—as a rule, with never a talk on the
matter, without any explanation and without a hearing. The man would be notified of the
decision, and that was that. Generally, Brezhnev tried to avoid unpleasant conversations
any way he could.
*Sometime later, on the occasion of his birthday or of some award granted to him, Bovin
and I sent Andropov humorous greetings in verse. Aside from other themes, we expressed our concern that his high position might spoil him, that he might become too
puffed up, since, as it is universally known, power tends to corrupt. And he replied with
quite a tidy little poem.

> Some scoundrel blurted out one day
> That power spoils people, so to say.
> And all the pundits have for years
> Drummed the same thing in our ears
> And, woe betide!
> They do not see the other side,
> It's the people that spoil power.

It's difficult to argue with this. It is also true—we have seen it more than once. Even
remembering Andropov in different periods of his life, one cannot but wonder about his
own example.

going reasonably well in the economy was very important. The economic debate that began back in Khrushchev's time with the publication of the article in *Pravda* by Professor Liberman from Kharkov continued and led, in the autumn of 1965, to a whole series of practical decisions that were unofficially called economic reforms.

And finally, Brezhnev's own political convictions and platform seemed to be evolving in a fairly positive direction. The year 1967 was particularly favorable. This is how it looked to us as we proceeded to work on his speech for the fiftieth anniversary of the October Revolution. (People of my rank had the chance to speak to Brezhnev about the substance of important political and ideological issues mainly on occasions when some major speech was being prepared.)

Nikolai Inozemtsev, Vadim Zagladin, Alexander Bovin, and I were assigned, as early as May, the task of preparing the first draft of the speech. We tried to raise what were, in our opinion, the most serious issues and provide answers to the most pressing and burning problems of the time. The result was a long and complicated draft of over a hundred pages, which we sent to Brezhnev, on his insistence, in its rough form. (Later, I remembered one of Kuusinen's favorite sayings: "Never show an unfinished text to your boss or to a fool.")

Brezhnev didn't like this version at all. Mainly, we thought, because it was overloaded with new ideas and the language was too serious for his tastes, and often too complex. We were shown some of his comments and suggestions and asked to hurry up and prepare a new version. Soon we learned that Brezhnev was so upset by the first draft that through Demichev he had assigned another group to write the speech. (That group was headed by Yakovlev, who was the acting chief of the Central Committee Propaganda Department at that time.) Eventually, both versions were somehow merged in the final text. They proved to be compatible, mainly because of Yakovlev's influence.

More important than anything else, however, was the final editing of the text; we did this with Brezhnev himself, so we had more than enough opportunities for debates and discussions. We spent a couple of weeks working in Zavidovo, Brezhnev's favorite retreat. The widest range of issues was discussed: Stalin and the NEP; the disfranchisement of the kulaks and economic reform; the Twentieth Party Congress and the role of the intelligentsia; questions of war and peace; relations with the West; and so on. Brezhnev would listen attentively, sometimes even suggesting new topics for discussion. At that time, you could still argue with him, even in the presence of others. In some instances he got angry and made cutting remarks, but in a couple of hours, or at the most the next day, he would make it clear to his recent opponent that he bore him no ill will, and while he would not exactly apologize, he would let him know that bygones were bygones.

As far as the speech was concerned, it did not turn out to be a very interesting one, even by the standards of those days. On the other hand, the debates with Brezhnev promised to produce results and seemed encouraging from the point of view of his "enlightenment." Since the reform was beginning to run into difficulties, this applied to the whole range of problems that concerned us: attitudes toward Stalinism; international affairs; the need to find major new economic solutions. The need to broaden creative freedoms for scientists, writers, and artists was also raised several times. At that time Brezhnev made some quite constructive statements on that issue as well. He once remarked that he remembered with shame Khrushchev's meetings with the intelligentsia. He promised that he would meet, without fail, with members of the intelligentsia after the October anniversary celebrations, yet he never did this. (On several occasions, though, when it proved possible to persuade him that his involvement was necessary, he did intercede on behalf of some theater producers and writers.) The fall of 1967 was the first time, I think, that he was directly confronted with the activities of Andrei Sakharov, in connection, as far as I remember, with Sakharov's first letter to him. Brezhnev said he would receive Sakharov, but unfortunately, delegated this meeting to Suslov, who never held it. I am not at all sure that a meeting with Sakharov would have had any positive result in terms of our leadership's enlightenment or in saving Sakharov from long years of persecution. But I felt that a chance was missed.

Anyway, we believed that the work we did and the discussions we had with Brezhnev were useful and could contribute to positive changes in policy. Unfortunately, 1968 saw a shift to the right, at least in domestic affairs. The events in Czechoslovakia were in this sense a clear landmark, if not one of the important causes. Our leadership started to get nervous about Czechoslovakia in January 1968. I learned only a few of the details of how the leadership finally made the tragic decision from my friends, because I had left the Central Committee apparat and in December 1967 was appointed director of the U.S.A. Institute of the

Academy of Sciences. I had practically no contacts with Brezhnev and other leaders until the next year.

But even without any inside information one could see how the political and ideological situation had deteriorated. I remember the Moscow City Party Committee plenum in February or March 1968, in which Brezhnev participated. The crackdown in ideology and culture was openly proclaimed there, obviously under the influence of the developments in Czechoslovakia. The roots of the dissident phenomenon probably go back to this period. Another new word appeared at the time: *podpisant* ("signer"); that was the label given those who signed letters and petitions in defense of people who were being persecuted, or of books that had been quashed by censorship. Dissidents and "signers" were mercilessly fired from their jobs and punished along Party lines. This affected the Academy of Sciences as well, all the more because the academy's president, Mstislav V. Keldysh, made a speech at the Moscow City plenum in which he denounced the "unfaithful." (The speech, which compromised him in the eyes of the intelligentsia, was partially explained by the fact that he was obviously shaking in his shoes because his sister had joined the ranks of the "signers" as well.) Censorship became harsher. Many books and articles that previously would have been accepted for publication were now barred.

The Stalinists immediately tried to exploit the situation. The most conservative members of the leadership—Suslov, Podgorny, Shelest, Grishin, Demichev, and the "storm troopers" of the conservative ideologues in the Central Committee apparat and among the social-sciences leadership—came out into the open and went on the attack.

As to the events of August 1968, there is nothing I can add to what is known already. I remember only that I was overcome by a burning shame over the policies of my country and what its leadership had done.

Therefore, when Georgi M. Kornienko, then head of the U.S.A. Department at the Ministry of Foreign Affairs, phoned on some routine matter and mentioned to me at the end of the conversation that he was editing a letter to President Johnson that explained the motives for bringing troops into Czechoslovakia, I was shocked. I could not even bring myself to go on my vacation to the Caucasus (I had planned to leave the next morning), where my family was waiting for me; instead I phoned my wife that night. I did not want to see anyone; I felt ashamed and bitter.

I came to be convinced that many members of the intelligentsia, among them Communists, including some whom I had previously considered to be quite orthodox, shared my feeling. A day or two after the invasion, I expressed my bitterness about our policy, heatedly and without mincing my words, to Tsukanov and also to Vladimir Kryuchkov, who had once worked with me in the Central Committee but had been transferred to the KGB. (This was the same Kryuchkov who became chairman of the KGB and in August 1991 was one of the leaders of the coup against Gorbachev.) Neither one of them sold me out to his bosses. I suspect, incidentally, that Brezhnev, and particularly Andropov, not only guessed but knew very well how I and many other intellectuals (including those who had continued to work for the Central Committee) felt about this action.

As many foresaw, the intervention in Czechoslovakia had a very negative influence on the whole course of our country's political evolution. It probably had an even more detrimental effect than the events in Poland and Hungary in 1956.

As for the intervention's effect on me, it made me think for the first time about how pernicious our ruling élite's imperial ambitions were, as were its attempts to keep the empire together by force. (Unfortunately, the élite often had supporters among the general population on these points.) At the end of the 1960s, we paid a high price for the Czechoslovak adventure. It played an important role in the growth of the conservative tendencies that eventually led to the period of stagnation.

The part imperial policies played in generating conservatism fully revealed itself at the end of the 1980s and the beginning of the 1990s. For the first time since perestroika began, open political opposition to Gorbachev consolidated because of the rapid, dominolike collapse of the socialist community. Conservative Party officials, part of the military, and part of the KGB joined this opposition. And when the collapse of the empire encompassed the Baltic states, Moldavia, and the countries in the Caucasus, this opposition gained popular support among extremists in the Russian-speaking populations in these regions. This subject requires special examination. For now I remind the reader that these opposition forces and the people who led them played no small part in the psychological and political buildup for the coup of August 1991. Imperial foreign policies and conservative, even reactionary, domestic policies are always linked.

I have already mentioned Khrushchev's statement that if Antonin
Novotný had listened to his advice and exposed the crimes his predecessors committed at Stalin's behest, the situation that arose in 1968 would
never have happened. I questioned this statement: mere exposure of past
mistakes and crimes is not enough, unless far-reaching reforms follow.
But if we consider the Czechoslovakian events themselves, Khrushchev
may have been right. Criticism of the past could have released pent-up
feelings and lowered the political pressure in society. This would have
been true particularly if everything had happened while Khrushchev was
still the leader: the changes in Czechoslovakia would have ridden the
wave of the Twentieth and Twenty-second Party Congresses and therefore would have been greeted in Moscow with understanding, perhaps
even with sympathy—not as a challenge, and particularly not as something that stirred up unwelcome internal problems. The political cycles
in both countries would have more or less coincided and the whole affair
might have been resolved easily without a confrontation.

But this did not happen. By the beginning of 1968, Moscow was de-
parting from the Twentieth Party Congress line. Naturally, the changes
in Czechoslovakia were regarded by conservatives with growing mistrust
right from the start.

The hostile attitude of our leadership to the events in Czechoslovakia
was formed, as I've said, as early as January 1968 and was undoubtedly
noted in Prague. And this hostility served to radicalize the moderately
reformist leadership of the Party and the country, and pushed it toward
those political forces in Czechoslovakia that were later called revisionist
and counterrevolutionary. This, in turn, fueled suspicion in the U.S.S.R.
and the other countries of the Warsaw Pact. Events went into a tailspin.

The matter was complicated by yet another factor, which I, having
worked for over three years in the Central Committee offices, understood absolutely clearly: the human factor in the apparat, the nature of
the people in the Central Committee who worked as specialists on specific countries. In those days there were people high in the ranks who
had been formed in Stalin's times, when the Central Committee "in-
structor" specializing in affairs of an Eastern European country not only
considered himself an imperial plenipotentiary, but was armed with an
unshakable conviction that as a Party official from Moscow he was the
ultimate arbiter of truth and authority. And anyone who disputed his
opinion was a foe or, at the very least, a "revisionist" (which was really

a bad word at this time—somewhere between "heretic" and "traitor").

Andropov understood the situation—and said frequently that such attitudes and such a mentality among officials were politically harmful, even dangerous, and hindered the development of normal relations with our allies. But unfortunately he sacked virtually none of these people. Thus, in 1967, many of the officials in the Central Committee department responsible for relations with allied countries possessed the same mentality as those who served under Stalin. Among the Party cadres in countries they dealt with, they had friends whom they trusted, on the one hand, and they had foes, whom they did not like, on the other. They began to look upon "their" country through the eyes of their friends, and favorites, who formed a kind of Moscow faction there.

But these officials, regarded as experts, reported to our leadership on the internal situations of the countries for which they were responsible. They were listened to, and more often than not they were believed. As a result, the leadership accepted information and assessments that were in no way objective.

At the beginning of 1967, our main experts on Czechoslovakia were the head of the relevant division in the Central Committee offices, Sergei I. Kolesnikov, and the minister-counselor of our embassy in Prague, Ivan I. Udaltsov. (Unlike Kolesnikov, Udaltsov was intelligent and even educated, but at the same time remained a supporter of the old dogmas). It's hard for me to judge what specific role they both played, but I think it was considerable.* Probably, the panic-stricken picture the leadership obtained of the events in Czechoslovakia was the cause of the rapidly growing tension in relations.

I do not know how the fateful decision to commit troops was made. According to the testimony of people I believe, Brezhnev postponed it for a very long time, and was simply afraid to make the decision to use military force. According to Irzhy Valenta, a Czech émigré and political scientist, Kosygin was against military intervention, but eventually gave his consent under pressure from the "interventionists." Both Mikhail Suslov and Boris Ponomaryov called for a political solution to the prob-

---

*Similar, almost complete monopolies on information and analysis were set up for other countries, too. For example, considerable political damage was caused by the group of Central Committee officials responsible for relations with China until 1986, and by another such group responsible for relations with Japan.

lem almost to the last moment, but for a tactical reason: the International Meeting of Communist Parties was scheduled for that autumn and a military intervention in the events in Czechoslovakia might torpedo it.

Among those who actively demanded a military solution Valenta (in a book based on his interviews with former leaders of Czechoslovakia, *Soviet Intervention in Czechoslovakia, 1968: Anatomy of A Decision**) names the following: Pyotr Shelest, Arvid Pelshe, Nikolai Podgorny, Pyotr Masherov, and Pyotr Demichev. Walter Ulbricht and Władysław Gomułka called for military intervention as well. János Kádár tried to avoid it.

On the basis of what I heard, I can also say that, unfortunately, Andropov had become intolerant of radical changes in the allied countries after the 1956 events in Hungary; he was among the supporters of "decisive measures," or at least he did not oppose them. Perhaps he was of the conviction that delay could lead to greater bloodshed. Dimitry Ustinov, as I heard, was of the same opinion. One fact remains undisputed: not a single member of the leadership protested when the decision was made. That I know for certain.

Later, I often asked myself: Why did everything happen the way it did? And I came to the conclusion that it is easier and simpler for a group to take "decisive" action. (I was astonished to discover that the same attitude was observed in the American leadership during the Cuban missile crisis of 1962.) To make an appeal to moderation, patience, and tolerance requires greater political courage. Therefore, in a moment of crisis, the leader has to play a particularly big part. Unfortunately, Brezhnev chose to hide behind other people.

Apart from misinformation and a false picture of the state of affairs, other factors played a large role in the leadership's fateful decision. One of them was the influence of imperial attitudes and ambitions that justify, or "sanctify," actions of this sort in regions regarded as one's "sphere of vital interests." Another factor is the ingrained ideology according to which any departure from your own perceptions of what is right or wrong for socialism becomes the equivalent of treason and a criminal act. I think Brezhnev believed this dogma and allowed himself to be convinced that he would betray the cause of socialism, or, at least, un-

*Baltimore, 1979.

dermine his position as leader of the Party and the nation, if he did not intervene. A former Soviet ambassador to Prague, Stepan Chervonenko, told me that while Brezhnev agreed that the search for a political solution should continue and any opportunity to avoid, or postpone, the use of military force should be taken, he told the ambassador in July 1968 that if the "revisionist" tendencies in Czechoslovakia were victorious, he would be forced to resign as general secretary of the CPSU ("After all, it will look as if I lost Czechoslovakia").

Today it seems to me that the optimism and hope among those who worked close to the government in 1967 either did not take into account or underestimated the deeply rooted attitudes and political tendencies of those who shaped our country's policies.

7 Creeping Re-Stalinization (1968–1974)

Stalinism had embedded itself in our society over a long period and by the most radical means. It had set deep roots, much deeper than Khrushchev probably thought when he addressed the Twentieth Party Congress. As we have seen, a great many people in the leadership adhered to the old Stalinist views, and it would have been difficult, if not impossible, for them to find a place in any other political and social structure; they were simply incapable of doing anything other than carrying out the will "from above." A significant part of our society was not prepared for change. A great number of people had been programmed by our whole history to behave in absolutely prescribed ways and were too afraid to show any initiative, to think and act independently, to assume any responsibility.

After October 1964, and particularly from the end of 1968 onward, two forces aligned themselves to encourage the re-Stalinization of the country. I describe this process as "creeping" precisely because it was not imposed by decree, but gradually extended its bounds. The Stalinists' efforts were channeled primarily in two directions. One of these amounted to measures taken against anyone who took an anti-Stalinist stance or dared raise his voice against the conservative offensive. While

arrests and trials were infrequent, the common practice was to fire people from their jobs; to mete out harsh punishments along Party lines,
including expulsion; to fabricate accusations against dissidents and per-
secute them in increasingly sophisticated ways; to compromise people
publicly and to hound them; to force them into psychiatric hospitals;
and to exile people and strip them of Soviet citizenship.*

What were the objectives of such a policy? The main one was the
defense of what the leadership thought were the foundations of true socialism and socialist order. But I doubt that these people realized that
the socialism they were trying to support was deformed and that they
were defending the authoritarian order—or, to put it more precisely,
their own power and privileges. As the ideological line moved right, the
number of people who were subjected to persecution grew, and the political, spiritual, and moral atmosphere worsened significantly.

Many fell silent. The bounds of "legality"—that is, the criteria for
what you could do without being shut out by the system—grew nar-
rower as this ideological-political struggle progressed. It was soon forbidden to talk about things that were common knowledge.

In 1971, my book *Ideological Struggle in Contemporary International
Relations* came out. Despite its somewhat dogmatic (or, I would say,
Marxist-theological) title, for the times it was broad in content and also
unusual for our literature on foreign relations. In this work, the pages
proving the lack of foundation for militarism, and its inevitable failure,
are particularly dear to me. Military power as an instrument of politics is
a subject that has concerned me for a long time. I wrote my first work on
it in the mid-1950s and returned to the theme in 1990–1991, whereby I
became engaged in sharp polemics with our generals and marshals.

The book contained quite an elaborate defense of the policy of peaceful coexistence (including a defense from the point of view of Marxism-

---

*The attempt to fan anti-Semitic feelings, cloaked under the need to combat Zionism,
played a very noticeable and unseemly role in all this, as did some strange political games,
which I did not understand then and do not understand now. The emigration of Soviet
Jews was allowed, for some reason, in those years—a circumstance for which we were
completely unprepared either morally or politically. But what was actually going on as far
as the so-called Jewish problem was concerned, I do not know and, therefore, I won't
attempt to talk about it in detail. One note, however: a base and an "infrastructure" were
being prepared and created for Pamyat and an organized anti-Semitic movement. Not
only did the authorities turn a blind eye, but certain officials and agencies actually helped.

Leninism, as was required at the time). In addition, it presented some unusually critical views of socialist ideology, including some passages that did not escape the attention of some favorably disposed critics in the United States (for example, the contention that the strength of the socialist example as a revolutionary stimulus also has its negative side, since the economic troubles and political arbitrariness of socialist countries undermine socialism's attraction and repel people from it).

Another book, which came out in 1981, contained a series of interviews I conducted with the Dutch journalist J. Oltmans. (It first appeared in the Federal Republic of Germany and the Netherlands, then in the United States, and then in a series of other countries; it came out in the Soviet Union only in 1982. In each case it had a different title.) It addressed Soviet foreign policy. And although it generally defended this policy, it was, in the view of many critics, exceptional for its great frankness and self-criticism, which were unusual at the time, and simply for its higher-than-usual level of skill, professionalism, and argumentation.

I wrote many articles. Mostly they were about foreign policy and military-political issues. These articles defended the ideas of détente, disarmament, and improvement in Soviet-American relations. However, they frequently also contained sharp criticism of various U.S. actions or of statements by American public figures and authors. In my opinion, they sometimes fully deserved this treatment. Not everyone in our country liked these articles. For example, my statement that there would be no winners in a nuclear war, that "no one will return" from one (1978) caused displeasure.

I would like to emphasize yet again that by today's standards all this may sound weak, even conformist, and not at all self-critical. But at that time timidity was forced on all of us, except for the publishers of *samizdat* and *tamizdat*—that is, people who had broken with official policy and those who tried to influence it from outside. As for myself, for reasons that I mention in other parts of this book, I did not belong to those groups. I am not sorry about this even today, although I respect many of the so-called dissidents (not all of them—there were differences among them).

One other observation. The pressure of censorship and the restrictions on the freedom of speech had one benefit. They forced you to become finely tuned, to write cleverly, to express important thoughts between the lines—through innuendo, through omissions, and through irony. To a certain extent I tried to do this, as did the majority of my colleagues at the institute.

But let me return to the beginning of this period of "creeping re-Stalinization." I think that these changes in the spiritual life of society caused great and prolonged damage, which eventually resulted in additional troubles for perestroika, too. When the truth about Stalin was revealed at the Twentieth Party Congress and when, for the first time, an effort was made to enlist honest Communists, non–Party people, and all the healthy elements of society in a struggle for its renewal, many people approached the project with enthusiasm and a sense of mission. The shameless attempts to pretend that no crimes had been committed and to resurrect the recently dethroned idols led to a serious decline in the public's trust in socialist ideals and in its readiness to serve the great cause. The next step in the public's disenchantment was a strengthened skepticism and cynicism, especially among the younger generation, and we faced the negative consequences of their passivity during perestroika.

The revival of Stalinism did encounter opposition. There were people who would not remain silent and compromise—the most famous being Solzhenitsyn and Sakharov, but one can name dozens of others. Many fought within the system. And many were persecuted. I will give just one example: Academician Pyotr L. Kapitsa. We learned about some aspects of his noble behavior only after the publication of his letters to Stalin, Khrushchev, Brezhnev, and Andropov. Some people bore a grudge against him for not signing collective appeals and complaints in defense of those who were persecuted or offended. As it turned out, it was not lack of courage that kept him from signing. He simply preferred another way, which he considered to be more effective: individual letters to the leaders defending some people or protesting some acts. He did it whenever he thought it necessary, and was ready to bear personal responsibility for them.

I am not saying this to make even the smallest claim to the courage and the great civic achievement of those people who openly challenged the forces of evil and joined battle against them as in war. However, social evolution is more complicated than war and requires a different combination of actions and efforts. In my judgment, the priority was to halt the restoration of Stalinism and prepare the groundwork for subsequent democratic reforms.

It is also important to remember that Stalinism's counterattack, which began in the second half of the 1960s, was aimed not only at people, but at ideas, at historical truth, and at any new outlooks people may have had on socialism, the world, and politics. As they launched their counteroffensive, the conservative forces had many possible options at their disposal.

The ideological positions had already been conquered. The Ideological Department set up under Khrushchev and headed by Leonid Ilyichev was divided into three. The first new entity was the Science and Education Department, which fell into Trapeznikov's hands and immediately became the mainstay of the Stalinists' counteroffensive. The second was the Cultural Department, headed by V. F. Shauro, former secretary of the Byelorussian Central Committee on Ideology. He was prepared to execute any policy prescribed from above. Although not very energetic himself, he gave free rein to his coworkers, who were out for blood and willing to do anything they saw fit in the area of culture. Since strongholds of Stalinism had already been established in the artistic unions and in a series of editorial offices, these people had little difficulty stopping any advance and opening up a wide front from which dyed-in-the-wool conservatives and Stalinists could attack.

Things were more complicated in the Propaganda Department, which had detached itself from "Ilyichev's Empire." After V. N. Stepakov's removal (apparently because of his closeness to Shelepin) this department remained without a director until the beginning of 1972. In the interim the acting director was Alexander Yakovlev, the first deputy chief. Only Yakovlev and a very few like-minded people in the Propaganda Department tried to do anything to stem the tide of conservatism. Yakovlev soon had to pay for this. His enemies found a pretext in his interesting article in *Literaturnaya Gazeta* (the *Literary Gazette*) on internationalism, which created quite a stir.

The article was the first serious public defense of internationalism against nationalism and Great Russian chauvinism. It strongly defended the ideas of the Twentieth Party Congress, and did not go unnoticed by either the Stalinists or their opponents. Golikov immediately wrote a refutation, which the Politburo scrutinized. I and several of my colleagues were present when Brezhnev reprimanded Yakovlev for this article. In the presence of one and all he told Yakovlev that he would forgive him "this time." Then he waxed sentimental about his own magnanimity and even embraced Yakovlev. But a few days later Yakovlev was appointed ambassador to Canada, and there he stayed until the middle of 1983. After that, the Propaganda Department fell into step with the others.

The situation on the ideological front was complicated by the fact that Pyotr Demichev, in his capacity as secretary of the Central Committee, was in charge of all three departments. Demichev was devoid of talent, though he was ready to undertake anything. I cannot remember a single instance when he came to the defense of someone or stood up for the truth. Many times he patronized bad people, supported dirty deeds, and perpetrated such deeds himself.

The person who replaced Demichev as Central Committee secretary for ideology was Mikhail V. Zimyanin, and at first everybody was pleased with that. His reputation was not bad; he had, in fact, clashed with Trapeznikov and Golikov during the preparations for the Twenty-third Party Congress. But something happened to him while he was a Central Committee secretary. Maybe he could not bear the burden of power, or maybe it was just his age. At any rate, he had changed completely and become a patron of the conservatives, taking an active part in some unseemly affairs (for example, the attempt to destroy IMEMO in 1982).

Somewhere up in the clouds sat the éminence grise and high priest of ideology, Mikhail Suslov, who made only occasional public appearances. Behind the scenes he always played a conservative role. His unequivocal stand against Alexander Tvardovsky, Alexander Solzhenitsyn, and Vasili Grossman is well known. Suslov's role in politics, I think, was more complicated—at least in those cases, of which there were more than one, where he spoke out against adventurists and extreme rightists. In such instances, Suslov's natural caution and his fear of causing problems often led him to exert a constructive influence. When the extreme rightists went into action on the ideological front, he sometimes exercised a restraining influence upon them.

In general, there was practically no one you could turn to. Faced with difficulties and critical situations in one or another facet of life, scientists and people in the world of culture tended to turn to Andropov (despite everything, his reputation was still good), or they went straight to Brezhnev.

The first victim of the right wing's inroads was history. The Stalinists achieved what they had set out to do in all areas of politics, ideology, and culture: to reverse the ideas of the Twentieth and the Twenty-second Party Congresses, and to return to an apologia for Stalin and Stalinism. Naturally, in all the editions of the nearly annual outlines on the history of the CPSU published during the 1970s under the editorship of Boris Ponomaryov, there were a few laconic paragraphs about the Twentieth Party Congress (without mention of Khrushchev's speech or his name) and about the decisions of the Central Committee on the personality cult and relevant subjects. But these comments did not dampen the impact of the pro-Stalinists.

There was a massive effort to pretend that the Twentieth Party Congress had never happened. A victimization campaign was unleashed against many honest historians. Pavel V. Volobuev, who had taken a principled stand in the academic world, was fired as the director of the Institute of the History of the U.S.S.R. at the Academy of Sciences. Alexander Nekrich, who was famous for his works on the history of World War II, was persecuted with particular viciousness. In the end, he was forced to emigrate. (This was an effective method. An émigré became, for all intents and purposes, a sort of traitor, and his position, his works, even his supporters were compromised.) Roy Medvedev was expelled from the Party. Many others suffered.

This helped to solve the main problem: in science, in literature, and even in the arts, a wholesale falsification of history began anew (although, all things considered, it had never really ceased; only the first few hesitant steps toward an assertion of historical truth had been made under Khrushchev). Special efforts were made to falsify the history of World War II and Stalin's role in it. I think this was because his apologists understood very well that in the soul of the nation, the war was the most emotionally charged chapter of Soviet history, and therefore the veracity of the Twentieth Party Congress's statements about it had been particularly effective in exploding the myth of the "Great Leader." So the easiest way to rehabilitate Stalin and to restore respect for him in the population at large was to give him the decisive role in the victory over Hitler.

I cannot pass over in silence the fact that, in their reprehensible efforts to falsify the history of the war, the Stalinists from the Ideology Department found eager allies among a significant number of our military leaders, including some who were truly distinguished and much decorated.

Such a development seemed crazy to me; after all, who had suffered more at the hands of Stalin than the military, particularly its high command? In December 1959, I first learned from Lieutenant General A. N. Todorsky the tragic numbers of higher military commanders who at Stalin's behest were either assassinated or arrested on the eve of the war.*

Unfortunately, as I found out from my personal conversations, many generals who were in military command positions during the 1960s and 1970s were not greatly concerned about the tragic fate of their predecessors. Why? Their military discipline played a great role in their behavior. Immediately after the Twentieth and the Twenty-second Party Congresses they adopted an anti-Stalinist line, as you can see from some of their memoirs. There were also generals who had moved rapidly up the ranks precisely because Stalin had removed the military commanders superior to them not only in responsibilities and rank, but in experience, talent, and intelligence. After Stalin's great pre-war bloodletting, the professional requirements for military commanders were drastically lowered. A mediocre C student or even an outright failure could pass for a skillful military commander, as we learned from bitter experience once the war started.

Many in the military were worried, I think, that if people seriously reported the history of the war and exploded all the accumulated myths (of which each war produces a surplus), it might affect their own reputations in combat. It was much more to their advantage to stick to the saying "Victors are not judged," to reduce the history of the war to a hymn of praise to a mighty, heroic achievement, mainly one of those

---

*This fact, too, was taken out of public and scientific circulation. Here is just one example: in the six-volume edition of *The History of the Great Patriotic War of the Soviet Union, 1941–1945*, which appeared in the early 1960s, is the following: "Between May 1937 and September 1938 about half of the regimental commanders, almost all the brigade and divisional commanders, all the corps and military district commanders, all the members of military councils and the chiefs of the political directorates of the military districts, the majority of corps, divisional, and brigade senior political officers, about a third of regimental commissars, and many instructors at the higher- and middle-level military schools were subjected to repression" (vol. 6, p. 124). In the twelve-volume edition, *The History of the Second World War, 1939–1945*, which appeared in the 1970s, even the word "repressions" was studiously avoided; it was replaced by "accusations." Thus, volume 2 contains this passage: "Between 1937 and 1938 a significant number of commanders and political officers were relieved of their duties [sic] in the army due to unjustified accusations" (vol. 2, p. 206). It was noted that the appeals of those who had been relieved were, supposedly, examined and the mistakes were, to a significant degree, corrected.

generals who survived and found themselves in favor. No doubt, some of them wanted the myths to go forth and multiply so that they could comfortably enjoy their glory without having to worry that historians might start analyzing their real wartime actions and decisions.

There were those, I think, who were impressed by Stalinism as the highest embodiment of what they imagined to be military order, but which was now imposed on the whole society.

The commanders' literary works and memoirs appearing from the end of the 1960s to the mid-1980s (they would fill a library) have created historical, political, even moral problems. The authors of these books are renowned and their views cannot be disregarded. But the majority are guilty of unforgivable omissions and blatant falsifications of the history of the war. Memoirs, after all, are documents, even if they are personal rather than analytical reports. No one has ever written a truly self-critical autobiography, though many individual works have been honest and have drawn conclusions based on facts. But in this case we have a whole series of books that contain obvious falsifications, often fabricated by ghostwriters.

One way or another, we will have to get to the bottom of who did what and why. There can be no doubt that the Chief Political Directorate of the Soviet army, Voenizdat,* and other publishing houses, played a major role, along with the Departments of Propaganda and Science of the Central Committee (which was responsible for history as well as other sciences) and, of course, the Institute of Military History. I think the techniques behind this production line of fakes, half-truths, and cover-ups should be exposed.†

I cannot help recalling one episode. In 1969, Marshal Zhukov's memoirs were published by the Novosti Press Agency. The book was a real sensation; everybody was trying to get hold of it. I remember how difficult it was to obtain ten copies or so from Novosti for some of our top scholars at the institute. Soon after the book was published, I ran into its chief editor, V. T. Komolov, the director of Novosti Press, in the foyer of a film theater. We started talking, and naturally the book became the main subject of our conversation.

*A military publishing house.
†In connection with this I have to say that truthful books about the war have begun to appear in recent years. Among these are books by well-known military authors, for example, D. A. Volkogonov's *Triumph and Tragedy: A Political Portrait of J. V. Stalin.*

Komolov complained that he had worked himself to death rewriting some of the main parts of the book. Zhukov, he claimed, was old and didn't understand anything about politics, and it was a good thing, at least, that eventually he agreed to all the corrections, cuts, and additions. After all, the memoirs had to be made to fit into the line, said Komolov. "Didn't you have any doubts?" I asked him. "After all, this is history, the memoirs of one of the important characters in the greatest drama of our country's history. And here you are, taking advantage of his illness and, perhaps, his weakness—going ahead and writing whatever you want to in his name." Unfortunately, Kolomov simply could not understand what I was driving at. He started explaining that he had checked every-thing with the Central Committee; he named some mid-level officials from the Science and Education Department. According to the mem-oirs of A. Ya. Mirkina,* who had also helped edit Zhukov's memoirs, the chapter on the repression of the Red Army High Command in 1937 was deleted from the text. If that is the way they treated Zhukov's mem-oirs, what can be said about those of figures who were less famous and more willing to compromise?†

S. M. Shtemenko's memoirs deserve special mention at this point. Shtemenko had very good reason to eulogize Stalin: he was one of Sta-lin's favorites during the war and was quickly promoted. According to Konstantin Simonov, the noted Soviet writer whose major theme was World War II, Shtemenko was close to Beria. In his memoirs, pub-lished in 1967, Stalin is described as a man endowed with "the high qualities of a military leader," as a commander who "made an inestima-ble contribution to the victory of the Soviet people in the Great Patriotic War," and as the brains behind almost all the great battles and opera-tions. At the same time, all the misfortunes that befell the nation and the Soviet forces, for which Stalin was responsible, are passed over in silence. According to Shtemenko, Stalin even fought against the per-sonality cult.

I don't want to create the impression that I am calling for the dismis-sal of all the war memoirs that appeared from the late 1960s onward. Probably there are some reliable facts and observations even in those books glorifying Stalin, but we must bear in mind how the Great Patri-

*Ogonyok, no. 17, 1988.
†The unabridged memoirs of Marshal Zhukov are currently being prepared for print.

otic War dominates our history. I think those memoirs should be evaluated objectively, and the mechanics of the operation to falsify the history of the war should be investigated.

The multivolume *History of the Second World War* was published in those years, and, like many other institute directors at the Academy of Sciences, I was a member of the editorial commission. This was a fundamental work and a vivid example of the irresponsible approach to history taken by the military leaders of the time. I witnessed many sharp exchanges on the editorial commission revolving around only one thing— the desire of one marshal or another to present his own actions and the actions of his units in the most favorable light. Each one of them wanted to bask in the limelight, and Brezhnev set the example by making a battle he took part in (Malaya Zemlya, near Novorossiisk) look like one of the decisive battles of the war.

But the worst was the tone set from the very start. As work on the first volume began, in 1972, it was to follow a shamelessly and cynically Stalinist line, aimed at a blatant falsification of the entire period of the war. I found myself thrown into a lion's den of seething passions. I was the object of an organized victimization campaign that was calculated, apparently right from the beginning, to teach the civilian members of the Chief Editorial Commission a lesson on how to behave. For the commission, it was easier to deal with the military: you simply issued an order.

The episode involving me started in a very routine way. I presented to the commission my remarks and proposals about the draft of the first volume. For example, I wrote that the extent of our defeats at the beginning of the war was downplayed and that the reasons for these failures were untruthfully presented in the introduction to the first volume. The introduction spoke only about "mistakes, which are generally known," after which emphasis was placed on the superiority of our military strategy, our operational plans, and so forth. I also questioned the judgment made in the first volume on the assistance given by American corporations to the German rearmament effort before the war, pointing out that "the issue of the aid provided by American companies to Nazi Germany is exaggerated." I also noted that during the 1920s the United States did not experience a fit of expansionism, as claimed by the authors of the volume; if anything, a growing pacifist spirit was more in evidence at the time.

A couple of weeks after I had sent off my critique, aides to the minister of defense, Marshal Grechko, who was also the chairman of the Chief Editorial Commission, started telephoning me at regular intervals, almost every other day, informing me about the forthcoming commission meeting and asking me if I was going to take part in it. I attributed this persistence to military discipline and zeal. In fact, a performance was being prepared that would make an example of me before the commission for my subversive remarks.

After opening the meeting with a short summary of the reviews that had been received, Grechko fired off a devastating salvo against me. He recognized two big guns and a third, smaller-caliber piece, who spoke in succession and laid down a barrage of criticism.

The first speaker was Pyotr N. Pospelov, one of the most odious high priests of Stalin's personality cult. The editor-in-chief of Stalin's official biography and formerly of *Pravda*, Pospelov had been the Central Committee secretary in charge of ideology for a long time. Here are a few quotes conveying the character of this meeting, which was very typical of this phase of Stalinism's counteroffensive. I made detailed notes of the meeting, almost like minutes in shorthand.

. . . The issues Comrade Arbatov raises in his review are not only dubious, but can be disputed absolutely. The overall value of the work is quite obvious. . . .

American and English monopolies rendered material assistance to Nazi Germany during the arms race. Yet Comrade Arbatov, who is an expert in international affairs, raises objections about this.

. . . Comrade Arbatov raises a fundamental point about our strategy at the outset of the war, but he raises it incorrectly. From the point of view of strategy and military capability, we were fully armed and prepared right from the very first days of the war. What were the reasons, then, for our retreat during the first months of the war? With two years of preparation behind them, the Germans enjoyed a threefold superiority in military equipment, having seized the economic base of all the occupied countries of Europe.* But we performed wonders

---

*Nowadays this thesis, originally proposed by Stalin, has been convincingly exposed by our researchers, who have shown that the Germans did not enjoy any superiority at all in the number of tanks, aircraft, and artillery pieces in 1941.

when we started evacuating our most important plants and enterprises in June 1941.

The second "witness for the prosecution" was army general Shtemenko. He spoke in a denunciatory tone:

> Comrade Arbatov has doubts about our superior strategy [although it was] based on the laws and principles governing historical and dialectical materialism, on Lenin's teachings about the defense of socialist society.

Marshal Grechko himself summed everything up:

> I think that, since Comrade Arbatov is not strictly a military man, he should not start giving advice and putting forward proposals on military affairs.*
>
> I listened to the statements made by the academicians with great pleasure and made a mental note of everything.

Marshal Grechko continued:

> For those of us who have spent all our lives in the army, it is sometimes easier to see how one particular military problem or another should be solved. But you are touching on problems of military strategy and doctrine. We are much better equipped to deal with problems in this area than anyone else. And we consider that the things contained in this volume are correct.

And that was that. Mind your own business—even if you happen to be the director of the U.S.A. and Canada Institute at the Academy of Sciences and are discussing the internal and ideological situation in the United States during the 1920s or the economic relations between the United States and Weimar Germany.

This attack was conducted before an ominously silent audience of about 100 or 150 military men, most of them high-ranking officials of

---

*This is typical of the advice our generals like to give to civilian specialists even today.

the Ministry of Defense, plus a couple of dozen civilian historians and political scientists. There were, of course, some very decent people among them, such as Marshal Bagramyan, who watched this spectacle in shame and who later called me and told me how he really felt.

The purpose of this confrontation, clear to me and to many of the others, was to set a special political tone for this multivolume work right from the start. That purpose was preserved when Marshal Dmitri Ustinov replaced Marshal Grechko as chairman of the Chief Editorial Commission after Grechko's death. They and the authors whom they assigned to work on the project saw as their mission the rehabilitation of Stalin and the glorification of the marshals and generals who had commanded the armed forces. They blocked an objective analysis of the history of the war and stifled questions that were unpleasant for the military leadership.

It's interesting that in 1991 there was a debate on the draft of the first volume of the latest version of the multivolume history of the war. This volume was to appear on the occasion of the fiftieth anniversary of the victory over Nazi Germany. Once again I found myself on the Chief Editorial Commission, headed by Dmitri Yazov, who was minister of defense at that time. (And once again all this was decided upon by the Central Committee in 1988, when the relevant resolution was passed. Even then this organization was the decision-making body on all questions of any importance in the country.)

This time, when I learned of the decision to publish the work, I thought we were talking about a real history that would eliminate the falsifications and mistakes made in the two previous versions,* both of which bore the same mark of Cain due to the Stalinist views and assessments that had not yet been overcome, and both were incredibly short on reliable factual data. (After all, the archives were still closed.) Moreover, these works had the stamp of toadyism, since the authors tried to magnify the "military exploits" and the contribution to victory of whichever of the two was leader of the country at the time, and, in his wake, of whoever was the minister of defense, the chief of the General Staff, and so forth. It seemed to me at the time that it would be all the easier to cleanse history of these blotches because the new generation of leaders either had not taken part in the war or (like Yazov and Akhromeyev)

*The first one was published under Khrushchev and his team.

had been of such junior rank that they could not pretend to a leading role in the victory over Hitler.

But these hopes proved vain for no reason other than that the new history of the war was being written at the behest of the Central Committee and, what is more, under the direction of the marshals and generals. And I'm not saying this just because Defense Minister Yazov, during one of the sessions of the Chief Editorial Commission, proposed to "strengthen the role" played by the engagement at Ponyri, in which he personally took part. In the long run this is just a minor thing, but it transpired that the Party and military leadership once again wanted to produce a falsified history of the war. This time, the chosen target of attack was not myself, but General Dmitri Volkogonov, whom I mentioned earlier.

The minutes of this secret session fell into the hands of a journalist and were published in *Nezavisimaya Gazeta* ("The Independent Gazette"). Sometime later (at the time of the debate I was absent from Moscow) I gave the paper an interview in which I said that a significant part of the military leadership opposed the whole policy of recent years and realized that the truth about the political leadership of those times, and about Stalin, would be yet another blow against the bulwarks of our totalitarian system. One of the main justifications for the crimes under Stalinism was World War II. It went like this: yes, there were repressions, there was the disfranchisement of the peasantry, but then we won, and saved Europe. But no one asks himself the questions: "But at what price? And was such suffering unavoidable? And why shouldn't we have won anyway?"

I also mentioned the fact that the military caste (that is, the generals) were trying to "privatize" the achievement of the whole nation, and because of this, they were defending the old legends. For this reason they needed an officially canonized history of the war, and an apologia, so that they could destroy the civilians' desire to meddle in their military affairs and judge them. Only marshals and generals are allowed to do this, you see.

During this interview I also officially announced that I was resigning from the Chief Editorial Commission and that I was urging my colleagues, at least the civilian ones (the military were subject to their own discipline), to resign as well. It is impossible to write a truthful history of the war under such conditions. Now I feel ashamed that I took part in the production of the previous twelve-volume history—that I lived according to the rules of the day—although I tried to protest. But I did not see the thing through to the end. I don't want to find myself in such a situation a second time.

To write an accurate account of the truly nonpareil achievements of the army and the nation and many talented commanders, it would have been necessary to bring to light many unknown facts and clarify the crucial issue: Why did we twice suffer near-defeat—once in 1941, and the second time in 1942? Why did we sustain such heavy losses, incomparably greater than those of the other powers?

The subject of the war became the main path along which those who sought the rehabilitation of Stalin and Stalinism set off. This applied not only to military historians, but to writers, playwrights, and film producers. And with Stalin in the lead, the names and images of others, including Molotov and his close comrades and principal accomplices in crime, began to appear in books and films.

But, of course, the neo-Stalinists' efforts did not stop with the history of the war. Once again a strict ban was placed on the subject of the purges. At first, this issue was avoided in articles that occasionally appeared about the innocent Party and government leaders destroyed by Stalin. At least the dates of their deaths were included, and people could figure out what those implied: that prominent leaders in the years 1937, 1938, and 1939 were simply not allowed to die a natural death. That is certainly the conclusion I reached when I read those dates and thought about why they had been inserted. Later, the dates stopped being mentioned.

The rehabilitation of Stalin in the 1960s, 1970s, and 1980s did not confine itself to Stalin's reputation as a "Great Leader." Far more ambitious, it was intended to preserve and rebuild Stalinist mechanisms, albeit without their more extreme, overt, and excessive forms. Clearly, the achievement of such strategic aims presupposed a conservative offensive not only in history but in other social sciences as well.

In economics there were open clashes of opinion. By the end of the 1960s there was an ongoing debate over which of the economic reforms of 1965 had been fulfilled. Despite the general stagnation of the late 1960s, there were some changes for the better in the field of economic research.

One of these was the establishment of the new Institute of Economics at Novosibirsk. A bright group of scholars came on the scene, among them Abel Aganbegyan and Tatyana Zaslavskaya. It was natural that economics as a discipline should flower in Siberia, far away from the Moscow institutions that were strongholds of politico-economic dogma, but even so, it would have been impossible without such brave and talented people. Despite regular attempts to victimize them, they held their ground and managed to make a significant contribution to the study of economics in our country.

The other development was the establishment of the Central Institute of Economics and Mathematics, founded by V. S. Nemchinov and later headed by Nikolai P. Fedorenko, with the active participation of the eminent mathematician and economist L. V. Kantorovich, who later received the Nobel Prize.

The conservative and traditionalist academic institutions offered fierce resistance to these centers and scholars. Among the conservative institutions was the Economics Department of Moscow State University, which for years had been a breeding ground for narrow-minded lecturers and dogmatists. Another was the I. I. Kuzminov Chair at the Academy of Social Sciences of the Central Committee, and, to a certain extent, the Economics Institute at the Academy of Sciences.

The general shift toward Stalinism could not but have an effect on economics. True, the conservatives were hindered for a while by the fact that, politically, it was clear that the country needed to be brought out of its growing economic difficulties. But the search for solutions to that dilemma demanded creative thinking. Through the joint efforts of a number of experts, the debate on how to expand economic reform and develop a structure for the national economy headed the agenda at the Twenty-fourth Party Congress, but, for all intents and purposes, there were no results.

As both a witness to and a participant in these debates, I can say that the desire to raise new issues did not come from the official centers of economics, politics, and science. On the contrary, they continued to provide traditional and absolutely sterile proposals for the leadership and tried to prevent any changes. Nonetheless, the leadership could not help but see how little promise these proposals held for the future. As a result, political leaders started to turn to those familiar with world economics—for example, to Academician Inozemtsev and the experts at his institute, to my colleagues and myself at the U.S.A. and Canada Institute, to one or two other specialists in international affairs. Gradually, an unofficial working group took shape; it was soon joined by Alexander Bovin, Stepan Sitaryan, and Boris Sukharevsky. Georgi Tsukanov was the official chairman and in difficult circumstances the main liaison to Brezhnev and other members of the Politburo. The group found itself in frequent conflict with officials of the Central Committee and the Council of Ministers: Kosygin and, particularly, Tikhonov, Kirilenko, Mikhail Solomentsev, the secretary of the Central Committee, who later became prime minister of the Russian Federation, and others.

Since we weeded out the panegyrics to imaginary economic successes as much as we could, and tried to concentrate attention on problems and failings, the apparatchiks soon invented a nickname for us: "the slanderers."*

By drawing on the good counsel and assistance of many serious economists in Moscow and Novosibirsk, this group counterbalanced the old way of thinking in economics and helped to generate and legitimize ideas that had long been considered seditious, as well as to introduce many correct and fresh ideas. The practical effect of our work, which demanded not only great labor and persistence but also involved a certain risk, was a different matter altogether. Here, we were to be deeply disappointed. Speeches were made, documents were printed—and then nothing, absolutely nothing, happened. The attempts to breach the stout walls of the administrative-bureaucratic fortress were fruitless, despite the fact that we often managed to scale these walls by means of instructions, persuasions, and proposals coming from the top leadership itself. But despite these efforts, which earned a lot of praise from the leaders, the real situation in the country was growing inexorably worse.

Even when successful breakthroughs resulted in some constructive official decisions, those decisions were quickly discarded by the bureaucracy through the force of inertia. The dismantling of the economic reforms of 1965 is one example.

---

*Sometimes these personal attacks even turned to the advantage of group members. This was because one of the favorite accusations against us was, How was it that "nobodies" were asked to perform responsible political assignments? Academic degrees, publications, reputations were, for these critics, indeed, "nothing." For them "something" meant at least election to the Central Committee or the Supreme Soviet. Therefore, the leadership showed an interest in promoting to higher political status various people who were asked to take such assignments.

From the late 1960s on, my institute, with Inozemtsev and several other colleagues, very persistently and repeatedly argued that a new scientific-technological revolution was under way in the world that would have tremendous significance for the Soviet economy and all other aspects of life. We were in danger of lagging behind, which might relegate our country to the sidelines of world development. Urgent measures were needed.

At first, these signals were ignored. Even the term "scientific-technological revolution" was not used until the 1970s and was carefully deleted not only from official documents, but from articles and books as well. But later, the facts that our scholars supported became so self-evident that it proved impossible to ignore them any longer. Shortly after the Twenty-fourth Party Congress, the Politburo decided to hold a special Central Committee plenum on the technological revolution. As usual, the preparations for this meeting were entrusted to a commission consisting of several secretaries of the Central Committee; it was headed by Andrei P. Kirilenko. A working group was formed to prepare the materials, including the draft of the general secretary's speech. Inozemtsev and I were assigned to head this group. Some prominent economists worked with us, including Academicians Fedorenko, Aganbegyan, and Ivan D. Ivanov. Upon request, the working group was given "extraordinary privileges"—the right to invite government ministers (including those from the defense sectors), directors of enterprises, and prominent scientists in a wide range of fields, and "interrogate" them. Many months of intensive work produced a thick—130-page—comprehensive economic-reform program that for those days was quite progressive. We had reached the conclusion that quicker progress in science and technology was simply unthinkable without radical changes in the economy.

The document was delivered to Kirilenko, Solomentsev, Vladimir Dolgikh, and others in May 1973, before the deadline. And there it died a quiet death. Nobody criticized it; some even praised it. But the whole idea of the plenum sank like a stone. I reminded Kirilenko several times about the Politburo decision and our document. Once I asked Brezhnev about the plenum, but I received no coherent answer. It's worth noting that the questions themselves, about the plenum and its fate, were greeted with a certain amount of irritation. Later I realized that the leadership was not prepared for any important changes in the economy, or for any kind of serious and complicated business. In this context, the document we had presented was simply an irritant. The authorities wanted something smoother, something more propagandistic that envisioned administrative measures for scientific and technological development; but in no way did they want fundamental economic reform.

Together with the authors who are still living, I have often compared the document's ideas with today's thinking and current debates on the subject. The conclusion is unanimous: had the analysis and the proposals we made at that time been put into practice, things would look very different today. It was very gratifying indeed to hear Mikhail Gorbachev say, during a meeting in October 1989, that an interesting document had been prepared in the early 1970s, but that, unfortunately, it had been quashed. I was told that the original was found in Leonid Brezhnev's safe after his death, and it apparently ended up in Gorbachev's hands. Gorbachev held the idea that conditions for reform were ripe almost twenty years ago and that appropriate reforms had, in fact, been proposed. But since they were never carried out, our problems only worsened, and today we must attempt to solve them under much more difficult conditions.

I totally agree with this assessment. But at the same time I see that it was simply impossible to hold the plenum and put the actions we were proposing into practice. Economic demands and the theoretical thinking behind them clashed with the insurmountable political realities of the time—the barriers of the absolute power of the bureaucratic and administrative system and the inertia of established mechanisms and concepts. This confrontation could not exist forever. The political system's rigidity suppressed thinking and theory and condemned the national economy to stagnation.

At the same time, of course, a new factor came into play, which allowed Brezhnev and the whole leadership to file reforms away in the bottom drawer. That factor was the rise in oil prices as a result of the Yom Kippur War of 1973. Suddenly we inherited a large and unearned fortune—and nothing spoils people more than unearned riches.

The wealth that rained down on us from heaven retarded economic reform (I will address this question later). The stagnation of the national economy and the endless postponement of reforms further exacerbated the crisis in economics and invited a conservative attack. A bitter fight was launched over market mechanisms. Firmly established in Stalin's time, the traditional school of thought denied the right of the market to exist. The top leadership, as far as I know, did not take sides, displaying an indecisiveness that in itself was very bad for the nation's economy.

These were hard times for our best economists. One problem after another descended upon the heads of Abel Aganbegyan and Tatyana Zaslavskaya. Fedorenko was under constant pressure from above. (Another reason for attacks against him was the fact that several of his co-workers had emigrated to the West—a political crime by the standards of that time.) Time and again, official wrath descended upon our well-known economist Stanislav Shatalin and upon Alexandr Anchishkin.

At the end of this period (1981–1982), the Central Committee Science Department tried to reorient economics as a whole away from the study of real situations and the ever-growing problems of the national economy and force a return to the scholastic shuffling of abstract quotations taken from the works of the founding fathers of Marxism-Leninism in their most primitive Stalinist interpretations.

But I will write later about the whole situation in the country at the peak of the crises that have acquired the name of "stagnation." Before that, a few words about the areas in which I actively participated—foreign policy and détente.

8 | The Short, Unlucky Life of Détente

B etween the late 1960s and the mid-1970s we scored some considerable successes in foreign policy. But from the mid-1970s until the arrival of perestroika, we managed to squander them and suffered some bitter defeats. The lessons of these successes and failures should not be forgotten.

In principle, it was easier for the Soviet leadership to change direction in foreign policy than in domestic politics, if for no other reason than that many fewer people took part in the shaping and conduct of foreign policy and it was easier for the leaders to plot its course. But from the first days of the October Revolution, our foreign policy found itself so tightly bound to our whole outlook, to our ideology, and to our internal affairs that its development was always an important component of our general political framework.

During the postrevolutionary period the leadership warred over two extremes in political thinking. One group saw the Russian Revolution as the first act of a world revolution and justified revolutionary war and the willingness to sacrifice even its gains, if necessary, for the sake of the triumph of socialism and communism throughout the world. The opposition made internal changes its main aim and offered peaceful coexistence with capitalism, believing the socialist example was the best way to further the cause of communism all over the world. But there was probably not a single Soviet official alive in whom both views did not coexist.

After the revolution and the establishment of Soviet power in Finland and the Baltic states, Soviet rule was established temporarily in Hungary, and major revolutionary events swept Germany and Eastern Europe. Not only revolution but counterrevolution, it seemed, had assumed an international character. Was this not demonstrated by the intervention of the Entente against Soviet Russia; by the German army's suppression of the revolution in Finland and the Baltics; by the participation of German troops, with England and Japan, in the suppression of Soviet rule in Ukraine, in Transcaucasia, and in the Far East; and, finally, by the West's support to the White Army and the forces of counterrevolution during the Civil War? All this seemed to support the traditional Marxist belief that the revolution in Russia was the first organic part of the global revolutionary process.

Much has been written in our history and literature on Lenin's arguments with the "leftist" Communists, the supporters of Trotsky during the talks on the Treaty of Brest-Litovsk. The prevailing belief has been that from the outset Lenin's policy was one of peaceful coexistence and of opposition to the exportation of revolution. Careful study shows that this is not true. A unique realist, Lenin was more concerned with concrete political situations than with abstract theories. He was pragmatic enough to participate in negotiations and enter into agreements with the "class enemy." He did not share the view held by a number of revolutionaries that at certain times a heroic suicide of the Russian Revolution was preferable to a "shameful" peace, since the former could ignite revolutionary fires in other nations.

I think that at the same time Lenin believed that the European revolution, if not the world one, had begun. Along with the overriding necessity of winning the Civil War, this conviction distracted attention from the challenge of building a new socialist society of universal justice and from the management of the transition period, including the long-range economic problems. Lenin often used to say it was up to us to start the revolution, but it would be easier for others to continue it. Perhaps he thought that once the revolution had taken place, it would be easier for Western countries to play the part of pathfinders and explorers, searching out the means to complete the transition from capitalism to socialism. If revolution had soon taken place in other countries, at least in Germany, it would have been possible then to work out plans for the political, economic, and social transformation of those countries. Judging by the general tone of Lenin's statements and those of other comrades-in-arms, such hopes remained high right up until 1921–1922.

The attitudes of the leadership, the Party, the army, and the public during the war with Poland are a clear example of this view. The country was inspired by the early victories; Mikhail Tukhachevsky led his troops forward under the slogans "Onward to Warsaw!" and "Onward to Berlin!" Many people in the Party, including the leadership, apparently believed that all we had to do was let the Red Army cross the borders, and the Polish and German proletariat and their allies would rise and claim a victorious socialist revolution. Things turned out differently. Tukhachevsky's troops never got as far as Germany, and their arrival in Poland united Poles of every class, who inflicted a bitter defeat on the Red Army. We had to surrender some of our lands in Ukraine and Byelorussia to the Poles. The Party also learned the practical lessons that you cannot export socialism into another country at the point of a bayonet and that national solidarity in the face of an external threat can be a greater force than class solidarity.* The illusion that one could establish communism by decree and military might and usher in a new society of plenty and justice for all was buried by harsh reality.

The issue of whether it was possible to build socialism in a single country became crucial to the U.S.S.R.'s domestic and foreign policy for purely practical reasons. Lenin and those who shared his opinions found a solution in their New Economic Policy (NEP), in peaceful coexistence and trade with the capitalist countries. At first, both policies were probably regarded as temporary retreats, providing a breathing spell.

This impression was short-lived. Judging by Lenin's last works, he was already beginning to understand that this new, "temporary" state of affairs was going to last for a long time and had to be confronted. Unfor-

---

*Here I have an apology to make. In my comments in *Ogonyok* in 1988, discussing an article by the astronomer Carl Sagan, I brushed aside his conclusion that Tukhachevsky's Polish campaign had been an attempt at exporting revolution. This was due to the usual defensiveness, which became a conditioned reflex, and the fact that we got into the habit over many long years (eventually it became second nature) of sweeping "inconvenient" facts under the rug. I, for example, have only recently studied these pages of our history with any degree of care.

tunately, fate allotted Lenin only a very short period to adjust Soviet policy. Stalin deftly put the former "revolutionizing" and "leftist" convictions to his own use, both in his struggle for power and in the establishment of his own policies.

The fact that the New Economic Policy was regarded as a "temporary retreat" helped Stalin create a military economy, which was later named the administrative-command system. People began to identify it with the very essence of socialism (and many still continue to do so), although it is much closer to a military-feudal or a bureaucratic-feudal system of government. The model for the "socialism" that began to take form under Stalin was that of an "emergency situation." It did not work too badly in wartime or during either preparation for war or postwar reconstruction, but it failed hopelessly under normal conditions.

For the purpose of establishing a totalitarian regime, nothing could be more useful than the political and psychological environment of an emergency situation. Normal problems and issues connected with economic development and social change were pushed into the background by the looming world revolution.

These attitudes presupposed a black-and-white division of the world into two halves—you and your comrades on the one hand and your relentless foes and their allies on the other. Such a stark view of the world lodged itself firmly in our consciousness. This concept evolved into a theory in which the world was divided into two hostile socio-economic systems, whose relentless struggle became the main axis around which life between nations revolved and developed. This concept was fated to have a long life—right until the mid-1980s. And in Stalin's time it proved very useful for the establishment and maintenance of a personal dictatorship and for the imposition of a repressive order.

This perception had implications of a revolutionary-messianic kind. Though such a view paid homage to the highest and noblest of human ideals, in reality it inevitably led to the rapid spread of violence.

Of course, aside from these messianic theories, such attitudes had other roots as well. Among them were the powerful yearnings of the people to find a special meaning for their unprecedented suffering and the destruction of their society's foundations. Revolutions are often accompanied by messianism. The great French Revolution was; and the American Revolution instilled in the minds of many Americans the idea of their country as a "shining city on the hill"; it led to the theory of

Manifest Destiny. These beliefs still exist in one form or another in the minds of much of the public and in the character of American politics. I hope many Americans are aware of this.

But to be fair, I must argue that the messianism born of the Russian Revolution was not a nationalistic one. It was initially internationalistic, imbued with the will to sacrifice everything for the freedom and happiness of a humanity fainting under the "yoke of capitalism."

Such messianism undoubtedly helped people bear incredible hardships and survive the gravest trials. Moreover, these attitudes also helped the Soviet Union gain high respect in the eyes of the leftist and liberal intelligentsia of the West—although, because of our sectarianism, that respect and sympathy did not last long. But, at the same time, this messianism strengthened the hostility of the West. Here, the pluses and the minuses balanced each other out. But there was another great and truly fateful minus—one that could not be balanced out by anything: Stalin manipulated internationalism to serve nationalism and imperial ambitions. These attitudes manifested themselves clearly in Stalin's foreign policy, beginning with the protocols to the Soviet-German agreement of August 23, 1939. Subsequent developments showed how willing Stalin was to violate publicly professed political principles and morals. During Molotov's visit to Germany, the Germans proposed that the Soviet Union join the Anti-Comintern Pact, which had hurriedly been renamed the Tripartite Pact by its members—Germany, Italy, and Japan. Soon an agreement to this effect was sent off to Berlin on the condition that Hitler not object to our expansion south to the Black Sea straits and the Indian Ocean.*

Lingering in the minds of our leaders and part of the population, these "remnants of the past" weighed like a stone on Stalin's successors. They prevented the country from breaking out of the dangerous Cold War policy that had evolved after the war and from dealing more effectively with the dangers of the arms race, even when conditions favorable to such changes began to appear. To undertake perestroika in our foreign policy we had to start with perestroika in our political thinking.

More likely than not, Khrushchev never could see this problem in all

---

*Valentin Berezhkov, who was Molotov's interpreter at the time and accompanied him on his trip, describes this meeting in some detail. See *Mezhdunarodnaya Zhizn'*, no. 8 (1989), p. 14.

its depth, but he quickly realized that we had to forgo at least some of the dogmas that hindered the conduct of politics. First of all, there was the dogma about the inevitability of war; second, the belief that a socialist revolution inevitably had to be violent. Third, we once again had to renounce the "exportation of revolution," and "revolutionary war."

These dogmas were abjured at the Twentieth Party Congress and after it, in connection with the polemics against Mao Zedong. Regardless of whether all this fell into a neatly intertwined Marxist-Leninist concept or whether it contained obvious contradictions, the Soviet people got more or less coherent answers to these burning political questions. And since the most urgent priority of the people, who had suffered so much in the last war was peace, they were ready to accept these answers. The decisions of the congress also made clear to the West that the new leadership had chosen not to bear responsibility for the words and deeds of its predecessors and had adopted a new foreign policy platform.

But the gremlin of "leftist extremism" turned out to be very tenacious. You chased it out the door, and it came back through the window, down the chimney, or even through the keyhole. Over the course of our long-suffering history, it proved incredibly difficult for most of us (above all, for my generation) to forsake our old dogmas, even when they no longer had any relation to reality. For example, many people, starting with those at the very top, were able to take a few bold steps forward in politics and theory, but soon fell ill with a sickness that I call the "revolutionary inferiority" syndrome.

After taking those few steps, we almost immediately started to look into our revolutionary theology for ways to somehow "compensate" for our realism, and were deeply obsessed with not "going too far." For example, we abandoned the idea of an inevitable—and armed and violent—path to revolution, and embarked on a policy based on peaceful coexistence; we made the first realistic attempts at arms reductions; and so on. But immediately we got scared of our own courage and developed a number of theoretical and political gimmicks that we hoped would allow us to continue on a realistic course in politics while preserving our ideological virginity, demonstrating our revolutionary faith and fervor.

It later became evident that these gimmicks could only harm our policies and undermine the new political credibility we had just started to win. I would not blame our "enemies" in the West for this.

For example, there were attempts to prove that, although war was not inevitable, it remained a threat as long as capitalism existed. And should capitalism start this war, it would end with its total defeat and, therefore, with the universal triumph of socialism. We understood what nonsense this was only when the Chinese repeated it in polemics against the Soviet Union.

For a long time the leadership never stopped repeating that peaceful coexistence did not mean an end to the ideological struggle. This point was the main theme of their propaganda. I must admit I found it difficult to understand why we were so insistent on this point. Maybe we persisted just to show our intransigence toward capitalism and, most of all, to justify the state of hostilities with real or imagined ideological foes abroad, and with those foes' "ideological diversions" on the home front. (This concept was put into political circulation by the KGB.)

Of course, as a socialist power and a member of the world community, we could not, and cannot, isolate ourselves from the world and, in particular, remain indifferent to colonialism. But I am certain that behind our aid to liberation movements there was also an element of compensation for some dogmas we had discarded. All the more so because the Chinese were constantly stepping on this sore toe of ours, slamming us right and left for our "betrayal" of the revolutionary and liberation movements.

Sometimes declarations about our adherence to the cause of revolution and liberation was a sort of verbal screen behind which were other political intentions. But I do not wish to imply that our leadership did not believe its words and actions. Therefore it is right to conclude that the Stalinist "relics of the past" hindered the development of a consistent new political course and helped our opponents to sow seeds of doubt about the Soviet Union's intentions. Most dangerous of all was the fact that, having given aid to liberation movements, we allowed ourselves to be drawn into competition with the Americans throughout the Third World, thus helping to internationalize regional crises and making them part of the Cold War. None of this benefited international relations or the true interests of the Third World countries. We got particularly vivid proof of this in the second half of the 1970s and at the beginning of the 1980s.

Nobody had any doubt that Brezhnev was a weak theoretician on foreign policy, but during the first period of his leadership he understood on a gut level that the chief priority of the nation was the preservation of peace. He took this position as early as 1967–1968. He saw quite clearly that discernible progress on that front was a sure way to win popularity for his policy and for himself.

At Gromyko's insistence, high-level contacts with the United States were initiated. President Johnson's visit to the U.S.S.R. was scheduled for the autumn of 1968, but events in Czechoslovakia forced the Americans to postpone the meeting. In general, the invasion of Czechoslovakia had a far greater negative impact on domestic politics than on our foreign affairs—perhaps because the American war in Vietnam was at its height. Under those circumstances, the President of the United States could not strike a moralistic pose, as he had on previous occasions.

Contacts with the United States continued, although they were not very active. At the same time an important breakthrough occurred in our relations with the Federal Republic of Germany; it was the Germans who initiated the move. The architects of the new *Ostpolitik* were Chancellor Willy Brandt and his aide Egon Bahr (whom I consider to be one of the most outstanding political minds of our time). The Soviet side quickly supported and broadened this initiative. Andropov; our ambassador in Bonn, Valentin Falin; and Brezhnev's aide A. M. Alexandrov played a large part. Falin worked directly with the Soviet leadership, sometimes bypassing our Ministry of Foreign Affairs. At first Gromyko did not actively support the German initiatives. I think this was because he put a higher priority on our foreign policy vis-à-vis America and had become accustomed to using the Federal Republic of Germany as a whipping boy to demonstrate his "class" and "anti-imperialistic" convictions, thereby offsetting the positive steps we were taking in our relations with the United States.* But eventually, the Ministry of Foreign Affairs also joined in. The so-called Moscow Agreements were signed

*There were some sharp clashes of opinion, apparently between Brezhnev, Andropov, and Gromyko. I remember that during Bahr's first visit to the U.S.S.R. I was even handed a request from Brezhnev to entertain our West German guest for a day so as to find the time to make Gromyko "shut up." That is when I got to know Bahr, with whom, over many years, I was to establish a friendship, which became particularly firm during our work together on the Palme Commission.

on September 3, 1971. At the same time an agreement on the complicated issue of West Berlin was signed by the four powers—the U.S.S.R., the United States, France, and Great Britain.

In 1969, the Soviet-American Strategic Arms Limitation Talks began, though somewhat later than had originally been planned.

On both the American and West German fronts it seemed that real opportunities were opening up and that we should take advantage of them. On the basis of conversations with Brezhnev, Gromyko, and Andropov, I believe it was still extremely difficult for us to pluck up the courage to become flexible and broad-minded enough to assess the international situation in a new light and to formulate an adequate policy.*

I see at least two reasons for these difficulties. The first one was basically ideological; it manifested itself in Brezhnev's and other Politburo members' lack of decisiveness about whether this new policy would conform to Marxist principles. Partly to blame was the fear that an insufficiently firm "class" attitude might cause opposition forces to coalesce within the Party or provide a pretext for them to attack the leadership. The October plenum and the subsequent debates on foreign policy were still fresh in everybody's mind.

The second reason was our lack of preparedness for a serious dialogue, and later, for serious action, in the area of arms control and disarmament. How did the U.S.A. Institute interpret Soviet-American relations and our political opportunities on this front? The institute prepared its first analytical report in April 1968, during the political upheavals in America that President Nixon called the gravest crisis in that country since its civil war. It was a presidential election year, and we made an attempt to forecast the impact of this extremely complicated situation on Soviet-American relations.

On rereading this report (it was stamped CLASSIFIED in accordance with the standards of the times), I was struck not so much by the fact that its main conclusions and forecasts turned out to be correct as I was by the boldness and even recklessness displayed by the authors. We drew some pretty categorical conclusions right at the start of our research.

Our main conclusion was that, regardless of who won the presidential

---

*Andropov dug in his heels on many issues (Germany was something of an exception) and displayed great caution. Today I think this was a tactic he used to avoid confrontations with his colleagues.

election, conditions were being created in the United States for changes in foreign policy that could, objectively, coincide with the Soviet Union's interests.

"For the first time the situation has arisen," we wrote in this document, which was forwarded to the leadership, "in which the U.S. government has encountered serious opposition, not only internationally but domestically, in conducting its global policy. For the first time, the United States has been confronted with the danger of serious internal upheavals, caused largely by higher taxes, inflation, the poverty of the minorities, and crises in the cities. The solution to these increasingly burdensome problems demands considerably more attention on the part of the government and a greater concentration of its resources on internal affairs." We thought the Americans' domestic problems would stimulate constructive new initiatives in their foreign policy. We also concluded that the U.S.S.R. could positively influence these processes.

At the beginning of 1968, such conclusions and recommendations were somewhat unusual. In presenting them to the Central Committee and the Ministry of Foreign Affairs, we were well aware that they could be received with displeasure and irritation, since liberation from the Cold War psychology turned out to be a painful process. In the contemporary evaluations of U.S. foreign policy, the Soviet perspective was dominated by formulas of irreconcilable hostility, such as "the main enemy," "hostile imperialistic policy," "military preparation." At the same time these evaluations were usually accompanied by rhetorical bows toward our policy of peaceful coexistence.

I do not wish to exaggerate the level of our understanding of America's domestic affairs and foreign policy. The institute was just beginning, and our first achievement was the decision to tell the leadership frankly (and write in the press) what experts who followed events in the United States already knew but were somewhat afraid to say. We were bold enough to discard ideological blinkers and base our conclusions on the practical interests of the Soviet Union. And as the knowledge of the staff members at the institute grew, our talk on this subject became more meaningful.

The opportunity for useful talks with the United States existed, but years passed without visible progress. We blamed them. They blamed us. I think we must both share the blame. A critical factor was that we were not yet ready to discuss the issue of arms limitation in a businesslike manner, if only because no one had ever demanded that the Ministry of Defense or the defense industry care about disarmament. They were concerned with catching up with the Americans in arms, not with arms control. Moreover, the people who worked in the Defense Ministry and in the military-industrial complex (as well as the majority of Foreign Ministry officials and even academic experts) were intellectually unprepared for a dialogue with the Americans and for serious talks going beyond the bounds of political declarations. At first they could not properly grasp American concepts and terminology concerning strategic and disarmament issues. I remember this vividly because of my frequent meetings with the members of our delegation before the start of the Strategic Arms Limitation Talks.* They were neither prepared for nor capable of seizing the initiative, of making their own well-grounded proposals, let alone of introducing new ideas.

But would any progress have been possible if the delegation had been ready? The military-industrial complex was a state within a state. All this was, and to a great extent still is, enveloped in a deep layer of secrecy. The spheres in which these agencies operated were absolutely sacrosanct: Brezhnev was indebted to the military for its support and liked to see himself as a war hero. Moreover, as second secretary of the Central Committee, he had run the defense industry for several years and had grown accustomed to granting the generals and the military industrialists anything they wanted. And the thing that they wanted most was no agreements tying their hands.

Some special circumstances were needed to overcome these obstacles and to pluck up the leadership's courage to attempt to replace the foundations of the Cold War with a new, less dangerous international system. This required more than simply working within the bounds of traditional diplomacy.

---

*I must say that our knowledge at the institute on this subject was rather poor. Basically, it was limited to what we could regularly read in the American literature on the subject (including trade literature) and to our discussions with some American experts, during which we tried, to the best of our meager abilities, to defend our country's position. From this we could at least gain an understanding of the terminology and the meaning of some strategic and disarmament concepts. But even this humble fund of knowledge made our institute unique and encouraged others to seek its help. Due to the institute's pioneering efforts, a new type of expert was created—the civilian expert on strategic-military, political-strategic, and arms-control issues.

Two such preconditions had appeared long before—the unacceptability of nuclear war and the burden of military expenditures. Khrushchev had realized this, as had Eisenhower and Kennedy. They made the first few steps, however modest, to start arms-control negotiations.

But toward the end of the 1960s, more concrete reasons for change had appeared. One of these was the prospect of improving our relations with the Federal Republic of Germany. Another important factor was China. During the late 1960s and the early 1970s our relations with China deteriorated, beyond theoretical differences and debates to increasing threats of a conflict. China had built nuclear weapons and started to produce missiles, albeit not very sophisticated ones. The Soviet Union increased the number of troops on the Chinese border. Proclaiming the danger of attack from the north, the Chinese dug in, building shelters, trenches, underground passages, entire underground townships. We, in turn, interpreted this as preparation for war.

In such a climate Sino-American relations acquired a new urgency. At the beginning of the 1970s, some serious changes took place, with great significance for the Soviet Union. As is well known, Henry Kissinger considers the use of the "China card" one of his greatest successes and achievements. But the credit for the diplomatic coup does not go to him alone. The idea of normalizing Sino-American relations had been lying dormant for a long time and was begging to be put on America's diplomatic agenda. I do not mean in any way to disparage Kissinger's skill and his extraordinary ability to assess a situation and act on it, but the political realities were still the main factor. By the late 1960s and the early 1970s there were simply no sensible reasons left for maintaining hostile relations between the West and China.

The one thing that remained unclear to the Americans was how the Chinese leadership would react to the idea of normalization. But this could easily be clarified. I never did understand why the United States took such a long time to establish the first contacts.

The only explanation I can find is that the Americans also suffered from a deep inferiority complex. For example, during the 1950s and 1960s they developed a fear (that had become almost an obsession) of not being sufficiently irreconcilable toward communism, toward the Soviet Union, and particularly toward China. Some remnants of this attitude were in evidence in the late 1970s and early 1980s.

One of them was the ever-present fear, inherited from the McCarthy era, of appearing "soft" on communism. During the McCarthy era, many outstanding American experts and diplomats who specialized in China were destroyed politically and morally. For a long time after that, the right wing regarded any attempt to normalize relations with China almost as high treason.

The second component was the psychological and political legacy of the Korean War, when Chinese troops fought a long battle with the Americans—and not without some measure of success. Anti-Chinese passions reached such a high point that even the use of nuclear weapons against China was debated. True, it all ended when General MacArthur, the author of this idea, was recalled to the United States and sent into retirement, but the political legacy remained.

The third factor was America's concern about the very active role China played in the liberation movements and civil wars in Southeast Asia and other regions of the Third World. I think this concern was heightened when the Chinese accused us of betraying the revolutionary cause and the liberation movements—they constantly glorified armed struggle. I can imagine that all of this seriously worried the Americans: it worried us! There was even concern that, with China's help, nuclear weapons would proliferate throughout the Third World. One should point out that the U.S. was justifying its military intervention in Vietnam primarily by the threat of Chinese, not Soviet, expansion.*

The fourth and related factor was, in my opinion, U.S. displeasure

---

*There is much evidence to support the contention that Americans thought that if you had to make a choice between the U.S.S.R. and China, China was the greater of the two evils. It was said that when the Vietnam War was already under way, the Americans were putting out cautious, unofficial feelers to learn how we would react to a U.S. strategic air strike against Chinese targets involved in the production of nuclear arms. Such feelers could have been a deliberate provocation; had we shown any interest in the idea, the United States could immediately have used it against us to create even greater friction in our relations with the People's Republic. Kissinger writes in his memoirs that Brezhnev, at his summit with Nixon in 1974, supposedly proposed to him some sort of joint action against China. I have the greatest doubts about this, although I do not exclude the possibility that Brezhnev could have criticized China's policies and told Nixon that they were harming the cause of peace and détente, as well as Soviet and American interests. In those years he constantly dwelled on these subjects during his talks, including those with the Americans, and thereby could have provided cause for such an interpretation.

with the aid the People's Republic was giving to Hanoi and the anti-Saigon forces in the South. Many Americans were convinced that the United States could not win this war—mainly because of China's direct aid to Vietnam. They believed that the competition between the U.S.S.R. and the People's Republic for the leadership of revolutionary and liberation movements was forcing the U.S.S.R. to increase our aid to Vietnam.

And finally, the fifth factor was the difficult obstacles in bilateral Sino-American relations—in particular the problem of Taiwan. The Americans naturally did not want to create the impression that they were betraying their old ally, fearing that this would demoralize other friends of America.

All of these circumstances may have postponed the ripening and inevitable normalization of relations between the United States and China. One of the reasons Nixon and Kissinger could do what their predecessors did not have the gumption to do was, I think, the solid reputation for being tough on communism that the administration, particularly Nixon, had earned and now could use to its advantage. (Let us recall that the friendship and support of Senator McCarthy gave Nixon the first boost to his political career.) Such a reputation immunized the Nixon administration from criticism by the right. And this was very important in the United States, just as in our country it was important for many years to have protection or immunity from critical attacks by the ortho-dox Communists and Marxist purists.

In this regard I cannot refrain from quoting the well-known American economist Professor John Kenneth Galbraith. Two fears, he claims, dominated American politics for a long time: the fear of communism and the fear that the liberals might appear to be too soft on communism. Nixon and Kissinger were too experienced to succumb seriously to the first of these, and their reputation as conversatives and anticommunists was impeccable enough to deter the second.

Nixon promised to find a quick solution to the Vietnam problem, but complicated it even further by deciding to bomb Cambodia, to over-throw the Cambodian government, and then to invade the country. Nixon and Kissinger's strenuous efforts to bring about a face-saving peace through military pressure combined with the reduction of American forces and American participation in the war—"Vietnamization"—

were fruitless.* And I think that by the end of 1970 they both realized this. But the 1972 presidential elections loomed ahead, and they needed to show some visible political successes.

Naturally, under the circumstances Nixon and Kissinger turned their attention to their relations with the U.S.S.R. and the People's Republic of China, the improvement of which would have been an acceptable alternative to "peace with honor" in Vietnam. Why did they decide to start with China? First of all, I think, Nixon and Kissinger must have come to the conclusion that the main enemy was no longer China, but the U.S.S.R. And in the spirit of Kissinger's long-held adherence to the "balance of power" philosophy, which was to replace the concept of the "bipolar world," it was logical to speed up the process of rapprochement with Beijing, thus putting more pressure on Moscow. In other words, in accordance with Kissinger's concept, there was apparently an effort to balance Soviet power with another weight on the other side of the scales.

*Before he joined the administration, Kissinger explained to me what was considered necessary for the United States to end this war while saving face. Kissinger had come to Moscow for the first time in December 1967, at the behest of the Johnson administration and Secretary of Defense Robert McNamara. Moreover, he came in what was for him an unusual role—as a member of the Pugwash group, a scientists' association, one of whose aims is nuclear disarmament. But his real mission was, as he told me privately, to feel out the possibility of gaining Moscow's support in solving the conflict on the following terms: a cease-fire, a peace agreement, and the withdrawal of U.S. troops. But Hanoi would have to promise to use only political measures over the next few years, and those only gradually. What happened after that didn't interest Washington. In the absence of other, higher-ranking contacts, Kissinger explained these ideas to me (on behalf of McNamara). I promised that I would pass them on to our leadership, but they did not make a great impression on anyone. Thus, for all intents and purposes, I became the first Soviet "political person" with whom Kissinger was acquainted. In February 1969 it fell to me to introduce Kissinger to the Soviet ambassador to the United States, Anatoli Dobrynin.

In 1967 I got the impression that this plan to find a solution to the Vietnam conflict, as well as the idea of going to Moscow, was Kissinger's, and that he had offered himself to McNamara to carry it out. But more to the point is the fact that after he became the President's national security adviser and then secretary of state, Kissinger took part in the peace-making process on very similar terms, although this did not bring success before 1973. But following the signing of the agreement the Democratic Republic of Vietnam gained control over the southern part of the country as well, and the U.S. ambassador in Saigon was hurriedly evacuated by helicopter from the embassy with the flag under his arm. The administration, Kissinger included, showed anger and regarded this almost as a breach of faith. Criticisms were leveled at us as well.

With my parents in Odessa in 1928, when I was five years old

In uniform in 1942

The tobacco pouch presented to my father by fellow prisoners in Ulyanovsk Prison on my parents' twentieth wedding anniversary. The pouch was embroidered with threads taken from the mattresses in the cells. The names on the pouch are, at the top, Yura (the diminutive for Georgi), and at the bottom, Sasha (the diminutive for the name of my younger brother, Alexander).

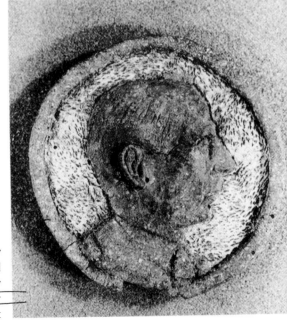

A medallion with my father's profile, molded from bread by a fellow prisoner; another anniversary gift

This photo was taken in 1962, when I received my first civilian medal. I am the second from left in the back row. Chernenko is on my right. At the time he was director of the Chancellery of the Supreme Soviet. Brezhnev, seated at the center, was then chairman of the Presidium of the Supreme Soviet. Standing at the far right is Alexei Rumyanstev, then editor-in-chief of the international Marxist journal *World Marxist Review* in Prague.

With Professor John Kenneth
Galbraith in 1970

With George Bush in 1972,
when he was chairman of the
Republican National
Committee

Poet Yevgeny Yevtushenko speaking at the Institute for the U.S.A. and Canada in 1973

With Brezhnev at the Winter Garden at Zavidovo in 1973, when he was still smoking, animated, and healthy

The first official U.S. Senate delegation to the Soviet Union in 1975. Members of the delegation seated on the right side of the table are, from the bottom of the picture, Ambassador John Stessel, Jacob Javits, unidentified delegate, John Danforth, Hugh Scott, and Hubert Humphrey; at the end of the table, from the right, Howard Baker, Patrick Leahy, and Gary Hart. On the Soviet side of the table, I am at the far left. At Brezhnev's left is Boris Ponomaryov, the secretary of the Central Committee, and on Brezhnev's right, Viktor Sukhodrev.

In Washington, D.C., in June 1973. Brezhnev and the rest of the Soviet delegation have just arrived from Camp David. Yevgeny Chazov, deputy minister of health, is standing behind Brezhnev. Nixon autographed the photo when he saw it in my office on his visit to Moscow in 1989.

With Senator Edward Kennedy in Moscow in 1973, when Kennedy lectured at the U.S.A. and Canada Institute

The Palme Commission meeting in Bonn, West Germany, in 1981. With Cyrus Vance

During the meeting, with Olof Palme, founder of the commission and prime minister of Sweden, and his assistant, Andreas Ferm

With Pope John Paul II in Rome in 1981. Behind me is Joop Den Uyl, former Dutch prime minister

With Walter Mondale in Moscow in 1981. He had come to Moscow to lecture at the Institute and was still considering running for president.

At the Great Wall of China in 1984. I am at the far left. Crouching at the center front is one of my students, Vladimir Lukin, who is now the Russian ambassador to the U.S.

At the Pendleton Stampede in Pendleton, Oregon, in 1985

This photo was published in the Soviet press at the time of a 1984 meeting with the West German Social Democrats. The photo played a positive role in my life, for it appeared at a time when I was under political attack and it showed that contrary to some rumors I had not yet become a "nonperson." Alexander Yakovlev, then director of the Institute of World Economics and International Relations (IMEMO), is seated on the right side of the table, third from the back. Marshal Akhromeyev, the chief of the General Staff and my would-be opponent, is on Yakovlev's left. After the failed August 1991 coup, he committed suicide. I am on Akhromeyev's left. Chernenko is second from the right.

With David Rockefeller at the Dartmouth meeting in June 1976

During a meeting of the Council on Foreign Relations. From the left, Vladimir Petrovsky, now the secretary of the U.N., me, Alexander Yakovlev, Gorbachev, and Anatoly Dobrynin

Eduard Shevardnadze at center left, in 1981, when he was first secretary of the Central Committee of the Republic of Georgia, receives a group of U.S. congressmen headed by John Brademas, third from right, and U.S. ambassador Malcolm Toon, second from right. I am third from left.

In Washington in 1983 in a working group of the Dartmouth Council dealing with arms control. From the left: Brent Scowcroft, me, and Paul Doty, an arms-control specialist from Harvard University

A meeting with Vice President Bush in September 1985

It was also easier to normalize relations with China since no nuclear arms limitation agreements were part of the agenda. Relations with the U.S.S.R. were more difficult. Here one had to go through complex arms-control negotiations, for which neither side was well prepared.

It soon became clear that, as far as domestic politics were concerned, Nixon and Kissinger had calculated absolutely correctly. In the wake of the summit in Beijing, China and everything Chinese—from food to art to pandas—became the rage in America. And, undoubtedly, the popularity of the administration rose all the more because the right (apart from a small band of absolute fanatics) was in no position to protest. After all, by improving relations with China, the United States was strengthening its position vis-à-vis the Soviet Union.

To what extent the U.S. attempt to play the "China card" with the U.S.S.R. proved effective is a more difficult question to answer. Personally, I never put much stock in the China card; in the absence of gross blunders on our part, any damage to Soviet interests seemed totally unlikely. Of course, the strained relations between the U.S.S.R. and China, and also the possibility of an American-Chinese pact against the Soviet Union, naturally prodded us toward better relations with the West.

At the same time, our real difficulties with China and our concerns about a Sino-American pact were not our main motive in seeking better relations with the West. A genuine desire to reduce the threat of war played a very big role; our leaders talked a great deal about this, but somehow the Americans never took us seriously.

In the light of the bitter experience of the Soviet people, the preservation of peace was in no way a propagandistic slogan or a populist tribute to the mood of the public, but a serious political motive of the top leadership. Even the generous financing of military programs at the expense of the most urgent social needs was done under the pretext of serving the cause of peace. More often than not the top people sincerely believed this. I often heard Brezhnev repeat the line "Defense is sacrosanct," explaining his generosity toward the military. At the same time, the leadership was beginning to understand that the Cold War and the arms race could, sooner or later, lead to catastrophe, although I am convinced that the leadership did not fully realize how unbearable our military burden was. (I am not sure that the leadership knows everything in this regard even today.)

In the summer of 1971 it was announced that Kissinger had been to Beijing and had reached an agreement to hold a Sino-American summit in 1972. This put many members of the Soviet leadership into a state of confusion, if not shock. I remember this well from my conversations with, among others, highly placed functionaries who sought my opinion and my advice. Perhaps at no time before that had I seen so much general interest shown in the U.S.A. Institute and its analyses.

The almost hysterical response to the summit seemed to me incomprehensible: why should this political step by the Americans come as such a complete surprise to so many people? There had been plenty of clear signals—for example, the "Ping-Pong diplomacy," when a Chinese Ping-Pong team was greeted on an exceptionally high level in the United States. Long before glasnost, the official press had written endlessly about the possibility of "an alliance between the Chinese leadership and world imperialism," and had accused both the Chinese and the West of planning such a thing. In our panic-stricken deliberations we may have been telling the Americans where they could hurt us most.

But then I began to see that there was another reason for our confusion: our leaders had finally started thinking about whether it was possible to be bound by dogma about "American imperialism" and do nothing to normalize our relationship with the United States. How long could a country keep its back turned on reality because of ideological prejudices and avoid the political decisions that had to be made? In this sense the Americans helped us, perhaps unwittingly, by shaking up our political thinking and many of our politicians and showing how unprofessional they really were.

I was very worried about our confusion and groundless fears; they could have harmed our policies and our interests. I then took the somewhat unusual step of requesting an opportunity to publish an article in *Pravda* about the forthcoming Sino-American meeting. Even though it would appear under my byline, I understood it would be regarded as representing an official point of view.

With Brezhnev and Suslov on vacation, I raised the issue with Kirilenko of reacting to the forthcoming meeting and the Soviet public's bewilderment over it. It was well within my rights and responsibilities as director of the U.S.A. Institute to send such a "signal." "Well, go ahead and write it, and I will inform *Pravda*," responded Kirilenko.

I wrote the article "in one sitting"—in a day and a night—and it was published on August 11, 1971. It was addressed mainly to the Soviet public, to whom I wanted to explain that nothing terrible, let alone tragic, had occurred, and that there was no ground for fearing the threat of an anti-Soviet accord, let alone a military alliance between the United States and China. What had happened, in fact, was something we should have expected ever since the hostility between those two countries had receded. I also drew the conclusion that our final evaluation of the Americans' motives would depend on the general political context in which the normalization of Sino-American relations took place. If similar shifts followed in regard to other socialist countries (I had in mind, above all, the U.S.S.R.), including arms control and the settlement of regional conflicts, we would interpret the American initiative positively, part of an overall change in global policies. If not, we would entertain legitimate suspicions about American motives and possible harm to other countries (including the U.S.S.R.). The Americans interpreted the article as an expression, if not of official opinion, then of a position close to it (which was correct; the article was sent to the Ministry of Foreign Affairs and to the Central Committee before publication).

Of course, I was not so naïve as to think that I could convince the Americans of anything one way or another—they could not have failed to notice our panicky reaction to the news about the meeting in Beijing. But by that time the institute and I had sufficiently wide and reliable contacts among the Americans to have a clear idea about how the situation was being appraised in Washington and the degree of importance attached to a normalization of Soviet-American relations. American regional interests, even important ones, basically depended on relations with China. And, of course, the Americans were aware of the pressure that, thanks to our own shortsightedness and propensity for panicky reactions, could be put on us. U.S. relations with the Soviet Union determined American global interests, including cardinal issues of national security. I thought it was important that the Americans know that we were fully aware of the hierarchy of their interests, and that we would not allow ourselves to be put under too great pressure as a result of the political game Washington had initiated.

The article caused an exceptionally wide stir in the United States and other Western countries. It was quoted extensively and was reprinted in detail. (I was also the subject of a *New York Times* "Man in the News" column.) This interest and some other signals confirmed my suspicion that the Americans were interested in the Soviet reaction to their improved relations with China primarily because this whole operation was intended to put pressure on the Soviet Union.

In the end, the Sino-American rapprochement turned out to be a blessing in disguise for Soviet politics: we began to move somewhat faster during our talks with the United States. By the time Nixon went to Beijing, his May 1972 visit to Moscow had already been announced.

Kissinger came to Moscow for preliminary talks that spring. At that time our leaders, particularly Brezhnev, did not have much experience in meeting with Western representatives. Brezhnev diligently prepared himself, and the U.S.A. Institute received quite a few assignments to assist him. He invited me, and we had a lengthy talk, mainly about Kissinger. Brezhnev was very interested in everything about him.

A group of veterans from the regiment in which I had served held a reunion in Moscow on May 9, Victory Day. That morning we gathered in the Museum of the Soviet Army, where (to my great surprise) the regimental banner was kept, and later we held a banquet in one of the restaurants of the Hotel Rossiya. We went for walks, came back to the hotel, and continued eating and drinking in the hotel rooms. (People turned a blind eye to alcoholic excesses in those days.)

I came home at about ten in the evening in a humor befitting the occasion, and learned from my wife that people from the offices of the top leadership—Andropov, Gromyko, and Brezhnev—had been trying to reach me since about midday. I called back right away and was told that everyone had gone home, but I was instructed to be in Brezhnev's office at the Central Committee at nine o'clock the next morning.

I turned on the radio and discovered why I had been summoned. On May 8, the United States had resumed the bombing of Hanoi and had mined the port of Haiphong. There were casualties. All this was just before the first Soviet-American summit since 1959!

The next morning, there was a meeting at the Central Committee (headed by Brezhnev with Andropov, Gromyko, and, as I recall, Ponomaryov, with a group of experts and consultants). Although the principal discussions had occurred the previous day, the debate remained very serious. The main question was whether to cancel the summit. As we know, it was not canceled, but the decision was difficult. Many of the leading officials, including some members of the Central Committee, demanded a cancellation. They believed that if we agreed to go through with the summit we would be politically humiliated and would lose our authority in the eyes of the world, particularly the Communist world, and with liberation movements. And we would encourage American imperialism to undertake further adventures. Most of the ranking officials kept silent, as usual, waiting to hear what the leaders had to say. Andropov later told me confidentially that great pressure had been put on Brezhnev for him to give Nixon a "suitable rebuke" by canceling the summit. Those who could, including the experts who took part in the discussions, did everything possible not to succumb to this pressure, and proposed to ignore the American challenge, and to stonewall.

How does all this look today?

From a military point of view, the American decision to resume the bombing was a useless adventure, which did nothing to change the course of events in Vietnam in America's favor. It was a symptom of America's uncontrolled emotions, rather than the result of sober calculation. Having no grounds for counting on even tactical military success, Nixon and Kissinger were seriously risking a diplomatic fiasco if we canceled the summit. William Hyland, who was Kissinger's assistant at the time and is a leading specialist in Soviet affairs, writes in his book *Global Rivals* that the majority of people in Washington, including Nixon and Kissinger, took into account the possibility that the Soviet Union might cancel the summit when they made the decision to bomb.

Hyland notes that the only hope was that Kissinger's policy of "linkage" and, above all, the China card might work. But that was a miscalculation. Although the Chinese factor was mentioned during the debate in the Soviet leadership over whether to cancel the summit, it was not seriously discussed, as far as I remember. Concern over the fate of the agreements with the Federal Republic of Germany, which were to be ratified a few days before Nixon's arrival in Moscow, played an incomparably greater role in the decision. Moscow realized full well that a deterioration in relations with the United States could get in the way of the ratification, which was already threatened by active opposition from the German right.

At the same time, Vietnam engendered additional uncertainties for the Americans by raising serious concerns among her allies. The United States was playing a risky game and ran the danger of losing control over the situation. If it was a matter of humiliating the Soviet Union and demonstrating to America our ability to counter provocative behavior, then this did not succeed either. The talks proceeded between two equals, and people in the West—particularly in the United States, where discontent with the Vietnam War was growing—came to regard the Soviet reaction to this challenge not as a show of weakness but as political common sense.

There can scarcely be any doubt that our decision was correct. The cancellation of the meeting would not have helped the Vietnamese people. It would have untied the hands of the United States, which might have embarked upon further expansion at the cost of more casualties. The lessening of tensions between the U.S.S.R. and the United States would have been postponed for a long time. Both powers could have been embroiled in a very serious military rivalry. You can say the same thing about regional crises and conflicts in the Middle East, for example. It proved barely possible to contain the Yom Kippur War, which erupted less than a year and a half later, just when we were at the height of détente and in constant communication. It will be recalled that during that war the United States went on nuclear alert. The conflict could have proved to be more dangerous in an atmosphere of tension. Another victim could have been negotiations on the security of Europe. And, last but not least, important treaties between the Soviet Union and West Germany would not have been ratified.

The argument popular among some of my hard-line countrymen—that our cancellation of the summit would have sunk all hopes for Nixon's election to the presidency—was floated by many opponents of the meeting, and I and other experts on the United States had our work cut out for us in discrediting it. Then, as now, that argument seems to me not only wrong from the point of view of the domestic political situation in the United States at the time, but false in principle. You just cannot make your own policies on the most vital security issues dependent on internal events in another country, or sacrifice your own interests for their sake. You cannot do this because you cannot forecast such events accurately, let alone control them. Nor can you foresee their consequences: Who could vouch for the fact that, if we had refused to have the summit meeting in 1972, Nixon would have lost the election? And who can say for sure that, even if he had, it would have been a good thing for us?

At that time I reached the conclusion that a moderate decision, a concession, requires far greater political courage than confrontation and negative "radicalism." This is particularly true when relations with a political adversary are involved. Experience, unfortunately, confirmed this several times over.

Be that as it may, the Soviet leadership, having decided not to cancel the summit, urgently convened a plenum of the Central Committee to put the whole issue up for debate. The fear of appearing insufficiently "revolutionary" once again manifested itself. Although he made the right decision, Brezhnev was not absolutely sure about it and, above all, wanted the plenum to share responsibility.

Much later I asked myself why a plenary meeting of the Central Committee wasn't convened when the decision was made to invade Czechoslovakia, or for that matter, to start a war in Afghanistan. Was it because in those cases nobody could question the Marxist and "revolutionary" orthodoxy of the decision makers? In presenting such arguments I am not questioning the wisdom of summoning the plenum. That was the right thing to do; a discussion of foreign-policy affairs was long overdue. This was so not only because of the American aggression in Vietnam or because of the forthcoming summit, but because of the great need to clarify many political issues and take the measure of new international realities. Also, the Stalinists, who had gone into action after Khrushchev's ouster, succeeded to no small degree in imposing a thick layer of dogmatism on the political thinking of society and the Party. Once the determination to follow through on the course of détente started to take hold, the leadership had to use its authority to clear the ideological atmosphere. And this was done by having the Central Committee plenum approve the new political line.

The plenum was a victory over the regressive policies that had haunted us for several years. It sanctioned not only the summit but the policy of détente. We were placing our confidence in the principles of peaceful coexistence. At last we had summoned up enough courage to proclaim boldly that we could and would reach agreements with the Western powers, that we would improve relations with them and would not allow ourselves to be thrown off balance by issues of ideology and "class solidarity."

At the same time, one has to admit that the plenum did not go far enough in getting rid of some of the old dogmas in foreign policy. It tried to bridge the gap between the old theories and ideology—which were not always properly understood—and the new policy.

I remember the summit very vividly. I had come to know many members of the American delegation quite well, but I must say that they arrived in Moscow lacking confidence and in a fair state of confusion, even fear. On his first day Nixon met with Brezhnev one-on-one—that is, with only interpreters present. The Soviet leadership hosted a state dinner that evening in the Kremlin's Faceted Hall. Observing the protocol of the time, the Americans remained on one side of the room and the Soviets on the other, waiting for their leaders, for quite a long time. It was clear that Nixon and Brezhnev had become involved in their conversation. Many of the Americans, Kissinger in particular, were nervous. He came up and asked: "Well, how will it work out, what do you intend to do?" I made quite an optimistic forecast.

The next day, I learned from the journalists why the Americans were so concerned. Apparently, a rumor had spread among them that the Soviet Union had agreed to the meeting for the sole purpose of humiliating Nixon.

In fact, though Brezhnev raised the issue of Vietnam, the meeting resulted in a real breakthrough in Soviet-American relations, marking the beginning of the period of détente.

In reviewing this diplomatic success one must keep in mind that equally important changes were taking place with respect to Europe. Without them, the normalization of relations with the United States could have hardly been possible. I have already mentioned the agreements with the Federal Republic of Germany, but our relations improved with virtually every Western European country and Canada as well. The development of contacts with the Social Democratic parties, and the radical changes in our relations with the international social-democratic movement and the Socialist International, also seem important to me. The so-called European process—the Helsinki Conference on Security and Cooperation in Europe, culminating in the signing of the famous Helsinki Accords in 1975—was also progressing quite successfully.

Why détente proved to be short-lived and by the late 1970s had been replaced by an increase in tensions, even a "second Cold War," is a subject that still needs to be researched both in the U.S.S.R. and in the

United States. Historians will need to base their work on many documents that still remain unavailable, but I can hazard one or two thoughts on the issue.

The first thing that comes to mind is the old question: Who's to blame? For a long time our columnists and historians heaped all the blame on the Americans. In more recent years, many of them have made a 180-degree turn and started to blame everything on us and the period of stagnation.

The situation was more complicated than that. And not only in the sense that the blame for the collapse of détente should be divided between both sides (historians have yet to establish the proportions). More important and relevant to understanding the past and the future is the fact that the change in relations was overdue, and even Khrushchev* and Eisenhower had begun to realize it at the end of the 1950s. But even twenty years later neither the governments nor considerable sectors of the Soviet and American societies were prepared intellectually or politically for such a change.

Of course, one cannot exclude the possibility that had it not been for historical accident—Nixon's resignation and Brezhnev's illness at the end of 1974—the governments of both countries would have found themselves in the middle of détente. They could have raised their respective policies to the level that realities demanded. This might have laid a sound foundation for new policies. History, unfortunately, does not recognize the subjunctive mood. It does not tolerate premises beginning with "If . . ."

I have very serious doubts about whether a change in Soviet relations capable of putting an end to the Cold War was ever part of Nixon and Kissinger's plan. Both of these politicians, by virtue of their intellectual makeup, their ideological sympathy, all their past experience, were products of the Cold War, although by this time they had adopted a quite realistic and pragmatic position. But I suspect that at the time the

---

*When relations between the U.S.S.R. and the United States once again started improving after 1985, an Indian expert on international affairs who had been close to Jawaharlal Nehru told me that after the Geneva meeting of the heads of state of the U.N. Security Council's permanent members, Khrushchev, who was excited about the prospects for the future that were opening up, said to India's prime minister: "Now the Cold War is over." To which, according to my informant, Nehru laconically replied: "I'm not so sure about that."

thought never even entered their heads that you could set the ending of the Cold War, the cessation of the arms race, and the renunciation of the use of force as even long-term goals. As far as I can see, such ideas were beyond the bounds of their practical politics.

I read and studied what they wrote and said, and I talked frequently with top leaders of the U.S. government. I am absolutely convinced that when these people planned Soviet policy, the question as to whether there should or shouldn't be a Cold War and an arms race never arose. They thought about how to solve America's day-to-day political problems, and the first one was how to end the Vietnam War as quickly as possible. They thought about how to gain the safest possible level of different types of strategic arms in the correlation of forces between the United States and the Soviet Union. Last but not least, they concentrated on restoring and strengthening America's position in the world, which had been undermined by the war in Vietnam, by a worsening domestic situation, and by the successes of America's economic competitors. In the context of such goals and priorities, talks and relations with the Soviet Union were instruments of controlling the Cold War and the arms race rather than means of ending them. At that time, only a very small minority of American politicians, Republicans or Democrats, conservatives or liberals, were opposed to the Cold War on principle and supported an end to the arms race. Those who opposed even the slightest improvements in U.S.–Soviet relations made during the Nixon administration were far greater in number.

I think also that the bitter experience of the Vietnam War relieved a considerable portion of the American political élite, and of the American public as a whole, only of some symptoms of imperial ambitions and dreams of an American century. It drove these symptoms below the surface but did not eliminate them. There was a lingering nostalgia for the post–World War II era and what seemed to be an American Century. That is probably the reason behind the enormous appeal of Ronald Reagan's call for America to "stand tall."

In the Soviet Union, détente and the foreign-policy course set in the 1970s were considered successes unparalleled in our postwar history. But they proved to be incomplete and impermanent. Important lessons can be learned from the analysis of what was left undone, of what prevented détente from becoming irreversible and confined it to such narrow limits.

Two factors, both traps we set for ourselves in the late 1970s, complicated the struggle for a consistent foreign policy. One was our ideological lack of vision—the "revolutionary inferiority complex" that was so deeply rooted in our consciousness. It was complicated by the relics of great-power claims and imperial ambitions. This combination of insecurity and arrogance would always lead politicians into a tight situation.

The second factor was that our military policy and arms industry had completely escaped political control. The leadership made the decisions, but the military and the military-industrial agencies prompted those decisions and even managed to "preprogram" the political leadership. Shaped and executed under the cloak of secrecy, military policy ceased being an instrument of our foreign policy and acquired a life of its own. Naturally, détente could not tolerate such a state of affairs for long.

9 The Years of Decline (1975–1982)

I f very high political and economic standards are applied to judging the development of society, the years between Khrushchev's removal and Brezhnev's death could be regarded as a period of stagnation. In those eighteen years, there were no memorable and historic milestones along our road toward a general improvement of society. The same can be said of a considerable part of Khrushchev's era. But according to more practical standards that take into account our trauma in the aftermath of Stalin, those eighteen years do not appear so uniformly gray. There were achievements in the economy, in foreign policy, and in other areas.

In general I would divide the period after the ouster of Khrushchev into two parts. The first was a direct continuation of the "Khrushchevian" period in our social development. Our society had to endure long years of internal struggle to find a way out of the economic, foreign-policy, and domestic impasse brought about by totalitarian rule. In some areas this search met with success; unfortunately, it usually proved to be only temporary. We did not have a feasible and comprehensive concept of reforms or sufficient know-how to free ourselves from the deformations of the past. Nevertheless, in some areas we managed to move forward. In others, this search was completely unsuccessful, and we had to pay a dear price for that. But the movement never ceased. The real period of stagnation came upon us in the mid-1970s.

The new sparks of energy that had been released by the Twentieth Party Congress, and that the fire brigades of conservatism were diligently trying to put out in the years that followed, were also spent. The leadership that came to power in 1964 did not even make an attempt to rejuvenate domestic policy. In the economy, reform turned out to be short-lived and was soon replaced by the greatest bureaucratic flourishing in our history.

The personal story of our leader was a truly symbolic expression of this process of degeneration. In December 1974, Leonid Brezhnev fell ill. For eight years our country had lived under abnormal conditions. While the structure of political power remained, Brezhnev was no longer capable of adequately fulfilling even the elementary functions of a government leader. The structure inherited from Stalin was geared to decision-making at the very top. The existing mechanisms, traditions, and political environment excluded the possibility of a "normal" succession in leadership. Besides, who could have replaced Brezhnev? Until May 1982* the potential heirs and candidates were Suslov, Kirilenko, Grishin, and Chernenko. Such a lack of alternatives was by no means accidental. The mechanisms that had been created with the personality cult not only concentrated power in the hands of the leader, but also consistently and deliberately knocked out most of his potential rivals in the very early rounds of the game.

For a long time Brezhnev's illness was a major state secret. This is what I know: In December 1974 Brezhnev fell ill at the air force base near Vladivostok while seeing off President Ford. The matter was serious enough that Brezhnev's tour of the town was canceled even after people had gathered in the streets for a ceremonial reception. The patient was put into intensive care, and the next day, despite his poor

---

*I mention this date because it was not until the May 1982 plenum that Andropov returned to the Central Committee as secretary. The election of a leader straight from the position of chairman of the KGB would have been unprecedented and almost certainly would have been stopped by the apparat. Nor was Andropov regarded as a contender in Party circles at that point. As far as Gorbachev is concerned, he was at the time simply too little known and did not have the necessary support either in the apparat or in the society at large.

health, left for Mongolia, where he made a speech at the Party Congress. When he returned to Moscow, he remained sick for such a long time that the first wave of rumors spread about his failing health.

Over the next eight years, there were times of some improvement, but Brezhnev never returned to normal. His poor health was aggravated by his habit of taking a lot of sleeping pills (he talked about this willingly and in detail with everyone) at night and sometimes during the day when he decided to take a rest. This occasionally affected his appearance and his speech. He grew tired quickly, lost interest in the subject at hand; his speech grew worse, and his memory began to fail him. Toward the end of his life even the most elementary information that he needed for a conversation or for an act of protocol was written down for him. He simply could not get by without these crib sheets.

During this period Brezhnev promoted a series of very weak people—Chernenko, Tikhonov, and others—while he distanced himself from, or quarreled with, some of his more sensible assistants—Tsukanov, for example. Normal governance was no longer possible, even by the most liberal criteria that made allowances for Brezhnev's less-than-modest capabilities. Under such extreme circumstances, the danger rose that serious political mistakes were waiting to happen.

From Détente to the Second Cold War

In the middle of the 1970s, the Strategic Arms Limitation Talks started going off track. Of course we were not the only ones to blame. During 1975 and 1976, President Ford, perhaps waiting for the forthcoming presidential election, hesitated; Secretary of State Henry Kissinger was the first to proclaim that SALT II would be signed before the election, but the next day Kissinger fell silent and lost interest in the subject.

When Jimmy Carter was inaugurated in January 1977, he hastily decided to start the rounds of talks all over again. Also, some U.S. congressmen and segments of the media put us on the defensive by actively using our human-rights record to apply political pressure. (As I will discuss, we gave them plenty of opportunities to do this; the whole issue had become a major irritant in Soviet-American relations.) But we on the Soviet side committed our own errors and political miscalculations, which were strongly in evidence from the mid-1970s on. One was our policy in the Third World, in particular our assistance to liberation movements; we went so far as to give direct military aid. This policy was loaded with revolutionary jargon and closely intertwined with imperial ambitions.

It led to serious complications. The first was when we brought Cuban troops to Angola to support the MPLA* in their battle for power following the departure of the Portuguese. As far as I know, Cuba initiated this action, but we found ourselves involved in it right from the start. We supported the Cubans politically and supplied them with arms, transporting Cuban forces to Angola and then providing large-scale aid, including weapons and military advisers, to the MPLA government.

The United States was intervening in Angola's affairs (secretly, through the CIA), as were China and a host of other countries. But our policy was incorrect, contradicted our proclaimed principles in conducting foreign policy, and had negative political consequences. I not only remained convinced of this, but made this argument at the time with members of our government.

I was concerned that we were embarking on a dangerous road by participating in this joint action with the Cubans. Moreover, we agreed to commit regular troops in these operations. In contrast, the U.S. Congress had refused to fund further support for the pro-American parties and factions struggling for power in Angola. I thought that this would not only reflect badly on our relations with the United States and with the West as a whole, but would also establish an unwelcome and potentially dangerous precedent.

We seemed to be setting a new example by such international behavior. What might have been natural at the height of the Cold War became unacceptable during a period of détente and normalization of international relations. I was not the only one to see this. I remember well how, in the second half of 1975, this was one of the important topics of conversation among our experts. Many of them understood that our involvement in Angola could seriously damage détente.

I spoke with Andropov about this several times. He would listen carefully, but would neither argue with me nor express his agreement. I also talked about it at length with Andrei Gromyko.

With Brezhnev I had a chance to discuss Angola in the presence of a

---

*Movimento Popular de Libertacão de Angola ("People's Movement for the Liberation of Angola").

whole group of scholars and officials from the Central Committee and the Ministry of Foreign Affairs who were preparing the documents for the Twenty-fifth Party Congress. As we discussed the foreign-policy part of the forthcoming address, the new subject of Angola and the very recent events there was raised. I told Brezhnev that, in my opinion, the involvement of Cuban troops in Angola and our support of the operation there could cost us very dearly and undermine the very foundations of détente.

My chief opponent on that occasion was Andrei M. Alexandrov,* who immediately objected to what I had said and compared Angola to Spain in 1935, insisting that we could not simply stay on the sidelines without fulfilling our duty. Brezhnev said: "Pretend you are members of the Politburo. Go ahead, argue, and I will listen." (Brezhnev used this method quite often. He would challenge someone to an argument, and then sit back and listen.) Andropov, Inozemtsev, Bovin, and Zagladin were among those present. Bovin wanted to join the argument, but he had just been through a long period of disgrace, so Inozemtsev and I motioned to him to keep quiet.

I argued that we had the right, and were even morally bound, to help the national-liberation movement, but that there were various forms of aid. Political support could not be questioned. Economic aid was also possible. One could not exclude help in supplying arms. But participation in military operations by regular military units in a foreign country would change the situation radically. The Americans had just left Vietnam, and now, during détente, we and our friends were trying to restore the worst traditions of foreign military intervention in a completely new situation.

Alexandrov opposed me on ideological grounds, arguing that we could not avoid our internationalist duty. Brezhnev interrupted us at one point and said he understood what I had in mind: the participation of regular military units abroad would be a violation of the Helsinki Ac-

---

*My relations with Alexandrov were quite complicated. A professional in foreign policy, he took an active part in détente, but he was one member of the intelligentsia who suffered from our "revolutionary inferiority complex." This trait showed itself quite frequently, as in the given case. At the same time, he was one of the few who had the courage to disagree with Brezhnev openly and unequivocally about important issues.

cords. Naturally, I vigorously supported this statement (although previously it had never even entered my head). At that point Alexandrov came up with an argument that caught me completely by surprise: "But do you remember, Leonid Ilyich, how the Americans behaved during the conflict between India and Pakistan?" Brezhnev reacted to this very emotionally and said something quite nasty about American policy. Then he suddenly fell silent and "switched himself off" for the remainder of the debate. (This happened to him more and more often after his illness began.) And then after a minute or so he said: "Well, you go ahead and argue while I go to my office." On that note, the debate ended.

Unfortunately, Angola triggered a chain reaction of similar events. As often happens in politics, if you get away with something and it looks as if you've been successful, you are practically doomed to repeat the policy. You do this until you blunder into a really serious mess. That is what happened in Angola. At the moment we did not expect big troubles, because the Americans were preoccupied with healing the wounds of Watergate and launching a heated election campaign.* Of course they protested, and some strong words were used, both through diplomatic channels and in the media. But relations remained more or less intact, and the fact that the Soviet Union became even more suspect and untrustworthy was hidden under the surface of what soon seemed to become business as usual.†

---

*This is exactly what some of our shortsighted officials hoped for. I remember how once my newly appointed deputy Radomir Bogdanov came to my office in a very agitated state. (According to the rules existing at that time, I had to have some intelligence operatives on the staff, including one deputy. I knew Bogdanov personally and agreed to his nomination, preferring him to an unknown.) He said that the day before he had been summoned to see Andropov in connection with his new job and had to wait for an hour in the reception room, where he happened to overhear some other visitors, among them the first deputy to Andropov, Semyon Tsvigun, and some generals from the General Staff. They were very excitedly discussing the coming adventure in Angola. All of them agreed that the Soviet Union had nothing to fear. "The Americans will swallow it."

†On October 29, 1990, the American periodical *The Nation* published the secret record of a December 1975 conversation between Kissinger and some of his State Department staff. That record testifies quite eloquently to the fact that my concern at the time was justified. While instructing his colleagues on how to brief American journalists about the events in Angola, Kissinger said: "I would like these people [that is, journalists and their

One could have thought, at first, that the Angola operation was a smashing success. This made the Americans even more angry. The MPLA came to power. The country seemed to have acquired a stable government. The way to independence and successful development seemed open. It also seemed as if the Cuban troops would not overstay their welcome. One could scarcely have foreseen that they would have to remain and fight for fifteen years.

I began to worry that our government would remember only the success of the action and the absence of serious international complications. Indeed, my concerns later proved to be justified.

We were unable to resist further temptation to become involved in the complex internal affairs of other countries. After Angola, we went boldly down the path of intervention and expansion that we had beaten so assuredly. It led us through Ethiopia, Yemen, a series of African countries, and, eventually, into Afghanistan.

There were factors common to all of these situations. I think that, above all, there was the desire to take part in the "anti-imperialist struggle." I keep returning to this because the motives that calmed our conscience also dulled our vigilance and elementary caution and blinded us to incontrovertible facts, such as the point that we were simply intervening in the internal affairs of other countries and not aiding national-liberation movements. We became enmeshed in various political forces' struggles for power and in their territorial and tribal disputes.

The Afghanistan revolution of 1978 occurred without our participation; we learned of it from Western news agencies. Our concerns about the danger of a region with which we shared a border were genuine. It was also true that the government of Afghanistan had asked us for help many times and had all the more reason to do this because its opponents were also receiving aid from foreign governments. But none of this justifies what we did or the very dear price we paid in human lives—both ours and the Afghans'—and in economic and political damage. To me and to many of my colleagues this was absolutely clear from the moment we sent troops into Afghanistan in December 1979.

---

readers] to know that our concern over Angola is not connected with economic wealth or a naval base. It's connected with the fact that the Soviet Union is operating thousands of miles away from home and the neighboring states are asking for our help. This will have an influence on the Europeans, on the Soviets, and on the Chinese."

The invasion was a great surprise to me. I was in the hospital, where I had been for a whole month, recovering from a heart attack. I learned the news from Anatoli Dobrynin, who was undergoing treatment in the same hospital and had heard the announcement on the radio early that morning.

In the autumn of 1989, I was chairman of the Subcommittee on Political Issues and Negotiations of the Supreme Soviet Committee on International Affairs. We prepared a report entitled "A Political Assessment of the Decision to Commit Soviet Troops to Afghanistan." Through that work I learned some details about how the decision was made. I emphasize "some," since this was not a real investigation; we knew beforehand that we would propose that the decision be condemned.

Much remained undocumented. It was even unclear whether the decision to invade was made at a meeting of the Politburo or by an ad hoc group of leaders. Valeri Boldin, who held the keys to all Central Committee documents and archives, officially told Alexander Dzasokhov, chairman of the Committee on International Affairs, that the decision was not made at a Politburo meeting, but I have my doubts about this, especially after the August 1991 coup, in which Boldin turned out to be a co-conspirator.* Existing documents (for example, the assessments and proposals made by the concerned government agencies on the eve of the decision) were given to us with extreme reluctance.

I remember the fairly frank oral statements made to the leaders of the Committee on International Affairs by the Soviet ambassador to Afghanistan, F. M. Tabeyev, and Marshal Akhromeyev (the first deputy chief of staff in 1979). Akhromeyev recalled how on December 13, 1979, the minister of defense, Dmitri Ustinov, returned from the decision-making meeting. Ustinov summoned three people—Chief of Staff N. V. Ogarkov; Akhromeyev; and General V. Varennikov—and ordered them to prepare the operation for December 28. Akhromeyev told us that he and other generals were against it. When we asked why, he answered that our troops were not yet ready and could not be prepared in such a short time.

Tabeyev, who had been appointed ambassador to Afghanistan in No-

*Later, documents were found that proved both Boldin and Dzasokhov had lied to the parliament.

vember 1979, told us his story. From his account one could deduce that the question of sending troops had, for all intents and purposes, already been decided. He was ordered to report nothing to Moscow, to send no assessments of the situation in Afghanistan, and to make no proposals until he received special instructions.

The conclusions of the Congress of People's Deputies in 1989 are a matter of record: the decision to commit troops was condemned. The people responsible, apart from Brezhnev, were named: Ustinov, Gromyko, and Andropov.

There can be no doubt about Brezhnev's responsibility, although I am not sure that he was physically capable of clearly understanding the situation in Afghanistan or the consequences of the decision. More likely than not, he caved in and allowed himself to be persuaded, agreeing to the proposal of Ustinov, Gromyko, and Andropov—the "Big Three"— who, after Brezhnev's illness, decided (or, more correctly, predecided— the decision was rubber-stamped by Brezhnev) all matters related to foreign affairs.

Evidently, the Ministry of Defense actively supported the intervention. This is confirmed by retired KGB general Oleg Kalugin, who recalls that "the chief of military intelligence, Ivashutin, insisted on military intervention."* Quite a few other pieces of information show that the ministry, and Ustinov in particular, adopted such a position. I don't want to paint him as a villain, but he played a crucial role. Here we are dealing with a pretty typical escalation of military aid. We started by supplying arms. Military specialists and advisers followed. By insisting that Afghan troops use armed force against the population, which was protesting against the new order of things, the latter helped to turn the spring 1979 events in Herat into a serious conflict.† As I was told by an eyewitness to the telephone conversation, Ustinov ordered his representatives in Kabul to "arm the working class." We then received the first request to send troops. The Soviet leaders said no, but events had their own momentum. We had to protect our advisers, our military prestige, and our interests, which we now regarded as important defense

---

*See *Moscow News*, May 24, 1990, p. 11.
†In March 1979, over 100 Soviets were killed (some were tortured) in a Shiite uprising in Herat. Government forces retook Herat, in the process killing several thousand people.

interests, and then we had to protect a friendly army in a bordering country.

It seems to me that Gromyko could not have been an active supporter of the intervention, but he did not oppose it on principle. According to all those who knew him, he was very afraid of Ustinov and the military. Perhaps he allowed himself to be persuaded that the operation would be short and successful. Gromyko was, after all, a product of his time. He had climbed the career ladder under Stalin and later earned the nickname "Mr. Nyet" among his Western colleagues. But he was always "Comrade Yes" to his superiors. If the "Yes" had been for détente, in particular with the United States, he would, I think, have welcomed it. If the "Yes" were for a cold war, he would have been disappointed, but he would have followed this command. In the case of Afghanistan, it probably never occurred to him that military intervention contradicted the political ideals preached by the government.

Andropov's position was more complicated. He was friendly with Ustinov. Until that autumn (Oleg Kalugin testifies to this, as do other sources) Andropov had been a definite opponent of military intervention, as was the leadership in general. Then he changed his position. Why? I think he did this not only because Afghanistan's president, Hafizullah Amin, who had killed his predecessor, Nur Mohammed Taraki (whom our government trusted), came to power in Afghanistan. Amin was a bloody killer and an unprincipled politician. In addition, there were doubts about his loyalty, fueled in part by rumors that he had been recruited by the CIA while he was a student in the United States. (Perhaps U.S. intelligence services intentionally spread these rumors.) This, together with the realization that Amin's domestic policy, which was marked by extreme cruelty and sectarianism, offered no promise whatsoever for the future, apparently made Andropov change his position.

Another reason for Andropov's change was that he put too much faith in Babrak Karmal. There were grounds for this. Karmal, one of the more moderate leaders of the Afghan revolution, had been driven out by Taraki and Amin. Andropov believed that if Karmal, who had been granted political asylum in the Soviet Union, became the leader he could achieve reconciliation in his country. Perhaps Andropov saw some resemblance between him and János Kádár in Hungary in 1956. I admit that this may well have been Andropov's greatest mistake. Even if his high esteem for Karmal had been justified (something I find difficult to believe in the light of subsequent events), Andropov should have taken into account the fact that the only way Karmal could have become leader of the country was with the assistance of foreign bayonets. This immediately excluded the possibility of internal peace, especially in a country like Afghanistan. On the contrary, the civil war could only be intensified by the invasion of foreign forces. But Andropov clung to these illusions for a long time.*

Thinking these events over later, I concluded that, of the four people who made the decision, two failed to foresee the consequences (Brezhnev because of his illness, and Ustinov because of his limited political vision). But for Gromyko, and particularly for Andropov, it was simply unforgivable—the extreme amorality of the decision aside—even from a point of view of pure political realities.

In general I, and many people around me, took the developments in Afghanistan as a great personal disappointment. Not since the 1968 events in Czechoslovakia had we felt such pain. After a few years I could approach such events more philosophically, reminding myself that once we had embarked upon a course of armed intervention, of prodding events along with military force, we were condemned to follow that road until it ended in a devastating defeat. And I could not help thinking that the very fact that we had gotten bogged down in Afghanistan may have helped us avoid an even more dangerous adventure: intervention in Poland during the political crisis in 1980. After all, this would have had truly catastrophic consequences.

But why did we become an expansionist, aggressive power in the second half of the 1970s? My guess would be that the military-industrial complex had grown to such proportions that it escaped political control. It had gathered strength and influence and had skillfully put Brezhnev's

---

*I remember how, returning from a Dartmouth meeting with American political experts and public figures in Italy at the end of May 1980, *Pravda* commentator Yuri Zhukov and I managed to get an appointment with Brezhnev. We told him how our intervention in Afghanistan was ruining détente and helping the American extreme right in the forthcoming elections. We persuaded him to make a symbolic gesture by recalling 10 percent of our contingent from Afghanistan. The next day, Andropov, having found out from someone about our conversation, chewed me out for this initiative. Evidently, he was still hoping for a quick victory.

patronage and weaknesses to its own good use. Moreover, the military leaders of the time had a monopoly on the leadership's ear. Of course, this loss of political control over the military leadership and the military-industrial complex had its causes. I am far from blaming only the generals, the admirals, and the military contractors. The political roots of the situation were very important.

From his first days in office Brezhnev treated the military as a very important power base. For him that alone was reason enough to give the military virtually anything it asked for. I think his earlier activities as Central Committee secretary of defense industries must have contributed significantly to this attitude. From then on he was under the strong influence of our defense-industry officials. To this you can add purely sentimental reasons, which grew in proportion to his age and illness. Brezhnev remembered his years in the military with particular fondness. He was very proud of those years, and regarded himself almost as a professional soldier. He had a passion for military ranks and awards, especially military decorations, something that made him the subject of ridicule.

Dmitri Ustinov, particularly after he became minister of defense, matched Brezhnev in his sycophancy toward the military. It seemed as if he were trying to prove that a civilian minister could get even more for the military than a professional officer could. Previously, when he worked for the Central Committee, Ustinov did keep an eye on the defense complex up to a point, and sometimes argued with Marshal Grechko, in particular on the subject of arms-control negotiations with the United States. I know this from firsthand observation. The other members of the Politburo (including Gromyko and, as far as I know, Andropov) simply did not dare to get involved in military affairs.

Brezhnev's illness also played a certain part here. On several previous occasions, not only had he raised objections, but he had gotten into conflicts with the military. That is what happened, for example, during the debates on the SALT I Treaty. At a Politburo meeting, Marshal Grechko, at the time the minister of defense, announced that as the man responsible for the nation's security, he could not agree to the text of the treaty that had already been decided upon. As chairman of the Defense Council and commander-in-chief, Brezhnev thought, and reasonably so, that *he* was responsible for national security. Therefore, this statement by the minister of defense hit a raw nerve; Brezhnev insisted on approval of the text and ripped into Grechko. Brezhnev recalled in my presence about a year and a half later that the marshal went to visit him to apologize and admit that he was wrong. As Brezhnev recounted it, he replied: "You accused me in the Politburo of neglecting the security interests of the country, and you did this in the presence of many people. And now you come to Zavidovo to apologize in a private, one-on-one meeting."

Brezhnev also had a long, very sharp disagreement by special telephone with the military leadership during President Ford's visit to the U.S.S.R. at the end of 1974. At that time the concept of the SALT II Treaty was being discussed. I know about this from the Soviet participants and from some Americans, who told me that at the decisive moment of the negotiations, the Soviet leader told everybody to get out of the room, and spoke for almost an hour on the telephone. He was talking so loudly and emotionally that you could hear him through the walls and the doors.

But such evidence of Brezhnev's willingness to argue with the military does not change the fact that they got away with a lot—particularly during the second half of the 1970s and at the beginning of the 1980s.

Ideology was one example. Frankly, we embarked on an unprecedented propaganda campaign in those years, trying to militarize the mentality of our people. Especially shameless were the attempts to play upon the themes of the Great Patriotic War, which was sacred for the Soviet people. The country was flooded with memoirs and fiction (more often than not this was simply hack work), feature film series, television programs, large monuments built at incredible cost; all sorts of ceremonies became part of life (including honor guards of schoolchildren, dressed in military uniforms and armed with submachine guns, at memorials and military cemeteries). For years all this overwhelmed the spiritual life of the country. Moreover, this was not at a time when such behavior could be justified by a looming military threat.

This was clearly the most negative, but by no means the most essential, psychological aspect of the military's deformation of our society. What was done in the area of armaments was even more important, both for the domestic economy and for international relations. Of course, much of this is still classified material. But it is clear from the latest Soviet publications, which have partially revealed our defense balance sheets, as it is clear from Western, particularly American, data that the 1970s marked the Soviet Union's most intensive postwar efforts to develop and accumulate arms of all types. These efforts occurred at the beginning of détente, during a time when we had achieved military parity in nuclear and conventional arms and in land, air, and naval forces. As a result, we reached absurdly high ceilings in many areas. This applies to such important components of conventional forces as the number of people under arms; tanks; artillery; tactical missiles; many types of aircraft; submarines; and many other weapons systems. As far as nuclear arms are concerned, we surpassed the Americans in the number of delivery systems, megatonnage, and throw weight in strategic arms, and also in medium-range weapons.

The Americans acted equally irresponsibly with regard to some other weapons. It really often looked like a competition in absurdity. The feverish accumulation of weapons beyond any needed numbers not only bankrupted the country's economy, but had a baneful influence on our political interests. First of all, it undermined Western trust toward us. Right-wingers and militarists in the United States and other NATO countries waged a successful campaign to create public mistrust of us and of détente. This became clear by the end of the 1970s, when ratification of SALT II ran into great difficulties in the U.S. Senate. After Afghanistan these difficulties became insurmountable. More than that, our actions encouraged Americans to intensify the arms race in response to Soviet efforts, which by Western estimations "went beyond the bounds of reasonable defense needs."

A second result was that during this period we showed the Americans and the NATO countries, more clearly than we had ever done before, that we were going to keep up with any of their new military programs—and sometimes even put two or three military programs into place for every one of theirs. The Americans soon figured out that the U.S.S.R.'s gross national product was three or four times smaller than their own and that of their allies, and this provided a completely safe opportunity to undermine the might of the Soviet Union, perhaps eventually to inflict a total defeat upon it through economic exhaustion. During the first years of the Reagan administration the concept of "competitive strategy" evolved, as did the plans for an arms buildup specifically aimed, according to an American document leaked to the press at the time, at "making previous Soviet investments in defense obsolete." Likewise, the aim of the American defense programs was to force us to compete in the most disadvantageous, expensive, and debilitating areas.

Though all of this was obvious, it seemed as if we had reconciled ourselves to following the American rules of the game by responding with a primitive concept of parity that deprived us of the opportunity to establish an independent military policy. It seemed as if this concept handed over to the Americans the key to our defense programs, giving the United States a guarantee that we would follow whatever course it set for us.

In addition, we made serious political mistakes concerning our defense in some key regions of the world. One of these mistakes was a faulty assessment of the threat from China, which forced us to concentrate very large forces in the Far East. This, in turn, was interpreted by the Chinese as a threat forcing them to increase both their nuclear and their conventional forces and their political and military cooperation with the West.

The other mistake concerned Europe. We were so smart that we managed to conduct two different, even mutually exclusive, policies at once. One of them was détente and the creation of a reliable cooperative security system. I'm referring to the so-called Helsinki process. The other one was a feverish arms buildup that was beyond our capacity and transcended all reasonable limits. In addition to this, we deceived both the public and our partners at the talks in Vienna as to the true size of our armed forces. Naturally, this undermined trust in us even more.

To cap it all off, during the second half of the 1970s we started deploying new medium-range missiles in Europe: the famous SS-20s. This scheme not only cost us many billions of rubles, it also unified NATO, which took a much more militant stand toward the Soviet Union. The SS-20s also provoked the Western countries into further military preparations and led, in turn, to the deployment of American medium-range missiles in Europe.

Since this problem has now been solved through the "zero option," we have demonstrated clearly enough that we now consider the decision to deploy the SS-20s to have been a mistake. I would like to say that quite a number of our experts realized this as early as the 1970s, as soon as they learned that deployment had commenced. (Most of our experts and diplomats found out about it through the Western press.)

I was among those who realized that the decision to begin deployment of the SS-20s was an error. I tried to express my doubts at quite a high level. I first did so during a conversation with Andrei Gromyko. He heard me out but did not respond. As I discovered later, he kept equally silent, or just kept saying yes, when this issue was discussed by the leadership. Many people said at the time that Gromyko avoided arguments and conflicts with the military because he was already thinking about what might happen after Brezhnev was gone.

I also spoke with Andropov. After hearing me out, he said with surprise: "What are you getting so upset about? We are replacing old missiles with new ones—that's natural." I pointed out that single-warhead missiles were being replaced by triple-warhead ones, which were, moreover, of a different range, and that this was causing serious concern in the West, even though that concern may have been artificially fanned by some people. This, I added, simply did not tie in with détente, the Helsinki Accords, arms-control talks—including those on Europe—or, in general, with the fact that a dialogue between us and the West was under way. And seeing which way Andropov was leaning, I "surrendered" and suggested: "Well, fine, if we really have to replace old missiles, then at least we don't have to do it silently and surreptitiously, as we did in the past. We have to explain to the West, somehow, what we're doing, what our aims are, and roughly how many missiles we are going to deploy. We simply cannot behave as we did before, now that we are in a period of détente and negotiation with the West. We cannot go on implementing big new defense programs without saying anything about it, and without explaining anything to the West or the world community."

At this point Andropov blew up: "What do you want us to do—explain ourselves to NATO and tell them what we want to do? That's almost as if we were asking them for permission. We are not doing it now, and we are not going to do it in the future." The conversation left a bad taste in my mouth. I could not understand Andropov's outburst, and later came to the conclusion that he got angry only because he did not have any convincing answers, though he knew full well how hopeless it was to raise this issue with the leadership. I did not exclude the possibility, as I do not exclude it now, that for some tactical reasons of his own he had already endorsed the deployment of these missiles. Perhaps, too, he did not wish to spoil his relations with Ustinov. (I must say that at that time personal relationships between members of the Politburo played a very large role—too large a role, often to the detriment of the common good.)

All in all, I failed to move either Gromyko or Andropov on this issue. It was discussed by the leadership. By this time the Western press had started to write about it, and it was debated during official contacts with the West. But the thought of restraint, of moderation in military affairs, was probably absolutely alien to our leaders. Possibly our own deeply rooted inferiority complex was the driving force behind our efforts to catch up with the United States in nuclear arms. I even got the impression that whenever a new weapons system appeared that caused an outcry in the West, we started to rejoice and say to ourselves: "Just look at us, how strong and clever we are. We've managed to outdo and scare even the Americans and NATO." During those years we were arming ourselves like addicts, without any apparent political need. We did this not because we expected war or were afraid of aggression from the West in any way. I remember a conversation I had in 1976 or 1977 with one of our leading arms designers and manufacturers. "Why are we doing this?" I asked him. "Do the generals really expect nuclear war at any moment?" "No," he answered. "If anything, the military leaders are convinced there won't be a nuclear war. And that's exactly the reason why they go on happily building the most dangerous new weapons systems available." Chief of the General Staff Marshal Kulikov also confirmed this suspicion. During one confidential conversation he described the explosion of a nuclear bomb and said he was convinced that anyone who knew what kind of weapon it was would never use it, including the Americans. But when I asked him why, in that case, we were producing such large quantities of nuclear weapons, he could not give a coherent answer.

Curing this "addiction" proved to be very difficult (and still is). I remember how I tried in vain to persuade Georgi Kornienko and Akhromeyev—this was already in Gorbachev's time—to slow down, if only a little, the number of SS-20s being deployed, bearing in mind that the Netherlands was committed to forbid the deployment of American cruise missiles on its territory if the number of our SS-20s did not go above a certain ceiling.

Another factor that helped undermine détente in the second half of the 1970s and the early 1980s was Brezhnev's illness. I, for one, feel that if Brezhnev had been well he would not have been persuaded that we needed to build the Krasnoyarsk radar station—particularly since, in presenting the issue to the top leadership, the Ministry of Defense did not hide the fact that the site chosen for the station was a direct breach of the SALT I Treaty.* Incidentally, Brezhnev thought this treaty was a great achievement—and he was right.

I think that the failure of the first contacts with the Carter administration can be to a great extent attributed to the fact that Brezhnev was ill, that he had set much business aside, and that he could no longer take direct part in negotiations himself. This became clear during Secretary of State Cyrus Vance's mission to Moscow in March 1977.

Of course, responsibility for the failure of this mission lies with the Americans as well. For example, great damage was caused when Washington suddenly reneged on the Vladivostok Accord in 1974, and the contacts that the President of the United States had with prominent dissidents caused a very nervous reaction in Moscow. But American mistakes do not relieve us of the responsibility for our inflexibility, for being incapable not only of quickly adapting to a changing situation, but of putting on a brave face when we found ourselves involved in a game that was going badly for us. We should have avoided the impression of failure during our first negotiations with the new American administration. These were the first high-level talks with the United States in which Brezhnev did not take direct part; they were conducted by Gromyko, Ustinov, and Andropov. As Andropov told me later, when they reported the results to Brezhnev, he said bitterly, "Here, for the first time, I appointed you to conduct the talks yourselves, and you ruined them."

The talks showed that government by committee, without a leader who is ready to accept full responsibility, provides the opportunity to discuss problems, but it makes decision-making very difficult. This is particularly true when negotiations are involved, for negotiations presuppose the inevitability of compromise, and concessions are always

---

*Academician Yevgeni P. Velikhov and I found out about this from Marshal Akhromeyev in 1986, while we were preparing materials for the finding by the Supreme Soviet Commission on Foreign Affairs on our compliance with international treaties.

painful. A leader will be more ready to make concessions than a committee will, for he has the power and bears personal responsibility for the whole.

The talks were a failure. True, we were later able to rectify the situation through a joint effort. (My colleagues and I at the institute informally contacted Dr. Marshall Shulman, then an adviser to Secretary of State Cyrus Vance, and told him that what was said in Moscow was not the last word and negotiations would continue.) At the same time we were lobbying our own decision makers. But precious time was lost; perhaps in those six or seven months that we needed in 1979 to ratify the SALT agreement, we might have avoided dangerous political situations, including the sending of our troops into Afghanistan.

Ridiculous events were occurring in many spheres of life. Take, for example, the crazy panic over civil defense, and the huge sums allocated to it, the endless exercises, the appointment of functionaries responsible for it in just about every institution and enterprise. It seemed as if we were expecting war to break out any day, a war that would be like the last one, and not a nuclear war, for which the proposed exercises were laughable. These stupidities were not only expensive but dangerous. They provoked the usual flurry of propaganda in the United States. At first, I thought this propaganda was baseless. I argued with the Americans until I was hoarse. Then, unfortunately, I discovered that they were correct in much of what they said, and about much that they accused us of.

Our military indulged themselves in any whim. The following is a small example from the work we did on the Palme Commission. One of the interesting ideas contained in the final report of the commission, which was endorsed in 1982, was the proposal to create nuclear-free zones in Central Europe, along the lines dividing NATO and Warsaw Pact forces. I tried to get the consent of our military men, particularly Marshal Ogarkov and Marshal Ustinov. Without providing any explanation, they answered with a categorical no. I tried to ask Andropov for help, but he just waved me off: "What do you want me to do, quarrel with Ustinov over you?"

The idea was rejected, despite the fact that it was in the interest of security in Europe and in our own interest. The main thing was, Why should the Soviet Union take the blame for this failure in the eyes of the European community? But who, in those days, wanted to listen to reason and common sense? I tried to find a way out of the situation by inserting a relatively innocent footnote in the reference section of the Palme report, to the effect that the proposal would not be effective enough: one could swiftly bring back weapons in case of a crisis. As I learned later, our generals were angry with it and, had Brezhnev not died a few months later, I could have gotten into trouble.

To conclude this episode, I would like to say that shortly thereafter, we gave our full support to the idea of a nuclear-free corridor in Europe and were prepared to go further, to agree to the withdrawal of a series of other weapons systems from this zone. And in 1991 we agreed to do away with all tactical nuclear weapons.

Unfortunately, the Palme Commission, like other international, non-governmental organizations, could not prevent a rise in world tensions, but its efforts played a significant role a few years later, amidst serious changes in international relations. In the early 1980s there was a swing to the right in the United States and in some other NATO countries. Due to serious mistakes, our foreign and military policies not only did nothing to prevent the deterioration of the international situation at the end of the 1970s and the beginning of the 1980s, but even encouraged it. We became participants in the dismantling of the détente we had launched a few years earlier. We helped the enemies of détente in the United States and other NATO countries to start another cold war. Moreover, the failure of our foreign as well as domestic policy in those years had a visible effect on the political situation in the United States, strengthening the position of the extreme right and the military. We helped to create an increasingly frightening image of the enemy in the eyes of the average citizen in the West. In this sense, Ronald Reagan—the "early" Ronald Reagan—came to power, together with a team of right-wing conservative cohorts, with our assistance. There was also an impact in the opposite direction. Engendered by a whole series of domestic and international factors, the strengthening and consolidation of the conservative forces in the United States exercised an influence on the political situation in the Soviet Union. This forced us to spend more on defense and to pay even greater heed to the opinions of the military.

In a word, by 1982 the results of our foreign policy left us little cause for comfort. The situation had not improved by 1985, when perestroika began. The Cold War was on again, and the arms race reached unprecedented proportions—a very grave defeat for the United States, for us, and for the world community.

Nonetheless, I think today that the détente of the 1970s was not totally in vain. For the first time in the postwar years, the politicians and the public had to face a very important question: What should we consider normal international relations? What was a normal relationship between the U.S.S.R. and the United States? Was it the implacable hostility that found expression in a "hot" or a "cold" war? Or could more civilized relations, which did not exclude contradiction, disagreement, even conflict, become the norm? Such relations had to be founded on a realistic appreciation of common interests, on a willingness not only to live in peace with and tolerate each another, but also to cooperate on an equal footing and to our mutual benefit.

At the very least, détente succeeded in undermining the conviction that we were inexorably doomed to bad relations, to cold war and military confrontation. It gave birth not only to hope, but to a faith that the search for an alternative was not senseless but realistic. And even in the most critical moments of the new phase of our relationship, many people no longer regarded a return to the Cold War as the norm.

This mood made itself felt in the West as well. First of all, there was the turbulent rise of the antiwar and antinuclear movements, which occurred during 1980–1982. The sharp swing to the right in American politics, the rising militarism, increasing tensions, and Reagan's rhetoric and that of some other Western leaders mortally frightened the Westerners themselves. In 1981 the largest antinuclear demonstration ever— with almost a million people—took place in New York City. The extent of the public protest made a deep impression on Reagan, and later, when some positive shifts were made in Soviet-American relations, some American conservatives accused their President of borrowing his slogans and policies from the antinuclear movement.

It is worth mentioning that International Physicians for the Prevention of Nuclear War was founded in 1981. The cochairmen were Dr. Bernard Lown of the U.S. and Dr. Yevgeni Chazov of the U.S.S.R. The activities of the organization had a dramatic impact on world public opinion and, in 1985, it won the Nobel Peace Prize.

Even official foreign policy did not revert entirely to the old positions of the classic Cold War. Noticeable legacies of détente were maintained in Europe. Most important, we preserved one of the most significant achievements of the 1970s, our dialogue with the European Social Democrats; we even maintained a level of political cooperation with them. All this facilitated the important changes in international relations that began to take place during the years of perestroika.

To this I would add another legacy of détente, which, in my opinion, played no small role in the Soviet Union: the evolution of Soviet political thinking in foreign policy. It had begun earlier, although it ran into great difficulties during the years of heightened tensions. Here, I think, one can trace most clearly a direct continuity between the ideas of the Twentieth Party Congress, détente, and the new political thinking.

As I explained earlier, the Institute of World Economics and International Relations of the U.S.S.R. Academy of Sciences was an oasis of creative thought in the late 1950s and early 1960s. During the 1960s, more institutes, dealing with Africa, Latin America, and the Far East—and including, eventually, the Institute for the Study of the U.S.A. and Canada—were founded. Not all of these institutes were equally successful. Nonetheless, from the 1960s on, modern political science began to develop in the U.S.S.R. For the first time the field was not merely scholastic or dogmatic, but aimed at real life, at political practice, and extended the area of research to subjects that in the past either had never been studied or had been forbidden. I have in mind the study of conflicts and international crises, and also the broad area of military-political problems, economics, and the policies of other countries.

Deterioration in the Land

It is difficult to identify triumphant moments along the road of progress during our post-Stalin history. There were periods of economic growth and success, but they were short, and the cycles of political and cultural advance did not always coincide with them. But it is possible to identify a period when there was a noticeable deterioration in all these areas. This was the second half of the 1970s and the early 1980s.

I would like to start with the economy. The modest economic reforms begun in 1965 had played themselves out. Despite their inconsistency, they did yield some results, but they could never have lasted for long, given the form they took at the start. They should have been developed further and promoted. This did not happen. Not only that, the conservatives compromised the reforms at every turn, using such underhanded methods as playing on Brezhnev's rivalry with Kosygin. (People associated Kosygin with reform.)

It is even possible to assign an exact date to the point at which the dynamics of economic development took a turn for the worse. The eighth Five-Year Plan was a success. The deterioration began with the ninth Five-Year Plan, and the turning point was 1972.

Was this unexpected? Generally speaking, it wasn't, not by the experts and not by some of the leaders. As I have mentioned, debate on the economy had been going on since the beginning of the 1960s. This gave birth to reform. Despite the success of the eighth Five-Year Plan, a series of questions concerning economic problems were raised at the Twenty-fourth Party Congress. Among these were the need for a switch to intensive economic growth factors, the need for an increase in the role of economic incentives, and other urgent problems concerning the improvement of planning and management methods, and so on. As I have already mentioned, shortly after the congress ended, preparations for a plenum on the technological revolution began. Had we not become so scared that we canceled it, this event might have played a noticeable part in our economic development.

This plenum, like the reforms of 1965, was yet another historic opportunity to embark upon serious and radical reforms in a relatively normal, even favorable, climate and from what might be termed a position of strength. But these opportunities were missed. I won't venture to judge whether this was inevitable, although that may well have been the case. Perhaps those people are right who think that the only way we can be forced to make truly radical changes is through a deep crisis. Of course that is a more painful, a more difficult, and in some ways a more dangerous way to go about things. We now have to go through economic reform, not from a position of strength, but from a position of weakness.

Why were these opportunities missed? Why have we so unforgivably delayed putting our economic house in order? The main reason, in my opinion, is that the leadership was not prepared for radical change. For that matter, the same could be said of a significant part of the population. This became particularly clear later, during perestroika.

As far as the leadership is concerned—and I include the whole stratum of central management of the economy—the main thing to remember is that the system Stalin created gave rise to its own brand of economic and managerial thinking and created its own type of economic manager. It was necessary, in fact, to renounce the entire economic model whose roots were in "war communism," although few people realized this at the time. We had to build a new model, which included economic components and institutions regarded as alien to socialism and even as capitalistic—for example, a market economy. We had to stop identifying public property, which was supposed to belong to every citizen, as state property managed by the bureaucracy. And we had to legitimize private property. This proved to be a tremendously complicated and painful process because it faced desperate opposition from the bureaucrats and ideological fanatics in the Party, as well as ignorance, prejudice, and suspicion among the public. We found out the real scope of this resistance later—in the late 1980s and early 1990s.

Therefore, the ideas that the most progressive reformers had been proposing for a long time simply found little support among society and were often misunderstood. People had been conditioned for decades to prefer a more-than-humble, but secure life, one free of any risk. When one considers the ordeals of our history, these attitudes may have been justified. Why, then, one might ask, did they not start changing when the faults and vices in the existing economic mechanisms became apparent?

First, I think that not only society but even the government did not fully grasp the real economic picture. Totalitarian traditions, the obsession with propaganda proclaiming our successes, the incessant desire to tell superiors what they wanted to hear—all this took its cruel revenge.

Of course, the leadership was told much more than the general public. But it was difficult to tell these leaders the truth, even if one wanted to. This was not only because the practice of twisting the facts began at the bottom—with the padding of figures at the workplace, to say nothing of the plant or enterprise, or the state farm or collective farm. The statistics themselves, the system of collecting statistical data, the selection of indicators, and especially their analysis were all adapted to fit the existing system and the existing model of economic management. I don't want to reduce everything to a matter of statistics cooked up to satisfy our managers' primary need to report successes. Yet another aspect of the system was that it provided only quantitative indicators (without taking due account of quality, losses, and expenses) and did not exclude double-entry bookkeeping and other fiddling. The most interesting aspect of all this was that many people in the leadership knew, or at least suspected, that the economic picture fed them by the bureaucracy was basically embellished, but they did not show any determination to get to the bottom of things. They felt that something was not right, that there were serious inconsistencies, but they lived in a world of artificial concepts and conventions. For example, one of the most cherished criteria of success was 100 percent fulfillment of economic plans. But what did this 100 percent mean in reality? Most often it was simply a bureaucratic compromise that had nothing to do with the real needs of society. Nor does such an approach say at what price this 100 percent was achieved.

Among the leadership there was no sense of an approaching crisis. My colleagues and I, who for many years had taken part in the preparations for the traditional annual Central Committee plenary sessions on the following year's economic plan and budget, saw this vividly even from the heavily censored documents we received and from the way the plan was discussed in the Politburo.

The most important and fundamental economic issues were rarely raised there. Mostly, the talk concerned relatively minor grievances between various government agencies and, above all, the imperative that there be no deficits in the balance of payments. If there was a discrepancy of eight to ten billion rubles, or even five billion, it became a huge problem for N. K. Baibakov,* for Kosygin (later replaced by Tikhonov), and for Brezhnev himself. Year after year, new plans for emergency measures were born, including price increases on various goods in order to balance the budget. To be fair, I have to say that even this was better than the budgetary anarchy unleashed later by Prime Minister Nikolai Ryzhkov, Valentin Pavlov, and especially Yegor Gaidar. But reducing the problem to one of fiscal discipline could never heal a seriously ill economy. Few in the leadership were concerned about the fact that, year after year, tens if not hundreds of billions were thrown away because of frightful losses or because of the "building projects of the century," or were frozen because of "uncompleted construction," or were wasted on production of unwanted goods. In addition, the military expenditures, which bled the economy white, were so horrendous that they were kept under wraps and not completely revealed even to most of the leadership.

Another reason why both the government and society failed to com-

---

*Then chairman of the State Planning Commission of the U.S.S.R., Baibakov was an intelligent man, although he was more an engineer than an economist.

prehend the scope and the swiftness of the approaching economic woes until the crisis hit them was the fact that the growing holes in the economy were being plugged by the barbaric plunder of our enormous, but not limitless, natural resources, by scrimping on environmental protection and social spending. This can be seen most starkly in the export of oil (and later of natural gas)—the main reserve used to plug such holes, especially following the Yom Kippur War in 1973 and the creation of OPEC.

After 1973, many developed nations, including the United States, had to pay high prices for oil, and at times they experienced shortages and irregular deliveries. The very name "OPEC" caused a certain amount of fear and loathing in the West. But trying to analyze these events many years later, I came to the inevitable conclusion that the main victim of OPEC was the Soviet Union. This was especially true because the high oil prices coincided with our development of the Tyumen oil and gas fields. We viewed the export of these irreplaceable resources as a panacea. And nobody, including me, understood that the old adage that nothing corrupts as much as unearned wealth applies to countries as well as individuals.

Why bother developing your science and technology when you can order entire plants from abroad? Who needs to find radical solutions to the food problem when it's so easy to buy tens of millions of tons of grain, and no small amounts of meat, butter, and other produce, from America, Canada, and Western Europe?

Who needs to salvage the dreadfully backward construction industry when there are Finnish, Yugoslav, or Swedish construction companies to build or renovate the most important sites, when you can import the materials in shortest supply—the plumbing and the fixtures from West Germany, the wallpaper and the furniture from other Western countries?

I want to be correctly understood. I do not in any way share the opinion of those in our country who oppose the exportation of oil and other valuable and unrenewable resources as a matter of principle. One has to be realistic. Of course, it's better to export VCRs, airliners, and if worse comes to worst, cars, lathes, and instruments, rather than oil. But if you don't have competitive, high-tech goods or even industrial end products, then there's no alternative.

One must not permit oneself to be lulled into doing nothing because of a temporary state of well-being. The massive exportation of raw materials cannot last forever. One must look upon this opportunity to earn convertible currency as a chance to put one's economic house in order. Of course, this includes special efforts to avoid hunger, but you cannot turn the importation of grain, food products, and industrial equipment into permanent policy. First, the money from oil exports should have been used to modernize critical parts of our agriculture and industry and to develop export branches in finished-product industries that could earn convertible money. But this was not done, largely because of the oil wealth that suddenly rained down on us from heaven; we ended up freezing our efforts to push economic reforms, and canceled the plenum on the technological revolution.

Second, we should have developed this priceless resource more wisely, not at such breakneck speed. We should not have allowed millions of cubic meters of gas to be burned off at the oil fields, poisoning the atmosphere. We should have developed the region and its infrastructure sensibly so that people there could lead normal lives. Aside from increasing oil production, we could have improved processing facilities. We should have built oil and gas pipelines solidly and safely and, once again, with maximum economic effect. We should have followed the same policy of radical energy conservation pursued so successfully in Japan and Western Europe after 1973. In this respect, we were probably the most backward nation in the world.

We were the biggest oil producer in the world, but each year, because of shortages of fuel, we experienced serious disruptions in air traffic and lack of gasoline for even our modest number of automobiles. In addition, we were losing a substantial part of our desperately needed grain harvest because of shortages of fuel for our tractors and trucks. This forced us to sell even more oil abroad in order to import the grain. Here is just one fact that demonstrates the scope of our hidden reserves. The Japanese research organization Torai calculated that if the Soviet "metallurgical" industry were to use the same technology as the Japanese (incidentally, a considerable part of their technology was built on Soviet licenses and patents), the savings in energy would be roughly equal to the whole energy output of the Soviet nuclear-energy industry. I reported this to the leadership, but the Ministry of Metallurgy skillfully put the issue under wraps. This was not during the "stagnation years," but as late as 1988.

At the end of the 1970s and the beginning of the 1980s I and many of my colleagues often thought that western Siberian oil was saving the country's economy. We gradually came to the conclusion that this wealth was seriously damaging the economy, because it was constantly delaying long-overdue reforms. In light of this bitter historical lesson, I began to realize that few countries had made real progress and had become prosperous thanks to their abundant natural resources. There are a few exceptions, as in the case of some Persian Gulf countries that have small populations but are very rich in oil and have managed their natural wealth wisely. But these are the exceptions that prove the rule demonstrated in Nigeria, Venezuela, Brazil, and many other countries that are also rich in oil but have been unable to attain similar levels of prosperity. Conversely, neither Japan nor West Germany nor South Korea, nor many other industrialized or rapidly developing countries have significant natural resources. Our country has an ideal combination of rich natural resources and high scientific and cultural achievements, manpower, and a population that, I am sure, is willing and able to work. The right material and moral incentives must be created, and, of course, entrepreneurship and competition as well as market reform have to be put into play.

Returning to the approaching slump in our economy and in all other spheres of our life, I would like to focus on another characteristic trait of the times—the double-dyed bureaucracy, the arbitrary but flourishing and all-powerful apparat. There was a sharp increase in the number of ministries, and probably a corresponding decrease in their quality and that of their apparats. Our management structures were top-heavy. All decisions were taken to the very top, but the top could not make a single decision properly. Each decision required approvals numbering in the dozens, and sometimes in the hundreds. Besides this, implementing any government decision once it had been made meant putting it back under the arbitrary control of the apparent. There were many number of functionaries who could spoil even a good project at any time, and very few of those were willing and able to help; practically none of them bore any real responsibility for anything. On the lower management level, the bureaucratic apparatus grew to incredible proportions. In agriculture alone the number of bureaucrats hit the three million mark—more than all the farmers in America put together! In a word, the economy was developing not according to the economic laws of socialism, as the high priests of political economics were proclaiming on every corner, but as predicted by Parkinson's Law—in accordance with the selfish interests of government agencies and the bureaucracy.

Politics, the State, and the Party

I think that after Stalin, one fundamental contradiction was becoming increasingly apparent in our entire political orientation and economy. The economic model and structure of political power and government rule that had been created during a time of emergency and under siege conditions ("hostile encirclement" was for a long time much more than a propaganda slogan or an obsessive idea of the leaders) suddenly found itself existing in a more or less normal environment. Now there was no war, and the chance of a war's breaking out was very slight, at least for the foreseeable future. The postwar rebuilding had been completed. The hostile "capitalist encirclement" no longer existed. There was no longer a godlike Leader whose will, desire, or even whim could turn everything upside-down.

It then became clear that the existing political system and structure could not function under normal conditions. Not only that, but the model of the system, along with its many redundant attributes, was being distorted, sometimes turned into a political monstrosity. These features were utterly useless from the point of view of "socialist principles" or even common sense.

Under these normal, nonemergency conditions, it became increasingly obvious that the political mechanisms we had created were better adapted to seizing and holding on to power than to governing the state for the common good and solving problems as they arose. There was no concealing this reality. The "dualism" of these mechanisms was also becoming increasingly apparent—their division into bodies that held real power (the Party bureaucracy, the central agencies, and the penal arms of the law) and those that were supposed to provide the democratic façade (the elected soviets, the trade unions, and the public organizations).

The existing political superstructure drove political life into very narrow confines. It simply was not geared to revealing and analyzing society's changing realities or the interests and opinions of various social groups, or to mobilizing the intellectual potential to solve problems as they arose. And this was all the more true because the dominant task of the policymakers was increasingly reduced to mounting an impenetrable defense against change, to preserve the status quo at any cost. This task completely overshadowed any other. Naturally, that was what the leadership demanded from the government and the Party structures, from various levels of the mass media, and from the social and political sciences, especially beginning in the mid-1970s. All of them helped cover up the increasingly serious problems with the illusion of stability, success, and progress. With this effort, the last little islands of open discussion, of what was later known as glasnost, began to disappear, and the sphere of secrecy expanded. Each time a debate became unpleasant for the leadership, new areas were "classified." After articles on the pollution of Lake Baikal had appeared and been widely discussed, for example, ecology was declared a classified matter. Censorship became more severe, particularly because editors, editorial boards, artists' and writers' unions, ministries, and other agencies took the role of censors for the sake of their own peace and quiet.

Through such policies, the great and powerful apparat of political power, both Party and government, was placed at the service of preventing change and preserving immobility and stagnation. As a result, during this period a specific political style evolved, which was extremely cautious, slow, and aimed at not rocking the boat. It was as if social and national problems, the ecological threat, the deterioration of education and health care, the poverty of a considerable part of the population simply did not exist. Primitive propaganda stereotypes were substituted for the discussion of these problems.

As for the institutions of power, conservative policies for preserving the status quo meant, above all, the impotence of all elected bodies, which were supposed to represent the public but which actually performed purely decorative and ceremonial functions. These bodies had very little influence upon the real life of society, though in a certain sense they remained important because in a normal, nonemergency period the issue of legitimacy assumes a new significance. The public wants to know why these particular people are ruling the country, why they are deciding their fates, who put them there, and who sets the course on which they steer the ship of state.

Of all the different ways of resolving this matter of right of succession (power by divine right; the right of an idea; the right of the people; and so on), we who had experienced the dictatorship of a class, which soon became the dictatorship of a tyrant, were left with only one option: power exercised by those who had been freely chosen by the people. But neither the leadership nor the public were properly prepared for this. The real mechanisms of democracy did not exist. Here is where the representative bodies and the electoral system, which had been created back in the period of Stalin's rule for purely decorative purposes, proved handy. While these mechanisms were hardly convincing, at least we were used to them, and they calmed people down.

For three terms I was a deputy of the old Supreme Soviet of the U.S.S.R. and I know its workings and its electoral system inside out. Running for election to the Supreme Soviet (in fact, running for appointment to it) was considered an honor, and an acknowledgment by the leadership of one's achievements.*

The representative bodies, including the Supreme Soviet, were simply not allowed to formulate or even discuss real policies—or, more precisely, they were neither invited nor disinvited. Sometimes, before a session, someone would call you up from the apparat and ask you to make a statement. The same thing applied to the Commission on Foreign Affairs, of which I was a member. And right away some unknown bureaucrat would send you a draft of your speech (true, you were not obliged to use it). A similar procedure, by the way, applied to the participants in Central Committee plenary sessions; the difference was that they would not send drafts of a speech beforehand, and once you were given the go-ahead for a speech, you were free to say what you liked. But if you got off track, there could be consequences; careers had been ruined by speeches that didn't go over.

But the decorum of a parliament, of general elections to representative bodies by secret ballot and of "the will of the people" was maintained. Appearances were kept up and, most important, there was a semblance of legitimization. And sooner or later, this unique parliament "anointed" the real leader of the country in the name of the people—the

*I and a few others had another reason for being so honored. During détente, our country started establishing contacts and exchanges among parliamentarians. In order to do this, some people were needed who were more or less professionally abreast of international and foreign-policy issues. So they picked a few of us; Inozemtsev, Alexander Yakovlev, and Yevgeni Primakov began their parliamentary careers in the same way. So did Yevgeni P. Velikhov and Roald Z. Sagdeyev, when arms-control issues entered center stage.

general secretary of the Central Committee, that is, the person who had been appointed to this highest position by the Party. For this purpose the Supreme Soviet elected the leader of the Party either as chairman of the Council of Ministers (Stalin, Khrushchev) or as chairman of the Presidium of the Supreme Soviet, as in the case of Brezhnev, Andropov, Chernenko, and, for a while, Gorbachev.

Of course, apart from meetings with foreign delegates the parliament presented a deputy with an opportunity to leave a mark, even if only on small matters, if he or she was willing and ready to put in some effort. The deputy could help constituents solve local problems, assist people who had been unjustly arrested, had been harassed by their superiors, or had fallen into misfortune. I devoted a great deal of attention to such things. Each matter handled immediately brought about an increase in the number of petitions and requests. Of course, I was also a busy lobbyist for social and economic issues in my electoral district. I might try to speed up the construction of, say, a school, or a hospital, a bridge, a road, or a railway line.

The pitiful weakness of representative bodies was in sharp contrast to the rapid growth and consolidation of the executive branch. (I saw with my own eyes how the sessions of the Supreme Soviet became ever shorter from the mid-1970s and how meetings of its commissions became ever rarer.) The number of ministries and agencies and their staffs grew constantly. You could tell just by counting the rapidly growing number and size of ministerial buildings. One side of Kalinin Prospect was completely taken over by them. During the 1970s and 1980s, dozens of old prerevolutionary structures, homes, and offices were converted to ministerial use, and new ones were built. I don't mean just the gigantic Ministry of Defense and KGB buildings. Everyone was putting up anything he could. No money was spared.

The Central Committee complex grew particularly swiftly and on a massive scale. I worked there when the apparat was still housed in three buildings on Staraya Ploshchad ("Old Square"). One wing faced Kuibyshev Street. By 1985 the committee had expanded into dozens of buildings, some of which had been taken over from other ministries and agencies; it also moved into new buildings that were constructed in backyards. A whole new city was thrown up. This was all the physical evidence of a phenomenon, the incredible growth of the Party apparat, not only in numbers but in the role it played.

This was not a new phenomenon. Stalin built the Party out of the "political vanguard of society" (the Party's mission, according to the Party Rules) into the principal instrument of power penetrating all regions, all levels of social life, all institutions and enterprises, all pores of government and society. The fact that Stalin also created a parallel and equally diverse structure of state security agencies to maintain his position—even against the Party—does not alter a thing. He regarded the Party apparat as an instrument of total power.

But important changes took place in the 1970s and 1980s. Power and the methods of maintaining it had become much less cruel. The power was now understood not just as a political instrument (the ability to make major policy decisions), but as a means of direct management of everyone and everything, including the economy, culture, and science. Party organizations began to replace other agencies. This inevitably led not only to overlapping, but to a decrease in the qualifications for management and to a rise in overall irresponsibility. There was the absurd decision to permit local party organizations to exercise control over the administrations of their various institutions. Apparently, this decision was borrowed from the most difficult and anachronistic years of the revolution, but it was against not only the law but even elementary common sense.

All this led to a further deterioration in the quality and level of administration. People who had made it to the top of the Party ladder had long since forgotten their former specialized skills. And as for new specialties, they were limited to leadership and command per se; ranking officials couldn't do anything, they could only "lead."

From among the public at large, "the System" selected people who were not very talented (there were, of course, rare exceptions), but who were obedient, ambitious, and unscrupulous—people who were not greatly encumbered by abstract notions of conscience and morality. Who in those years typically went to work for grass-roots political organizations, in most cases for the Komsomol? It was hardly your best student, your best young agronomist or engineer, journalist or scientist. But it was precisely at that entry level that a young person got onto a conveyor belt that carried him and his political career higher and higher, first up the Komsomol ladder, and then up through the Party hierarchy.

You could climb very high, even as far as secretary of the Central

Committee, or as a minister, as a leader in science or culture, to say nothing of positions in the KGB, police, and judicial bodies.

Having begun to mind other governing organizations' business, the Party started to mind its own less and less. With time, even Party functionaries got more and more confused on this issue. Virtually all matters were purely Party matters. There were several dozen issues on the agenda of each meeting of the Central Committee Politburo or Secretariat. Most of them concerned the economy, administration, foreign policy, or defense, but rarely were any issues considered that had anything to do with the Party except for the nomination of officials. Long resolutions were issued on any matter from agriculture to public health. These were quickly forgotten, rarely checked, and even more rarely fulfilled. One of the major vices of such a government mechanism is absolute irresponsibility. This begins at the very top. Who, except for one or two functionaries, even knew the names of those who had initiated one resolution or another? Who had actually voted yes or no, and why, remained an eternal mystery, even for the initiated—say, members of the Central Committee, who by charter had access to the thick volumes of the minutes of the Central Committee Secretariat and the Politburo meetings (which were not real minutes, but contained only proposals prepared or approved by the apparat). Not once in my memory was anyone called to account for a wrong decision.*

What was the reasoning behind the inexorable growth of the administrative apparat, and what made it tick? What was the reasoning behind the growth of the bureaucracy at a time when the dynamics of development in the economy and other spheres had begun to fade away? I have

---

*I won't hide the fact that for a long time I, like others, did not give much thought to the monstrous absurdity and the inadequacy of such a method of decision-making. It was a method of mutual guarantees. I became conditioned to accept it as a fact of life—like snow in the winter and rain in the fall. We all started thinking about this and asking ourselves questions only with the coming of perestroika. These questions included one that in each given case was by no means superfluous or useless: Who is to blame? It is with that question that personal responsibility begins. So far, we have not received an answer. This includes mistakes committed after perestroika had begun. The main thing is not just to uncover the names of those who were to blame for wrong decisions made in the name of the Party, for which the whole nation had to pay a very dear price. It is far more important to understand the fault of the whole system, under which a few high-ranking officials could make decisions without answering to anyone.

already mentioned that Parkinson's Law provides the closest answer to
the truth. According to this law, social goals and social good are lost in
big bureaucratic structures, which start working more and more for
themselves, for their own self-aggrandizement. Bureaucracy, as a social
institution, acquires independence. In other words, it acquires its own
driving forces and motivations for growth that have no connection with
the outside world or with the subjects of government. This revealed itself particularly clearly during the years of stagnation.

These years were a true golden age for the apparat and the bureaucracy. Stalin used to weed out the apparat occasionally through merciless
purges, and Khrushchev would shake it up. He was endlessly reorganizing and would frequently replace people in high positions. Brezhnev
proclaimed the slogan "Stability" and served as its incarnation and
image, if by "stability" we mean immobility.

In fact, positions of responsibility were transformed into lifelong appointments, and the bureaucrats became impossible to replace. Many
regional secretaries, ministers, and highly placed officials of Party and
soviet apparats held their jobs for fifteen to twenty years. A very sophisticated technique was developed for shielding even totally incompetent
officials from any responsibility for their actions. If there were reasons
for expecting an unpleasant situation in the next elections in a region, a
regional secretary who had to be "saved" would be transferred, say, to a
job as inspector in the Department of Party Organizations and Cadres
at the Central Committee. After two or three years he would be recommended (for all intents and purposes, appointed) as secretary in another
region. An incompetent minister would either be shuttled from one
ministry to another, or some new ministry would be created under him.
And if someone turned out to be an absolute failure, he would be given a
sinecure, or if none existed, one would be created for him. Often, he
would be appointed ambassador to some country. (In Brezhnev's time
people who had fallen into disgrace would also be placed in such jobs).

In this way, high officials and the higher echelons of the *nomenklatura*
were finally separated into a special caste during the stagnation years.
(The same development applied to officials on the republic, regional,
and district levels, who formed their own "mini-castes.") Theirs was
something akin to an aristocracy—a life peerage associated with honors,
with a high standard of living (at least, as judged according to Soviet
criteria) and a good assortment of privileges (from the cradle to grave).

The gap between this caste and the rest of society was widened. The caste was isolated from the rest of society. It had its own health care. It had its own resorts. It formed its own clannish ties. Its children spent time together, got to know each other, and often intermarried. Moreover, it was precisely during stagnation that the next logical step was taken. The apparat tried to set up a system of inherited power, or at least privileges, through an exclusive system of education and then through a system of appointments and promotions. The leaders set the example: Brezhnev's son became the deputy minister for foreign trade, and his son-in-law became the first deputy minister of the interior. Of course, we never went as far as the Ceauşescu clan in Romania, whose reign turned into a complete caricature. Yet there can be no doubt that a privileged caste was forming. But you cannot associate these unwarranted privileges only with Brezhnev and the period when he was in power. These were widespread practices that began with Stalin.

Of course, the asceticism of many of the Old Bolsheviks and the "Party maximum" (that is, a quite modest income ceiling for all Party members, however high their position, which existed until the beginning of the 1930s) were a reality during the first postrevolutionary years. But the fanatical élan of revolutionary idealists does not make a system. The poverty of society made privileges practically inevitable. Special food-distribution outlets for officials in responsible positions appeared very early on. (There is a well-known, sentimental story that was used to justify the special Kremlin food outlet; while attending a session of the Sovnarkom—the early name for what later became the Council of Ministers)—People's Commissioner for Food Tsurupa fainted from hunger. At that point Lenin supposedly ordered the creation of a "Dietetic Food Cafeteria." This name disguised a kind of special food allowance that existed until 1988 and under some other guise exists even now, although on a much smaller scale). The top officials were, at first, provided with special housing in the Kremlin and in the so-called Houses of Soviets. There were several of those in Moscow, located on Granovsky Street, on Komintern Street (now Kalinin Prospect), and elsewhere. This housing was not too luxurious, but it was incomparably better than what most people had. That was the time when government dachas (with servants) appeared for the bosses. Special clinics, hospitals, resort homes, and sanatoriums also appeared, as did, of course, chauffeured cars for personal use.

All this had evolved into a whole system by the 1930s, and the system had its own hierarchy: members of the Politburo, candidates and secretaries of the Central Committee, ministers, department chiefs, and so forth. Each category had its own assortment of privileges. Before the war, the number of people who enjoyed those privileges was quite small, but the privileges were considerable. As for the very top leadership, their privileges boggled the mind. I remember one incident. During the 1930s, one of my classmates used to go with his parents to the dacha of Jan Rudzutak, who was a candidate-member of the Politburo. I was simply astonished by his stories of what was there, how they entertained themselves and what food they ate.

During the war, the economic and social gaps between the top leadership and the rest of the population grew enormously. This was particularly true toward the end of the war, when booty appeared and American aid began to flow. (Part of this aid—whether the organizers of Lend-Lease knew it or not—went to feed the upper strata of Soviet society.) Meanwhile, the rationing system reached the apogee of sophistication. I want to emphasize this particularly, since some of our current populists have recently spoken about rationing as if it were the height of social fairness. There were various categories of ration cards. Not only was there a category for dependents, for employees, for people at the workplace, but there were several special categories for management, the so-called lettered cards. In addition, there was the system of coupons and cards for various kinds of goods. There were also coupons for consumer goods, but vodka coupons served as the most stable currency in those days. The profiteering in knitwear, galoshes, footwear, which you could get for coupons, became almost a part of daily life for the families of high- and sometimes middle-ranking officials. Gradually, the top military brass started increasing its lead over the rest in this field. Some generals went so far that even Stalin, who looked upon this corruption with a blind eye, dressed them down and had some of them arrested. It was a real "Feast in Time of Plague," since the nation was absolutely impoverished. In my judgment, the period marks the breakdown in moral standards on a massive scale. Although at first glance it seems absurd, the end of rationing actually lowered the standard of living for a broad section of the *nomenklatura* and reduced its privileges.

But soon, privileges began to increase again. They took different forms—virtually free use of dachas; official cars; free breakfasts; free lunches; generous travel subsidies for trips to resorts and sanatoriums; and "recuperation money" (one month's extra salary paid when going on vacation). In Stalin's time, the best perks of all were the so-called packets, that is, salary bonuses for high officials. These could amount to several hundred or several thousand rubles, depending on your position. These bonuses, issued in envelopes (packets), were handed out secretly, were tax-free, and were exempt even from Party dues. Officials of lower rank were also paid proportionately. In addition, noncash privileges were thrown in.

I am convinced that this was a calculated policy of Stalin's, aimed at bribing the top levels of the Party and the Soviet apparat and at turning it into a sort of Praetorian Guard. I am convinced his aim was to ensure absolute obedience of the class of government employees, and guarantee its active service to the regime by way of direct bribery and the fear that, along with your job, you could lose your privileges—and, in Stalin's time, your freedom and even your life.

The privileges that the various ranks of the administration enjoyed after World War II had not been seen in the U.S.S.R. since the revolution. The fact that they were less talked about and people knew less about them was another matter. Many privileges were a secret, and anyone who revealed their existence could be severely punished. Another reason was that the number of officials who had these privileges was noticeably lower than in later times—as was the number of people who crossed the lines between the haves and the have-nots. Those who were sacked from their jobs were often arrested. And those who were not, kept quiet. To get to the top was very difficult. And those who got there, as a rule, led very closed lives.

Khrushchev embarked upon his first campaign against privileges on his own initiative and without any pressure from below. When I started working for the Central Committee apparat in 1964 the old officials there still could not get over the shock of having lost some of their privileges. Apparat officials called the cancellation of these privileges Khrushchev's Ten Blows, after Stalin's Ten Blows, the ten biggest battles of 1943–1944. Yet the number of people who received various perks grew constantly under Khrushchev and Brezhnev, keeping up with the growth in sheer numbers of the apparat. People abused these privileges shamelessly, even flaunted them. Quite often they built houses for themselves, to say nothing of their access to constantly expanding guest houses, "official" hotels, sanatoriums, and resorts. They lived with an incredible extravagance and a luxury that bordered on the absurd.

I would like to turn now to an important part of the political super-structure and the state: the law enforcement, or penal, apparat.

This apparat was born in the revolutionary years, during "war com-munism," and the Civil War, when the Soviet government used dictato-rial means, including at times the so-called Red terror. The first steps in drafting more or less normal criminal legislation, together with a judicial and police system, were taken in the same year. The economy was then switching over to the NEP (New Economic Policy) and there was a rad-ical reduction in the armed forces, from several million to 500,000. For-eign policy's mission became to secure a peaceful respite (the leaders did not count on much more than that) and to establish normal relations with other countries.

But our progress in the realm of legal defense did not get very far. Soon a huge political-police apparatus was created, and extrajudicial means and methods of enforcement were established (although the courts were also, in fact, obedient instruments of administrative and at times arbitrary power). The staged public political trials of the late 1920s and the early 1930s, the ominous years of 1937–1938, the disfranchise-ment of the kulaks, the deportation of whole nationalities, and the waves of lawlessness and repressions that followed one after another until Stalin's death were all integral parts of that process. This included the use of the law and the police, of the courts, of the correctional sys-tem, of the prisons and camps for economic purposes. (Discipline was maintained by forced labor and criminal prosecution; this included harsh punishment for the "theft" by hungry peasants of a handful of wheat or a small bucket of potatoes from the fields, for being late by more than twenty-one minutes, for producing low-quality goods, for storing raw materials or goods of one sort or another at a factory above the permitted norm, and so forth).

After the death of Stalin, and particularly after the Twentieth Party Congress, political repressions were sharply curtailed, if not entirely stopped. At the same time punitive practices were liberalized somewhat. But the machinery itself, together with its legal, normative, and practical components, was not destroyed. Political repressions, illegalities, arbi-trary actions under the guise of criminal prosecution did not cease under either Khrushchev or Brezhnev, even if they were on a smaller scale and were not widely publicized (or were even kept secret). It was not until perestroika that people started talking about radical legal reform and about the creation of a state and society based on law. (So far, as these words are being written, there has been more talk than action, unfortunately.)

Naturally, conservative policy, which is directed at preventing change, demands greater use of punitive force for the sake of suppression. And that is what happened. To some extent this suppression assumed a direct form. People were put on trial for various kinds of "anti-Soviet" activity—most often for propaganda and slander. People were sentenced to prison terms, sent to the camps and into exile. But, of course, after the Twentieth and the Twenty-second Party Congresses and after the exposure of Stalin's crimes and the gulag, the government did not want to resort to widespread use of such repression. Nor did Brezhnev, who remembered how history had repaid Stalin for his crimes, personally want this. That was even truer of Andropov. As head of the KGB, he did not wish to end up in the same category as Lavrenti Beria or Nikolai Yezhov.* Andropov complained to me on several occasions about the almost constant pressure from diehard Stalinists, including members of the Politburo, to "Lock 'em up!" The leadership yielded on quite a few occasions, but did not allow itself to be dragged into a policy of massive repression.

Massive repressions become possible, and all the more probable or inevitable, when the public has someone or something to hate, or to believe in with a blind faith. In the Brezhnev years, I believe there was neither of these, although several attempts were made to organize campaigns of public hatred—against modern artists, against Solzhenitsyn, and against Sakharov. But the spirit behind them was gone.

Mass political repressions became a thing of the past, but the policies of repression and their attendant apparat got a new lease on life. Arrests continued to be made from time to time, as punishment or as a warning. The public either was unaware or could see nothing wrong with the practice, and even often thought that it was natural and normal.

Nevertheless, blocking a change whose time has come inevitably requires adequate and effective measures of coercion and intimidation. It

---

*Yezhov was the commissar of state security in 1937–1938, during the worst of the purges. He disappeared in 1939.

also requires the application of these measures to a growing number of people. As it turned out, the threat of Party punishment against Communists, or of their exclusion from the Party, so effective in the past, proved insufficient. The same was true of threats to fire people who were not members of the Party from their jobs—that is, to deprive non-Party people of their means of support. The apparat had to find something in between these administrative measures and the downright repressions of Stalinist times. One has to admit that the new coercive measures developed in the Brezhnev years were rather ingenious.

A new sociopolitical phenomenon—the dissident—was born, as was a new array of measures against him: social isolation, sophisticated slander organized by experts in this field, concentrated efforts aimed at completely compromising an individual, the misuse of psychiatric wards, expulsion from the country and the revocation of citizenship, and, to a limited extent, arrest and conviction.

These "new" and sophisticated repressive methods affected more people than did the threat of courtroom reprisals. And they proved effective up to a point, although in the long run we paid for them dearly. We paid a particularly high price in the attitudes of the world community toward the Soviet Union and its policies. This was a key component of our Cold War relationships. You can start a cold war and sustain it as the centerpiece of relations for decades under only one condition: that people believe in the existence of a fearsome enemy and, if possible, a repulsive one. The fear of the enemy has to be great enough for people to be willing to spend exorbitantly to continue an arms race, to risk war, even to waive their rights to an independent policy and their national sovereignty. In the West the popular saying "Better dead than Red" expressed the fear rampant at the time.

I do not, of course, discount the effects of hostile propaganda toward us. Its contribution to the growth of distrust, fear, and even hatred toward the U.S.S.R. was always great and, as a rule, we were not very good at countering these propaganda attacks. I did not approve of the West's effort to organize political games around the fundamental issue of human rights. This campaign had quite a few negative side effects. In particular, the campaign made it easy for our conservatives to identify the democrats, the dissidents, with foreign powers—which often *were* very hostile to the Soviet Union. While putting additional strains on relations, the West's position often undermined the reputation of dissidents in the eyes of our less sophisticated citizens. But here, as well, we can't blame everything on foreign propaganda, particularly since no propaganda can be effective without justification, or at least good excuses, for its existence.

The campaign against the dissidents involved only a relatively small number of people. But it had a noticeable negative effect abroad, and it poisoned the political atmosphere at home, worsened the already repressed circumstances in culture, in social thought, and in the attitudes of all thinking people. They could not regard this as being anything other than a rebirth of the Stalinist practices of political persecution, intimidation, and pressure, even if the methods were milder and less sweeping.

For many people, even for those who were not direct victims, the struggle against the dissidents meant serious personal trauma. Forcing prominent scientists and cultural figures to sign letters damning other scientists, writers, and artists who had incurred official displeasure became common practice. Those who refused to sign could expect trouble; often this was the first step on the road to disgrace. Those who signed could expect the contempt of their colleagues and friends.

But it was not just a matter of moral damage. Hundreds, perhaps thousands of people found themselves direct targets of the antidissident policy. The search for dissidents, and their persecution, required enlisting the whole secret-police organization. This meant hiring more agents, encouraging people to make denunciations, opening private letters, and bugging telephones. Everyone, including highly placed people, was wary of bugged telephone conversations, of surveillance, of denunciations. Frequently, high officials in the Central Committee, even secretaries of the Central Committee, would glance at the telephone, make an obvious sign, and put their finger to their mouth when the conversation in their office started getting hot. According to one rumor, some of our well-known journalists (one of them the deputy editor-in-chief of a leading newspaper) had said something he shouldn't have (most probably, something personal about Brezhnev, which was the most dangerous thing); the culprits were caught by "technology," as they used to say—that is, by the microphones of the KGB—and were fired on the spot. The same thing supposedly happened to a couple of senior KGB officers who did not exercise due care during a conversation in a restaurant; they were sitting at a "radio-active" table. As a result of a denunciation for an "unorthodox" conversation, the chief of one of the important Party institutes, Fyodor D. Ryzhenko, admired by many who knew him, was forced into retirement.

These isolated incidents only confirmed what people already suspected: that the situation was growing worse, that you had to keep quiet and be careful in other people's company. You cannot blame just the security organizations in this instance. On direct instructions from the Moscow City Committee, a case was being prepared to expel from the Party Igor Kokarev, a scholar at the U.S.A. and Canada Institute. The only thing of which Kokarev was "guilty" was that during a lecture on movies, he had made some favorable comments about the wonderful (but free-thinking) singer, poet, and actor Vladimir Vysotsky, and had written, for his son's school, a little amateur play in which Vysotsky was either mentioned or quoted. At the cost of some very harsh words and considerable effort on the part of the institute, this act of vengeance was stopped. (We probably succeeded only because the Moscow City Committee got frightened that I might take the case "up to the very top," where they might find themselves on the wrong side.)

On one occasion, at the height of the SALT II talks, two of my colleagues gave an interview to an American paper in which they spoke of the possibility of compromise. This was simply an off-the-cuff remark, but it must have been close to our fallback position. After all, my colleagues were experts and could imagine what was possible—and even probable. There was a violent reaction at the Politburo meeting. A leak was suspected; a special investigatory commission was appointed (Ustinov, Andropov, and Central Committee Secretary Mikhail Zimyanin). And although no leak was discovered, the commission had the men fired, despite all my protests—just like that—for "superfluous" words. (I succeeded only in putting off this process for a year.)

In those same years, Alexander Pumpyansky was a U.S.-based correspondent for *Komsomolskaya Pravda* (today he is the very successful editor-in-chief of *Novoye Vremya* ["New Times"]). Pumpyansky incurred Zimyanin's uncontrollable rage when he wrote that there were 100,000 millionaires in America. He was recalled urgently and fired.

Along with an increase in political persecutions during the years of stagnation, it also became common practice to use the police apparatus to settle scores with people who simply had gotten in the way of local authorities (for the most part, secretaries of regional and city committees, and so on) either by criticizing them or getting into a conflict with them, or even because, in the opinion of the authorities, they posed a challenge to the established order of things through their desire for changes and unorthodox solutions to problems. The successful acts of such a person could be interpreted as a guilty verdict on the indolence, mistakes, and professional ineptitude of the people around him. Therefore, the bosses would try to rein such a person in, to cut him down to size, or to crush him. When society and government are not based on law, when investigation, prosecution, and trial are all subservient to the Party bosses, the leadership and its opinion outweigh the force of law. Thus, we were presented with the cases of collective-farm chairmen Ivan Khudenko, Ivan Snimshchikov, and Victor Belokon; plant directors like Alim Chebanov from Cherkassy and Vladimir Chebanenko from Gorky; and prominent scientists and inventors, for example, the Estonian Iohanes Hindt. Of course, these trumped-up cases were based mostly on criminal charges, rather than political ones. With our contradictory laws, our obedient investigators and courts, it was not all that difficult to make those charges stick. But the motivation was almost always political—to preserve the status quo, to defend the system.

In general, the decline of the economy corresponded to the state of the political and legal system. You could see with your own eyes how the management of public affairs was disintegrating. With shame, you had to admit that in the eyes of the rest of the world, we suffered from intellectual impotence in both domestic and foreign policy. The quality of the leadership fell relentlessly because the existing political mechanisms precluded a natural selection of good people. There was a sort of "reverse natural selection," which promoted people who were mediocre, weak, and often dishonest. Important decisions were made by a very narrow circle of underqualified people, often on the basis of unverified information that was incomplete and even false. Add to all this the fact that the leaders were growing senile before our eyes.

Culture, Ideology, and Social Thought

As far as political and ideological repressions were concerned, of course we had known worse times in our long-suffering history. But the repressions of our intellectual life were particularly repulsive. In the years since Stalin, we had become wiser, and were no longer so cowed that we did not realize what was going on. Therefore, although life was safer than under Stalin, and in some ways safer than under Khrushchev, one had a particularly sickening feeling inside because of the intolerable propaganda. For example, who could believe that I. Stadniuk or M. Alexeyev, servile hacks who enjoyed the full support of the ideological tsars of that time, were better writers than Solzhenitsyn, and that Trapeznikov or Fedoseyev were of a higher intellect and more honest than Sakharov? Gone was the previous belief, or perhaps hope, that the leadership was always right, or that if it did not always see things right, then it must simply have been hoodwinked for a moment. Many people were beginning to lose hope.

There was a sour mood, combined with cynicism, among the intelligentsia. Which feelings predominated differed from person to person, depending on the individual's character, circumstances (good or back luck), and the degree of his ideological commitment or, sometimes, his naïveté. Nonetheless, many people remained willing to fight stubbornly for every inch of idealistic ground, even without much hope of victory.

Some abandoned the fight, while still others chose another battleground, having concluded that one had to fight not to reform the system but to destroy it. I did not agree with them, but I do not want to criticize them here. At that time it seemed that those who fought to improve the system and those who fought against it were divided by a deep gulf. On the other hand, in recent years I have also begun to question whether one can say with absolute certainty that the system can be changed for the better. Today, it is beginning to seem as if sometimes, although not always, you can build bridges across this gulf.

As for the social sciences, stagnation was not merely a period of marking time, but of noticeable regression. At the beginning of the 1980s, the conservatives increased their attacks on the economic front as well.

There were still some "oases" of creative thought left, but an ever-increasing number of these now found themselves under siege. I have already mentioned Aganbegyan's institute in Novosibirsk and the Institute of World Economics and International Relations (IMEMO) at the U.S.S.R. Academy of Sciences in Moscow.

I would like to discuss the latter in somewhat greater detail. For a long time, some people had been sharpening their knives to settle scores with this institute. The fact that there were quite a few creative and progressive scholars working there was not the only reason. The institute, together with its director at the time, Academician Inozemtsev, was closer than many others to power and to the people who made policy. Therefore, they posed a particular danger in the eyes of the conservatives, as sources of a "pernicious influence" on the leadership.

The real trouble started at the final stage of stagnation in 1982.

The first bad event occurred at the very beginning of that year. The deputy administrative director of IMEMO was arrested. At the same time a fact-finding commission on the institute's administrative affairs went into action. The commission didn't turn up anything political, just a matter of economic administration. It soon transpired that the question at issue was what had happened to some old furniture that had been left behind during a move from the old building to the new one. Since it was forbidden by law (one must say, a strange law) to sell the furniture or to give it away, according to regulations, it therefore had to be destroyed, but now suspicion had arisen about whether anyone from the management of the institute might have acquired some of it.

This would have been a stupid, but routine matter, had it not been for the fact that the investigation was being conducted by a special investigator from the prosecutor's office (either of the U.S.S.R. or the R.S.F.S.R.) for particularly high-priority cases. But the investigation failed to find any material compromising the institute's management. The case was closed, and the deputy director was released from prison and went back to work.

We soon learned, however, that this had been only a prologue. In the spring, the KGB arrested two young scholars at the institute—Fadin and Kudyukin. They were supposedly part of a group that, among other things, had distributed leaflets criticizing the official version of the events in Poland and favorably portraying the Solidarity movement. In short, they were "dissidents" by the standards of the time. They were also accused of an unauthorized meeting with the secretary of one of the Latin American Communist parties, at which they had assessed the situation in the Soviet Union and Soviet government policies "from a dissident point of view."

In those years, an arrest of a dissident or dissidents who were employees of an academic institute was not all that unusual an event. Normally, this did not have any grave consequences for the institute or its administration. The case of the IMEMO scholars took on a completely different and unprecedented aspect. A Central Committee commission, headed by Politburo member Viktor Grishin, was formed to investigate the affairs of the institute. Central Committee Secretary Zimyanin and a number of senior officials from the Central Committee and the Moscow City Committee were also on the commission. Clearly, the aim of the commission was to publicly discredit the institute and its director. It "investigated" everything—the personal affairs of its employees, the academic output of the institute; it talked to people in the administration, in the Party committee, and to the heads of the various sections. They were all asked whether they thought what had happened was sheer chance, and how they rated the ideological environment at the institute.

The commission produced a document and organized a meeting with a few leading members of the institute staff. The document was read out aloud and no one was even shown a copy. In it, the institute was accused of ideological failure, of allowing a pollution of its staff to take place (among the pollutants were "Zionist elements," that is, Jews), and of misleading the government about processes taking place in the world. During the meeting, the head of the Economics Section of the Central Committee Science Department, Mikhail I. Volkov, announced that "our enemies were praising" the institute. (He had in mind an article in the foreign press that expressed respect for IMEMO.) During behind-the-scenes talks, Party officials (for example, Ponomaryov, the secretary of the Stavropol Regional Party Committee) advised the leaders of the institute's Party Committee to plead guilty to the accusations and thereby to "save their skins."

Inozemtsev suffered badly throughout these events. His health declined sharply, and he existed on an ever-increasing amount of heart medication. I think his illness and his feeling of malaise affected his behavior. He was quite passive and avoided a decisive fight, although he was well known to many of the country's leaders, including Brezhnev, and enjoyed their trust. At the final session of Grishin's commission in the Central Committee building, Inozemtsev did not speak at all, according to people who were there. V. N. Shenayev, the secretary of the institute's Party Committee, denied many of the accusations. Zimyanin made the following remark: "Things are even worse than we thought. You haven't understood a thing."

In general, the case proceeded according to the old, classic canons, which many people, including myself, found astonishing. I tried to persuade Inozemtsev to go to Brezhnev, Andropov, and even Suslov. Contrary to Inozemtsev's wishes, I talked with Andropov myself. In the summer, the situation eased up a bit; perhaps Andropov's return to the Central Committee in May 1982 had something to do with that. None of the directors or the institute's Party Committee members were sacked. Soon after, Inozemtsev was even included in the U.S.S.R. Supreme Soviet delegation to Brazil, and later was asked to give a report to the Politburo about the delegation's visit. The report came off well, and Inozemtsev thought that the whole business had blown over.

But the institute had suffered serious losses in its political prestige, and the team spirit had taken a blow. Directors of divisions, sectors, and grass-roots Party organizations that had employed the arrested persons were punished. Party proceedings were started against them.

Following the sudden death of Inozemtsev from a heart attack in August 1982 (I and the doctors I spoke to saw a direct connection between the campaign against his institute and his death) another attack was attempted on IMEMO. A plan was drawn up in the Moscow City Party Committee to disband the institute's Party Committee and replace its head. At the time, this was almost an unprecedented vote of no confidence in the whole institute; it also meant the start of another victimization campaign against the administration and the staff. The plan came close to succeeding. I recall that one Sunday in the second half of October, a close friend of mine who worked at IMEMO called me and said that a Party meeting had been called for the following Thursday. The Moscow Party Committee had demanded the meeting, and people from the Science Department of the Central Committee and the Moscow City Committee were planning to turn it into a boisterous spectacle during which they wanted to discredit the institute politically. I was out of town, working with a group that was preparing materials for the next Central Committee plenum on the budget for the following year. Before his death, Inozemtsev had always been invited to work with this group. On Monday Alexander Bovin and I thought up a plan. During our first meeting on the economic plan, scheduled for the following day with Brezhnev, we would try to talk to him about this whole affair, provided the state of the general secretary's health allowed for a serious conversation.

The meeting with Brezhnev took place that Tuesday, two days before the Thursday Party meeting at IMEMO. Brezhnev was feeling moderately well, and after the business part of the discussions was over, Bovin and I asked him to give us a few minutes of his time on a "personal matter." Georgi Tsukanov and Nikolai Shishlin, who had participated in the discussions, left the room. We told Brezhnev about the troubles that had descended upon Inozemtsev and apparently hastened his death, and also about the fact that a Party meeting was planned for the day after next, at which they would try to sully Inozemtsev's memory and also to carry out a pogrom at the institute.

Judging by his reaction, this was news to Brezhnev. He asked, "Whom should I call?" We suggested Grishin, because he was chairman of the Party commission investigating this affair and because the directive to hold the Party meeting had come from the Moscow City Party Committee. Brezhnev made a sign to us to keep quiet and pushed a button on his house phone. (It linked him to twenty or thirty officials. You didn't have to lift the receiver, it had a sound system.) Grishin's voice came over the phone: "Good morning, Leonid Ilyich."

Brezhnev told him (without naming his sources) that he had heard that there was some plot surrounding IMEMO and Inozemtsev, and that an investigative commission headed by Grishin had been formed. And now, on instructions from the Moscow City Party Committee, a Party meeting was planned for the institute; the plan for this meeting was to work Inozemtsev over posthumously, and to look into the Party organization and the staff at the institute. "So, what's the problem here?" he asked.

I have to admit that, having rehearsed all the possible scenarios for the conversation, Bovin and I never expected the answer Grishin gave. "I have no knowledge about what you are saying, Leonid Ilyich," Grishin replied. "This is the first time I've heard about a commission to investigate Inozemtsev's institute. I don't know anything about the Party meeting either."

I almost exploded from indignation. With my emotions running high, I opened my mouth to say something, but Brezhnev put a finger to his lips and told Grishin: "Viktor Vasilyevich, you go and check everything. If anyone gave instructions to work the late Inozemtsev over, cancel the affair and report about it to me later."* This call put the matter to rest for a while.

Why did the conservative officials attack IMEMO so viciously? It was perfectly understandable. The institute tried to concentrate the leadership's attention on reality, and on the problems that demanded radical changes in economics and domestic and foreign policy. The conservatives wanted to silence those who were constantly bringing up that reality and the necessity for change. Herein is the root of the campaigns against the economists in Novosibirsk, against the Central Economics and Mathematics Institute in Moscow, and against Soviet sociology, which was young and just getting on its feet. Herein lie the roots of the criticism and persecution of a considerable number of Soviet experts and scholars who wanted to tell the truth.

I was convinced then that the next target of attack, after IMEMO and Inozemtsev, would be the Institute for the Study of the U.S.A. and Canada at the Soviet Academy of Sciences, and myself personally. In fact, the attacks had already begun. In January 1982 I learned that Mikhail Suslov had criticized me (for my articles) and the institute at a meeting of the Central Committee Secretariat. Evidently the apparat was preparing in earnest.

I hope that the reader will not find me immodest for including the academic institution that I had headed since its inception among the "oases" of creative thought. The new political thinking, the new eco-

---

*Quite recently I got to hear another version of the events surrounding IMEMO. According to this version, Inozemtsev could not turn to the leadership for help because the campaign against him was at least sanctioned, if not actually instigated, by Brezhnev. Supposedly, Brezhnev was irritated by IMEMO, due to the worsening international situation and the failure of détente, of which the institute was an active supporter. This interpretation does not stand up to criticism. Brezhnev could not but have known the real reasons for the failure of détente. Apart from the political changes in the United States, they included our foreign-policy adventures, culminating in Afghanistan; the out-of-control arms race, including the deployment of SS-20 missiles in Europe; and the reaction of Western public opinion to the conservative offensive and the rise of repression in the Soviet Union. Brezhnev also knew very well that neither IMEMO nor Inozemtsev had had anything whatsoever to do with this. The leadership did not seek the advice of experts on such matters in any case—expert opinions on preserving détente and making it irreversible were simply ignored. All decisions were made under the cloak of secrecy. Most probably this version was floated by those interested in rescuing from criticism the real culprits in this ugly affair.

nomic and social ideas that later became the impetus for perestroika, did not just come out of thin air. They were incubated in the depths of our life experience, its problems and misfortunes, its disappointments and mistakes. Many of these ideas were born in discussions of the teams of specialists I have mentioned. The U.S.A. and Canada Institute was one of them.

I would like to conclude this section on a personal note. How did I and people in positions like mine react to this general deterioration in the country? Did we feel then, and do we feel now, any responsibility for what was going on?

These are difficult questions. In answering them, I will speak only for myself.

Yes, I did see the deterioration clearly. I felt it and I was troubled by it. At the same time you have to keep in mind that I did not understand or know everything. I was very pessimistic about what the future might bring, at least until the moment Andropov appeared on the political horizon as a possible heir. (And this was to happen only in May 1982.) I was afraid that after Brezhnev's death there would be a Stalinist coup.

But wherever I could, I, like many others, tried to the best of my abilities to resist this deterioration. This calmed my conscience but it did not bring me any greater confidence about the future. When we took action, we could hope only to limit damage. There was no way we could hope for a major change in the course of events, and, even less, hope for the recovery of a very sick society.

Of course, no one who was active during the years of stagnation can wash his hands clean of personal responsibility for what was happening. But at the same time, much depends on how each one behaved in a given situation. Here, the differences were very great. Often, I reviewed in my mind what I did in those years—at the institute and as a political expert during my debates and quarrels with members of the leadership. Of course, there are many things I would do differently today. There are some things that I now regret. But I do not know of anything for which I feel ashamed, or which I would have to hide.

I have to say that all of us who had believed Khrushchev, who were aroused by his speech at the Twentieth Party Congress and his bold exposure of Stalin, should have been bolder ourselves. This is our sin. We should not have allowed ourselves to be intimidated; we should not have been afraid of getting into trouble (particularly since the consequences could not have been so fearful as before). And we should have recognized more clearly the abyss into which the country was slowly sliding. The great majority did not display sufficient courage (perhaps the memory of the past weighed on everyone), including those who, by the standards of the time, were not cowards.

At the same time I do not think it is right to condemn everyone who did not follow the path of Sakharov, Solzhenitsyn, General Pyotr Grigorenko, and some other famous dissidents. This is not only because you cannot demand such self-sacrifice from everyone.

People had different convictions and outlooks on the world. After all, fighting against a social system and world outlook that you think are fundamentally flawed is one thing. Trying to reform a system and a world outlook in which, in principle, you have not lost faith is another.

Both those who sought to reform the system and those who fought against it played a role in subsequent events. Each in his own way was preparing for the radical changes that started a few years later.

Finally, it was no accident that Gorbachev and his comrades-in-arms who started de-Stalinization and perestroika came from inside, and not from outside, the system. These also were people burdened with past sins and limitations, imposed by that very system.

I pay tribute to the courage and fearlessness of those who, like Andrei Sakharov, risked taking an uncompromising stand. These people were heroes, even martyrs. And if they had not done what they did, I think the changes in our country would not have gone forward so quickly. But had it not been for the many hundreds and thousands who worked inside the system, fought routine skirmishes, tried to stop the pressure of Stalinist conservatism, and defended and promoted the ideas of democracy and peaceful economic reform, the process of revitalization would not have been possible at all.

On Some Leaders of That Period

One of the most frightening consequences of any despotism, of any totalitarian dictatorship, particularly such a long and all-embracing one as Stalinism, is the impoverishment and deterioration of the intellectual potential of a nation. And the higher you go in positions of leadership, the greater is the deterioration. A dictator is naturally afraid of strong and bright people around him. They can become rivals and, in any case, they cannot be relied upon as obedient and mindless executors of his orders. Such people are moved three, four, or five rungs down the ladder. All the conditions of life and all the rules for promotion stunt the growth of talent—particularly political talent; more, they discourage people from climbing the ladder of a political hierarchy. Totalitarian dictatorship also makes irresponsibility on the part of the leaders inevitable. Those in the highest posts dictate their writ, and this alone prevents them from being held accountable for anything. The rest are not held responsible, because all they do is follow orders from someone above. They are given great rights, but bear no responsibility.

For that reason an extreme paucity of talent and vivid personalities among the leadership was the natural price of Stalinism, and it had long-lasting consequences. One wave of human casualties followed another because totalitarianism, mass repressions, and the specific criteria and rules of selecting "the best" combined mercilessly to cut off heads at all levels of the political leadership along the way—starting at the bottom, with the district committee level, and going to the Politburo at the top. For bright, gifted people to manage to slip through the traps laid at every step of the way was a miracle, which happened only through a rare combination of good luck and extraordinary ability.

This explains the extremely low level of intellectual and managerial skills among the people Khrushchev promoted to the Politburo. They are almost all forgotten—the Frol Kozlovs, the Kirichenkos, the Ignatovs, the Mukhitdinovs, and God knows who else. They were several rungs higher up the ladder than they should have been. The same applies to the leaders in Brezhnev's incompetent entourage. (True, he inherited a considerable number of people from his predecessor.) First of all, these people were, with rare exceptions, absolute mediocrities. The education of such a "leader" usually consisted of a correspondence course when he was already ensconced in a major executive position (I can imagine how such people did on their examinations!), or some provincial institute or "Higher Party School," where the person devoted more effort to political ambition than to study. On a cultural level, can you really expect much from a person who was raised in a semiliterate family, went to a second-rate school, and has spent most of his life among dull and half-educated bureaucrats? To blame him for that would not be fair. These were objective circumstances, not acts of which he was guilty. He was selected for promotion precisely because only his obedience and discipline made him stand out from the masses. He managed to survive and navigate all the zigzags of a difficult, shattered epoch because he did not have any firm convictions of his own. He got to the top mostly because the people above him did not see him as a rival.

Against such a backdrop, Kosygin looked like an outstanding personality in 1964. He was literate, he was experienced, but he was mediocre by the standards of any high-level person in government leadership. The same could be said for A. N. Shelepin, a person who, apart from his student years (he, too, was not much of a student), had spent his whole life in the apparat—first in the Komsomol and then in the Party as a "leader," aside from a short stint as chairman of the KGB. And Shelepin, after all, was also a pretender to the "throne"!

The lives and careers of others—in particular Kirilenko, Chernenko, Polyansky, Shelest, Voronov, Solomentsev, Grishin, Demichev—all had one thing in common. They were all mediocrities who were able to rise to such a level in a great country because of the historical circumstances created by Stalin's despotism. This applied to practically all of them despite some differences in character and opinions.

More important than social background, perhaps, was social position and social perception of the world. I think that, in this respect, our post-Stalin political élite had one thing in common: basically, they all belonged to the petite bourgeoisie, or to the *meshchanstvo,* to use an old Russian word—such was their outlook on life, their ideology, their psychology, their ideals. Yet most of them tried their best to look like "great revolutionaries" and "fighters for the worker-peasant cause."

Leonid Ilyich Brezhnev

In assessing any political leader, it is important to control one's emotions, to stick to the facts and keep everything in perspective. In the case of Brezhnev, a negative assessment of him as leader of the Party and the country is perfectly justified. But one can hardly agree with the attempts to portray him as ominously as Stalin. (The expression "Stalinism-Brezhnevism," by the way, is becoming common usage in speeches and articles.) I think the reason for this emotionalism is a feeling of shame over our own silence; although we knew better, we still obediently applauded as this very little man was glorified, decorated, and praised to the skies, even as he fell into senility toward the end of his life. The main misfortune of that period, which is now called *Brezhnevshchina,* lies in the fact that Brezhnev was elevated by the course of our history and by the existing political mechanisms to a position for which he was quite unsuited.

History's paradox was that despite the wealth of evidence of Brezhnev's negative qualities, even during the long period of his decline and senility he had no rivals. The country, the Party, and the leadership were unable to produce anyone better.

I have already argued that before his illness, Brezhnev was better than the alternatives, or more correctly, he was the lesser evil. This is not the equivalent of a positive assessment of his rule, but a comment on the grievous consequences of Stalinism.

Thus we have to learn one of our most important lessons from the forty years of the post-Stalin era: the old political mechanisms had to be smashed and new ones created. Democracy, a new political culture, and an enlightened social awareness were not luxuries, but necessities. I am convinced that recognition of this has been the main mission of perestroika. Our future as a world power—even whether we *have* a future—depends on whether we fulfill this mission or not. We must look facts straight in the eye. The same applies to socialism and the socialist idea, which we have deformed to their very foundations.

Brezhnev was a typical product of the political élite of the times. He had a university diploma but was poorly educated and not really very literate. His abilities were average, his cultural level was low. On those occasions when he did read something for his own pleasure, it was usually a magazine like *Circus.** He preferred films on nature and animals, and *The Traveler's Film Almanac.* He could rarely sit through a serious film to the end. Perhaps one exception was an excellent movie about the second world war, *The Byelorussian Train Station,* which deeply moved him. I don't think he had been inside a theater for years. His greatest weaknesses as leader were his almost total ignorance of economics, his conservatism, his traditionalism, and his downright allergy to anything new.

But this does not mean that Brezhnev lacked a positive side. He was particularly artful in apparat infighting, where he showed sophisticated

---

*An obscure magazine that detailed the lives of circus performers, listed programs and appearances, etc.

cunning. In the final analysis, he managed to elbow out all his rivals and ill-wishers from the leadership. He did this slowly, without exposing himself to the risk of crises and conflicts and without using bloody repressions as Stalin had done, even without destroying his rivals verbally in public, as Khrushchev was wont to do. He obtained total obedience and submission from his comrades, and even instilled fear in them. Even such people as Andropov, Suslov, and Gromyko feared him; at least, that was my impression.

Brezhnev manipulated power very cleverly. He kept each person in the slot that he deemed most useful. Take, for example, the post of second secretary of the Central Committee. This office was never given official status, but it was essential owing to the enormous power wielded by the Central Committee Secretariat. An entire range of affairs was delegated to the second secretary by the mighty Party apparat. The position was also very uncomfortable for the general secretary (or first secretary) of the Party, since the second secretary served as a strong magnet for the apparat and Central Committee members, regional Party secretaries, and so on. The second secretary was in charge of the Secretariat, which dealt with most of the issues important to Central Committee members, regional secretaries, etc. He had to deal constantly with day-to-day affairs, large and small. By gathering senior functionaries around him, the second secretary inevitably became a potential rival to the first secretary, or at the very least was a person with whom the first secretary had to share power.

Khrushchev, after experimenting with Kozlov and Kirichenko—experiments that clearly failed—established a system whereby Central Committee secretaries and Politburo members were put in charge of the Secretariat on a rotating basis. When Khrushchev was being relieved of his power, Nikolai Podgorny started talking at the October plenum about establishing the official position of second secretary of the Central Committee. Brezhnev, I think, never forgot this, and soon transferred Podgorny to the Presidium of the Supreme Soviet.

After that he wasted no time in setting things up the way he wanted them. He always appointed two men to run the Secretariat or, at least, to lay claim to that right. They competed, not with the general secretary for power, but with each other for the right to be more second-in-command than the other. (At first these men were Suslov and Kirilenko, and then, when Kirilenko fell ill and virtually dropped out of the system, Konstantin Chernenko was promoted to his position. When Suslov died, Andropov was immediately handed the role of one of the two second secretaries.) In the realities of the apparat's power politics at that time, Brezhnev was far from being a simpleton. On the contrary, he was a grandmaster in these political chess matches. Not everyone understood this immediately, and later they had to pay for their lack of insight.

In questions of power Brezhnev was a great realist, but one who understood life within the political parameters that had taken shape under Stalin—that is, at a time when the power of the leader was determined not by the success of the economy, the people's standard of living, the popularity of the policies of the leadership, or favorable public opinion, but by force—real, brute, physical compulsion.

Brezhnev was very concerned about maintaining control over the army and the KGB. He had this control because since 1967 the loyal Andropov had been head of the KGB, and because after the death of the not very dependable Grechko, his man, Dmitri Ustinov, became minister of defense. In both places and at different levels he had more of his own people, and the leaders of both departments knew this, and daily felt themselves under his control, and therefore were doubly loyal.

Brezhnev also understood the significance of the mass media in maintaining power, especially the most important of the media—Gosteleradio and *Pravda*. In both places leadership positions were held by people who were 100 percent under his thumb.

These were powerful qualities that were important to Brezhnev himself. But did he have any positive qualities that were important to society? I am convinced that he did, at least in his first years and, of course, until he fell ill. First among them I would cite an absence of any inclination toward extremist or adventurous decisions. In his foreign policy this developed rather quickly into sincere support for the relaxing of international tensions.

In domestic affairs Brezhnev displayed the same moderation and reluctance to take a tougher political stance, even if his position may have been dictated by indecisiveness and cowardice. And this was at a time when many in the leadership were drawn to the old methods. But he sometimes gave way to the pressure. Nevertheless, he realized his responsibility and he feared sullying his name by following their lead. In many instances, he resisted this pressure from the right.

Until his illness—once again I must include this caveat—Brezhnev was not without a certain charm. He was not cruel, although in my opinion he was rancorous enough. He was a simple man and on many subjects, especially his wartime reminiscences, he was even sentimental.

He had a decidedly suspicious side; perhaps it was not innate, but stemmed from his many years in the apparat. From this, I believe, came his ability to use other people to achieve his goals, especially the more unattractive ones.

As long as Brezhnev was healthy, these negative qualities were not so noticeable. But things changed radically when he became sick. I have always said that I knew two Brezhnevs—one before and the other after his health failed.

Suspicion and love of gossip took over. At first these traits were carefully concealed, but they soon blossomed with the help of fawning sycophants. More than once it occurred to me that perhaps he suffered from something that accelerated the disintegration of his personality.* I wondered whether perhaps a disease was at work after I read a detailed description of Alzheimer's disease.

Unfortunately, Brezhnev's other negative personal characteristics had public consequences. Much rumor was stirred up by the financial abuses commonly attributed to Brezhnev. I do not think that there is any foundation, much less political sense, in launching a posthumous special investigation. But grounds for the rumors were without a doubt provided by Brezhnev himself, and especially by members of his family.

Before the eyes of millions of Soviet television viewers he openly and with obvious delight admired the famous diamond ring given to him in Baku by Geidar Aliev, the Azerbaijan party boss, Muscovites, and then the inhabitants of other cities and regions, learned of the dachas built for his son and daughter. And, of course, there were the much-talked-about "imperial hunts" and the "shooting boxes" (which were, in fact, mansions with a winter garden, a pool, and other amenities, paid for out of the defense budget. To this very day millions of rubles are being spent on the enormous complex in Zavidovo, which is maintained by the Ministry of Defense).

---

*It became absurd and funny when this formerly hospitable host (especially since the "grub" was paid for by the state) acted like Plyushkin, a greedy character in Nikolai Gogol's *Dead Souls,* vigilantly making sure that the menu for a group of specialists working with him at Zavidovo was as Spartan as possible. He would instruct the embarrassed administrators to order only soup, a main course, and cranberry pudding.

There were many facts and even more fantasies and conjectures, all of which undermined the authority of the government, the leadership, and the Party.

I would like to point out that it is impossible to attribute the financial abuses and graft, which have afflicted us like a dangerous disease, solely to political arbitrariness, unlimited power, and absence of leadership. It seems to me that this disease is a part of the genetic code of the system of economic management that has become firmly established since Stalin's time and that traces its beginnings back to "war communism."

Even now, in discussions about paths to economic reform and a market economy, attempts are made to link these manifestations of corruption to capitalism—either to the vestiges of capitalism, or to its underground forms inherent in the shadow economy, or to market relations themselves. In fact, although capitalism provides no insurance against corruption and white-collar crime, and is not devoid of numerous scandals, it is not so organically connected with corruption as the Soviet Union's administrative-command economy. The latter is a system where, on the one hand, everything belongs to the people, which turns out to mean that it belongs to nobody. From top to bottom, the temptation arises to appropriate something for oneself. On the other hand, an enormous, and parasitic, apparat is created. It gives or takes away, permits or prohibits, takes care of everything, can fire anybody, demote anybody, often even throw him in prison or, on the contrary, raise him up. And who with such power at his disposal can resist temptation?

Hence it follows that no matter how important it is to intensify the struggle of law and order against corruption, this effort is doomed to failure until we do away with the old economic model that grew out of war communism and Stalinism, which surprisingly reached its peak during Gaidar's reforms, where it was in some way married to the robber-baron period of capitalism.

I have already mentioned that in all of the unseemly affairs sowing mass dissatisfaction in the soil, a not insignificant role was played by Brezhnev's family. Of course, it is hard to dispute the argument that he bears the responsibility—for he not only tolerated but may even have encouraged the low morals of members of his family, especially his children. A chain of corruption linking his family, numerous relatives, and also people who were close to him stretched to Moscow from all his former places of employment in Ukraine and Moldavia.

There were some things he could not help but see. They used to say, for example, that he often bitterly complained about his daughter's behavior and his son's heavy drinking bouts. (In general he tried to spend a minimum of time at home; my impression is that his frequent trips to Zavidovo, where he tried to stay as long as possible, were mainly an escape from his family.) But this did not prevent him from trying to cover up his daughter's scandalous behavior. And without his knowledge and consent, her last husband—Churbanov—simply could not have achieved such a head-spinning career.

Within only a few years Churbanov became a lieutenant general, and from an ordinary political-police worker he became first deputy minister of internal affairs. He was elected to top Party positions and received awards, cars, dachas. The same applies to Brezhnev's son, who was appointed deputy minister of foreign trade. While heading crucial trade negotiations, the son used to wear dark glasses to hide the evidence of his hangovers.

This nepotism wasn't limited to Brezhnev's family. As often happens, the positive trait of supporting one's comrades developed into a more negative one: patronage awarded to old friends. To a certain extent, this was part of his clever personnel policy. He wanted to place his own people in key positions, and was able to, even if they were completely unsuited. The main thing was that they be devoted to him. To this was added a lack of willpower when he was put under pressure from relatives, friends, and acquaintances straining for power and perks.

Either consciously or intuitively, Brezhnev avoided strong, bright personalities, preferring gray, mediocre people and those with extremely questionable morals. Shchelokov was one such person. Brezhnev understood perfectly well where the levers of power were located, and therefore he was quick to name his own man to the post of minister of internal affairs, the major state body for the protection of law and order. He had known Shchelokov for a long time, and apparently was convinced of his devotion. Shchelokov was not only a mediocre, worthless person, but also amoral and criminal, having misappropriated museum treasures and stolen jewelry that had been confiscated from criminals by his ministry. Under his leadership, the corruption of the Ministry of Internal Affairs reached the broadest possible scale. Honest employees were persecuted and there was evidence of serious embezzlement.

Evidently Shchelokov sensed that he had gone too far and, like a man on thin ice, tried to slide forward as quickly as possible. He wanted to assure himself immunity under Brezhnev and, as much as possible, after him. It was his dream to become head of the KGB and a member of the Politburo. Perhaps at some stage of his illness Brezhnev would have given in to the frantic pressure of his old friend and appointed him to the KGB. But most of the members of the leadership were horrified by such a possibility.

Several times I heard, in particular from Andropov, about how he agreed with Arvid Pelshe, the head of the Party Control Committee, a watchdog over Party morals, and Suslov that together or separately they would, as resolutely as possible, raise the question of Shchelokov with Brezhnev. They believed that his career had to be stopped, or, best of all, that he should be removed. I know that this question was put to Brezhnev, though I am not certain it was presented with sufficient vigor. As a result of these efforts, they may well have put a stop to Shchelokov's forward run, although he had achieved more than enough: he was a general of the army, a member of the Central Committee, and a Hero of Socialist Labor, and he even had a doctorate in economics.*

Shchelokov was, of course, an odious figure; it's hard to compare him with anybody else. But Brezhnev placed other unappealing people in key positions. For example, he considered it necessary to have several personally devoted, absolutely trustworthy people in the KGB, and he kept them in high positions as deputy chairmen. Even though he trusted Andropov, he still wanted to keep him in check. After all, Andropov was not 100 percent Brezhnev's man, not someone whom Brezhnev had elevated through the ranks, as were Semyon Tsvigun and Georgi Tsinev. Both these men were also generously given awards and titles, and both were disliked and feared by honest people. One of them—Tsvigun—

---

*After Brezhnev's death Shchelokov was removed from his job, and then reduced in military rank. He was stripped of the title "General of the Army." His wife soon committed suicide. And then he did. The military authorities had called him to warn him that they were coming to take away the special medal of a general of the army (a gold star with diamonds). But he had apparently decided that they were coming to arrest him, so he shot himself.

killed himself while Brezhnev was still alive. (The Western press somehow connected Tsvigun's suicide with some criminal cases involving Brezhnev's daughter, but I am not about to judge that.) Tsinev continued to work in the KGB for several years after Brezhnev's death, and then, as a general of the army, he joined a special retirement group in the Ministry of Defense.

I am deeply convinced that the most harmful appointment, one that was absolutely monstrous for the country, was the one elevating Nikolai A. Tikhonov, a semiliterate, untalented man and one of Brezhnev's old buddies, to the critical position of chairman of the Council of Ministers of the U.S.S.R. Tikhonov made no small contribution to the economic decline of our state.

Brezhnev's vanity, always a strong component of his character, assumed outrageous proportions in his last years. The most absurd manifestation of this was his passion for awards. I was amazed at how this man, who was perfectly familiar with the entire award-giving system and who himself had conferred many of them on numerous people, could attribute such enormous significance to them. It reminded me of the passionate desire of young officers during the war to return home with a chestful of medals. But it became almost a craze—he ceased to realize that he was conferring awards on himself, while those around him kept feeding him pretexts for new ones to further their careers.

Brezhnev's literary exploits were another result of his inner circle's fueling his pathological vanity. I don't know who initiated it, but Chernenko and supposedly Ustinov, Leonid Zamyatin, and Vitali Ignatenko played a big role and advanced themselves nicely. Brezhnev was not a bad storyteller; before he got sick he had a good memory and often shared witty and gripping stories from his youth, his years at the front, and his later experiences. He often repeated himself, but his audiences listened, laughed, and expressed their approval. The sycophants often suggested to him that he write all these stories down. He would not be doing the actual writing—he generally never wrote anything—but would dictate it, and then someone would put it in decent shape. This idea remained a bad joke until it was transformed into a nightmarish reality. A small group of writers was put together and supplied with documents and the tapes of Brezhnev's dictated "fairy tales." Of course, they were given the opportunity to talk with some of the witnesses of those events they intended to include. The whole project was kept strictly secret, so that I learned of it only a few weeks before part one was to be published in the journal *Novy Mir*.

The most monstrous part of the affair was not the ghostwriting, but what followed publication. All three parts of this notorious trilogy—*Malaya Zemlya, Virgin Soil,* and *Rebirth*—were greeted by a deafening roar of well-organized ecstasy. The issues of *Novy Mir* containing part one and the two parts that followed became virtually obligatory reading within the Party education system. The Writers' Union immediately nominated the work for the Lenin Prize, which was hurriedly awarded. A significant number of famous writers published enraptured reviews of this trash, which had been created by the hands of others, and often unskilled hands to boot. I do not criticize or justify these reviewers, who were asked to write reviews and were afraid to refuse; they remembered that such refusals had often led to ostracism in the past. The reviews laid emphasis on the literary qualities of the work, even though literally every person in our enormous state, even the worst simpletons, knew that not a single page of this literary chef d'oeuvre had actually been written by Brezhnev.

In and of itself, this literary epic had not been all that expensive compared with other enormous costs incurred at the whim of our leadership. At the same time, I am convinced that the moral blow it dealt to our social consciousness was enormous: a shameful spectacle had been staged before the entire nation—a spectacle in which neither the audience nor the actors believed (aside from the main actor, the author). This episode added a large dose to the public's distrust of the government and encouraged the apathy and cynicism that were already eating away at people's souls. In a symbolic sense, the episode was an epitaph to a tragic period in our lives. This was stagnation in the true meaning of the word, and I would say its peak was 1975–1982.

Yuri Vladimirovich Andropov

I have already commented on Andropov's remarkable mind, his political talents, and his intellectual bent, which was so unusual for a political leader of the day. Although he did not have a formal education, Andropov stood out among the ruling class, some of whom had university diplomas and even scientific or scholarly degrees. I might note that this distinction was not always useful for his career.

Perhaps understanding this, perhaps out of an inborn modesty, he was a little shy and attempted to conceal his learning so as to appear simpler and more primitive than he actually was. He was known for his personal selflessness, which on occasion even extended to asceticism. Andropov also stood out morally among the members of the leadership. In political matters, the qualities that displayed themselves in his personal life coexisted with a more flexible reality; he was exceedingly permissive with regard to unattractive, even ugly "rules of the game," and to the low standards for personal relations that prevailed in higher political society for many long years.

I must note that my appraisal of Andropov, objective as I may strive to be, may not be totally unbiased. At times my attitude toward him was so positive that I knew it bordered on reverence, while at others I was full of disappointment, even bitterness, when he caved in at important moments. I was not blind to his inadequacies and mistakes. I not only noticed them, but I also pointed them out to him, and that occasionally led to a cooling of relations, to hurt feelings, and even to quarrels.

On the whole we enjoyed good relations, although differences in our positions and views naturally prevented us from becoming particularly close. In the presence of others, he always addressed me by my first name and patronymic—the most formal form of address in Russian. Only during rather rare intimate discussions did he address me by my first name only. For my part, I permitted myself no such familiarities with him; indeed the very temptation did not exist. On the other hand, I frequently spoke openly with him. He realized that, and when he wanted to get an utterly frank opinion, he would try to tease that frankness out of me—usually with success. At times I would use the same ploy with him, but, I have to admit, with less success; he was by far my superior in life experience and in dealing with people.

Our acquaintance, arranged by Otto Kuusinen, was a long-standing one. In the early 1960s I was asked to participate in one of the analytic groups he was directing. From 1964 to 1967 I served under him at Central Committee headquarters, first as a consultant, and later as director of a consulting group (which made me something like his deputy). When Andropov was appointed chairman of the KGB, he kept up friendly relations with me and some of his other former employees at Central Committee headquarters, frequently telephoning and from time to time calling us into his office. In my case that was usually once every couple of months. I have to admit that I went to those meetings at Lubyanka with some consternation, remembering what those walls had witnessed. After Andropov returned to the Central Committee in May 1982, I met with him more frequently, at both his initiative and my own.

This relationship of more than twenty years was based on sincere respect. It did not waver despite my understanding of Andropov's weaknesses or my disagreements and even quarrels with him on a number of questions, including some of major importance. I was also prompted by a sense of duty. I believed that when I set forth my opinion or supplied him with information I could, to some minimal degree, induce him to make what I considered the correct decisions and prevent him from making those that to me appeared incorrect or dangerous. Finally, there were people whom I wanted to save from threatening situations or protect from unjust persecution—where possible, reestablishing justice.

Through him I managed to cancel jail sentences for some people, including Belokon, a famous director of an Odessa collective farm who had been unjustly convicted. Belokon was a war invalid and a Hero of Socialist Labor. I also managed to help a number of people who were in trouble over having signed petitions and were considered dissenters. Never once did I ask him for anything for myself, although on occasion he did fend off slanderous denunciations against me. He even showed me some of these denunciations (probably to ensure that I didn't get too careless).*

---

*On one occasion he called me in and gave me a long, unsigned letter to read. (Later I learned the author's name; he was a prominent Soviet journalist and an acquaintance of long standing. I don't want to name him, since he's dead now, but he was a KGB informer, as many who knew him surmised.) In the letter, which described his conversation with a certain American, I was described as "Rockefeller's man," and even as a possible CIA agent. The text struck me as familiar, and I realized that it was a rehash of an article from a tabloid published by Lyndon LaRouche, an extreme right-winger—in my opinion, a fascist. After I had read the denunciation, I asked Andropov if I should attempt to clear myself and write an explanation. "No, of course not," he replied. "I just wanted to show you for your own information." I answered: "And I would like you to know the true nature of your informers." I told him the source of the accusations, and he was somewhat embarrassed. The next day I sent him a photocopy of the article, together with a transla-

At the time I did not give any particular thought to the reason for his interest in good relations with me. First, Andropov knew (and on one occasion even said to me) that I would not tell him lies out of a desire to please him or to avoid upsetting him (even though he knew that I would not tell him the *entire* truth in all instances). Back then that was an unusual attitude for someone who had regular dealings with the leadership and, judging from what I know of his close contact with other colleagues, he valued it.

Second, he must have felt a measure of interest and confidence in my judgments (although he frequently checked them)—primarily in questions of foreign policy. Third, he was interested in my opinions (and those of others) to get firsthand knowledge about the mood of the intelligentsia. Obviously he did not want to rely on the KGB reports alone. Fourth, like anybody else, he liked heart-to-heart chats. In time he came to realize that I never deceived him and that I knew when to keep my mouth shut on delicate issues.

On a personal level he was virtually irreproachable. He stood out among the leaders of the day in his indifference to luxury and his determination to keep his family out of the limelight. His son worked in my institute for several years, drawing a salary of 120 rubles, but whenever the conversation came around to him, Andropov would invariably say, "Give him as much work as possible." At one point he indignantly mentioned that his son's expectations had gotten ahead of his needs: the man had requested a two-bedroom apartment instead of a one-bedroom, even though he and his wife had only one child. However, the children of other Politburo members with families of this size had two- and even three-bedroom apartments.

I remember another episode: I mentioned to him that a certain scoundrel had bought up a shipment of Mercedeses and Volvos, which he sold to children of prominent politicians. The proud new owners were driving around town, inspiring resentment and hard feelings among those who were unable to afford such luxuries. Andropov grew red in the face and said: "If you're hinting at anything here, you should know that I have only one domestically produced Volga for my entire

---

tion. I might note here that Lyndon LaRouche's organization made me the object of harassment. They would send their agents to disrupt my lectures and set up pickets—not only in the United States, but in Western Europe as well.

family, and I bought it eight years ago for cash." A few moments later, when he had recovered his composure, he said that such a practice was not only an example of sheer degeneracy, but also an instance of political indiscretion: "But you can see yourself that it makes no sense for me to raise a row over this, with virtually all our top officials involved."

Andropov knew how to put the people he met at ease. This was not a game for him, but rather reflected the attractive side of his personality. I know of no instance when he intentionally committed any base act for its own sake.

At the same time he was fully capable of abandoning a person, even someone he liked. He had other negative traits—indecisiveness, faint-heartedness, and cowardice—which frequently came to the fore not only in political matters, but also when he should have defended this or that person, or this or that idea, more strenuously. I don't believe that this was an innate defect. I believe, rather, that like the majority of his generation who made their careers under Stalin, he had been deeply traumatized, frightened for life, by the experience. This trauma was present in Andropov, albeit possibly to a lesser degree than in many other politicians, but it seems to me that this weakness drew him into a readiness to agree too easily to serious compromise.

In his heart, Andropov seemed to recognize this; he attempted to justify it. Such compromises, concessions, withdrawal from the fight were rationalized as "tactical necessities." He was not at all loath to discuss such necessities out loud. He would frequently rebuke me: "You see things correctly and you're not a bad strategist, but you're a lousy tactician." ("Lousy" was one of the more genteel terms he used.) Sometimes I would agree with his criticism, sometimes not. On one occasion I couldn't restrain myself and told him that the approach he always suggested (it was a question of internal affairs) would get bogged down in endless tactics, with a total loss of strategy. Andropov was offended; for a time our relations cooled, but they were later reestablished.

Another of Andropov's weaknesses was his serious misappraisal of people. On some occasions he got too carried away by tactics. And there were times when these misappraisals were the product of his own contradictory political views.

He mixed his successes in selecting the appropriate people (he made some real finds!) with serious mistakes. While working in the Central Committee, he did manage to gather a strong consulting group around him.* But if one considers his recruitment and promotion of people while he was part of the political leadership of the Party and the country, one is confronted by political contradictions that are difficult to explain.

Andropov was one of the first to appreciate such an outstanding political figure as Mikhail S. Gorbachev. I know that for a fact, having first heard his name from Andropov in the spring of 1977. I remember the date because we were discussing the results of the Cyrus Vance visit and Brezhnev's illness. At that point I remarked bluntly that we were on the road to major problems, since everything I knew indicated that our up-and-coming Party functionaries were weak and politically suspect. The comment made Andropov angry (perhaps because he basically agreed with my appraisal of the situation), and he began to object harshly: "There you go, running off at the mouth, but you don't know those people and just want to criticize everything. For example, have you ever heard the name Gorbachev?" I had to admit I had not. "There, you see? We have entirely new people coming up, people who can bear our hopes into the future." I don't recall just how that particular conversation ended, but I heard Andropov mention Gorbachev's name for a second time in the summer of 1978, just after the death of Fyodor D. Kulakov, the former secretary of the Central Committee responsible for agriculture.

After a lengthy, businesslike conversation that touched upon my appraisal of the situation in the United States and the American reaction to our deployment of SS-20s in Europe, the talk shifted to domestic questions. At that point Andropov suddenly, without any direct connection to the thread of the conversation, said as if thinking out loud: "Those bastards don't want Gorbachev transferred to Moscow." In re-

*Incidentally, when a Soviet journal published an excerpt from my memoirs, I was asked: Why did Andropov need such a strong consulting group? I have discussed one of the reasons. Given the polemics being conducted with the Chinese leadership, the complicated situation within the Communist movement, and the political entity that at the time was called the socialist commonwealth, there was a real need to develop a knowledgeable discipline in both theory and politics. Another reason may have been more personal. As a creative person, and one who was still buoyed up by the direction of the Twentieth Party Congress, Andropov wanted to gather around him intelligent and educated people with whom he could work out the problems that troubled him. But only recently have I realized that he may also have wanted to assemble a strong brain trust, having in mind his future political career, although it is difficult for me to imagine him considering being leader of the government at that early date.

sponse to my bewildered question, he explained that he was thinking of appointing Gorbachev to Kulakov's position. Then he changed the topic. But in the fall of that year (I can't say for sure just how circumstances developed) Gorbachev was given the appointment. (Not long after that I met him for the first time, during preparations for the latest plenary meeting of the Central Committee.)

Gorbachev's appearance in Moscow as secretary of the Central Committee was undoubtedly an event of historic significance. And Andropov's role in bringing about his appointment was one of his real coups (although this does not exclude the possibility that such an outstanding man as Gorbachev might well have found other ways into the leadership).

But Andropov's fortunate selection was balanced by several failures. Among other things, he invited to the Politburo the odious Grigori V. Romanov from Leningrad. He made Geidar Aliev his protégé, simply not knowing of, much less having been a part of, that extreme corruption and abuse of power of which Aliev was later accused (I am absolutely convinced of this); he simply failed to understand the man's abilities and character. Finally, it was Andropov who brought Yegor K. Ligachev from Tomsk to Moscow and appointed him chief of personnel of the Central Committee. (True, in his memoirs Ligachev credits his appointment to Gorbachev, but I am certain that Andropov would not have appointed anyone to that crucial position who did not enjoy his total confidence, no matter what backing the person had.) Evidently, Andropov chose Ligachev because of his intolerance of corruption.

As far as I could tell, Andropov did not suffer from any excessive ambition or careerism, from any striving to be "first," even though he played the game according to definite rules and must have thought of career and power. I do not exclude the possibility that he had begun seriously to think of himself as Brezhnev's successor chiefly because he saw no other worthy candidate.*

The absence of worthy contenders for leadership must have led him to think that he could become the political leader of the Party and the country, regardless of his personal desires. Besides, given our cruel polit-

---

*Andropov was plagued by poor health. On one occasion, in 1981, I noticed that under his cuffs he had gauze bandages on both wrists. Only later did I realize that the bandages hid the devices by which he could be hooked up to a dialysis machine.

ical system and its traditions, none of our leaders could help but fear the next ruler, who might make short work of him. The inevitable conclusion is that, if possible, it is better and safer to end up on top of the heap yourself.

I believe that the prospect of leading the country was crystallized for Andropov in early 1982, after Suslov's death. As early as February, rumors began to circulate that Andropov was being groomed to take Suslov's place. Soon after that I had the opportunity to ask Andropov whether these rumors were at all justified. In asking the question, I quipped that since taking up my duties at Central Committee headquarters I had ceased believing rumors about personnel shifts, and after I became an academician I was able to justify my lack of faith scientifically: rumors were based on common sense, but Central Committee personnel decisions followed different, "more lofty" paths. Andropov laughed and said that this time the rumors were correct. Just a few days after Suslov's death Brezhnev asked Andropov to return to the Central Committee as secretary. Brezhnev formulated his offer in the following words: "Let's decide it at the next meeting of the Politburo, and you can move into your new job the following week." "I thanked him for his confidence," Andropov confided, "but I reminded him that the Central Committee secretaries had to be elected at plenary meetings of the Central Committee, and were not appointed by the Politburo. At that point Brezhnev suggested that a plenary meeting be called the following week. I remarked that it made no sense to call a special session just for this, and that the election procedure could be conducted at the next meeting, scheduled for May. Brezhnev growled a little, but agreed."

The impression I got from the conversation was that Andropov had mixed feelings about the proposal. I could guess at his reasons. On the one hand, he wanted to return to the Central Committee, if only because he realized that after the next change in leadership (Brezhnev's illness was progressing) the chairman of the KGB would find himself in an exceedingly vulnerable position. To appoint the head of the secret police to be the leader of Party and country, as I have written earlier, would have been a violation of all tradition, and our leaders were very traditional people. So someone else would have become Brezhnev's successor. But no matter who it turned out to be, the new leader would first of all replace the chairman of the KGB, since that person knew too much, including personal information about the leader. Besides, the new leader would prefer to have his own man in that position. In that sense there were a lot of arguments in favor of accepting the new appointment. On the other hand, Andropov told me directly that he could not but have been troubled by the question of Brezhnev's reasons for making such an offer. Brezhnev seemed never to have given any thought to his own death and possible successors. Did Brezhnev really want Andropov to head the Central Committee, or was he simply attempting to remove him as KGB chief?

Had I known certain other details, I would have harbored still further doubts about Andropov's attitude toward this offer. I have in mind the fact that Brezhnev did not heed Andropov's advice about Andropov's replacement; instead of Viktor Chebrikov, Brezhnev appointed Fedorchuk, who had formerly headed the Ukrainian KGB. There was also the circumstance that certain criminal cases had touched upon Brezhnev's immediate family (as I wrote earlier, there were people who linked the death of Andropov's deputy Tsvigun to this circumstance, and Tsvigun was very close to Brezhnev).

Regardless of the real motives behind this affair, Andropov changed jobs that May and ensconced himself in the fifth-floor office formerly occupied by Suslov. (In late 1982 his chair was taken by Chernenko, then Gorbachev, followed by Ligachev.) I am convinced that Andropov understood very well that he had moved into a position that made him the most probable successor to Brezhnev as general secretary of the Central Committee. By then events were impelling him to seek the position of number two man in the leadership. A struggle ensued over the appointment, even though Andropov did not seem to have a single worthy opponent.

This was a curious period. Brezhnev, as well as his cohorts, some acting out of a sense of self-preservation and others out of a fear of people who had formerly competed with Brezhnev, established power in the hands of a small group of leaders dominated by the general secretary right up until his last days. Every person in that group had what amounted to life tenure as long as he could more or less stand upright. They were also so old that sheer physiology came to play a crucial role in politics. Sometimes it was simply a matter of who would outlive whom.

For example, if Chernenko's health had been better, or if Suslov had lived for another year, it is entirely possible that Andropov would never have become general secretary, as he did in November 1982. His move back to the Central Committee was essential for taking over the post of general secretary. But of course it could not resolve all these problems automatically. In the summer and early fall of 1982 I frequently spoke to Andropov, even though he usually displayed a good deal of reserve in talking about what was taking place among the leadership, and especially about any internal struggles.

Almost immediately after Andropov became secretary of the Central Committee, Chernenko and Brezhnev went on vacation. Andropov utilized this situation for his own purposes in a number of ways. Among other things, he pushed through the transfer to Moscow of Sergei Medunov, who had been first secretary of the Krasnodar Regional Party Committee; this was a man who, together with Shchelokov, had become a symbol of unrestrained corruption. The transfer had enormous practical significance; while in Krasnodar, Medunov had been able easily to block the investigation of misdeeds in his region. Andropov, on the other hand, was eager to lance this boil, hoping thus to defuse the political situation and encourage the fight against corruption in other areas as well. True, from their vacation spots in the south our leaders issued signals of displeasure. And those signals came not just from Chernenko but from Brezhnev as well, even though Andropov said he had gotten Brezhnev's approval by telephone for the transfer.

As far as I am able to determine, at that moment Andropov had lost his former close contact with Brezhnev and could not be confident that his enemies were not hatching intrigues against him behind his back. Among other things, the new chairman of the KGB, Fedorchuk, initiated a restructuring of the organization, which troubled Andropov. (Just why, I can't say, but he was noticeably nervous when talking about it.) And there were other matters that angered Andropov. In the summer and fall of 1982 he was frequently in a bad mood.

Later—I believe it was the twentieth of October, just a few days after Andropov had returned from his holiday—I was summoned to his office (I had requested a meeting the day before to discuss a replacement for Inozemtsev, who had just died). I had never before seen Andropov in such an elevated, excited mood. Just two hours earlier he had had a heart-to-heart talk with Brezhnev. "I got my courage up," he said, "and stated outright that I did not understand my position and that I wanted to know what it was that the leadership, and Leonid Ilyich personally, wanted to achieve in moving me to this new job—to remove me from the KGB or to entrust to me more important Central Committee affairs." Brezhnev heard him out and told him that he wanted him to take control of the entire establishment: "You are the number two man in the Party and the country, so base your actions on that and make use of your authority." And he promised him his full support. This untied Andropov's hands—in the Politburo, in the Secretariat, and at Central Committee headquarters, where Chernenko's position was particularly strong and Andropov's was not at all simple.

Barely three weeks after that conversation Brezhnev died and Andropov became his successor. Perhaps Brezhnev foresaw his own death? Or was it sheer chance? I don't know.

More important, however, is the political evaluation of Andropov's role throughout the period during which he was in the leadership. I will express my own views and suppositions, but there are a number of details that I simply do not know, particularly with regard to Andropov's work in the KGB. He almost never spoke with me on that topic, even though I could infer certain things and compare them with what I learned elsewhere.

The first position Andropov held that made it possible for him to influence politics was that of Soviet ambassador to Hungary. He occupied that post from 1954 to 1957.

All my Soviet informants agree that the cables sent by Andropov to Moscow during the months preceding the armed uprising of enemies of the Rákosi regime in the fall of 1956 were unusually frank and even blunt. (Possibly this reporting saved his political career after the Hungarian events, when, in his own words, his communiqués home "were studied in microscopic detail.") Among other things, Andropov referred critically to Rákosi and other Hungarian leaders, warning that if we continued to stake our policy on them, everything could turn out catastrophically. At the same time, I do not exclude the possibility that his recommendations also contained proposals to strengthen "law and order," conceivably by building up our military presence in Hungary.

This would not surprise me, for the simple reason that it would have fitted our imperial thinking at the time, chiefly with regard to the countries of Eastern Europe, which were called socialist thanks to us. In the late 1940s, these countries had a political regime and an economic model imposed upon them that corresponded to our ideas about socialism. That was one of the major failures of our policy. Rather than strive toward good relations with our neighbors on the basis of mutual respect, we opted for a military-political union accompanied by crude interference in their internal affairs. The price for that decision was revolt—in Berlin in 1953, in Hungary in 1956, and in Czechoslovakia in 1968. But the true hour of reckoning came in the late 1980s, when this entire structure collapsed like a house of cards.

The abnormal and dangerous situation that had developed after forced "socialization" of the Eastern European countries in the late 1940s did not go unnoticed. As early as the first years following Stalin's death, an understanding developed, albeit with difficulty, that we had to take into account the economic and political interests of our allies. That understanding could have led to a new approach in our relations.

Andropov was probably unable to free himself from the contradictions of the Stalinist and post-Stalinist approaches. But judging from what I know, he stood out among the other ambassadors in his greater openness to new ideas. Also, he was quicker than his colleagues to realize that in the country in which he was an ambassador he could not behave as if he were a party boss in his region back home.

The tragic events in Hungary in late October and early November of 1956 made a deep impression on Andropov, for he found himself at their epicenter. He really did understand them (he told me this himself) as an armed counterrevolution that had to be suppressed, and that appraisal influenced his political thinking. At the same time, I am certain, he realized better than others that the collapse of the Hungarian government and the scope and intensity of the mass discontent were not so much counterrevolutionary conspiracy and dirty tricks played by foreign countries as the result of Stalinist perversions transplanted to Hungarian soil, where they took on an even uglier form (if that was possible). He was also aware of the effect of problems created by the inequitable position of Hungary in trade and economic relations with the Soviet Union.

Andropov's attitude toward the developments in Hungary must have been influenced by personal and deeply emotional impressions. He received a flow of reports about the activities of the rebels, about how mercilessly they settled scores with Communists, Party workers, and civil servants. He suffered a number of attacks himself. I knew that the events had caused the serious, life-long illness of his wife. There was shooting all around the embassy, and Andropov came under fire as he headed to the airport to meet Mikoyan.

One should not overestimate Andropov's intellectual and political maturity in 1956, when he was a forty-two-year-old provincial Party functionary who had grown up in the Stalin period, who still had had no international experience, and who had been brought up on ideological dogma. I had the impression that the peculiarities of Andropov's intellectual baggage, together with the historic events at whose center he found himself, had created in him what people who knew Andropov later called the Hungarian syndrome. This they defined as a guarded attitude toward domestic difficulties in the socialist countries. I interpret that to mean an excessive readiness to make very radical decisions to prevent these tensions from escalating into a severe crisis. At the same time, one must admit that, unlike many other Soviet politicians, he took an attitude toward such crises that was by no means primitive, for he perceived their deeper economic, political, and ideological components and, while he did not exclude the use of force, he did not limit himself to it.

This last quality is related to another element that distinguished Andropov from many of his colleagues. Once the armed opponents of the government had been crushed, Andropov's first thought was not of vengeance and settling scores, but of quickly reestablishing civil peace. That was why he supported, as far as was possible, the candidacy of János Kádár to head the Party, which meant that Kádár would be the new leader of Hungary. Rákosi had had Kádár imprisoned, tortured, and threatened with execution. I know that there were many in Moscow who did not look favorably on Andropov's recommendation. The very fact that Kádár had been imprisoned and felt himself wronged was sufficient in their eyes to influence his attitude toward the Soviet Union, since he knew that Rákosi must have received Moscow's approval for the arrest. Did that not mean that Kádár might turn out to be an unreliable ally who would lead Hungary down a path hostile to Moscow?

There were such doubts in the Kremlin—similar to the doubts harbored by the Soviet leadership with regard to the Polish leader Gomuľka, whose fate was not unlike that of Kádár. Andropov, however, managed to convince Moscow that Kádár should be the leader. Kádár's assumption of power helped to extract Hungary from its deep crisis and make it a healthier society.

I was able to observe Andropov's activities at closer hand at Central Committee headquarters while he was in charge of relations with other allied countries. On the whole, I believe that he exercised a positive influence on our policies during his term in this very important office. We must take into account that he acted within the framework of political concepts that were considered irrefutable.

The period following the October 1964 plenary meeting of the Central Committee was a very complex one. Andropov, who had been out of favor and seriously ill, actively supported the more progressive line and attempted to influence Brezhnev in that direction. I believe that in this respect his role within the leadership was unique; I know of no other person in a similar position who at that moment would have openly opposed Stalinism and supported a policy of reform and peaceful coexistence. At the same time, Andropov was very cautious, observing all the rules of tactics (on occasion even overusing them).

As far as I am able to tell, his leadership of the KGB had both negative and positive sides to it.

First of all, one must bear in mind that during that period the leadership was inclined to return to Stalinism at least partially, albeit not to its extreme forms. A few times I heard from Andropov, and I was informed by other trustworthy people that some in the Politburo were insisting on the arrests of dissidents and of persons who criticized the system and openly expressed critical opinions. For example, I know there were demands that important members of the cultural and scientific communities, such as Solzhenitsyn and Sakharov, be arrested. These demands were accompanied by harsh remarks about the "liberal" attitudes of the officials in charge of law enforcement and state security.

Andropov did not want to go along with this, and probably did everything he felt he could to resist it. He was in part motivated by moral conviction, for he had been molded of different clay from the Yagodas (Genrikh Yagoda was head of the secret police in the early 1930s and the predecessor of Yezhov), Yezhovs, and Berias who preceded him in office. And he was also cautious, for he had learned the lessons of the Twentieth Party Congress, which exposed the misuse of power by the security apparatus. He was protecting his good name, and he was thinking of the future.

Nevertheless, the KGB not only arrested and convicted people who were later found innocent and rehabilitated, but it initiated revolting practices to suppress dissidents; these new methods were becoming widely known.

Andropov had to bear the responsibility for this. And it is extremely difficult—even for people who respected him—to justify this on the grounds that he engaged in such practices—sanctioned them—in order to avoid the harsher measures demanded by some of his colleagues. It is true that such demands were made, and Andropov was thus able to justify his actions to himself. It is by no means my intention here to play the role of moralist. For example, I have no doubt that he agreed to head the KGB in 1967 not only out of loyalty to Brezhnev and his own ambitions, but also because it would have been dangerous to yield this crucial, strategic position to someone else. He must have understood that there was a price to be paid for this decision. As head of the KGB, Andropov had to carry out certain tough actions with regard to spies, traitors, and irreconcilable enemies of the regime.

But the fact remains that, passively or actively, Andropov allowed himself to be drawn into some very nasty affairs. Despite what he wrote in the poem I quoted earlier about power corrupting people, he was not an exception to the general rule; he succumbed to the moral corruption that emanates from power and high position.

I must mention one project that was very dear to him—the idea of organizing within the KGB structure a so-called Fifth Directorate. (I think the idea originally came to him from some of the older employees of the KGB, but that, of course, in no way clears him of the responsibility.)

I first heard about this plan soon after Andropov had been transferred to the KGB. One day he stated with pride that he had separated out "work with the intelligentsia" from counterespionage. He said it was not permissible to treat writers, scholars, and scientists as potential spies and hand them over to experts in counterespionage. Now, he said, things would be different; the intelligentsia would be entrusted to different people, and the emphasis would be on the prevention of "undesirable phenomena."

At that time it was easier to disagree with Andropov; he had just left the Central Committee and still did not feel that he was one of the leaders. I worked up my courage and voiced an objection. First of all, I said, I did not understand why the KGB had to "work with" the intelligentsia. After all, it did not "work with" the working class or the peasantry. I conceded that if certain members of the intelligentsia, just like any other social class, were to take the path of crime, the path of counterrevolutionary conspiracies and anti-Soviet activities, then that might be a matter for the KGB. But it seemed to me that the rest should remain within the sphere of other institutions—the Central Committee, the creative organizations, and so on, but no punitive bodies, whether they were classified as counterespionage groups or given some other new name. Second, I did not like the idea of "professionalizing" KGB agents in their work with the intelligentsia, of entrusting the intelligentsia to some specific body in that organization. Would they not end up like the tsarist gendarmes who "worked with" the intelligentsia and were described by Maxim Gorky in his novel *The Life of Klim Samgin*? Would they not follow the practices of Benkendorf? (Benkendorf was head of the tsarist secret police, and Pushkin and other writers were forced to endure a great deal because of him.) Andropov was offended by this comparison, and said I was out of touch with reality and did not understand what was going on in society; his plan represented a significant step forward, it was a rejection of the bad old practices—and was not in any way a return to "gendarme" activities.

Nevertheless, I expressed still another doubt—that the creation of a special directorate would not lead to a reduction, but to an increase in the number of problems with the intelligentsia. My logic was quite simple: this was not the basic responsibility of counterespionage, whose chief mission was to catch spies. Once we created a special directorate, it would have to justify its existence. If it had no real work, it would have to invent work, and that could create serious problems.

Andropov did not agree with these objections; he said that I was a stranger to this field (something I could not help agreeing with), but that I would in time see that these changes had proven beneficial.

Later I got the impression from Andropov and others that he was keenly interested in the work of this new directorate. Still a neophyte in KGB affairs, he was carried away sometimes and had too much confidence in its employees. But the activities of the directorate were far from benevolent and added one more shameful page to the history of the KGB. There were a number of personal tragedies. The moral and political climate in the country had worsened, and our image was damaged still further in the eyes of the world community.

Andropov bears responsibility for many injustices in the 1970s and early 1980s: for persecuting dissidents, for political arrests, for deportations, for the misuse of psychiatry, for notorious cases such as the persecution of Academician Sakharov. There is no escaping these painful facts. At the same time, he pulled individual intellectuals out of scrapes and protected them.

Under Andropov, especially as his political influence increased, the KGB grew noticeably in political power, in personnel, and even in the number of buildings it occupied in Moscow and outlying areas. However different it was from the KGB of 1937 and of other periods of Stalinist repression, such an enormous growth in a punitive body's influence was abnormal, and it had a negative impact on society. In promoting the expansion of his empire, Andropov was probably not deliberately pursuing any intentionally evil goals and was not attempting to create a greater police state; more likely, his actions were simply a question of gaining administrative turf—a temptation from which even the greatest political figures are not immune. Objectively speaking, however, nothing constructive could have come of this. Growing bureaucratic structures always search out activities to occupy their energies, and when they don't find them, they invent them. When one is dealing with punitive bodies, this is particularly dangerous.

I do not wish to justify Andropov's activities, but to be objective I must note that in exercising his leadership within the KGB, Andropov never felt himself to be "master in his own home," even though he enjoyed a good deal of independence during Brezhnev's illness. I have already written that Brezhnev attempted to put in high positions people who were close to him personally and reported directly to him, bypassing Andropov. And that put Andropov under constant pressure.

The following is a typical episode. One day Andropov asked me to come to see him on an urgent matter. He showed me a piece of paper, about which I was to tell no one, but about which he wished to consult with me. It was a copy of a letter written by a very close friend of mine and intercepted by the postal censors. Andropov himself not only knew the man well, but enjoyed good relations with him. The letter was written in a very sincere tone. The man touched upon not only his personal, but also his political anguish, which, he wrote, stemmed from working under what he described as "worthless" and "stupid" people and wasting his energy and time.

Since we were dealing with a man who was well known to the leadership, Andropov said he had no choice but to hand the letter over to Brezhnev, who would assume that he himself was being referred to. For that reason Andropov expected the most negative response against the writer (which was how things turned out). What should he do?

I attempted to dissuade him: Why should he show Brezhnev the letter, especially because the name of the person whom the author considered "worthless" was not mentioned and it was possible that he did not have Brezhnev in mind but someone else? God only knows that we had plenty of worthless and untalented people. Dismissing this argument as naïve, Andropov remarked: "I'm not certain that a copy of this letter has not been handed over to Brezhnev already. After all, the KGB is a complex institution, and its chairman himself does not escape its attention." Then he added: "All the more so since there are people who would be delighted to compromise me in the eyes of Brezhnev for having concealed from him something touching upon him personally."

I left that conversation depressed. What sort of world of trick mirrors were we living in, where disgusting and politically amoral customs prevailed at the very top! They were opening personal letters, reporting them to the most powerful figure in the country! As if that weren't enough, they were scrutinizing the very person the leader had entrusted with watching everyone else! This episode revealed a great deal. Even though he headed the KGB, Andropov himself could not escape the watchful eye of that institution. It must not have been an easy thing to remain true to his principles while constantly facing the seamy side of political, civil, and personal relations and having no choice but to hunt through the soiled linen of society.

At the same time I believe that if another person had been given the position of chairman of the KGB—and I mean practically anyone on the political horizon at the time—events might have taken a much more oppressive turn.

Over the course of many years in the KGB Andropov was part of the political leadership of the country. He was first a candidate-member of the Politburo and later a full member, and one of the most influential, at that. In this respect, there is no denying that he bore responsibility for the state of the country and the growing momentum of its decline. Nevertheless, knowing the political mechanisms and mores of that period, I would caution against broad generalizations about his responsibility; the atmosphere within the political leadership was such that one did not interfere in affairs not directly subject to one's control; certainly one did not quarrel with the general secretary. Thus, any evaluations or appraisals must be specific in nature. If we are to speak of the government's policies at that time, one major sin on Andropov's soul was truly Afghanistan.

More than once I had the opportunity to discuss the war in Afghanistan with him (unfortunately only after it had begun). And I could see his evaluations of the situation change, but not in the sense that he judged the decision in which he himself had taken so active a part to have been mistaken, not to mention criminal. It would have been unrealistic to expect that sort of reappraisal. But Andropov's assessment of the progress and the eventual outcome of the war changed.

I recall first discussing the war with him in 1980; by then he had already realized that hopes for a quick success had been false, but he did believe that the problem would be resolved in a year or so. After a year and a half had passed, he began to criticize our military more and more frequently. (The chief players were Ustinov's protégé Akhromeyev, who had received the title of marshal and the Star of a Hero of the Soviet Union for his actions in Afghanistan; the "hero" of the August 1991 putsch, General Varennikov; and later Sokolov, who in 1984 served as minister of defense for a short period.) Andropov criticized them for doing a bad job of running the war and for getting involved in politics; he believed they were conducting themselves as self-proclaimed rulers, infuriating the populace and making the political climate in Afghanistan still more precarious.

By the time another year had passed, he had begun to speak of a political solution, and was ready to hear my thoughts on that question. Using this as tacit approval from on high, I attempted to do what I could to help stop the war: I had regular contacts with the Pakistani ambassador, and on occasion with the Pakistani foreign minister. I also had contacts with Prince Saddrudin Agha Khan, a member of the royal family that had ruled Iran until the 1925 coup. The prince was well acquainted with the key people of Afghanistan, including some of the leaders of the exiled opposition.

On the other hand, the brief period in Andropov's career between his return to the Central Committee in May 1982 and Brezhnev's death probably should be given a positive rating. Having become essentially number two in the Party during Brezhnev's illness, he began to feel a greater sense of responsibility for the general situation in the country, and not just for his own narrowly defined obligations. (At least, that was my impression, although he naturally never discussed this with me.) This was all the more the case because he must have known better than others the difficulties and challenges facing our country, thanks to the steady stream of information he received while heading the KGB.

Once he returned to the Central Committee, Andropov tried to hit the ground running. As I understand the situation, one of the problems that troubled him the most was the corruption and decadence that had permeated society. First and foremost, there was the corruption of the leadership at various levels. I never heard him mention Brezhnev's family's involvement, although a good deal had been written on this topic in the West. I cannot exclude the possibility that he simply would not discuss this matter with me. But I do know from our conversations that he was particularly troubled by the activities of Medunov and Shchelokov—people who, as I have noted, graphically illustrated the flourishing criminal corruption among the leadership. Moreover, they were close to Brezhnev and compromised him.

In the spheres of culture and social sciences, Andropov also tried to revitalize normal activities, and we had rather frequent meetings on the subject during those months. He had no plans at that time for any dramatic changes, but he clearly wanted to stop the active offensive of conservatives and neo-Stalinists.

In the six months between the time Andropov took up his new job in the Central Committee and Brezhnev's death, many people, including me, noticed that the atmosphere was changing. Those who were aware of this began to look more hopefully to the future. For the first time there was a real alternative to the Chernenkos, Grishins, and Tikhonovs.

By then Andropov had clearly become the most likely candidate to succeed Brezhnev. It was probably during this period that he began to think more broadly and boldly of the problems confronting the entire country, including its politics, economics, and ideology.*

People have begun to forget that once the era that we justifiably call

---

*By November 1982, when Brezhnev passed away, Andropov was the most probable successor, but he could not be certain of this. I know that because I was in Austria when we learned the news of Brezhnev's death; I was urgently recalled to Moscow. Andropov wanted to have as many persons as possible whom he could trust at the plenary meeting of the Central Committee. (I was then a member of the Central Committee and, if the need arose, could speak out.)

the period of stagnation had ended, perestroika did not immediately commence. There was a hiatus of nearly two and a half years, and part of this crucial period included Andropov's term as general secretary of the Central Committee. It lasted only some fourteen months, and if we subtract the time he was critically ill, one is left with little more than a half-year. But even taking into account Andropov's modest accomplishments, these were important months. They symbolized a break in our malevolent uniformity, our seemingly endless slide downward.

For one thing, in his very first speeches Andropov promised change—to fight corruption, the decline in discipline, and the generally slipshod way of doing things; he set as his goal a revival of the country, the resolution of difficulties and problems (he spoke of these problems with an unaccustomed frankness, although nothing like the openness achieved under glasnost). For another, people could see that real things were being accomplished, and these were perceived as harbingers of even more significant changes down the pike. Odious individuals (including Medunov and Shchelokov) were fired; the war on bribe-takers and embezzlers was intensified; an effort was launched against corruption; law and order began to get a foothold; and discipline was strengthened (although this was sometimes discredited by local authorities, who made use of foolish methods such as dragnets, checking the identification of restaurant and movie-theater clientele during working hours).

During Andropov's first months in office, all this ensured him enormous popularity. All strata of society—the workers, the farmers, and the intelligentsia—expected a great deal of him. (He was particularly popular among intellectuals, despite their traditional suspicions of the KGB.)

Is it possible eight years later to assess how justified these hopes were? Had Andropov lived longer, what would his program have been, and where would he have led the country?

I have already discussed the fact that Andropov perceived the country's problems with great clarity, but that does not mean that he was aware of all of them or of their true dimensions. He had developed some plans before Brezhnev's death. They went much further than simply instituting order or punishing the more blatant embezzlers.

Judging from some of our conversations, he seemed to understand that society still had not recovered from Stalinism; having suffered all kinds of frustration and humiliation, it was in need of serious reform and rejuvenation. But Andropov had been taught by experience to be a cautious politician, and it is my belief that he was overly wary of rapid, major reform. That included the most obvious issues—the overdue questions of personnel and purging the Party and the government bureaucracy of incompetent, stupid, and mediocre people, who were often very old and hardly capable of work.

On one occasion, in Andropov's first days as general secretary, we argued this point. I maintained that he would be unable to accomplish anything without radical reform. He agreed that many senior officials were inefficient and unreliable, but argued that he was not about to replace them immediately because he did not want to end up with a hostile Central Committee. As for violating the Party Rules by calling a congress three years early, or using plenary meetings to kick people out of the Central Committee, as Brezhnev had done, he did not consider those actions possible. While believing that Andropov did not want to violate the CPSU Rules, I am not convinced that this was strictly a matter of finickiness on his part. I have the impression that Andropov simply did not know who could replace the government members he had inherited. Weak as he thought many of these men were, he not only understood them, but even felt they were kindred spirits. It is my opinion that, as before, confronting personnel problems was one of his chief weak spots. He had lived and developed for decades among our Party bigwigs, and I believe he simply could not imagine replacing them en masse. He was more inclined to draw several individuals close to him and thus attempt to compensate for the weakness of the others, to solve problems at hand. But now that he had to operate on a national scale, this line of attack was doomed to fail in bringing about serious reform. In addition he was guilty of some out-and-out mistakes, such as the appointments of Romanov and Aliev to the posts of secretary of the Central Committee and first deputy prime minister, respectively.

But I cannot exclude the possibility that with time Andropov might have adopted a quite different posture. Circumstances would have left him no other recourse.

But personnel is still only a means—although a very important means—to achieve a goal. What goals did Andropov set for himself?

I am convinced that he was aware that the state of the country, not only under Stalin but under Brezhnev, had been abnormal, and that something serious had to be done, beginning with the economy. Here we see a definite weakness, one that I believe would have become more evident had he lived longer. Andropov had no interest in economic problems, nor did he understand them, and his solutions were limited to the traditional ideas of enforcing discipline and perhaps utilizing moral and material incentives. Of course, if life or fate had allotted him a little more time, his views on these questions might have changed.

Unquestionably, the new general secretary had his own program on foreign policy, a subject in which he was an expert (although such professionalism can also be a barrier to innovation). I know for a fact that he harbored no doubts about the country's need for peace, détente, and the development of mutually beneficial ties with other countries. At the same time he did not always understand how to reach these goals, partly because he did not fully realize how much of the difficult international situation was attributable to our own policies.

He did understand our relations with countries of the "socialist community." As far as I can tell, his thinking reached an important turning point after the events in Poland and our failures in Afghanistan, for which he, Gromyko, and Ustinov bore particular responsibility. The proposal we initiated in January 1983, in which the Warsaw Pact and NATO would agree to renounce the use of military force, was a crucial breakthrough. According to this agreement, both sides would commit themselves, first of all, not to use force against any country *belonging to its own bloc;* second, not to use force against any country of the opposing bloc; third, not to use force against any other country. I believe that this proposal reflected Andropov's "new thinking," signifying a break with the "Hungarian syndrome" that had so plagued him. Of course, it was also a break with what was known throughout the world as the Brezhnev doctrine.

Unfortunately, neither the United States nor the West paid sufficient heed to these proposals, possibly because they considered them to be mere propaganda. But what else could you expect of America when the Reagan administration was in the throes of a wildly anti-Soviet mood?

Andropov also saw that the changes in China were clearing the way for a normalization of our relations. He even made a statement to that effect in one of his first speeches as general secretary. (In all candor, I proposed it to him, as I had some time earlier to Brezhnev, because I considered our relations with China anachronistic and irrational.)

As far as the United States and the West as a whole were concerned, Andropov was a proponent of détente and improved relations. Still, he had deep doubts that much could be accomplished on that front during Reagan's administration. After the U.S. government's violent anti-Soviet reaction to the tragic incident involving South Korean Airlines flight 007, these doubts hardened into certainty.

I do not believe that Andropov was prepared to go as far down the path to common sense as was Gorbachev. Nevertheless, he did sense the need for serious changes, for some movement away from our fossilized political position (to which he himself had contributed). Despite close personal relations with Ustinov, Andropov began to have doubts about our military programs and the stand of the Ministry of Defense on arms control. I think that if he had lived longer, our position at the disarmament talks might have changed, although not as decisively as it did during perestroika. He regarded certain military leaders, including Nikolai Ogarkov, as politically unreliable. Once, while talking to someone by phone in my presence, Andropov called Ogarkov a "little Napoleon" (I remind the reader that soon after Andropov's death Ogarkov was removed from his position as chief of the General Staff.)*

As far as domestic affairs were concerned, it seems to me that Andropov intended to solve a number of serious problems in the socio-political sphere, where he felt more at home than he did in the economy. Judging from our talks and other evidence, he considered some degree of democratization essential. At the time, his ideas were bold, although now they would appear quite modest indeed. He was troubled by the tensions between the various nationalities making up the U.S.S.R.; evidently, as chief of the KGB, he was more aware than others of the danger they presented. Andropov considered it essential that relations between the leadership and the intelligentsia be improved and that a cooperative environment of trust and mutual respect be encouraged. These plans, however, were still on the road to fruition. It was a slow process, since Andropov was distracted by the purely internal affairs of

---

*Later I thought that perhaps it was Ustinov who had set Andropov against Ogarkov. Ustinov clearly disliked Ogarkov's independence and sense of self-esteem. That was why he advanced Akhromeyev so insistently, in violation of all traditions of the military establishment. He awarded Akhromeyev, who had been deputy chief of staff, the title of marshal. I know how displeased many of the generals were over this. Still, it enabled Ustinov to replace Ogarkov with Akhromeyev in 1984. But Ogarkov's views turned out to be harmful in many respects; he encouraged the growth of the army and increased defense expenditures.

the apparat, which exerted pressure on him from all directions (chiefly from the right), and he was not always capable of—or, sometimes, even interested in—resisting.

This became evident to me only after my great quarrel with Andropov was over. The quarrel erupted in late December of 1982 and was most likely precipitated by a note I sent him. The note was returned to me the very same day with an angry rejoinder, delivered by a KGB officer who arrived without warning at my home. This incident put an end to the comradely relationship we had enjoyed for a number of years. I was happy that my wife was not at home. She would have been frightened by the appearance of the KGB, especially since she knew nothing of our quarrel; I told her about it only much later.

I had written to Andropov that many intellectuals were disappointed with the appointments he had made during his term, in particular the nominations to the Central Committee Cultural Section and to a number of publishing houses and newspaper and magazine editorial boards. "Parallel to all of this," I wrote, "a number of theatrical plays are being forbidden, including some that earlier had been permitted" [the Satire Theater and the Mayakovsky Theater had already been affected, not to mention the Taganka Theater]. I appealed to Andropov to "put a halt to the activities of certain officials until you yourself get around to looking into this area."

I mentioned the efforts of our bureaucrats to return economics to the bosom of classical Stalinist dogmatism.*

---

*Among other things, I wrote about the "directive" lectures being delivered in all the major academic institutions by Mikhail I. Volkov, who headed the Central Committee Economics Department:

> According to Volkov, the alleged source of difficulties is that people have been carried away with specific research projects, such as those on economic mechanisms and management, instead of concentrating on the study of the classical concepts of political economy. For instance, Volkov, a Stalinist dogmatist, praised the economic discussion of 1951, which was, according to him, a model of creativity and practicality, Stalin's article, "Economic Problems of Socialism" (which, in the opinion of real economists, was one of his worst works, one most divorced from reality). Volkov also preaches a lot of other foolishness. The scholars who attended his lectures interpreted them as an attempt to isolate economics from practice, and to prevent the study of our more severe and complex problems. At the Institute of World Economics and International Relations, and at his own

In response, Andropov rebuked me for my "amazingly undiplomatic and subjective tone," for "playing the mentor," and for a lack of objectivity. In conclusion, he wrote that this was "not the tone in which you and I ought to converse with each other." He wrote to me using the formal variety of Russian address, the first time he had done so since 1964. As for the substance of the questions that I had raised, he rejected all my arguments about what I saw as a clamp-down on culture* and did not take the trouble to check the facts I had given to him about our economic situation.

"I don't know what Comrade Volkov was preaching," Andropov wrote, "but even if I take on faith everything you write, I see no cause for panic. If he is in error, he should be corrected, and that is the end of it." (Such a comment from an experienced politician, who knew all too well the pecking order between Central Committee headquarters and scholars!) Andropov continued: "You write that there is a lot of agitated

---

institute, Oleg Bogomolov has preserved notes taken during these lectures, so your aides can request them. There is a lot of agitated talk—people don't understand what such speeches by an important member of the Central Committee mean. There is also a lot of guessing going on about the planned meeting of economists. Is it not intended as a stick to be used against many scholars and scientists in order to strengthen dogmatic positions? In a word, the impression is that all of this is a harmful and dishonorable affair.

*In responding to my remark about the three Moscow theaters and the public indignation caused by withdrawing the plays, Andropov wrote,

I have looked into the question carefully, and I can say that the play Valentin Pluchek wanted to stage at the Satire Theater [Erdman's *Suicide*, which has since become part of the repertoire of all our theaters] was recognized to be anti-Soviet as far back as 1932, and its content has not changed since then. While in principle I regard Yuri Lyubimov [the director of the Taganka Theater] positively, I never gave him, or you, carte blanche to put on *any* play. The play *Look Who's Coming* has not been forbidden at the Mayakovsky Theater, but has only been held up until revisions can be made. Moreover, Goncharov, the director of the theater, was in full agreement with the criticism leveled against the play. It is incorrect that these plays were formerly permitted and have now been banned. The play *Boris Godunov* has not been forbidden at the Taganka, but is now being prepared for staging [the premiere took place in 1989]. The Moscow City Soviet has leveled certain criticism at it, but that is within the competence of that body.

talk—people don't understand where this turn is leading us. . . . Is not the planned meeting of economists intended as a stick? On what basis do you draw such conclusions? Has the Central Committee 'beat up' on anybody of late? People who have nothing else to do with their time can engage in all the guessing they like." I felt that this too was an unfair comment. Andropov knew better than anyone else how Central Committee staff members could ruin the futures of people and even of entire branches of science.

But the most crucial part of Andropov's response was reserved for the end: "I write this to let you know that such notes are of no assistance to me. They are not founded on facts, are irritating, and, most important, do not permit one to draw the correct practical conclusions." I understood the letter—not as an attempt to correct me (which I was willing to accept), but as a declaration that our former relations had come to an end. Moreover, this was not done in person (or at least by telephone), but "documented" in writing.

This was a major quarrel, and it was extremely troubling to me. And surprising, as well. Neither the tone of my letter nor the questions that I raised were in any way different from the other notes I sent Andropov from time to time. Our relationship of more than twenty years was such that I did not pay particular heed to ceremony, but wrote what I thought without being overly concerned with matters of form. My comments had never produced such anger before.

At that point I called Alexander Bovin, the only person to whom I could show both letters, and asked for advice. We met at a trolley stop on Kropotkin Street. It was raining and, covering the letters with my hand, I read them to him under a streetlight. Bovin, who also knew Andropov very well, agreed with me that it was not my letter itself that had caused such a reaction. Andropov had used it as a pretext to distance himself from me. Bovin also agreed that I should not apologize, explain myself, or attempt to smooth over the incident. That left only one option—to understand and accept the signal that had been sent, and not to get underfoot. Several days later an analogous clash took place between Bovin and Andropov, which confirmed my suspicion that the letter was not the root of the trouble.

What had been the real reason? More and more I came to the conclusion that efforts by certain members of the leadership to isolate the new leader from independent opinions were at the root of the matter.

Among others, that meant Zimyanin, Ustinov, and perhaps Chernenko. I learned that a rumor had been launched (and, of course, conveniently passed on to Andropov) that certain persons who had formerly worked with him (including Bovin and me) were bragging of their long-standing friendship with the general secretary and had expressed hopes of profiting politically from it, even laying claim to high positions.

Of course that leaves open the question of how Andropov, who had known us for so many years, could have fallen for such nonsense. One explanation lies in Andropov's inclination to listen to gossip, which was deepened by his suspiciousness and his work at the KGB. Sometimes he would heed that gossip. He was also loath to spoil relations with the sources of this hearsay, especially if they were highly placed. Second, Andropov was already seriously ill, and this frequently affected his judgment. The following events convinced me that the illness had played a role and that Andropov was not in full control of himself.

I was at a diplomatic reception in January when I was called aside by my good friend, the noted interpreter Viktor Sukhodrev, who worked at the Ministry of Foreign Affairs. He recounted how he had been sitting in an office with Zimyanin's son, who told everyone that Andropov had "chewed out Arbatov" for interfering in matters of culture and art, and had broken off relations with him. Aside from Andropov's bad health, I could find no other explanation for the indiscretion and the personal betrayal it entailed, since Andropov had told me several times that he despised Zimyanin. Somewhat later Andropov, who had believed an allegation that I had said something out of line to some Americans visiting Moscow, had his successor in the KGB, Viktor Chebrikov, call me in for an official reprimand and warning. Considering our long-standing friendship, I could explain this only as a symptom of his illness. After all, he could simply have asked me directly what happened once he received the allegation—if not personally, then through any of his aides, and not through the chairman of the KGB.

Months passed. In May 1983 Andropov called me unexpectedly to congratulate me on my sixtieth birthday. Although the conversation was brief, almost official, I got the impression that he had "cats scratching at his soul," as we say in Russian; certainly that phrase applied to me as well. I could not help thinking that now, when normal working relations with this man were particularly important, he and I were quarreling, or had allowed others to bring that about.

Soon after that—it was either July or early August—we made up. Mikhail Gorbachev called me one day (he knew of our quarrel) and said with joy in his voice: "Phone Yuri Vladimirovich immediately; he'll receive you. And then drop in on me." I did so, and we had a warm meeting that moved me deeply, although some harsh words were said on both sides. I later went to see Gorbachev, who had been upset over our quarrel and had evidently contributed to ending it. Soon thereafter Andropov and Bovin made up as well. Andropov's health had improved, and he began to think seriously about his next steps—in both foreign and domestic policy.

During a meeting on those subjects he entrusted me with preparing a memorandum on a major talk about relations with the intelligentsia. At the same time Bovin received an analogous assignment on the nationalities question. One had the impression that Andropov was abandoning his original intent of focusing on minor affairs and preparing to take up questions of vital importance.

Soon after I had sent him a memorandum, he called and thanked me, saying that he had found much in it of interest. He said he hoped to be able to discuss it with me soon and to put my proposals into motion. But soon after he fell ill again, and did not return to work.

A few days after his death, one of Andropov's aides returned the memo to me. I was interested to see which passages he had marked. Among other things, he had noted my reflections on the leadership's attitude toward the intelligentsia, sixty-six years after the revolution. Both in a sociopolitical and a moral sense, "while there is nothing left of what was the bourgeois intelligentsia, it nevertheless remains as the last, least necessary, and least important of all the three basic strata of society."

"Of course," I continued, "this stratum is occasionally referred to in a positive sense—after the workers and the peasantry. But this is always done with a certain condescension, even with reservations. And in conversations with officials, if they feel unconstrained, the word 'intellectual' remains virtually a term of abuse."

He had also marked a reference to an "innovation" that I believed was proposed by Yegor Ligachev, who had been appointed secretary of the Central Committee, with responsibility for organizing Party work and personnel:

Just recently a decision was taken not to bring into the Central Committee persons without previous professional Party work experience. That automatically excludes specialists in international relations, scholars and scientists, journalists, cultural and artistic figures, doctors, teachers, and managers. In essence, we are establishing a sort of bureaucratic sectarianism. Once the republic and regional committees have drawn their own conclusions from this ruling, the Party hierarchy will end up consisting exclusively of persons who from their very youth have selected a bureaucratic career with the goal of becoming bigwigs. Usually they begin in the local committee of the Komosomol and move up in that organization, step by step. It seems to me that it is extremely dangerous to transform work in the Party bureaucracy into a stand-in for the peerage. . . . This is a broader question than that of the intelligentsia, but is nevertheless related to it. I do not believe that anything bad resulted in the 1960s from bringing into our international and other Central Committee offices scientists and scholars, journalists, and diplomats. Perhaps it would make sense to try them out in other fields as well—as secretaries of regional committees in positions of economic responsibility, etc.?

Judging from the marks Andropov made in the margins, he was also intrigued by my thoughts on "relations between the creative intelligentsia and the leadership." Here are a few of them:

There are two important political points here. First, we need to understand that it is best to limit "the leading role of the Party" in culture and art to political and ideological issues.

Second, there are different methods of leadership. Here, first and foremost, we must make the effort to persuade people, to show respect for them in doing so, to display professionalism and knowledge of the subject at hand.

Andropov had noted other passages dealing specifically with relations between the leadership and the intelligentsia. Among other things, I discussed the necessity for

a dialogue, a normal and systematic interchange (not to "work over" the intelligentsia, as Nikita Khrushchev did, and not just for show, as was Stalin's practice). This interchange should not act as a semiconductor, but should function in both directions. The leadership should inform the upper intelligentsia of problems of which it is important for them to know, but at the same time should lend an attentive ear to what they have to say. And one other thing. We have many talented people, but we also have a few figures who are unquestionably great: Chingiz Aitmatov, Sviatoslav Richter, Georgi Tovstnogov, Yevgeni Mravinsky. They must be protected and cherished. Even Iosif Vissaronovich [Stalin] maintained such a circle of persons and tended to overlook their sins, not to mention any denunciations of them that he may have received.

Andropov also showed interest in a number of passages in the note dealing with the considerable difficulties of a broad group of educated people, chiefly doctors and teachers. He had marked the spot where I wrote that a 10 to 15 percent salary raise would not do much good, and that something more radical had to be done.

The time is probably ripe for a deep reform of both spheres [education and health]. Among other things, we need a sort of "industrialization" and perhaps even a scientific-technological revolution; for example, modern electronics and communications permit our best teachers to give state-of-the-art lessons and even teach other instructors (such opportunities are especially useful in medicine). As for health care [Andropov specially noted this passage], if there is no other solution to the situation, it would probably be better to permit private payment for medical services (especially in the case of those persons who enjoy a decent salary) instead of the hideous forms of bribes and gifts that we have now.

Andropov also noted the following point:

Our large contingent of engineers poses a problem similar to that of our teachers and doctors. They have their own specific concerns, but there is much in their work and living conditions that does not correspond to the lofty calling of engineer. Obviously, they are underpaid, so they underproduce in return, and the gap between what they could and do accomplish is considerable. Perhaps this would be a good topic to talk over with our specialists.*

Had Andropov lived longer, he might have attempted to push through at least some of these ideas, but I am not certain that he would have taken up the task with sufficient persistence if he had encountered serious resistance.

It seems to me that fate wasted this unusual and politically talented person by assigning him to secondary roles for too long. Perhaps he had burned out, and by the time he became a political leader it was already too late. Then, too, he had been molded by the political traditions and mores that had dominated the country for so long.

Andropov had very little time remaining to him. I saw him for the last time in early January 1984. A group of us had been entrusted with drafting a traditional speech for the February elections to the Supreme Soviet. It was assumed that Andropov would either read the speech at a voters' meeting or, if his health did not permit this, deliver it on television from the hospital.

At one point, an Andropov aide phoned and asked me to visit Andropov in the hospital to discuss certain questions about the speech.

I found him sitting in his room in an ancient dentist's chair with a headrest. He looked terrible; I realized that I had a dying man before me. He spoke little, and I felt extremely awkward. To avoid the difficult pauses, I talked at him uninterruptedly. When I was about to leave, he leaned over and we embraced. Only after I had left did I realize that he had summoned me to say good-bye. Later I learned that he had met with several other persons whom he had known and worked with for a long time.

A few weeks later Andropov died.

As far as I could tell, most people sincerely grieved at his passing. Upon coming to power, he had awakened many hopes, and his hurried departure left the people with a sense of uncertainty and disappointment. These feelings were deepened when Konstantin U. Chernenko became his successor.

---

*I have dwelt in such detail on this memorandum because, to my knowledge, it is one of the few documents that at least indirectly testify to Andropov's political plans—plans hatched during that brief period when he was leader of the country.

Death Agony

The period of reforms and perestroika could have begun right after the death of Andropov. I heard that not long before he died he had had a lengthy meeting with Ustinov, who was at that time the strongest and most influential man in government, both because of his character and because he had many military divisions at his disposal. Gromyko, himself an arrogant man, as has been mentioned, practically cowered before him. This was even truer of the other Politburo members at that time. It was therefore probably Ustinov who had the last word in resolving the problem of a successor. I think, although I cannot substantiate this assertion, that Andropov discussed the problem of the succession with him. I'm sure that Andropov couldn't have recommended Chernenko; he probably named Gorbachev.

Why, then, didn't Ustinov heed this advice, why didn't he even listen to the opinion of the doctors? (At that time Yevgeni Chazov headed the "Fourth Directorate" of the Ministry of Health, which was responsible for treating members of the leadership. When he and I were coming back from Red Square after Chernenko's funeral, Chazov swore that he had warned the Politburo members a year before that Chernenko was hopelessly ill, incapable of work, that he would soon die, and that therefore it was impossible to name him to the post of leader.) I think purely selfish motives were at play: Ustinov himself was already an old and sick man (he died six months later). He probably feared the young and energetic Gorbachev and felt more comfortable with the dying Chernenko.* These feelings might have been

---

*This assumption was confirmed by Arkadi I. Volsky, who was Andropov's aide at the time. In an interview granted to *Literaturnaya Gazeta* on July 4, 1990, he said: "I remember the day when the Politburo met after the death of Andropov: Ustinov and Tikhonov walked by us into the hall. The minister of defense, laying a hand on the shoulder of the prime minister, said: 'Kostya [Chernenko] will be easier to get along with than the other one [Gorbachev]. . . .' " This is how the question of choosing the leader of a great power was decided.

Andropov, by the way, viewed Gorbachev as a successor. In an interview in the weekly *Nedelya* (no. 36, 1990, p. 7), Volsky recounted how, not long before his death, Andropov inserted into the text of his memo, which was distributed to the members of the Central Committee, the following paragraph: "Comrades and members of the Central Committee of the CPSU, for reasons that are well known to you I cannot at this time take an active part in the leadership of the Politburo and Secretariat of the

shared by several others. Once more the impotence of our political mechanisms was revealed.

What was Chernenko like? In order to answer this question, it isn't necessary to have known him and his work personally, or to have carried out a serious investigation of his activity. With him everything was completely transparent.

Chernenko was a professional clerk, an average bureaucrat, and not a statesman. He really should never have gone further than assistant head of the Documentation Department of the Central Committee, or manager of the chancellery of the Supreme Soviet. There was no reason to expect anything valuable from him as a leader, although he was not a malicious person. But he could have caused a lot of harm if he had had more time and been in better health. The health factor was important not only because he could have done more, but because those surrounding him would have taken him seriously, would have feared him, and would have obeyed him. They would not have wavered in the face of approaching changes.

In reality everyone understood that Chernenko's was a transitional and very short-term rule. Some came to the conclusion that it was necessary to get through this period with minimal losses and, as much as possible, to prepare themselves for the serious changes that were imminent and long overdue. Mikhail Gorbachev, without a doubt, was one of these people. He virtually became the second secretary of the Central Committee, since he chaired the sessions of the Secretariat and, in the absence of the general secretary, the sessions of the Politburo as well. And he was not only conscientious, but he also did everything he could to maintain the dilapidated government machinery, while at the same time showing loyalty toward the sick general secretary.

He continually met with specialists representing various disciplines,

---

Central Committee. . . . I consider it necessary to be forthright with you; this could last for an extended period of time. In connection with this, I would like to ask the plenary meeting of the Central Committee to examine this matter and to entrust the leadership of the Politburo and the Secretariat of the Central Committee to Comrade Mikhail Sergeyevich Gorbachev." This, in point of fact, was his proposal for his successor. According to Volsky, however, this paragraph was eliminated from the text of the memo distributed to the members of the Central Committee by the troika of Chernenko, Tikhonov, and Ustinov. This, as Volsky tells it, provoked Andropov's anger.

listened to them, and not infrequently argued with them, defining his position on the basic issues of domestic and foreign policy. Only after the death of Brezhnev, I think, did Gorbachev consider it possible to show an open interest in foreign policy. Prior to that he was secretary of the Central Committee, assigned to agriculture, and such an interest would have been understood by his associates as a claim to the leadership. Under Andropov he stopped worrying about this, and under Chernenko he was forced to take part in international affairs. His heading up parliamentary delegations to Canada in 1983 and, especially, Great Britain in 1984 were perhaps the most visible of his foreign-policy actions in those years.

It was, in fact, during the preparations for the first of these trips that I noticed that Gorbachev had begun to be interested in foreign policy. My institute was charged with preparing material for the parliamentary delegation's trip; the material was sent to the leader of the delegation. A couple of days later Gorbachev asked me to come see him. When I asked him whether he was satisfied with the material, Gorbachev answered: "Yes, but everything in it is about agriculture. I have competence in that area as it is; it would have been more important for me to talk about and get materials on foreign policy." I took this request as a signal, and from then on did not forget Gorbachev's ever-growing interest in the subject. I also did a few things at his request during preparations for his trip to Great Britain in December 1984;* after that trip he began to be per-

---

*He phoned me roughly a week before his trip and asked me to drop by. When I arrived, he handed me the typed texts of the speeches he was to deliver in England and asked me to comment on them. I said I would do so, but that I was leaving for the United States in three days. He was disappointed and said: "What an annoyance," possibly in the hope that I would be able to delay my departure. I said I couldn't do so, but that I would have everything done by the next day. I wrote out my opinions of the papers Gorbachev had given me; I was sharply negative. The authors of the speech wanted Gorbachev to take "vengeance" for Reagan's recent trip to England and the anti-Soviet speech Reagan had delivered in Parliament. I wrote that Reagan's actions had not been circumspect, but that was no reason to respond with the same lack of circumspection and tact. How would Gorbachev react if an American politician were to visit one of our allies and deliver an anti-Soviet speech there? Why put Thatcher in an awkward position? I advised, therefore, against any anti-American sorties and in favor of a constructive approach with a view to the future. I also presented him with passages that might be included in his speech in Britain. Evidently all this jibed nicely with

ceived around the whole world not only as the most probable next leader but also as a Soviet statesman from whom one could expect new approaches to the most significant issues of policy.

Other problems also attracted Gorbachev's interest. During the agonizing months of the Chernenko period, a group of people gathered around Gorbachev who supported the idea of renewal, a policy that later got the name of perestroika. The bulk of the leadership—the members and candidate-members of the Politburo and the secretaries of the Central Committee—bided their time during this period. The approaching demise of Chernenko was never in doubt.

Judging by the rumors I heard, some people were maneuvering without any justification in the hope of becoming successors to the gravely ill leader; they were, so to speak, "trying on the ermine robe." But could they be seriously blamed for this? Almost every one of them—Grishin, Romanov, Gromyko—could ask himself: Why not me? Am I any worse than Chernenko? Such an atmosphere had an extremely negative effect on public morale.

The situation at that time was one of complete stagnation and decline. Given the extreme crisis, you had to wonder what the leadership was doing, and what the Central Committee, which held the real power, was doing.

The real manifestations of decay were two television appearances in the beginning of March 1985; the dying Chernenko, lifted from his deathbed, was supported under the arms and led over to the camera. As far as I know, Grishin (from the Moscow City Party Committee), and not the Secretariat of the Central Committee, personally took the initiative for this. In any case, Gorbachev, to whom I expressed my negative reactions after the first of these broadcasts, simply didn't know anything; he hadn't watched the program. These pictures were broadcast around the world many times, apparently as a symbol of our weakness—indeed, of our death agony.

The desperate state of affairs was obvious to virtually everybody. And it's difficult to believe that in that period there were so many people staking their future on Chernenko, trying to use him to pursue their

---

Gorbachev's inner convictions, and he proceeded exactly in this way. And when I returned to Moscow, he invited me to visit him, specifically so he could thank me.

own ambitions. But there were such people. First of all, I would like to name Richard I. Kosolapov, at that time the editor-in-chief of the journal *Communist,* but before that a longtime employee in the Propaganda Section of the Central Committee and a deputy in the Supreme Soviet. Chernenko trusted him completely. I don't know why. He considered Kosolapov our leading ideologue and theorist, and constantly kept him nearby.

Kosolapov was a dogmatic Stalinist (although literate, and well read in the literature of orthodox citations), and he used his position as editor-in-chief of the theoretical and political journal of the Central Committee to propagandize and disseminate his views. This didn't surprise me. What I failed to understand was his scheme to use his closeness to Chernenko to make his way up, to become the main ideologue of the Party, and to elbow his way into the leadership.

Now Kosolapov and his friends were racing with death. They set their sights on the Twenty-seventh Party Congress, which, according to Party regulations, was supposed to take place in February or March of 1986. But by the end of 1984 and the beginning of 1985 it was clear that Chernenko would not last that long. So, under pressure from the young careerists, the congress was moved forward to the fall of 1985. In March 1985 a group of Central Committee staff members headed by Kosolapov was supposed to leave town to prepare for the congress. But Chernenko's death forestalled their departure.

During the years of perestroika Kosolapov became one of the ideologues of the ultraconservative opposition—the so-called United Workers' Front (OFT), created by the conservative wing of the Party, the state apparatus, and the trade-union leadership and aimed at attracting workers with demands for the "dictatorship of the proletariat" and with right-wing populist slogans. These slogans were not simply Stalinist, but even fascist in their implications.

After publication of the abbreviated version of my memoirs in a Soviet journal, Richard Kosolapov and Vadim Pechenev (former assistant to Chernenko), who had been stripped of political posts under Gorbachev, rushed to react. Kosolapov published three articles in a small newspaper known for its unrestrained style and reactionary, anti-Semitic leanings. (Formerly *Moskovsky Stroitel'* ["The Moscow Construction Worker"], the paper was now named *Domostroi,* from the title of an ancient Russian guide to running a family in the most patriarchal fashion.) The articles "exposed" me completely, from my political views to my morality. At the same time they were intended to serve as a denunciation of my "pro-Westernism." Kosolapov wrote that I was "inclined toward convergence"—that is, that I favored the convergence of the U.S.S.R. and the West. Kosolapov also allowed himself a clear hint at my half-Jewish origins: he claimed that Brezhnev, in sentimental moments, used to call me Abrasha, which is a Russian diminutive for "Abraham" and is used as a synonym for "Jew." (Incidentally, I can recall no such instance, but evidently Kosolapov had been unable to come up with a more convenient form in which to launch his anti-Semitic diatribe.)

In his memoirs, published soon after Kosolapov's articles, Pechenev went into great detail to disprove the facts I have mentioned, claiming that it was not he and Kosolapov, but the leadership of the Party, who had changed the date of the congress. Pechenev, quite a different person from Kosolapov, did not mount any vicious attacks on me personally. Despite his ill will toward me, he nevertheless attempted to appear objective. Among other things, he mentioned that Arbatov "had played an active, and in my opinion, useful role—one that was progressive for that period."*

For me the Chernenko period was very difficult. I was acquainted with him and, in general, felt no ill will from him. Ill will was, however, shown to me in spades by one of Chernenko's relatives, Mikhail I. Volkov, who remained as head of the Economics Section of the Science and Education Department of the Central Committee. I have already mentioned the large-scale attack, with his active participation (under the leadership, apparently, of Grishin and Zimyanin), on the economic and international institutes of the Academy of Sciences.

I was also attacked personally. One fine day Zamyatin asked me to come and see him. He let me look at a letter that had been sent to the Central Committee by a person I did not know, accusing me of praising Reagan. (The accusation was based on the fact that in one of my Soviet television broadcasts I had half-jokingly said that Reagan had frightened the American people with his saber-rattling and militaristic

---

*V. Pechenev, *Gorbachev: To the Pinnacle of Power* (Moscow, 1991), p. 42.

speeches and had thereby given a powerful boost to the development of the antinuclear movement, so perhaps he deserved a peace prize—though maybe not the Nobel). Zimyanin (the Central Committee secretary for ideology) and Zamyatin had been charged by the leadership to ask me to explain myself.

I was indignant. Did he and the leadership really fail to understand the irony? How could they take seriously a stupid letter written by somebody completely devoid of a sense of humor? Zamyatin clearly felt uncomfortable, but kept repeating that he was fulfilling his charge.

In the spring of 1984 a real provocation was set up against me. In an article about Konstantin Chernenko that appeared in the West German magazine *Stern,* I was quoted as saying that Chernenko was an uneducated peasant in no way suited to his high position. Of course, I had said nothing of the kind; the very notion of criticizing people for their "non-aristocratic" origin is alien to me. Knowing the Moscow connections *Stern* had at the time, I came to the conclusion that this was disinformation consciously fed to the Germans by a Soviet who wished me ill. And this disinformation, as I soon found out, was immediately reported to the leadership and became the subject of lively discussions in the corridors of power.

Soon thereafter, Gorbachev took the opportunity to raise this issue with me. Gorbachev told me that he'd heard about the quotation, and that there was no need to convince him that it was spurious: "There are some things that Arbatov can't be accused of," he noted, "including being such an idiot that he would say this sort of thing to foreign journalists." Promising to talk with Chernenko, he advised me to ask Chernenko to receive me. I did so and soon had an appointment. I sat for about twenty minutes in the waiting room. (This also was useful: about ten staff employees who were scurrying back and forth saw me and quickly told others.) Then, for about twenty or twenty-five minutes, I talked with Chernenko. About business—about relations with the United States and about the necessity to develop a more active policy in the Pacific region. Chernenko listened, coughing the whole time and spitting into a bottle (I remember the same kind of bottle from the tuberculosis hospital during the war). He was quite friendly; he said that basically he agreed with what I was suggesting, and told me to submit a note to the Central Committee. I did so, but while Chernenko was still alive the note produced no effect. Quite honestly, I didn't expect any. My personal problem was resolved at that moment and for some time I was left in peace, while the political situation remained dismal, as before.

At the same time, an understanding was growing that the country could no longer endure another man of Chernenko's intellectual and political weakness. And although it was not in our tradition to discuss which political figure might become the next leader, the country was so tired of the gray anonymity of the leadership that the problem of a successor to the general secretary was on everybody's mind. And by the time of Chernenko's death the prevailing opinion was that the only worthy candidate was Mikhail Gorbachev.

News of Chernenko's death caught up with me in San Francisco, where I had arrived that morning with a parliamentary delegation headed by Vladimir V. Shcherbitsky. That same evening we broke off the trip and started home. Everybody was wondering who the successor would be. People in the delegation were of different political views. But on the five-and-a-half-hour flight to New York that night, nobody maintained the usual reticence, engendered by decades of fear. They all talked out loud, and they all agreed on one thing. Gorbachev, and only he, must become the leader. The five Central Committee members on the plane even threatened that if it didn't work out that way they would protest at the plenary session.

In New York, where we had to change to a Soviet airliner, our delegation was met by U.S. congressional representatives, our ambassador to the U.S., Anatoli F. Dobrynin, and the Soviet representative to the U.N., Oleg A. Troyanovsky. As we were coming down the ramp they whispered to us: "The plenary session has already met; they've chosen Gorbachev as general secretary." There began a general rejoicing in the delegation. I said to my colleagues, half in jest: "Wait until we're in the plane to express your joy; after all, the nation is in mourning!"

How can one evaluate such a short historical period in history as that of Chernenko? At first I had a simple answer: over thirteen months had been lost in a difficult period for the country. Then I began to assess the situation more carefully. Maybe those thirteen months hadn't been lost after all. Maybe they were even necessary after the stagnation, and after the light shakeup we received under Andropov, to come to an under-standing of how much the country was in need of radical reform. In this sense, perhaps, the very dolefulness and despair of the Chernenko reign paved the way for perestroika.

10 The Institute: How We "Discovered" America

I n May 1967, the Academy of Sciences of the USSR had decided to establish an Institute of the U.S.A. Alexei Rumyantsev, at that time vice president of the academy, called and offered me the directorship of the institute. I was interested immediately. First of all, I would have a chance to return to the field I had chosen as a young man—the study of America. Second, I very much wanted to take on a project of my own— especially since I was then forty-four years old, so I was getting a rather late start on such an undertaking. But at that point in my career I had earned myself something of a reputation as a potential specialist on the United States. I read and wrote professionally about America and I had completed two dissertations on related subjects: a master's in law and a Ph.D. in U.S. history. I also began to write two books—one about the Bill of Rights and another on Thomas Paine—though I wasn't able to complete these projects because my time was taken up with other responsibilities. And, perhaps most important, by then Andropov had left his Central Committee post. His most probable successor would be Konstantin Rusakov, and I was absolutely certain that I would not be able to work with him.

I immediately told Rumyantsev that I would do it and asked him how the idea for the creation of the institute had come about. He told me that it had been developing for a long time, spurred on by the government's knowledge that dozens of institutes in the United States were studying the U.S.S.R., while we didn't have any investigating the United States. Finally, both the Ministry of Foreign Affairs and the Academy of Sciences introduced the appropriate proposal to the Central Committee. Like almost all large and small questions in those days, this matter was considered by the leadership of the Party; it received a positive response.*

Several days later a letter from the Academy of Sciences arrived at the Central Committee, asking that I be transferred to the new institute. But the decision was not made for six months.

Brezhnev's aides told me that he was wavering; he simply couldn't come to a decision. Finally, during a break in a regular work session in Zavidovo, I asked if I could have a personal appointment with him. He immediately guessed what I wanted to talk about, and muttered, "Is it about leaving the Central Committee again?" But he didn't refuse, and invited me to his apartment.

In answer to my question whether he would let me go, Brezhnev said, "I consider the establishment of an institute to study America extremely important. After all, Americans have many institutes studying the U.S.S.R." This argument had made an impression on him, too. It was like the arms race: if the Americans had something, then we should acquire it, too. "But at the same time," he continued, "Andropov has just left the department, his former deputy Tolkunov has recently been transferred to the position of editor-in-chief of *Izvestia,* Fedor Burlatsky left even before that, and now Arbatov wants to leave, too. Wouldn't this weaken an important sector of the Central Committee?" I could not make him budge from this position until I resorted to my last and, apparently for him, most convincing argument: I was going to have to

---

*Many Americans have asked me about the reasons behind the creation of the institute. Was the leadership planning an improvement in relations with the United States, or had it foreseen the deterioration of these relations? (The United States began to finance Sovietology generously during the Cold War.)

I can state for the record that the creation of the institute was not connected with any political plans. Rather, it was a somewhat belated response to a growing interest, initiated as far back as the Twentieth Party Congress, in the outside world and in the development of social and political research.

leave in any case because of my bad relations with the new head of the department, Rusakov. Now Brezhnev could let me go in a gentlemanly fashion. Otherwise I would have to leave unpleasantly or even with a scandal. Finally he promised to let me go, but only after I finished work on his report for the fiftieth anniversary of the October Revolution.

On December, 20, 1967, I became the director of the Institute of the U.S.A., and for about two weeks was the only member of its staff. The study of America had finally become my full-time job.

Was I prepared for it? To a certain degree, yes—because of my education, my interest in serious political and economic literature, and my long fascination with the country and its politics. At the same time I knew my own weaknesses and deficiencies. They were not confined to the fact that the study of the United States had, until then, not been my principal discipline and so my knowledge was insufficiently deep and systematic. I had never been to the United States. I had no contacts or acquaintances among Americans (given the restrictions of those times, as an employee òf the Central Committee apparat I didn't even have the right to initiate such contacts). As a specialist I was unknown to my American colleagues—a circumstance that initially gave rise to curiosity, bewilderment, and gossip in the United States, in particular as to whether or not I had come from the KGB. Therefore, during my first contacts with Americans I had to assure them that I was not a member of that organization.

My lack of acquaintances and contacts was quickly rectified. Meetings began immediately. The first person I met was the governor of Michigan, George Romney, who was then considered to be one of the possible candidates in the 1968 presidential race. At the December 1967 Pugwash meeting in Moscow I met with a group of distinguished American scholars that included Henry Kissinger, who at that time was still a professor at Harvard University. In January 1968 I gave my first interview to correspondents from *Business Week* who were visiting Moscow, and in my extremely modest apartment I entertained my first American—the well-known entrepreneur and multimillionaire Cyrus Eaton. My wife was at a loss: What should we serve him? As a guest he turned out to be kind and good-natured; he ate with gusto, praised the food, and inquired about all the dishes. Then visitors began coming by the trainload.

Of course I got to know the U.S. ambassador in Moscow, Tommy

Thompson, and his wife. I was impressed and charmed by them. And I am grateful to Ambassador Thompson; I have the feeling that it was he who explained to some of his compatriots who I was and what my institute represented, and he did it in such a way that our ties and contacts with American colleagues began to develop.*

What was harder to acquire than acquaintances and contacts was a *feeling* for the country, a partly rational, partly intuitive sense that we could acquire only through regular professional contact with a wide variety of specialists from the United States and with representatives from government and business. Such contact was really the only way we could begin to understand how political mechanisms worked in America, how the centers of power operated, and, of course, how the public reacted to various developments—and how all of this influenced political decision-making. Even more important, as we began gradually to understand how different types of people think, we no longer attributed our own stereotypes to another society.

In contrast to the United States, basic and fundamental research in our country is concentrated not in universities but in the Academy of Sciences. This tradition has existed since the beginning of the eighteenth century, when Peter the Great founded the Academy of Russia. All fields of knowledge were treated equally—from mathematics and physics to philosophy and linguistics—including economic and political research on the Far East, Africa, and America.

The academy is, on the one hand, an organization of leading scholars. Not so very long ago the members numbered several dozen; when I was

*I took my first trip to the United States in January 1969 and immediately expanded my circle of acquaintances both in the academic world (I visited Harvard, the Massachusetts Institute of Technology, Columbia University, Berkeley, Stanford, the Rand Corporation, the Hoover Institute of War, Peace and Revolution, and others) and among politicians (once again I saw Kissinger and his colleagues, including Bill Hyland, and met Averell Harriman, with whom I maintained good relations until the very end of his life. I am much obliged to him and to his advice, and also to his widow, Pamela, for her help. I met Gerard Smith, who then headed the Arms Control and Disarmament Agency; Under Secretary of Defense David Packard; Robert McNamara; John McCloy; Cyrus Vance; and others. And I also met prominent senators and congressmen) and members of the business world (I especially remember David Rockefeller, Norton Simon, and Tex Thornton. It was then that I first came to know the famous impresario Sol Hurok and one of his friends, the greatly talented violinist Isaac Stern).

made a member there were 200, and now there are 350. The academy, in turn, consists of more than 150 institutes.

The Academy of Sciences is concerned chiefly with research, although it offers postgraduate studies and awards doctoral degrees and professorial ranks. The results of its work are summarized in books, academic journals (many institutes, including mine, publish their own journals), in various projects, and in policy and economic recommendations. The number of employees varies dramatically—from several dozen to several thousand people.

When I was leaving the Central Committee, many apparat employees couldn't understand what I was doing: why, they asked, leave an important position for something obscure and unknown? But I had no doubts whatsoever. First of all, I saw an opportunity in the work. One rarely gets the chance to initiate and develop a new research institute. And studying a topic of such vital importance as the United States (I added Canada in 1975) inevitably meant involvement, not only in research, but in policy as well, and even in drafting economic decisions.

In the fall of 1991, a Soviet interviewer asked me: "You have been working for twenty-four years as the successful director of the institute, and you've become extremely well known; has anyone during this time ever offered you a higher position, say, the ambassadorship to the U.S., or even the foreign ministry?" I answered him candidly that I was offered the ambassadorship when Dobrynin was stepping down, but I refused it.* And I would have refused the position of deputy

---

*This offer, by the way, was made by Dobrynin himself, who had been appointed to the high position of secretary of the Central Committee and head of its International Section. Quite a bit has been written in the United States about our enmity, or rather about his jealousy of me (for example, by Zbigniew Brzezinski, in his memoirs; by Jerrold Schechter, in an article in *Esquire;* and by others). I never wanted his job. I never wanted to be ambassador, nor did I ever want to diminish his role in policymaking. In principle, as far as Soviet-American relations were concerned, we shared the same views, we were allies. But from time to time I did sense his hostility, which I attributed mostly to the attempts of our ranking officials to deny other, independent opinions even the possibility of access to the leadership. Two or three times Dobrynin even denounced me directly in coded cables. (I had supposedly made disloyal comments or divulged something to American representatives.) Once this led to a serious conversation with Brezhnev, but I managed to convince him that Dobrynin's denunciation, referring to a conversation of mine with William Hyland, was groundless. And a couple of times Gromyko protected

minister and even that of foreign minister, had they been offered to me.

I would have refused, not because I'm not ambitious; my ambition has simply turned in another direction. It is reflected in the institute and its successes, in *my* institute. I didn't come simply to be director for a while and then go off and find myself a better or higher position. I wanted to create the kind of institute I'd dreamed about. It seems to me that that has been achieved, and so I consider myself a happy man.

Developing the U.S.A. Institute was a complex task, and not only because there had never been a great demand for such specialists so there hadn't been a great supply of them. I understood that it was not only a matter of a lack of knowledgeable and well-trained people. The overwhelming majority of our specialists (and to some degree I include myself) as well as all of our social scientists, were spoiled, overwhelmed, and deformed by the pervasive ideology and the dominance of propaganda, by the fear that has become an integral part of our national psyche, by timidity of thought, and by conformism. At that time I was repelled by those aspects of our social consciousness; I understood that real research is incompatible with these barriers and I wanted as much as possible to try to overcome them. This was probably extremely presumptuous, but it is what I wanted to do—not to defy the system and its policy. I honestly didn't even consider such a tactic. I was simply unhappy with what was being written and thought in our country about foreign policy and foreign countries. I wanted to demonstrate that foreign policy could be conducted in another way, but I remained confident that reforming the system (and achieving success in the wake of reform) was possible.

At the time, I had to search out people one by one. I had to try to convince them to join me, to lure them into the institute. There were ludicrously few candidates, so I created the principal staff from my home-grown personnel, the young people whom I invited into the institute directly from college.

---

me by simply not distributing Dobrynin's dispatch to the leadership. He had no particular liking for Dobrynin and viewed him as a rival, and therefore the latter remained in Washington for almost a quarter of a century. I did not allow myself any disloyalty toward Dobrynin, especially in conversations with foreigners. But I did express to Gromyko and Andropov my skeptical attitude toward the "second channel" (that is, the special channel connecting the leaders through Kissinger and Dobrynin).

Our first projects were to write some analytical papers and the book *Who's Who in U.S. Political Life.* As the chief, I had to create and train a working group and at the same time direct the research. I managed to unite the young and the old and to promote an environment for common work, free discussion, and intensive thought, without which creative work cannot flourish.

I toiled for many weeks and even months before achieving the first modest results. I tossed and turned all night, wondering whether the institute would take shape or not. And then I was told that Brezhnev had said, either as a joke or seriously, that "if Arbatov doesn't have any success with the institute, we'll send him back to the Central Committee." And I thought: Would I really have to return in disgrace?

Much later, when it became clear that the Institute of the U.S.A. and Canada had become well established (although not everybody liked it), I often asked myself how a collection of independent research scholars could have developed in the very bowels of a regime that bore the scars of its recent totalitarian past. Even by today's standards, this was unusual. And how could such an institute not only function but flourish under such restrictive conditions while constantly maintaining a decent and sometimes progressive political stand?

I had absolutely no experience as the administrator and leader of a large, important group and an absolutely independent establishment (independent, of course, not of social conditions and political limitations, but of direct administrative control). I had, however, worked in the press, in the Academy of Sciences, and in what was the main political headquarters of the country—the place where policy was made—the Central Committee. I also had some international experience; this background provided a number of opportunities to make up for my lack of administrative skills.

My work experience on research and writing teams, beginning with that of Kuusinen, taught me that one must try to do absolutely everything to permit people to realize their potential.

One of the reasons for our success was that I honestly understood that a fresh spirit in political thinking was needed, and I very much wanted the institute to become a center of liberated thought. Further, I knew the rules of our political game well enough so that the institute's work could be integrated into the process of formulating policy and wouldn't be thwarted by the existing mechanisms of power. At the same time I was not a prisoner of those rules (partly because I worked in the apparat for only a short time, and partly because I intuitively resisted it). To become one would have meant crossing the boundary beyond which political tact and tactics are transformed into unprincipled politics, politics as an end in itself. If I had done that, I would not have been able to influence policy. The institute could have achieved success under such conditions, but it would not have lasted long, especially if there had been abrupt changes of policy and of political leadership.

This meant that from the 1960s on I worked with the leaders of the country and did not hide my differences of opinion from them—a practice that sometimes led to arguments or a noticeable chilling of relations, but that allowed me to remain true to myself. That policy, in terms of the institute, found expression in a rather steady level of activity (and, probably, usefulness) throughout all the political changes. Even so, the institute found itself a target for sometimes malicious attacks, though fortunately they did not cause too much damage.

My first two major tasks were to provide the money, space, equipment, furniture, and conditions for the rapid training of qualified specialists and to develop a new concept of the institute as a growing research center. I must admit that to complete the first task I made full use of my connections with the leadership. I simply went to the leaders and raised questions; I begged, even demanded. After working for a long time with members of the leadership I was not afraid, when it was a matter of the institute, to appeal to them, particularly to Gromyko (later I got to know him better), Kosygin and his deputy Kirill T. Mazurov, Suslov, and others.

Being persistent, I got quite a lot: better salaries than usual, and, by our standards, significant financial support (including a modest but adequate hard-currency allocation for business trips, books, journals, and newspapers). Also, a first secretary in the embassy in Washington was assigned to represent the institute, and we were allocated four internships in New York and Washington. (Later, several other institutes took my cue and got the same perks for themselves.)

A plan for the institute's activities gradually developed. I also began to formulate a concept of the institute. It would combine purely academic research and writing books and articles with drafting practical recommendations for policy (chiefly in Soviet-American relations) and the economy. This work was to be conducted on an interdisciplinary basis—

by economists, political scientists, historians, sociologists, military specialists, and so on. These activities were part of the institute's basic mandate. I wanted it to go further.

I wanted the institute to lay the groundwork for serious research on current foreign-policy problems. And not only historical studies or propaganda intended to support Soviet diplomacy, as was always the case in our country, but research on vital policy, taking into consideration economic, military, and even psychological questions. I wanted the institute to participate in policy-making.

Second, I wanted the institute to initiate serious research on military policy in order to help liquidate the military's monopoly on such questions, on the political aspects of strategy, and on arms-control problems. We were so far behind the United States and the West in this area that as contacts, discussions, and dialogue became more and more intensive, we often failed to understand the other side, or even explain our position to them. I am ashamed to admit that at that time even our specialists did not know our real position, beyond the limits of propaganda, on the most important issues of military policy. On many questions our position was simply not thought through. Soviet specialists knew even less of what lay behind the decision-making process; in our system those details were extremely secret. When our staff experts began to figure them out and to master not only the concepts and the terminology but also the essence of the problems, for a long time they had to be satisfied with only American and Western data. More often than one might have expected, the data would turn out to be reliable—provided, of course, that we didn't rely on one source, that we knew the value of each source and compared its data with others'.

None of this encouraged confidence in our results, either within the country or abroad. But people learned, and with the advent of glasnost, when our data became available, we already had a strong team of experts. The leadership began to reduce the number of secrets as perestroika was introduced; our own data on an expanding number of questions slowly appeared. The U.S.A. Institute was a pioneer in this area, and other institutes concerned with international problems followed its example, in particular IMEMO and, later, the Institute of Europe. In time, a group of scholars who represented the exact sciences (as distinct from the humanities and social sciences) and were also interested in policy and disarmament began to play a significant role in this research. In par-

ticular there were the academicians Yevgeni P. Velikhov, Roald Z. Sagdeyev, Yuri A. Ryzhov, Vitali I. Goldansky, Boris V. Raushenbakh, and
several others.

During the perestroika years, several of this new breed of civilian experts participated in Soviet-American summit meetings, and others became advisers or members of our delegations at disarmament negotiations. True, the traditional forces—the generals, representatives of the
military industry, the Party leadership, and the KGB—soon pushed
them off to the sidelines in real policy-making. But an important change
had been accomplished: real independent experts in different fields had
emerged, and a certain reservoir of knowledge had been created.

Third, I wanted the institute to a certain extent to become a "dis-
turber of the peace" in developing our economic concepts and our understanding of the role of science and technology. I wanted it to challenge our established methods of economic and public management, as
well as some social, political, and cultural matters. I wanted it to become
a source of expert knowledge based on the study of the American, but
not only the American, experience. It therefore seemed important to me
to create subdivisions of applied research that would study the influence
of the revolution in technology on society, the problems of agriculture
and food production, and public administration and social policy.

Of particular importance was the fact that in the autumn of 1968 the
institute made one of the first reports to the leadership, and then to the
public at large, on the international scale and significance of the new
scientific and technological revolution. The specialists stressed the need
to create favorable conditions for speeding up this revolution in the Soviet Union. Unfortunately, the situation that developed in our society
during those years prevented these efforts from being realized.

Fourth, I wanted the institute to separate science from propaganda
and to study the United States not through the distorted prism of
dogma but in its reality. We managed to do that within the existing
limits, although we often had to compromise. In spite of these compromises, the institute's scholarly output—dozens of books; the monthly
journal, *U.S.A., Economy, Politics, Ideology;* and articles by institute employees in other publications—was noticeably different in both content
and form from most of what was published at the time. This new approach often provoked unpleasant responses from the ideological departments and censors. Today these achievements seem more than

modest. But in the depths of the period of stagnation, we took a step forward, and perhaps to some degree helped set the stage for glasnost.

Fifth, I wanted the institute to communicate with the Americans and the Western community in a way they would understand. I wanted to talk about the Soviet Union, about its policy, about Soviet-American relations, and also about what we liked and didn't like about the United States and its policy. At the same time we had to take into account the domestic Cerberuses who zealously guarded our "ideological purity," so that courage and readiness to take a risk were often demanded of us. In order to talk to the Western audience, it was necessary to deviate from many dogmas, stereotypes, and the usual clichés. Many of my colleagues and I took this risk. The singularity of the style and writing of the institute employees soon began to be noted not only by the Soviet public, but also by the Americans. They naturally interpreted it in various ways.

During a formal dinner at the American Embassy during the first summit meeting in Moscow in 1972, Henry Kissinger, answering an observation of mine, joked that I understood the "masochistic" essence of the American soul, and that I made clever use of this understanding.* While sensing some irritation behind this joke, I must confess that I was flattered by such an evaluation. In general, the Americans had a very easy time arguing with us. And the more dogmatic and crude we were in presenting the Soviet point of view to the West, the easier the Americans' job became. Therefore it was pleasant to hear that our opponents were having more difficulties with my colleagues and me in the institute.

Only later was this point corroborated in the Americans' attempt to brand the institute a propaganda organization, created especially to deceive and trick them. This is one of the most absurd misperceptions concocted about the institute, and it has been repeated from time to time by fairly serious authors. The leadership did not set us such propagandistic tasks. All of the institute's appearances in the American media were at our own initiative, without any government directive; moreover, they were accompanied by certain personal risk. I see nothing shameful

---

*"Arbatov knew a lot about America and he skillfully tailored his arguments to the prevailing fashion. He operated particularly subtly, appealing to the inexhaustible masochism of American intellectuals, for whom a symbol of faith was their conviction that all the difficulties in American-Soviet relations were caused by the stupidity or the intractability of the U.S.A." Henry Kissinger, *The White House Years* (Boston and New York, 1979), p. 112.

in our efforts. We simply took a serious approach to American democratic institutions and to American public opinion and understood how serious their influence on policy could be.

Sixth (last in number, but not the least), I wanted the institute to become the alma mater of a new type of contemporary Soviet Americanist and political scientist. I wanted it to gather together creative people and to provide scope for their abilities. I wanted it to foster specialists capable of rendering assistance to their nation. And—please excuse the lofty words—I wanted it to help them become real peacemakers in their modest way. It is not for me to judge how successful all of this was, but I must say that I am extremely proud of the group that the institute assembled.

Four of my five deputies came to the institute right from college, and of those who grew up in the institute, Academy of Sciences member Vitali Zhurkin created the Institute of Europe. Another former deputy, Andrei Kokoshin, recently became first deputy defense minister of the Russian Federation. Three staff members became deputy directors of large and important institutes; one occupied a ministerial position in the government; one became the head of the Russian Central Bank; another was (besides myself) a people's deputy of the U.S.S.R; and another became both a people's deputy of the Russian Republic and the head of the Committee on International Affairs and Foreign Economic Relations of the Russian parliament and is now Russian ambassador to Washington. The present deputy of the Minister of Foreign Affairs of the Russian Federation worked on and defended his dissertation in the institute.

What did I do to ensure that the institute had a highly qualified staff? First, of course, I carefully selected staff members on the basis of their knowledge, intellect, personal qualities, and political convictions. We were prepared to resist the pressure of certain officials, and sometimes influential organizations, who wanted to place their people in the institute. I will not say that we managed to do all this without compromises and without mistakes, but as a whole I think we were successful. We created the appropriate conditions conducive to continual discussion: democratic, benevolent, and competitive. We also fostered loyalty, protecting people even if they made a mistake. (In difficult times I managed to protect a fair number from trouble and to guard them against persecution. And, in defending my people, I did not fear even the wrath of the leadership.) As a rule, the employees pay back such loyalty with loyalty to the institute. Finally, I created equitable conditions for the rapid growth and advancement of our employees (especially the young ones) providing them with responsible tasks, trips, promotions.

We did have our failures. Some politically dishonest, reactionary people, like Nikolai Yakovlev and Yuri Katasonov, did work with us, but the institute later got rid of them. One employee, Vladimir Potashov, volunteered to become an agent of the CIA, was arrested and convicted, and caused us trouble. But these were exceptions.

The most important successes of the institute influenced political knowledge and political practice. Our work has made a substantial contribution to "demythologizing" our foreign policy, to stripping it of ideology, to applying common sense. Soviet policy was deeply steeped in myths and ideology (to a significant degree this applies—I'll say this to be fair—to American policy as well). One must not think that these myths and ideologies were only a soup that we fed the masses, while the "high priests" ate completely different food, and coldly and rationally calculated policy on the basis of some higher interests visible only to them. Maybe Stalin was like that. But not those leaders whom I knew.

Of course, they were far from believing everything they said, and far from saying everything that they believed in and thought. They were no strangers to healthy and sometimes not so healthy cynicism. But despite this, their thinking was thoroughly littered with ideology and the myths that ideology created. Their long-held belief was that the capitalist "imperialist" West was innately and irreconcilably hostile to us, and that this hostility was the main military threat.

I had more than one occasion to raise this subject with Brezhnev, Andropov, and other leaders, who varied in their culture, intelligence, and global awareness. Their ideas varied, too. But distrust of the West, and the fear that the threat of war came from the West, united them. True, when I managed to get deeper into the subject and ask a question about which rational interests in the West could demand war, or even an irreconcilable hostility toward the U.S.S.R., they came up with new themes: yes, the times have now changed, nobody could want war, and so forth. Nevertheless, there soon followed the arguments that we have to be prepared, that the imperialism of the West is a reality, that it can be restrained only by our strength, and so forth and so on.*

Such considerations, however, should be understandable to the Americans. It seems to me that American society is very ideological and is subject to myths (though Americans are still way behind us). I've based this conclusion on many meetings, conversations, and speeches in various settings. At times during the years at the institute I came up against open, sometimes almost fanatical, hostility, but I was more often met with guardedness if not suspicion and distrust. (I don't want to imply that we didn't give the Americans any reasons to distrust our policy, just as they provided their share of reasons for our distrust of theirs.)

The biggest and most harmful myth was the belief that we could ensure security and resolve, if not all, then almost all, political problems with military strength (a mirror image of this myth existed in the United States as well). At work here were the powerful forces of an inertia that dated back many years, even many centuries, and psychological baggage that was common to both of us. At fault were our bolshevized thinking and the Americans' history of conquering the "Wild West," of wars that were almost always perceived as messianic, conducted in the name of a noble idea or cause.

My colleagues and I at the institute were neither dissidents nor prophets who were able to discern the new political realities from the very beginning. If we saw deficiencies and threats, we tried to eliminate them; to the extent that reform of the system was possible, we saw it as the route to that goal. Sometimes today we are reproached for this, but I do not consider such reproofs to be justified.

In the final analysis, all reforms and changes in our country arose from what appeared to be a totalitarian monolith. And it seemed, by all indications, to be Communist. But, from the very beginning, within the idea of communism was the idea of justice as an alternative to tsarist, arbi-

---

*The people who, in my opinion, were the least prejudiced of all and the most cynical were our generals. I remember a conversation I had with Marshal Kulikov when he was still head of the General Staff. The talk turned to nuclear war, and for a long time Kulikov gave me his personal impressions of a nuclear bomb blast. He said: "Whoever has seen one knows, and the Americans know no less than we do, that they are not going to fight. If things get as far as nuclear explosions, everybody will scatter." But when I asked him why we were so seriously concerned with various scenarios of nuclear war, he moved the conversation to a different subject, noting only that the Americans had started it.

trary rule. Immediately after the revolution Soviet leaders tried to unite this idea with that of a strong state (a concept that was in defiance of the "founding fathers" of Marxism, who believed in the withering-away of the state) and also with the idea of empire. The latter two ideas overwhelmed the first, and the regime became totalitarian.

But the idea of justice, and of democracy as well, still existed in the depths of our consciousness. And it turned out that the democratic alternative to Russian communism could sprout only from within Russian communism itself, from its deeply contradictory legacy. These sources united the forerunners and the leaders of perestroika, from Khrushchev to Gorbachev and Yeltsin, as well as the most famous dissidents, beginning with Sakharov and Solzhenitsyn.

The overwhelming majority of Soviet reformers and dissidents started with a belief in the age-old promises of communism—justice, liberation from all types of oppression, and the dignity of the individual. (According to Marxism the highest goal of communism is "complete freedom for the development of the human individual.") When they realized that totalitarianism had ascended the throne instead, their first objective was to force the system to live up to its ideals and promises. I believe that we in the institute share responsibility with the overwhelming majority of our fellow citizens for our loyalty to the system.

At the same time, I consider it extremely important that the struggle to force the system to live up to its ideals, to turn policy toward realities, and to approach things pragmatically was accomplished not only from outside but from within the system. This was true in the achievement of noticeable, if not long-lasting, progress during the years of détente.

Our anti-Stalinist position and pragmatic approach to policy allowed the institute to play its own role in these matters. Another factor was our broad connections with specialists, politicians, and public figures in the United States and in other countries, and the readiness, desire, and ability we developed to listen to and understand them.

Of course, we did not agree with everybody. But a thorough introduction to other points of view, the exchange of opinions, and the discussions freed up our thinking, and many of our foreign colleagues came up with ideas and approaches that stood us in good stead.

The institute participated in three forums for regular meetings that were especially important.

The first was the so-called Pugwash movement. This forum of scholars from the Soviet Union and the United States began years ago and later included scholars from other countries as well. It was particularly important to us in the sixties and seventies, when we had few other possibilities for meetings and discussions with foreigners. For me and for many of my colleagues the Pugwash movement was our first course in Western thinking on security and disarmament. Our discussions gave birth to a number of interesting technical and political ideas. One of them was the idea of moving to a *defensive* defense policy. We came to a broader realization that our adversaries should not interpret the strengthening of our own defenses as an increase in offensive capabilities. We moved toward the concept of a minimally sufficient defense—which, under Gorbachev, became a part of our official policy.

The second forum consisted of the Dartmouth meetings. President Eisenhower proposed the idea of meetings between prominent public figures from our two nations. (The first of them took place at Dartmouth College—thus the name.) The first organizer was Norman Cousins, and the administration and funding have been borne by the Kettering Foundation, whose president, David Matthews, has made a great contribution to the mutual understanding of both powers. The meetings were held even in the most difficult periods of Soviet-American relations, and they played a useful role. They seriously helped my institute, and me personally, to become familiar with various American points of view on extremely important questions of foreign, military, and economic policy, and they became valuable sources of our education in these areas.

Third, there were the meetings of the Soviet and American U.N. Associations, in which my colleagues and I also took an active part. (In 1986 I became head of the Soviet U.N. Association.) These meetings were similar to the Dartmouth meetings, but the existence of two such forums allowed us to meet more often and to take part in discussions with a wider circle of people.

I would like to mention another forum that played an important role, not only in the evolution of my own views, but in the changes of our political thinking. And that is the Palme Commission, with which I had the honor to work throughout its existence. Its official name was the Independent Commission on Disarmament and Security. It was created in 1980 on the model of the Brandt Commission (which dealt with is-

sues in the developing countries), just as the second Cold War was starting.

My work with the Palme Commission became an important aspect of
my life and exerted a great influence on my understanding of politics and
international relations, if for no other reason than that for several years I
was in constant contact with a whole range of prominent politicians,
with people who were unusually perceptive and original thinkers. I had
to argue with them and to find points of common ground. The groups
included Olof Palme, Cyrus Vance, Gro Harlem Brundtland, Egon
Bahr, David Owen, Johann Holst, and also people who were not directly associated with the commission but who worked closely with it—
Rajiv Gandhi, Bruno Kreisky, Pierre Trudeau, Bettino Craxi, and the
former Swedish prime minister Ingvar Carlsson.

The commission became a unique research institute. In the midst of
once-again-tense international relations, new ideas and thoughts were
born from collective experience and in open, honest, and sometimes
heated debate. The most significant was the idea of "common security,"
the essence of which was that we cannot guarantee our own security at
the expense or detriment of someone else's, but only on the basis of mutual interests. Also, a new approach to nuclear arms emerged. The commission questioned their value as a deterrent and as a factor of military
stability, and so-called tactical nuclear weapons were classified as de-
stabilizing. The proposition to create a nuclear-free zone 300 kilometers
wide along the borders of the two military blocs came out of this position. Perhaps this became one basis for the 1991 agreement to eliminate
most of the U.S. and Soviet tactical nuclear weapons systems.

The publication of the report on this subject, in translation and without any deletions, allowed us to introduce this idea to the Soviet public.
(At that time, this caused us a lot of trouble and involved a certain political risk for me.) In addition, our people became acquainted with Western estimates comparing U.S. and Soviet armed forces. These estimates
showed that we had a great advantage in certain areas, which made a
considerable impression. They also proved to be very useful in 1985,
when we started reexamining our political thinking.

In general, my work with the Palme Commission became an important part of my career, both as a researcher of foreign-policy problems
and as a practitioner of politics. But it sometimes put me in a difficult

spot politically. By this I do not mean merely that it incurred the displeasure of several senior Soviet officials or caused problems connected
with its postulates.

There was displeasure and suspicion among some of our people over
the very fact that I became a member of the commission, not because I
was sent there by the "directive bodies" (that is, the Central Committee), as was usually the case, but because foreign statesmen, specifically
Willy Brandt and Olof Palme, asked our government to send me there.
(At the time I did not know them personally; they judged me by my
publications, public appearances, and reputation, and probably on the
basis of personal recommendations.) One day, about a year or a year and
a half after the commission was founded, Boris Ponomaryov had a frank
talk with me about this. At that time he was a Central Committee secretary and head of the International Department. He asked me, with apparent displeasure, "Why did they have to pick you in particular?" I
grew indignant and said that if I was not trusted in my own country I
would resign from the commission immediately, and would write to
Palme that very day. Ponomaryov, clearly scared by such a declaration,
started dissuading me from doing such a thing. ("After all, the Central
Committee did agree to your taking on this work!")

I did not resign. But the episode was a lesson for me and a reminder of
the political mores of the time. My colleagues on the commission did
not even suspect that I had such problems. But it was a great pleasure to
hear many of them, including Cyrus Vance, say later that they greatly
appreciated my efforts to bring the basic ideas and conclusions of the
Palme Commission Report to the attention of the Soviet public and the
new Soviet leadership. They also noted their deep gratification that
many of the ideas of the Palme Commission and of the new Soviet political thinking proved to be in harmony with each other.

The institute's contacts and meetings with foreign representatives and
colleagues became a very important channel for our information and enabled us to get a feel for America. From 1968 on, the institute opened its
doors to visitors and guests. Among those who lectured at the institute
and took part in seminars and detailed discussions were dozens of U.S.
senators and congressmen, political and public figures, prominent busi-
nessmen, and, of course, colleagues from the academic world: Richard
Nixon, Walter Mondale, Harold Wilson, Pierre Trudeau, Cyrus Vance,
Robert McNamara, Henry Kissinger, Brent Scowcroft, Harold Brown,

Zbigniew Brzezinski, Peter Peterson, Tom Watson, David Matthews, Edward Kennedy, Howard Baker, Gary Hart, Alan Cranston, Charles Mathias, John Danforth, John Tower, John Kenneth Galbraith, Seymour Lipset, Paul Kennedy, Robert S. Tucker, Marshall Shulman, Ed Hewitt, Alan Wolfe, William Maynes, Seweryn Bialer, Robert Legvold, Samuel Huntington, Charles "Tex" Thornton, Ted Turner, Armand Hammer, Roy Ash, Michael Blumenthal, Felix Rohatyn, Duane Andreas, Edgar Bronfman, and many, many others.

In its twenty-five years, the institute has known prosperous times as well as times of trouble and even decline. I think that following the first year or eighteen months, up to the mid-1970s, our efforts were quite successful. As we learned how to articulate our ideas, people began to listen to us. But to an even greater extent, we benefited from the favorable conditions that began to prevail in the mid-1970s, even if we had only a small window of opportunity. The conservative agenda had not yet gathered enough strength to completely swamp the evolution of free thought. In turn, the feeling that we were a presence during important shifts to détente greatly helped in establishing the institute and hastened its coming of age.

From the mid-1970s on, the period of stagnation made it increasingly difficult for us to put ideas into practice. More and more often, the institute encountered hostility from conservative officials in the Party apparat, the military command, and the government. Admittedly, these people did not dare to launch open attacks, as a rule, since they were not sure whether the top Party leadership would support them. But it was through their efforts that the institute acquired the reputation of being "pro-American" and ideologically and politically unreliable. We felt the pressure, but we never doubted that we were doing the right thing.

With the exception of a short breather when Andropov became leader of the country and our hopes began to rise, the first half of the 1980s was a difficult time for us. We were expecting some sort of crackdown on the institute, and realized that we could not escape it unless the general situation changed. The shake-up of Inozemtsev's institute demonstrated that even good relations with the leadership would not necessarily help if things came to a head. When Konstantin Chernenko became general secretary, those good relations ceased to exist.

March 1985 was the start of our most fruitful, if most complex, period. As democracy was being born and a polarization of political forces was taking place, the institute found itself involved in a bitter political struggle.

It would not be an exaggeration to say that the institute wrote a new chapter in the development of my country's political, military-political, and applied economic research. It nurtured some important and, in some cases, even brilliant experts. The leadership paid attention to our institute, particularly during periods of active policy toward the United States. Our reports were read, circulated, often taken into account, and we received quite a number of serious assignments.

The public was also interested in the activities of the institute. I judge this by subscriptions to our journal (up to 30,000), by the fact that the majority of the books we published did not collect dust in the bookstores, and also by the large number of invitations our colleagues received to deliver lectures. Of course, the reviews of our activities were not always positive. Quite frequently we got into trouble. Sometimes it was our fault but, more often than not, it was because of overzealous censors and ideologues. Apart from all this, the activities of the institute were defined clearly enough, ideologically and politically, for the conservatives to suspect its motives and to attack it. On one occasion in 1973, Demichev and Kirilenko tried to plant a powerful mine under the institute and me. (The pretext was a common one—Zionism. Too many Jews. Moreover, the director was not pure-blooded "Aryan.") But it never went off. Their denunciation did not produce any response from the government leadership, particularly since denunciations of this type were then only too common. In general, I have no grounds for complaint. Other institutes and specialists suffered greater troubles and tribulations.

The institute evoked the hostility and suspicion of conservatives not only because of its publications but because of its pragmatic style, the behavior of its people, and the uninhibited atmosphere that had developed within its walls. Very many of us, if not all, lived in the hope that the period of conservatism and stagnation would not last and that the processes of democratic change would gain strength. This defined the attitude among the best researchers at the institute; like all creative people, they sought intellectual and spiritual freedom, and the institute served as a kind of refuge for them.

The fact that for a long time the average age of the researchers was not above thirty played no small part in the openness of the institute's atmosphere. Young people at the institute were presented with broad opportunities and they showed great motivation. Of course, to maintain such an environment, you often had to defend your colleagues. Sometimes you had to defend them from conservative attacks and accusations that did have some basis—for example, sympathy for the leaders of the Prague Spring, refusal to go along with the persecution of our dissenters, moral and material support for our dissidents, and unguarded political statements. And sometimes the attacks were completely groundless— pure slander, passed on, nonetheless, to the Central Committee or the KGB. For example, one of my employees was alleged to have a large foreign bank account whose source was unknown. All this proved to be untrue. Another example: someone at the institute was said to maintain dubious moral and political connections. I dismissed this denunciation as a reflection of the accuser's political agenda. Since these accusations were made officially, I had to provide written and verbal explanations, which I found utterly revolting. But I nearly always managed to ward off the attacks on my people.

I'd like to turn now to American attitudes toward us.

At first, there was simple curiosity and, of course, suspicion. There were attempts to find out who we were and what the institute was doing. In January 1968, *Business Week* asked me for an interview, and others followed. An article about the institute was published by *Time* magazine. I also began to appear on television. Due to specific traditions and unwritten rules of conduct, I could not, for instance, tell of my work for the Central Committee. (In May 1985, Andropov expressed his anger in front of me and my colleagues in the apparat because the journal *Soviet Life*, which was published for an American audience, had printed short interviews with us and indicated where we worked. Andropov's outburst came after a special Politburo discussion of the interviews!) We also could not give specific answers to some questions about the activities of the institute—for example, whether we worked for the government or received assignments from it.

The Americans soon started to assess our activities. *Time* noted that Soviet newspapers were now finding it necessary to draw a distinction between "sober-thinking" and "realistically thinking" imperialists on the one hand, and the more common and more hostile characterization of imperialists on the other; according to the editors, this was attributable to the work of the "new observers" of America.*

Later, specialized works about us began to appear and, with time, even whole books were published devoted to the studies of Soviet Americanists and foreign-policy researchers. Let me refer to some passages from the U.S. Library of Congress report *Soviet Diplomacy and Negotiating Behavior: 1979–1988. New Tests for U.S. Diplomacy.* This report emphasizes that the U.S.A. and Canada Institute played a leading role in the "intellectualization" of the Soviet Union's foreign policies and, "despite admitted shortcomings," was "the main force" behind the transformation of "the Soviet perception of the American political system and particularly of the Congress." It went on to say, "Those who carefully follow the activities of the U.S.A. Institute consider that this organization" is known for its "professionalism and ability to influence" the foreign-policy apparat, while others stress "the propagandistic role of the Institute."†

In 1984, Neil Malcolm's book *Soviet Political Scientists and American Politics* was published. Basically, the book is devoted to the work of our institute. I first saw news of it in the British *Times Literary Supplement,* where the Sovietologist Archie Brown described the essence of Malcolm's study in the following words:

> Though relations between the superpowers have had their ups and downs over the past twenty years, Soviet knowledge of American politics has steadily increased. . . . If Soviet leaders have learnt much about American politics and society, this is in large measure due to the work of Soviet Americanists whose writings have increased both in volume and sophistication since the foundation of the USA Institute in 1967. . . . Though the work is uneven in quality and by no means uniform in the views and interpretations it offers, it does enable Soviet leaders and the educated stratum of Soviet society to be considerably better informed about American politics and society than their American counterparts are about the Soviet Union. . . . The work of the Soviet Americanists . . . is both an integral part of, and

*Time, Feb. 7, 1969, p. 23.

†*Soviet Diplomacy and Negotiating Behavior: 1979–1988. New Tests for U.S. Diplomacy.* (Washington, D.C.: U.S. Government Printing Office, 1988), pp. 563–64.

makes a significant contribution to, a much better-informed intellectual milieu than existed in the Soviet Union a generation ago.

But we also encountered totally different attitudes toward the institute from some Americans. They regarded us as political enemies, which was understandable given the chill in Soviet-American relations. But there were also some very malicious attempts to slander and discredit the institute and me. I had encountered personal instances of this long before on the part of some individuals and organizations. (I have already noted the incident with Lyndon LaRouche's organization.) From the beginning of the 1980s, however, the attacks assumed the character of an orchestrated campaign. I could explain this partly by the general deterioration in Soviet-American relations, but I soon realized there were other reasons. I believe that some influential people, including some inside the Reagan administration, had become concerned about the impression the institute and I had made in the American media. Evidently, they thought we were exerting a harmful influence on public opinion in the United States and in other Western countries, and they decided to counteract it.

I will list some of the most visible articles that were written specifically to discredit the institute: "The True Face of the U.S.A. Institute of Moscow," published by the Heritage Foundation, a right-wing conservative group (1982); an article by John Rees, "Moscow's Friends at the Institute of Policy Studies," in *American Opinion* (1983); an article by William F. Buckley, Jr., "Waiting for George," in the *National Review* (1983); and a pasquinade by John Brennan, "A Little Visit with Yuri Andropov," in *American Opinion* (1983). There were others. This is to say nothing of references to us in books such as John Barron's *The KGB Today: The Unseen Hand* (1983), extracts from which were printed in the mass-circulation *Reader's Digest.*

One day I complained to Norman Cousins about this stream of "anti-Arbatov" articles, and he said to me: "Don't take it to heart. This probably won't last very long, and, anyway, they're not harming your reputation. This is all part of the game of American politics." He reminded me of the old joke "Any publicity is useful, with the exception of an obituary," and added that this press attention could make me famous in America. The only things missing were cartoons and a novel.* I told him that the first "cartoon," and quite a vicious one, had already appeared, in the form of an illustration accompanying Jerrold Schechter's extremely unfair and dishonest article in *Esquire*. (When a copy of this magazine arrived in the institute's mail, our censor stamped it "top secret.")

These articles contained worn-out, slanderous themes. For example: the institute was an instrument of the KGB† and I was "a Soviet intelligence official." This campaign also attempted to undermine the scholarly reputation of the institute and its staff by portraying us as "functionaries" attempting to mislead and confuse Americans. The American mass media were sharply criticized by the authors of those articles because they so willingly provided us with an outlet and were billing us as "leading Kremlin experts on American affairs." We were accused of having "created" the antiwar movement in the United States, Canada, and Western Europe (this is very flattering, but unfortunately the peace movement was not our doing) and of sowing the seeds of a nuclear freeze on American soil. In point of fact, things were, of course, the other way around—the idea of a nuclear freeze came to us from the United States. The hostility toward us was not limited to words. Some members of the Reagan administration had very strong negative attitudes toward us. This administration was obsessed with advertising, propaganda, and public relations, and was more controlled by ideology than any other. They came to the conclusion that the institute's people were too effective on TV and in the press (perhaps because the American media saw me as one of the unofficial spokesmen and advisers of the Soviet leadership). Many of my American acquaintances told me about this. How similar it all was to the "Suslov syndrome" that I knew so well—the fear that, God forbid, some "evil idea" might penetrate people's minds!

---

*Donald Freed, *China Card,* New York: Arbor House, 1980. In this novel, I was given the somewhat flattering though unaccustomed role of savior of the world and romantic lover—both caused jealousy in different circles (including in my wife).

†I can say that our relationship to this organization was no greater than that of other institutes of the Academy of Sciences. (And in certain respects even lesser; considering my connections with the country's leadership, the KGB was hesitant to put too much pressure on me.) It is true that several of their people worked at our institute—I knew it officially. The situation has changed, and today, to my knowledge no one from the KGB is on the staff of the institute.

At the beginning of the 1980s, the American authorities began to put all sorts of obstacles in the way of the institute's scholars and myself, mainly to prevent us from making appearances in the American mass media. In 1982, for example, they cut my visa short in order to prevent my appearance on Bill Moyers's TV program. In 1983, they gave me a visa on the condition that I would have no contacts with the media. (This resulted in tremendous publicity for me. The U.S. State Department handled the affair clumsily, and the story became the subject for one of ABC's *"20/20"* programs.) At the same time the relations between the institute and the U.S. Embassy in Moscow became strained.*

A little later, when the first positive signs of change in our relations began to appear, Charles Wick, the head of the United States Information Agency, even offered to lift my visa restrictions on the condition that I arrange some "compensation" for the Americans—that is, in return they could also make appearances on Soviet television. (I responded that I had no interest in making American TV appearances, that I was being invited to do this, not trying to foist myself on anybody. Therefore, there was no basis for compensation. Besides, I had no power over Soviet television.) My colleagues and I regarded this worsening of relations with the Reagan administration as something natural, even as a kind of compliment, if you consider the extremely hostile positions toward our country that the Reagan administration adopted at first.

*Of course, some of the difficulties arose out of pure misunderstanding. One day Jack Matlock, then a minister-counselor and later a very successful U.S. ambassador in Moscow, called me and asked for a meeting. I invited him over to the institute. A very awkward conversation followed in which he told me that the U.S. government was fully satisfied with the existing lines of political communication with the U.S.S.R. and did not need any additional ones, and that he had been authorized to tell me this. I was at a complete loss as to what to think. It was only later that I discovered that certain Americans who had visited the institute had started the story in Washington that there was a possibility of opening up a channel of political communication parallel to the one through the embassy, and that the institute was prepared to take on this role. My relations with U.S. Ambassador Arthur Hartman were becoming complicated.

As mentioned, I was skeptical about "second channels," including the one that went through Kissinger and Anatolí Dobrynin. I think this channel benefited the United States more than the U.S.S.R., and I think Kissinger invented it to exclude the U.S. State Department and Congress from the game, since there could be leaks from Foggy Bottom to the Hill. As for us, our second channel worked the same as any other: according to what Andrei Gromyko decided, everything was sent either to the whole Politburo, or to a part of it, or to Brezhnev alone.

I would like to note that my personal relations with Ronald Reagan were friendly, if very superficial. We happened to meet in Washington in 1979, while I was standing outside the Soviet Embassy waiting for a car. He, his wife, and someone who turned out to be Michael Deaver walked by. They stopped beside me, and Deaver said to the future President that this was the Soviet Embassy. I recognized Reagan, greeted him and introduced myself. Strangely enough, he remembered this meeting; three or four years later, he wrote about it in a letter to one of our mutual acquaintances, jokingly asking him to "explain to Arbatov that I [Reagan] don't eat children." Later, when I would walk up to him in the receiving line at receptions during summits this became a standard joke. "So you don't eat your children, Mr. President?" I would ask. "No, no, Mr. Arbatov," he would reply. Or sometimes it was the other way around. He would start: "So now you know that I don't eat my children . . ." and so on. All this was quite friendly.

On one occasion he did get upset with me. Someone at the Geneva summit asked me at a press conference whether Mikhail Gorbachev had seen any films with Reagan in them while he was preparing for this summit. I said I didn't know. And besides, I added, those were B movies. It leaked to Reagan and, as I soon heard, this upset him. He even told Gorbachev: "Tell Arbatov that I've played in A movies as well—for example, *Kings Row.*" To his credit, he was not really offended; it was just a joke.

But there were people in Reagan's entourage who disliked me intensely. (Two notable exceptions were Vice President George Bush, with whom I became acquainted in 1971 when he was U.S. ambassador to the U.N., and Secretary of State George Shultz, whom I also had known professionally for a long time.) My "enemies" in Reagan's camp decided to offend me publicly by not inviting me to the U.S. Embassy reception when Reagan came to visit Moscow. This did not upset me; to a certain extent, it was even useful. Like the abundant "anti-Arbatov" publications in the U.S., it undermined the allegation by my conservative foes that I was "pro-American" and "pro-Western."

Another question often put to me both in the United States and at home, regarding my pre-perestroika relations with the U.S. was, Why did the institute and I criticize American policy in public, sometimes harshly, and why did we try to justify our own policy?

I would divide the answer into two parts. Yes, I tried wherever possible to defend Soviet policy. (I did not justify our invasions of Afghanistan and Czechoslovakia.) I agreed with many of our government's foreign-policy positions (for example, its objections to the neutron bomb and Star Wars); also, there were many things in our policy of which I was unaware. Moreover, I relied on official information (this applies, particularly, to our military affairs, the numbers of weapons, the violation of treaties, the feverish civil-defense program). Sometimes I simply found it difficult to believe that we were, in fact, doing the stupid things that people in the West were accusing us of doing. Unfortunately, as I discovered later, people in the West were right. I was also defending my country and its policies against unjustified attacks by American conservatives, which increased in the late 1970s and the early 1980s. And part of my position was, I admit, the result of conformism, a dose of which was a condition of survival. This may not excuse my weakness, but it explains it. Under the harsh conditions of totalitarianism and post-totalitarianism, if you wanted to do something useful and preserve what you had accomplished, you had to give some ground.

The second part of the answer concerns my criticism of American policy. I don't think that there is anything in my attacks on American policy in the early 1980s that I have to repent. People have accepted as received wisdom the idea that it was Reagan's political toughness and his decisive steps to increase America's military power that helped alter Soviet policy and demonstrate the futility of its warlike course. This is absolute nonsense. Those changes not only ripened inside the country but originated within it. The hostility and militarism of American policy did nothing but create further obstacles on the road to reform and heap more troubles on the heads of the reformers. It posed additional threats to democratic change, justifying both the harsh regime within the country and new Soviet efforts to increase the size of our own military-industrial complex. The reaction to America's military buildup brought out a real Frankenstein monster, which got out of control and undermined the new policy even during perestroika. In August 1991, this monster made an attempt to reverse the course of events by force, and we have not yet brought it entirely under control.

The early policies of the Reagan administration evoked hostility and genuine indignation in me and many others. I honestly condemned extremist conservatism, militarism, hatred toward other countries, and military blackmail, and I have seen how negatively such policies can influence events in the Soviet Union. Knowing the situation my country was in, and Brezhnev's deteriorating health, I had no doubt that the process of change would soon begin, but I was afraid, as were many of my friends, that matters might take a turn for the worse, ending in a swift restoration of Stalinism and a more adventuristic foreign policy. An extremely hostile policy in the United States would have also contributed to this. In this sense, the United States was playing a very dangerous game, and there is no way it can claim that it helped us lay the groundwork for perestroika.

This stage of American relations with the U.S.S.R. and our institute is over; our contacts with the Americans have been normalized. The good reputation of our institute in the eyes of our American colleagues has been preserved; the efforts to discredit it proved unsuccessful.

Still, I was surprised recently to read some quite flattering lines about the U.S.A. and Canada Institute in the entry about me in the *Biographical Directory of 100 Leading Soviet Officials,* published by Radio Liberty. Radio Liberty had been quite hostile to me and my colleagues in the past (and we reciprocated in kind). Now I am called the chief Soviet expert on the United States and "the director of a major Soviet political research institute that generates careful analyses of American politics and provides useful information about life in the United States to the Soviet leaders."*

I attribute such shifts in assessments of the institute to the radically improved relations between our countries which allow us, indeed compel us—both Americans and Russians—to judge each other, our leaders, our institutions, and our procedures more soberly, honestly, and wisely than before. I would like to return Radio Liberty's compliment. Its excellent broadcasts in the days of the August 1991 coup made me change my opinion of it.

I would not like what I have said about the institute to be interpreted as self-congratulatory. During the years of perestroika my colleagues and I began seriously to reassess our work. We have looked for and found plenty of faults in what we had been doing. What were the major mistakes and misconceptions? I have mentioned that in the 1970s I was

A Biographical Directory of 100 Leading Soviet Officials. Compiled by Alexander Rahr, Westview Press (Radio Free Europe/Radio Liberty), 1990, p. 16.

too optimistic about détente's irreversibility, despite some obvious blunders in our policy.

I was also reluctant to acknowledge the growing threat of the swing to the right in the United States in the late 1970s, although some of my colleagues at the institute had warned me about this in good time. I think that one of the reasons was that I was not fully informed about our military buildup and for a long time did not believe the West's statements about its dimensions; it inevitably strengthened the hand of the American extreme right. I also underestimated the adverse influence our uncertain political situation (the growing economic difficulties, the sick and aging leadership) had on the policy of the West. None of this predisposed America and its allies to develop better relations, to reduce arms, and increase cooperation.

Our forecasts of U.S. domestic developments were not always accurate, although neither Soviet nor American experts can claim to have been 100 percent right all the time. Despite some mistakes, the institute and I had a pretty good record. That is, of course, if you do not apply today's political and ideological standards to our work. For many years we were trained (often by very cruel means) to have a rigid mind-set. One of its characteristics was to defend Soviet policies and our way of life unquestioningly and unconditionally, however bad they may have been. But there were certain things I never defended publicly or in private: our military interventions in the postwar years; the arrest and persecution of dissidents; suppression of ideas, books, and free thought; attempts to justify Stalinism; militarism; and the like. We were also trained to have the most negative attitudes (they were called "class" or "Party" attitudes) toward the other side, and particularly toward "American imperialism." At the same time I do not want to deny my critical attitude toward certain aspects of the American way of life and especially of American foreign policy. I still think that dangerous imperial trends and ambitious tendencies existed, and, in some form, still exist in U.S. policies, U.S. political thinking, and some American economic and political institutions (including the military-industrial complex). But even in those days I rarely called America and its policies imperialistic as a whole. I avoided such political slang and the misuse of such terms.

We were trained not only to have a particular mind-set, but also to use specific language (the German Communists jokingly called it Party

Chinese—"Partei-chinesisch") that was horrible to those who were not
conditioned to it. You felt this when confronted with translations of Soviet articles or political documents into another language.

In addition, practically all of us, including people in my position, simply did not know many things concerning both domestic and foreign
affairs. Neither I nor any other specialists or political scientists were ever
invited to any meetings of the top leadership at which critical military-
strategic questions were discussed. Soviet positions and proposals at
arms-control talks were also kept secret, although we were assigned to
defend those positions during meetings with parliamentarians and in
public statements. We had to depend mainly on the Western press,
which we were trained to treat with suspicion but which, as we later
discovered, was, unfortunately, often right.

Apart from the errors imposed by stereotypes in thinking and even in
language, the basic lack of information incapacitated even our most per-
spicacious researchers. Therefore, I just cannot accept it when some critics now rebuke people like me, saying: "Earlier, you wrote that there
was, say, military parity in Europe, and now you indignantly protest
against a policy in which the U.S.S.R. has many more arms than the
West. Then where's the truth?" To this I would like to reply: "And
when did anyone ever tell us the truth? And do they tell the whole truth
today?"

But this is relevant only to some of my own and my institute's efforts,
mainly those dealing with military problems. On political and economic
issues we were relatively well informed and have to take responsibility
for what we wrote and advised. Some of my advice might not have been
too wise, but I do not remember ever having given any advice that damaged our country. And though in giving recommendations and making
proposals I did not always tell the whole truth as I understood it, I never
told lies or accommodated the moods of my superiors, nor did I slant my
arguments to please them.

Although our record is good overall, we realize that it is impossible to
live on just our old capital—especially these days when our country and
its policies are being redefined. It was hard enough for the institute to
survive as a refuge of pragmatic expertise and new thinking during the
period of stagnation. It is going to be no less difficult to remain productive and useful and to preserve our professional identity in the present
economic austerity and absorption with domestic problems, and with

growing competition from other centers of information and analysis about the outside world. Still, we are doing our best to adjust to this new reality, and I am sure that the institute will be able to respond effectively to the new challenges ahead.

Conclusion

Did my colleagues and friends ever count on the possibility that a hopeful new era would dawn after the political frosts of the late 1970s and early 1980s? To be honest—both yes and no. From the point of view of long-term prospects, yes. A totalitarian system is doomed to failure, since it contains the seeds of its own destruction. But short-term prospects looked far from simple. I have to admit that it often seemed to us that the Brezhnev era, even at its demise, probably represented the last awakening of our society. We feared the darkness of a new and merciless dictatorship that would not spare us, for by Stalinist criteria we had been too bold, too free-thinking, and too provocative.

For me this was an extraordinary paradox. While I was being "exposed" in the United States as a servant of Soviet totalitarianism, a threat to Americanism and a "subversive element," portrayed in cartoons as a cunning wolf, smiling and baring his teeth, I and many others were living in fear and foreboding of victimization and reprisals. This fear was exacerbated by a traditional and important element of Russian politics: those who worked directly with, or were regarded as being close to, the former leader (Brezhnev) were obliged to lay their heads on the block with the coming of the new one.

But who can foresee the odd and ingenious course of history? Suslov died, and Andropov took his place, suddenly becoming the heir apparent. This alone was cause for hope. When Andropov died, this hope seemed to fade. But things were not as gloomy as before. Somehow people understood that changes were possible—that, more than likely, change would come. Therefore, people did not think Konstantin Chernenko represented a long-lasting victory for conservatism. When he died, the grim forebodings and forecasts went with him.

We made great progress in the first years of perestroika. But the situation remains unsettled. Our future depends on what we do today—and to that end, the lessons of the past are crucial.

The first lesson that the post-Stalin years have taught us is that a lack of resolve, as well as excessive caution and delays, lead to a swift decline of reforms. Until the public establishments and institutions are overhauled, significant progress is impossible. Until fundamental changes are promoted and instituted by the unceasing efforts and encouragement of the top leadership, grass-roots reforms will not take root and survive.

Time plays an enormous part in the speed of reforms. If reform is prolonged, it risks falling to the side like a top that has stopped spinning. Certain sociological laws are probably at work here. When society rejects overdue reforms out of hand, revolution, with all its destructive consequences, becomes inevitable. But reform also means rapid change and not a slow, drawn-out evolution; so, when momentum is lost, the old conservative elements quickly adapt themselves to the situation and find ways to combat change effectively.

The second lesson concerns the fact that it is impossible to progress and develop successfully without opening oneself to the rest of the world, without becoming an active participant in the international division of labor, without making use of all the benefits of economic, scientific, and technological cooperation, and without taking full advantage of the world's economic, social, and cultural experience. At the beginning of the 1950s, a critical landmark in the history of our social development was the death of Stalin. But many countries that today astonish the world with their successes and are now on the leading edge of progress were in 1953 far behind the Soviet Union in their socioeconomic development. Japan's gross national product, for example, had only reached its pre-war level and the country was just beginning to restore its pre-war reputation as a producer of second-rate consumer goods. Few people could have envisioned in the early 1950s that West Germany or Taiwan, let alone South Korea, would be a serious economic power. I simply cannot imagine how many of these countries, or any country that achieved economic success after World War II, could have done so without active participation in the world market.

Fear has been and still is the barrier in the way of our decision to enter the tough world economic market. For some it is the fear of betraying the traditional values and "principles" that took root in Stalin's time. For others, it is the fear of the unknown.

Those who fear the risk of the unknown have to realize that every endeavor, every attempt to find a new way, involves risk. But today a refusal to strive for something new involves an incomparably greater risk, since the old way leads inexorably to further decline and catastrophe. Franklin D. Roosevelt's words are true in this context: "The only thing we have to fear is fear itself."

The third lesson is that we will never be able to put society on a normal track without overcoming militarism in our foreign and domestic affairs. We grew accustomed to this abnormal condition, and perhaps we would have tolerated it right until the final Day of Judgment and universal catastrophe, had it not been for economic realities. This burden of enormous military budgets has become intolerable not only for us, who spend up to 25 or 30 percent of our gross national product on defense, but also for the richest country in the world, the United States of America.

There is a fourth lesson to be drawn from the historical experience of the post-Stalin years—the effect of reciprocity on competitive international relationships. The essence of this is that whenever you take some action that involves your opponent's interests either in some region of the world, or in his new defense program, or in his military doctrine, or wherever else, you can expect a reaction from him. If you don't take this reaction into account beforehand, your action can backfire. In the world of global politics, no big power can remain the clear winner forever, or even for very long. Things are even more complicated where there is a clear loser. Inevitably, scores have to be settled.

This interdependence has existed mainly in the arms race and the Cold War. In recent years we have seen that it is possible to have a peaceful rivalry, even a disarmament race. This process, instead of a hostile military one, is moving my country and the United States from the latter to the former. And even at this very early stage, there is hope for the future.

At last we are beginning to understand that the real mission of foreign policy is not to conquer others or to build empires. It is to create external conditions that allow each country, each nation, to concentrate not only its might and resources but also its attention on solving its real problems, to concern itself with economic and social issues, with the spread of culture, science, education, health care, ecology, the quality of people's lives and the betterment of their well-being.

Now that the Cold War has ended, for the first time in decades we have the opportunity to change our priorities. History has once again provided us with a unique opportunity to solve our real problems. Will we make use of it?

PERESTROIKA AND AFTER

Volumes will be written on the collapse of so unprecedented and ominous a system as Communism in the Soviet Empire. But my history of the Soviet system would be woefully incomplete if I failed to comment on the historic period of perestroika, especially since in those years I played a more active political role than I had before. As I have noted, by the time Mikhail Gorbachev was elected General Secretary of the CPSU Central Committee, I had established a good working relationship with him. While I was working under both Andropov and Chernenko, he would often invite me to meetings or for one-on-one conversation, to seek my advice or just to talk things over.

When Gorbachev was made General Secretary, I decided that my most important task was to help introduce him as quickly as possible to foreign policy realities and ideas. (I have already described a couple of times when I helped him, including his preparations for his visits to Canada and Britain as head of delegations of the U.S.S.R. Supreme Soviet.) I must say that he had already made considerable progress understanding foreign policy, having apparently used the years between the deaths of Brezhnev and Chernenko to study.

But now he had become a leader who could work out and pursue his own foreign policy agenda. I wanted to help him at a crucial moment and spent several days and nights on a detailed forty-page memorandum on the key international issues. Gorbachev received the paper in early April 1985, and apparently thought it was worthwhile because he asked me to continue advising him.

Today the memo does not appear to me too wise or too bold, but by the standards of 1985 it was very unusual. First of all it was almost completely liberated from ideology, and amidst the prevailing climate that was a significant step forward. It began with a series of general observations. I wrote that the arrival of a new leadership always promises great new opportunities in political affairs—if only because the incoming administration was not bound by the old policy's inertia. But there is also a danger of disappointment, if new initiatives do not begin to materialize soon enough. I wrote, "If we face the facts, we will have to admit that, regarding our policies, the recent years have been a period rich in failure and poor in success." Associating the failure with both economic problems and "the loss of dynamism in leadership," I warned that "we are about to cross the line beyond which serious troubles may begin."

These general observations were reinforced by a critical analysis of the arms control talks and a proposal that we change our negotiating style and take unilateral measures, including issuing a moratorium on nuclear testing and reducing our armed forces in Europe. I was and remain convinced that unilateral measures were at this time among the most effective actions toward disarmament—attempts to negotiate a painstakingly accurate parity had already led the talks into an impasse. I then addressed the crisis in our relations with the United States and the West in general—a crisis for which I refused, as I refuse now, to blame the Soviet Union alone, though it carries its share of the responsibility—and with a number of regional conflicts and problems. There was a special section on the need to change drastically our relations with the countries of Eastern and Central Europe. Its main conclusion was that it was no longer tolerable that "the domestic stability in the allied countries be upheld only through the presence of our troops or the possibility to dispatch them there."

I would like to quote a passage from that document, one dealing with Afghanistan. "The war has been going on for five and a half years [longer than World War II lasted for us], but the situation is not improving. It costs a lot in blood and in material resources, it is damaging us politically, undermining our military prestige. If the present situation drags on for years, the costs may become prohibitive. . . . To withdraw the troops from a war you cannot win is always hard and unpleasant, but to be too late to withdraw is even worse." I mentioned the probability of changes in Afghanistan's government and reminded Gorbachev that, "we used to have fewer problems and troubles with Afghanistan when it was headed by the king and later by a bourgeois government than with 'revolutionaries' like Taraqi, Amin, or Karmal." Soviet and Cuban presence in Angola and Ethiopia and our unconditional support of the Vietnamese in Southeast Asia were discussed along similar lines.

Following that memorandum, I wrote to Gorbachev regularly, discussing both foreign policy and domestic affairs. When we met, we would often debate issues, at times heatedly. I am not suggesting that I was always right. But I wrote and spoke what I really thought. And I have a feeling that Gorbachev understood it. During these years, Gorbachev and somewhat later (from 1986) Shevardnadze were open to new ideas, including those put forward by people respected for their fresh approaches and by international organizations like the Palme Commission and the Organization of Physicians and Scientists. This meant a radical change in Soviet policies.

The first years of perestroika were unforgettable. Supporters of reforms and opponents of Stalinism were full of hopes and Gorbachev's popularity soared. We whose history had taught us to assess our leaders with caution and not to grant them big advances not only trusted him but came to love him, even when we saw some of his mistakes and weaknesses. The latter were fully revealed only much later and brought bitterness and serious disillusionment.

Before I write about them, I would like to make some general observations. In coming to terms with its Stalinist past, the Soviet Union had three major chances for salvation. The first came at the twentieth Congress of the CPSU, at which Nikita Khrushchev made his famous speech exposing Stalin's crimes. It could have become the turning point in Soviet history but did not for several reasons, the main one being that neither our leadership, the political elite, nor the public was prepared for serious changes and reforms.

The second great chance was perestroika. In the course of just a few years, the leadership managed to affect a substantial part of our society (though, perhaps, not as large as it seemed to us at the time). It also made significant strides toward freedom of speech and of the press and made the first steps toward political reforms. But we did not go far enough. Soon the pace of reforms slowed, the leadership retreated on a number of important issues, and a rightward political shift picked up momentum, culminating in the August 1991 coup.

The victory over the coup presented us with the third chance. It brought an unprecedented surge of democratic sentiment, a wave of optimism, even enthusiasm, and a sense of unity among the larger and better part of our society. That euphoria was fully justified, for unarmed citizens had just overwhelmed—or so it seemed—the world's largest armed forces and secret police. Supporters of totalitarianism were demoralized, discredited, disorganized, on the run. There was a real opportunity for great changes. One could move mountains. But before I describe what did happen, I think it is important to say a few words about the deterioration of Gorbachev's policy, for the failure of perestroika presents an historical lesson that should not be forgotten.

As with previous periods of revolutionary change in our history, perestroika began with its romantic phase. Then, following the usual pattern, this phase gave way to political polarization. By 1990 the battle between the hard-liners and the reformers was rapidly evolving into a crisis that put the future of perestroika into grave doubt. And today I must bitterly admit that we have forfeited this rare second chance.

Of course, there were early indications of the impending crisis. The first thunderclap of the approaching storm was published in *Sovietskaya Rossiya* in March 1988 by Nina Andreyeva, called "I Cannot Compromise the Principles." It was a real neo-Stalinist manifesto, printed with the authorization of Yegor Ligachev, a leader of the Politburo hardliners.

Meanwhile, most observers both in the Soviet Union and abroad failed to appreciate the significance of another, earlier event: the dramatic resignation of Boris Yeltsin at the October Plenum of 1987 from his influential post in Politburo and as the first secretary of the Communist Party's Moscow organization.

Yeltsin's move was in protest against the slowdown of perestroika and the conservative style of the Central Committee's Secretariat, headed by Yegor Ligachev. The plenum was also significant in that it shed a new and not very flattering light on Mikhail Gorbachev, who organized a strong attack on Yeltsin,* giving the first evidence that Gorbachev was

---

*I was a member of the Central Committee at the time and participated in the plenum, and remember very vividly how the hint to attack Yeltsin, made by Gorbachev, was understood. One after another, Party bosses rushed to the floor. They lashed out at Yeltsin in the spirit of the best Stalinist traditions, sparing no abuse. I could not stand it and asked for the floor, too—not so much out of sympathy with Yeltsin, whom I did not know personally, but simply because I felt that I would be ashamed later if I kept my mouth shut. I said a few rather timid words in Yeltsin's defense, but as far as the bosses were concerned, my statement was not only out of order but also revolting. I said, "Actually, the very fact that one member of the leadership says something critical about the work of another is not against the Party rules. I think that, to some extent, it is a result of

the kind of politician who would be prepared to make compromises on matters of principle for the sake of a power struggle.

Of course, at first everyone, including me, regarded such actions of Gorbachev as a tactic and believed the common wisdom that, in order to save perestroika and secure its success, he was compelled to keep maneuvering between conservatives and liberals, the right and the left. It is quite possible that initially Gorbachev really was aiming at far-reaching changes and was using all kinds of tactics to do so. I was prepared to believe him when he began saying in the late 1980s that power meant nothing to him, and that had it been otherwise, he would have never started perestroika—for who in the Soviet Union had more power than the Communist Party's general secretary? But the more he repeated this statement, the less credible it sounded. Gorbachev's ambition could not possibly be satisfied by power alone, by the very fact of becoming general secretary, especially after Brezhnev and Chernenko. He wanted to go down in history as a great reformer. And he was not alone in that de- sire—the whole country and even the Party wanted it, for by 1985 they were sick and tired of leaders who consolidated their personal power but did nothing else. That was the reason Gorbachev received so much sup- port.

With time, there were more and more signs that the problem was larger than just questionable tactics. Increasingly, the new Soviet leader's strategic line was given to vacillations that led to a very significant shift to conservatism and authoritarian rule. Frankly, I was so fascinated and enchanted by Gorbachev—even enamored of him—that I was slow to take note of his strategic ambivalence and lack of political scruples. But when I noticed them, I could not and would not conceal my opinion, which later caused a break in our relationship.

What were the reasons for Gorbachev's strategic deviations from the policy he set forth? Why did he betray his own best principles?

---

perestroika and a businesslike approach to work." I also said, "It would be wrong to try to picture whatever Comrade Yeltsin has ever said or done as bad. We are used to such a style, we remember how it was practiced in the past, and we must not revive it. By the way, you have to grant Yeltsin civic courage. His was not an easy step to take." That statement, the only one veering off the Party line, and which therefore sounded rather loudly, was immediately attacked by Ryzhkov. And, in the opinion of some of my friends, it was then that my relations with Gorbachev began to cool off.

Soviet intellectuals, especially those close to policy-making, have been debating those points over the past three years. One view, the one most critical of Gorbachev, is that all of us were deceived, having mistaken him for someone he was not. According to this view, he did not have deep reforms in mind, and while he ambitiously sought the fame of a bold reformer, his main goal was power.

Others hold that Gorbachev did want to achieve deep reforms, but only up to the point that they not disrupt his cherished institutions—preservation of socialism, though with a human face; preservation of the Soviet Union, as a system not as despotic and centralized as before, but still controlled in all its parts from one center; preservation of the Communist Party's power as the leading force in Soviet society.

According to a third view of Gorbachev, he did seek radical changes, but had to knuckle under to the pressure of conservative forces in the Party, the army, the KGB, and other state structures and renege on his original plans. Above all, even if he did decide on far-reaching reforms, he did not have the guts to change the key bureaucratic stratam. And when he did make such changes, he replaced the old officials with younger and sometimes even tougher versions of the same kind of people.

Each of these three hypotheses is plausible, but the truth probably lies in some combination of them. Whatever the reasons for Gorbachev's vacillations, his inconsistencies as a leader were becoming more and more manifest. And I often asked myself: What is it that Gorbachev ultimately wants? What does he really think? What is he trying to achieve?

Among the things that confused me were his frequent double standards. For instance, as early as 1986 Gorbachev started making sharp criticisms of *Ogonyok* magazine and the weekly newspapers *Moscow News* and *Argumenty i Facty*—the radical democratic media. But I cannot recall one instance when he would single out as worthy of condemnation any periodical of the right-wing bent—the daily newspaper *Sovietskaya Rossiya,* magazines *Molodaya Gvardiya* and *Nash Sovremenyik,* or even decidedly neo-fascist tabloids, despite the invective and slander that they kept heaping on his people, on perestroika, and often on his own person. Likewise, he would resort to harsh, often unjustified attacks on political leaders from the democratic camp, but would not utter a discouraging word about archconservative and even extreme right-wing groups and leaders, sometimes creating an impression that he was flirting with them. I do not know whether he was afraid of offending the right or, indeed, was more scared by the democrats and thus tried to keep his right-wing support—or whether, perhaps, as was widely rumored, his actions were influenced by his wife. But I was often puzzled by his behavior. I did talk to him about it a few times, but he would not give me an answer.

Even more serious doubts concerning Gorbachev's political integrity appeared in the spring of 1990, when with his consent an "Open Letter of the Central Committee to the Country's Communists" was published. This was the opening salvo in a campaign of persecution of all Party dissidents and liberals. As a member of the Central Committee, I received the draft in advance and immediately sent a very tough letter of protest to the Secretariat and to Gorbachev. Alas, in vain. As a result, control of preparations for the Twenty-eighth Party Congress was captured by conservative bureaucrats, the liberals and progressives were purged, and the Party irrevocably fell under right-wing control, which, in my opinion, predetermined the ensuing turn of political events against perestroika. This danger became obvious. During the party congress I wrote another letter to Gorbachev, trying to persuade him to resign the post of general secretary. I received no answer. It looked as though the party leadership's radical swing to the right was predetermined.

Soon afterward, around September 1990, it became evident that Gorbachev, too, had turned to the right. His rejection of the "500 days" economic program drafted by economists Stanislav Shatalin and Grigori Yavlinsky was the first signal. Troop movements near Moscow on the eve of a scheduled mass demonstration of the democrats were especially ominous. Then Gorbachev named conservative Leonid Kravchenko as head of the All-Union Broadcasting Company. Kravchenko, who announced that he "came to execute the will of the President," was quick to clamp down on radio and TV, which led to resignations or firings of their best journalists and the closing of some of the most popular public-affairs shows. At the December Congress of People's Deputies, the President requested and was given emergency powers that he immediately began using.

At that congress, Eduard Shevardnadze announced his resignation as foreign minister and made his dramatic warning of an impending threat of dictatorship.

I recall another characteristic episode of the December 1990 Congress. During a break, the President "went down to the people"—strolled around the hall, stopping to chat with deputies. He stopped near my row, too, and was surrounded by deputies who queried him about the reasons for his policy shift. He replied that, since the society had moved to the right, government policy had to follow suit. That response caused a lively discussion. I deeply disagreed with Gorbachev and soon found an opportunity to express my view to him in a letter. I wrote him that he misunderstood the changes in public opinion. Yes, the people were tired of chaos, confusion, ineptitude, and rising crime, and they did want some kind of order. But they certainly did not want order at the expense of a budding democracy. Aside from that, policy should not always obediently trail the changes in public mood; indeed, often it must resist those changes.

Meanwhile, harsh words were increasingly turning into repressive actions. The President began issuing orders, invoking his emergency powers—on joint police-army patrols in city streets, on the right of the police and KGB to conduct searches in offices without a warrant and to confiscate and impound documents at their discretion. Deployment of troops in peaceful cities was becoming a regular occurrence.

In January 1991 the Soviet army and internal troops of the U.S.S.R. Ministry of Internal Affairs were sent into the Baltic states, and government buildings, TV stations, and other important installations were seized. There were violent confrontations between the public and the military. Human blood was spilled—first in Vilnius, then in Riga.

Soon it became clear that we were witnessing not outbreaks of passions but, rather, the execution of a well-designed plan. Anonymous "committees of national salvation" were set up in the republics, and the central government was widely expected to intervene on their behalf, installing them in power and deposing the legitimate parliaments and governments.

Citizen protest prevented these actions from succeeding. Mass demonstrations began, barricades were erected around parliaments, and thousands of people stood guard on them. Hundreds of thousands of Muscovites filled the streets in solidarity with the Balts. A mass rally took place in Leningrad. Boris Yeltsin flew to Tallinn and signed important political treaties with Estonia and Latvia, and later, Lithuania.

The massive military operation did not take place. Hard-liners close to the national salvation committees were quick to charge Gorbachev with treason. One of them, Lieutenant Colonel Viktor Alksnis, stated publicly that Gorbachev at first sanctioned the move by the Baltic putschists, but then left them without support.

But Gorbachev continued to keep silent. After about ten days, he made a statement expressing his regret (though some also saw in it a share of condemnation) concerning the bloody events in the Baltics. But no real investigation took place. Neither was there any inquiry after journalist Yuri Shchekochikhin published documentary evidence in July that among the troops responsible for bloodshed in Vilnius were KGB special forces, the so-called Alpha Group, which reported directly to the head of the KGB and, through him, to the President. Shchekochikhin's article evoked no official reaction, despite the fact that a number of Soviet deputies, including me, made an open appeal for an investigation, which was publicized in newspapers and on TV. No wonder rumors began to circulate that Gorbachev himself played a role in the Baltic events: could it be, for instance, that he gave those who were planning putsches in the Baltics (and perhaps in other places) reason to think that if they should win, he would join them?*

Creation of a presidential "garrison state" was going ahead at full speed. Gorbachev obviously participated in that process. Why? I do not have an unequivocal answer to this question. But I think it quite possible that Gorbachev became frightened by the demise of the old structures of power and the growth of democratic trends beyond his control, and this pushed him to the right.

He treated these political developments not as a natural manifestation of the society's becoming democratic, but rather as a result of the intrigues of his political rivals, the democrats. He increasingly focused on the personality of Yeltsin, viewing Yeltsin's growing strength as a threat to his own power. Conceivably it was that personification of complex political processes developing in the country that explained many of Gorbachev's mistakes. The President's struggle against Yelt-

---

*Later, many came to view the January events in the Baltics as a rehearsal of the August putsch.

sin had become an obsession, and he stubbornly tried to "expel" the Russian leader from political life. Of course, opponents of perestroika skillfully played on that obsession, calculating that if those two most popular politicians should destroy or undermine each other, an avenue of attack would open up for the hard-liners. Such a threat was quite real, and it gained especially serious proportions in the winter and spring of 1991.

The political battle that pushed Yeltsin to some ill-considered statements—a call for Gorbachev's resignation, a public "declaration of war on the center," though at that time it would have been more accurate to say that the center had declared war on the Russian leadership and the democrats in general. Gorbachev, not to mention his associates, gave us enough reason to draw such a conclusion. His speech in Minsk in March 1991 was almost slanderous in its references to democrats with its veiled hints that they were tools of hostile foreign intrigues.

The conservatives quickly used Yeltsin's statements to mount another attack against him. They gathered enough votes in the Russian parliament to convene a special Congress of People's Deputies of Russia, at which Yeltsin would have to give a progress report on his policies. The plan was to oust him as chairman of the Russian parliament—after all, he had been elected by a narrow majority, while the parliamentary conservative faction, called Communists of Russia, was very strong.

Yeltsin and the democrats saw through the plan and called for mass demonstrations in Moscow, Leningrad, and a number of other cities on March 28, the first day of the congress. The Gorbachev government declared a ban on demonstrations in the capital and ordered troops into Moscow (estimates of their number varied from fifty to seventy thousand). Huge numbers of vehicles, including armored personnel carriers, cordoned off the city center.* Moscow was set for a showdown. But when it came, it was Gorbachev who lost.

One of the results of his defeat was that the demonstration did take

---

*Much later, in the fall of 1991, I learned some details of those events. It turned out that KGB chief Kryuchkov reported to Gorbachev that the demonstrators were planning to storm the Kremlin, using special hooks and ropes to mount its walls (those walls are so high it's impossible to throw a stone over them). Incredible as it may seem, Gorbachev apparently did believe that absurd disinformation borrowed from descriptions of medieval battles! Or could it be that he only pretended to believe it, trying to persuade his colleagues in the Soviet leadership that bringing troops to Moscow was justified?

place—if not in the very center of Moscow, then in other big squares. But there was a more important reason. Such an arrogant use of military force in politics shocked and angered even those people who up until then had remained neutral. The Russian Congress, on which Gorbachev pinned such hopes, voted to annul the government's ban on the demonstration, to suspend its session in protest against the ban, and to resume it only after the troops were withdrawn.

By the next morning, the troops had left, and the Russian Congress resumed its work. Yeltsin now had a majority firm enough to win the crucial vote on the establishment of the Russian presidency. The parliament scheduled the presidential election for July 12.

Miners' strikes were gaining strength throughout the country, this time demanding the resignation of President Gorbachev. Massive strikes hit even Byelorussia, traditionally considered a bulwark of conservatism.

A Gorbachev defeat was inevitable. And to Gorbachev's credit, he understood it and did change his course.

I felt Gorbachev's political waverings in my own dealings with him. As early as the summer of 1990, Yeltsin invited me to join his Supreme Consultative and Coordinative Council. I agreed, not regarding it as any betrayal of Gorbachev, especially since it happened during a period of cooperation between the two leaders. But in the fall, as Gorbachev turned right, my association with Yeltsin apparently served as cause for a sharp deterioration in our relationship.* In early 1991 I began to feel

---

*It so happened that I had my first opportunity to sort things out with Gorbachev in October 1990, when I was invited to participate in his meeting with Ted Turner and Jane Fonda (I introduced Turner to Gorbachev in 1988 and organized their first meeting). On the way to the meeting, Gorbachev dropped a few irritated phrases: "I wish you did not distance yourself, Georgi"; "don't fall off"; "you will regret it." He would not explain what he meant. During the conversation with Turner, Gorbachev complained that some people were predicting gloom and doom, looked at me and said, "Georgi here, too, is saying the same things." I interrupted him and asked again, "What do you mean, what are you talking about?" but still got no answer. Jane Fonda sensed the tension and tried to ease it. As she was saying good-bye to Gorbachev and wishing him success, she said, "But after all, I am encouraged. Dr. Arbatov told me that perestroika is doomed to success." (Indeed, in my previous conversation with her, discussing the difficult situation in the country but emphasizing that we must move forward, I said, "We are doomed to success—sooner or later"). Gorbachev looked somewhat surprised and asked her, "Did he really say so?" After the Americans left, I suggested to Gorbachev that we discuss our differences.

outright hostility, which spurred on my personal enemies. Press attacks on me became especially vicious, threatening letters and phone calls became more frequent.

On March 22, 1991, I got a call from Alexander Yakovlev, who was still a Gorbachev adviser, though on the verge of resignation. Yakovlev invited me to come over and have a chat. When we met, he told me of a long telephone conversation with Gorbachev in which they had discussed me, among other subjects. The President had said he was surprised and concerned that an old friend like Arbatov would be telling everyone that he was "all rotten" and "decayed." Yakovlev, according to his account, told the President that, while he would grant that Arbatov disagreed with many aspects of Gorbachev's policies and would even speak publicly about it, he could not believe that Arbatov would ever say anything offensive or derogatory about the President. Then Yakovlev said to Gorbachev, "By the way, Mikhail Sergeyevich, why don't you discuss it all with Arbatov personally? After all, you have known him well for a long time now." Gorbachev agreed and asked Yakovlev to offer me the opportunity to outline my disagreements with the President and my views on major policy issues in a letter, with the possibility of a subsequent meeting. Yakovlev promised to relay the message to me, as he was now doing.

On April 2, I sent Gorbachev an eighteen-page letter. I did not know that he was then mulling over his further actions in the wake of his failed ouster of Yeltsin. Referring to my conversation with Yakovlev, I repudiated the rumors of my alleged offensive remarks about the President, and expressed a fear that we were once again confronted with a situation when a political leader is gradually being isolated not only from independent-minded people but also from the facts of life. Mentioning that I had just finished my memoirs, I wrote that I had "long been pondering these things in the context of the fates of your predecessors. And I must say that I find quite a few analogies between recent events and the times

---

He replied that he had to attend a Supreme Soviet session, but promised to give me a call. Of course he did not call, and that was the end of it. But since that episode I have become convinced that some people around Gorbachev were constantly misinforming him and setting him against those who they thought had "a bad influence" on him. And, as I found out later, after the putsch, the main source of that disinformation was the KGB, with its wiretappers and sleuths.

of Khrushchev. I think it quite possible that a conspiracy against you is already being hatched and that among the conspirators may be people on whom you have been relying of late."

I drew Gorbachev's attention to the danger that, at his request, the presidency had been given truly dictatorial powers: "Many, including myself, consider Gorbachev morally incapable of becoming a despot and a dictator. . . . But what if something happens to him or he is deposed? Can one be confident in Lukyanov, who is clearly moving toward the No. 1 post, or in Pavlov* and Yanaev?"

I wrote to Gorbachev that whatever the reasons for the shift in his policy may have been, "it is extremely dangerous to continue the course of a close alliance with the right, a policy which resembles a game of yields† with militarists and reactionaries. I consider it my duty to speak out frankly on this issue, since I am deeply convinced that a continuation of the policy of recent months will inflict great damage to perestroika, to our country and society."

I concluded: "Today there is still time to exit from crisis. . . . It could be done through a return to the policy of perestroika and reforms, to an honest policy of democratization. That would require Gorbachev to re-unite with his natural allies—the democrats. Your reunion with the democratic segment of the public would not demand capitulation from either side. It would be a compromise based on a recognition of a few principles which seemed acceptable to both.

"First, putting top priority on the economic reform. Second, in order to save the Soviet Union we must reform it radically by going a long way to meet the republics' demands, agreeing to a serious decentralization and starting a dialogue with them on the basis of goodwill, rather than diktat.

"Third, we must renounce violence as a means of political struggle. And, of course, the current war between the President of the U.S.S.R.

---

*In September 1990 I was invited for the last time to take part in a policy discussion chaired by Gorbachev. About thirty people were present, including Valentin Pavlov, then minister of finance. We discussed economic issues, and Gorbachev asked me to speak. At the end of my remarks, I said, "Mikhail Sergeyevich, there is a special danger emanating from the Finance Ministry and Minister Pavlov. If you let them have their way, they will explode the society."

†Yields *(poddavki)*—a checkers game popular in Russia, in which a player wins by being first to yield all his pieces.

and the chairman of the Supreme Soviet of the R.S.F.S.R. [that is, be-tween Gorbachev and Yeltsin] must be stopped. Whoever takes the first step on this path and shows more tolerance and flexibility will gain politically. What is more important, it will be the nation's gain. Fourth, the process of democratization must be unfrozen."

I realize that these citations may sound self-serving today, but I must set the record straight.

I sent the letter with some inner unease, but also with a sense of ful-filled duty.

About three hours later, my special government phone rang, and a voice said, "Mikhail Sergeyevich will speak with you." Then I heard Gorbachev say, "Hello, Georgi. I have received your letter and book [the memoirs]. I haven't read the letter yet. As to the book, I looked at the contents, it seems interesting, thank you, I'll make sure to read it." I strongly doubted that Gorbachev had not read the letter before calling me, but I asked him to do so. "Yes, yes," said Gorbachev, "of course. But don't you fall off, Georgi." I expressed a hope that we would soon meet and clear things up. Gorbachev responded: "Mind you, I'll never draw back from my policy of perestroika, I have nowhere to draw back to. What is happening now is a tactical maneuver."

That conversation left me feeling ambivalent about Gorbachev's thinking. It was good news that he considered his shift to the right as just a tactic. But didn't he see that even as a tactic it went too far?

Our meeting never took place, but our relations thawed somewhat. And I wrote the President two more letters. In the first one, dated April 12, I urged him to "urgently state your readiness to sit down at a 'round table' and cooperate with republics and their leaders, including Yeltsin, and to restore your relations with the democrats. Otherwise, it may be too late."

Gorbachev called me at home the day he received the letter. He said, "I have received it, read it, and understand your concern. This is a re-flection of the ongoing developments, which concern me, too. Some of them you are not even aware of—you cannot imagine what is happening now in the Communist Party." Since we were talking on an open line, I did not ask him to clarify. I reiterated my opinion that the situation was very disturbing and that he must act without delay. He said, "Yes, I have already written to republic leaders, including Yeltsin. On my return from Japan, we will sit down at the table and talk."

I wrote my third letter on April 22. It was motivated by a concern that the right-wingers would mount an assault on perestroika at the Central Committee plenum, which was to open in two days.* I cited facts in support of such a forecast and argued that he was making too many concessions to the right, and made yet another appeal to him to return to his natural allies, the democrats, and to establish at least some kind of cooperation with Yeltsin.

At the same time I, as a member of the Consultative Committee under Boris Yeltsin, thought I had the right and duty to address him, too, recommending him to offer Gorbachev and republic leaders his readiness to cooperate for the sake of the country's salvation.

I am sure that other people, too, were giving the country's leaders similar advice. The leaders themselves could not fail to see what the situation required and what the nation was expecting of them. Finally, at the end of April, at a government reception house at Novo-Ogaryovo, near Moscow, where Nikita Khrushchev received Vice President Nixon in 1959, leaders of nine republics and the Soviet President started talks, which became known as "the 9 + 1 formula" or "the Novo-Ogaryovo process." It was a major step forward. The Novo-Ogaryovo process encouraged many of us to hope that the President of the U.S.S.R. had returned to his policy of perestroika, and that an agreement with the republics could be worked out, which would be critical to leading us out of the crisis.

To Gorbachev's credit, he was the first to state that we had a unitary (monolithic) state rather than a union, and that we needed to move toward a real renewed federation. But as in a number of other instances, he made a statement, repeated it several times, but then for a long time did nothing. Events were beginning to overtake the progress of policy-making.

---

*The assault did not take place. And Gorbachev finally did raise the question of his resignation from the No. 1 party post. His opponents immediately shut up. Both then and even during the putsch, Gorbachev, contrary to the opinion of some Sovietologists, remained absolutely necessary to his opponents on the right. Without him, they would have lost their legitimacy. It seems to me that Gorbachev, provided his concessions to the right were truly tactical, failed to appreciate that strength of his and to use it, just as he failed to use his enormous power in the first years of perestroika—the power historically inherent in the post of the general secretary of the Party—to advance the policy of change more resolutely.

Gorbachev's quest for an agreement with the republics met powerful resistance from the forces embodying the imperial traditions and ambitions—the Party leadership, the military-industrial complex and a large part of the top brass, the KGB, and the "generals of industry"—the top management of U.S.S.R. ministries that controlled the economy. They were supported by a political movement of a segment of the ethnic Russian and Russian-speaking population in non-Russian republics, fearful of becoming ethnic minorities in foreign countries, should the U.S.S.R. break up. Those fears were stoked quite effectively by local Party and military leaders and chauvinists from Moscow, trying to form a mass base for "the Russian party," made up of Russians living outside the republic—much as the Algerian *piedas noirs* formed a dangerous opposition to General de Gaulle in the early sixties. Still, despite the opposition, April 1991 brought a political spring to Moscow. The Novo-Ogaryovo process revived hopes that now, even without the Baltics and on a confederative rather than federative basis, we might be able to solve the critical problem of our state's future.

In the crucial area of economic policy, there were also some reasons for hope. Our economist Grigori Yavlinsky, together with a group of Harvard professors ("the Graham Allison group"), had worked out a new economic plan, which sought to tie in economic reforms inside the U.S.S.R., designed in stages, with large-scale Western aid. But soon, apparently influenced by the "Ryzhkov-Pavlov mafia," which he for unclear reasons favored, Gorbachev rejected this plan. As a result, the London G-7 meeting in June produced almost nothing.

The President remained just as indecisive (or was it his ill-fated tactic again?) in the political sphere. In June, the third dress rehearsal for a coup took place at a session of the U.S.S.R. Supreme Soviet. Addressing the session, Prime Minister Pavlov demanded emergency powers, including some presidential prerogatives. The imperial-minded Soyuz faction in the parliament supported him. The session was then declared closed, and the deputies heard the statements of KGB Chief Kryuchkov, Defense Minister Yazov, and Internal Affairs Minister Pugo. Somebody taped the Kryuchkov speech and publicized it. It was a real call for a coup. The whole story made an awful impression. But the next day, Gorbachev came to the Supreme Soviet and declared that there was no need to worry, that everything remained under control, and that he and Pavlov were in full agreement. Pavlov spoke next, professing puzzlement at all the fuss over his statement, which allegedly had been misunderstood.

I still fail to comprehend just what happened and why Gorbachev chose to downplay the scandal and not to break with those who were soon to head the conspiracy. The only explanation I have heard— namely, that he did not want a scandal, which would confirm the rumors of domestic instability in the U.S.S.R. on the eve of his visit to the London G-7 meeting—does not seem convincing to me. First, one could hardly expect to allay the Big Seven's concerns by sweeping the already publicized scandal under the rug. Second, this version fails to explain why Gorbachev maintained the status quo after his return from London.

Gorbachev refused to take a clear position and to heed numerous warnings, some of which, as it was recently reported, came from President Bush and Secretary of State Baker. In the Soviet Union, statements concerning a possible coup d'état and reports of the unreliability of many high officials, including Pavlov, Kryuchkov, and the leadership of the Defense Ministry, were featured prominently in the media. I also warned Gorbachev personally, more than once.

I cannot help recalling President Bush's visit to Moscow less than three weeks before the putsch. On his second working day in Moscow, George Bush gave a reception at the U.S. Embassy. Premier Pavlov was seated at the remotest table. Meanwhile, the resigned Yakovlev, the writer Tatyana Tolstaya, who had the reputation of a diehard "dissident" in Moscow, and I found ourselves at the same table with Gorbachev and Barbara Bush. In the course of the conversation Gorbachev said that he had read my memoirs and liked them very much. Then, looking me straight in the eye, he added, "I have read your letter, and on the whole you are right." Since everyone at the table was listening to that remark, I felt too uncomfortable to ask him any further questions, but his comment had to mean that he was aware of the danger. Nevertheless, a few days later, he left Moscow for a vacation.*

---

*In December 1991, I saw the BBC documentary "The Second Russian Revolution," and learned that during July, Yeltsin and Kazakhstan's President Nursultan Nazarbayev were also warning Gorbachev that Lukyanov, Pavlov, Yanaev, Kryuchkov, and Yazov were unreliable. Gorbachev promised to replace some of them after the signing of the Union Treaty, scheduled for August 20. In the film Nazarbayev relates that Yeltsin was worried during that meeting with Gorbachev that somebody might be eavesdropping on them. As it turned out later, he had good reason to worry: Kryuchkov had the room bugged and

On the day of the putsch, August 19, 1991, I was in Helsinki deliver-
ing a lecture and working on an assignment for Yeltsin. I will not go into
a detailed account of those three nerve-racking, dramatic days. Let me
just point out that my first task was to establish communication with
Moscow, which turned out to be quite difficult. I was able to make my
first call on the morning of the nineteenth via the Estonian foreign minister Lenart Meri, who came to Finland to head a government in exile in
the event that Estonia was occupied: the Estonians had wisely taken
steps in advance to set up autonomous lines of communication (in 1992,
Meri was elected President of Estonia). After that, I was able to communicate regularly with the institute and my family. I also managed to
get in touch with Ruslan Khasbulatov, chairman of the Russian parliament. I was categorically warned not to return to Moscow (which was
my first impulse on the morning of the putsch), but rather "to help from
out there." The idea was that I should facilitate a better understanding
of Moscow events by Western leaders (at first, it looked as if some of
them leaned toward political recognition of the conspirators, viewing
their success as inevitable), as well as mobilize Western support for the
resistance to the putsch. I worked at it as best I could.*

For me those were days of great personal anxiety. Frankly, when I

---

recorded the talk. I thought that this episode might have strengthened the conspirators'
decision to go ahead with the putsch faster and to accomplish it before the treaty's signing.

*Meanwhile, in Moscow, the U.S.A. and Canada Institute was the first and almost the
only one of the academy's institutes to adopt a formal resolution condemning the putsch,
declaring support for Gorbachev and Yeltsin and going on political strike. The resolution
(actually a manifesto) termed the coup "a criminal attempt to overthrow legitimate government in the country and throw the nation back to the times of dictatorship and lawlessness," and called on all "to support the legitimate authority and prevent the establishment of a dictatorship by the criminal clique." On August 23, I received a letter of
commendation signed by Ruslan Khasbulatov. It said: "On behalf of the Supreme Soviet
of the Russian Federation, I express gratitude to you and the staff of the Institute for the
Study of the U.S.A. and Canada for your activities during the attempted coup d'état of
August 19–21. Those activities were a logical continuation of the great work the institute
has been doing to help develop democratic processes in the country and implement
Russia's radical economic reforms. . . . I congratulate the institute's staff on the great
victory of democracy and wish you new success in your work." The letter made a special
note of those members of the institute's staff who participated in the defense of the
White House on August 20.

heard about the composition of the committee which headed the coup (the army, KGB, Ministry of Internal Affairs, and so on), I was almost sure that they had won their battle for power. What forces could possibly defeat this group, which commanded the country's monstrous apparatus of armed violence? Despite this accumulation of force, the conspirators were not likely to stay in power. But what suffering and bloodshed our people would have to pay for their clinging to power! Personally for me it would also be a tragedy. I would not be able to return to my country; the generals, the head of the KGB, and the prime minister saw me as a sworn enemy. The coup would have tragic consequences for my family, my son and my brother in particular, as well as for many people in my institute and many of my friends. The same fate would await hundreds of thousands if not millions of citizens, and military and police actions would be taken against the rebellious republics. The country was sinking into darkness.

But a few hours later, I felt some relief when CNN reported that Yeltsin was in the White House, [headquarters of Russian government] and had publicly denounced the leaders of the putsch as "a gang of criminals." I felt an even greater relief when I saw the trembling hands and meaningless blather of the putschists at their televised press conference.

Why did the putsch fail? I would like to add two reasons to the conventional wisdom that the putschists were inept and stupid and that perestroika had brought about great changes in the attitudes of the people.

First, it was sheer luck. My fellow citizens had a remarkable escape from a terrible disaster. They were lucky to have a fearless Boris Yeltsin as Russia's President, who became the rallying point for the resistance. They were lucky that the putschists either failed to arrest him early in the coup or did not dare to do it. And they were lucky that no provocateur or panicky citizen in the street opened fire on the soldiers, who were on the verge of a nervous breakdown themselves. The list could go on and on. And I emphasize this so that there will be no euphoria either in Russia or abroad. Luck is great, but you cannot stretch it too far.

Second, the conspirators suffered from a lack of legitimacy, which they needed to be accepted by their own country and the outside world. That explains why they sent their representatives to Gorbachev on the eve of the putsch to persuade him either to yield power to them or to join them in some capacity. Even after he rebuffed them, they were still hoping to "conquer" Gorbachev later, after they had seized power. Conceivably, that was the reason why they failed to give the order for large-scale shooting.*

The putsch's failure was a dramatic watershed for the country. It marked an end to the more or less evolutionary course of events and brought about a revolution that turned the country in a direction opposite to what the putschists had tried to achieve. They stated that they were determined to preserve the U.S.S.R. and therefore had to move fast, attempting to co-opt the signing of the Union Treaty at Novo-Ogoryovo. But actually the putsch touched off the U.S.S.R.'s fast demise.

The coup's organizers were careful not to talk openly about socialism, Marxism, and preservation of the Communist Party (their statement was the utmost hypocrisy in this regard). Of course their major purpose was to restore the Communist Party as an instrument of total political control. The putsch, however, had the opposite effect—the coup d'état became the Party's coup de grace. And its disbanding was not the final point in its dismantling. Many episodes from the Party's history still await scrutiny. For example, investigations of the use of Party funds are proceeding. And no doubt there are many other skeletons in the closet.

The system has fallen apart. One unquestionably positive ramification is that many totalitarian structures ceased to exist. But in the wake of this collapse, events became chaotic and unpredictable. The West focused primarily on just one element of this situation—the fate of nuclear weapons. But there are others: the still existing monster of huge

---

*The putsch was certainly a test for Gorbachev. And it is to his credit that he rejected the conspirators' demands on the eve of the putsch and thus denied their legitimacy. But he also shares a great deal of responsibility for the fact that the country found itself on the brink of disaster. It was he who put and kept in top positions, despite numerous warnings, political hustlers, opponents of perestroika, reactionaries, and immoral people. He also prepared and established through presidential orders or legislative action a whole package of emergency measures, which he apparently expected to use himself if the worst should come to worst (but which actually were used by the putschists). He even conducted a few "dress rehearsals" for the use of those measures, like the January events in the Baltics and the troop deployment in Moscow on March 28 (though as a result we had rehearsals of resistance, too, and people at least were not afraid of tanks and soldiers). Finally, he failed to heed numerous warnings and went on vacation despite the obvious danger of a right-wing move. And he had to pay a very high price for his long flirtation with the right, which he tried to justify as a tactical necessity.

armed forces and arms industries; the rapid and deep changes in the whole Eurasian geopolitical situation; the emergence of many sovereign and semi-sovereign states and statelike formations, where national independence has far outstripped democratic developments; and the threat of economic catastrophe.

This situation poses many complicated problems for the Soviet Union's successors—above all, for the largest states like Russia and Ukraine. It is in the West's interest to help them, and not just economically. It is very important that the states of the former Soviet territory are quickly integrated as full and respected members of the world community. But they must understand very clearly what they must do in order to achieve this.

Out of power along with the U.S.S.R. was President Gorbachev, since the state he had presided over had ceased to exist. His departure was also a proof that his highly reputed tactics had failed. When he shifted to the right and then tried to switch back to the center and the democrats, he found out after the coup that the democrats no longer trusted him.

As I have mentioned, history generously gave us a third chance for significant progress: the defeat of the August 1991 coup de'état, which paved the way for the democrats to gain power and seriously undermined their adversaries. In the aftermath of the coup's defeat, the leadership lost precious time immersed in a power struggle. Two centers of power were formed—one around Gorbachev, the other around Yeltsin—and the deep mutual distrust of the two men prevented them from working together.

The post-victory euphoria engulfed large numbers of democrats, apparently including some leaders, clouding their ability to face reality. Crucial strategic mistakes were made. One of them, which I will detail later, was a misunderstanding and neglect of top priorities, particularly the most urgent among them, far-reaching political reforms. In addition, Yeltsin, to everybody's surprise, left for a vacation at a crucial moment, and soon his ability to disappear at critical junctures became famous.

As a result of delays, loss of momentum, and the unfocused political program, the government was soon at a standstill, and its disintegration could be felt across the territory of the former USSR. The depth and speed of the breakdown of many social and political institutions was intense. The dismantling of the whole system of government and ideology produced a vacuum that everybody tried to fill—nationalists and even anarchists and monarchists. The ruling elite was also in turmoil. Some of the newcomers were quite intelligent, others not. A lot of new people who were coming to power lacked experience and well-formed views. They possessed varying degrees of honesty, too. Alongside them, the old elite continued to function. Only a small part of it organized itself into open opposition. Most of its members willingly integrated themselves into the new system—such as it was—trying to adapt to it but trying even harder to adapt it to themselves.

None of these developments changes the answer to the question I keep asking myself: Was it possible to make the transition from totalitarianism to normal democratic society less painful, more stable, and more orderly? My firm belief remains—it was possible at least until Gorbachev's mistakes and the August putsch destroyed the evolutionary process and provoked a revolution. And any revolution, even though it radicalizes and speeds up social change, also makes it unpredictable, uncontrollable, and highly contradictory.

How have the events of the winter and spring of 1993 affected the course of this second Russian Revolution? It is too early for final conclusions. Only the outlines are visible, but to my great disappointment and regret it seems to be a period richer in failures than in success. And not all the failures were inevitable.

Boris Yeltsin—a leader neither I nor most others fully understand, and indeed, a leader who most likely does not yet fully understand himself—is still evolving. I think it is too early to pass final judgment on him, but ultimately we will have to ask whether this politician was ready for the great mission history assigned him. Was he prepared to lead the country through a period of complex reforms, safeguarding it from disasters and upheavals, to build, in place of the old USSR, a federation of states, and above all, to secure civil peace in a society permeated with conflicts, distrust, and intolerance?

I saw him more or less regularly after August 1991. I have been impressed by his simplicity, directness, and readiness to hear things he might disagree with. On the other hand, he has struck me as stubborn—especially when convinced (sometimes wrongly, as it would later turn out) that he was right—and too quick to make decisions. His way of selecting his inner circle, or rather, of letting it form by itself, has not been terribly impressive either. He can be easily swayed by its members. And he can just as easily dismiss loyal and useful people—sometimes very rudely—without explanation.

Nevertheless, the country (and the whole world) is obliged to Yeltsin for halting the rightward shift to orthodox conservatism in Soviet politics and for defeating the August 1991 coup. He has made his way out of many very difficult situations due to his extraordinary political intuition. But it is still an open question whether he will be able to set up a responsive, professional government, guarantee that it will carry out its work properly and honorably, select and lead an administration of public officials capable of governing the country democratically, and help create a democratic society in Russia that is based on the force of law rather than the law of force.

The nature of the system, as we have seen, has determined that Yeltsin, like Gorbachev, Brezhnev, and other Soviet rulers before him, arrives at the head of the leadership with limited governing skills and economic knowledge. And while people can grow, especially at history's critical junctures, they can just as quickly disappoint. So, what awaits us now?

Having pondered this question, I came to the conclusion that Yeltsin's main weakness as a leader is that he has not prepared himself to respond to the spontaneous course of events with well-thought-out and well-designed policies, relying too much on improvisation and his own political intuition. I am mystified that the President, confronted with a formidable array of events and problems, has not made proper use of the country's very substantial intellectual capital, which is always at his disposal. Among his many resources, aside from the Presidential Consultative Council,* are scores of specialists at the Academy of Sciences and elsewhere with both theoretical and practical knowledge. There are also trustworthy reformers of the "first wave" who became prominent under perestroika, like Alexander Yakovlev, Vadim Bakatin, and others.

---

*Soon, many of us learned that even this quality did not last for long. When the Council was reorganized in the winter of 1993, a few of its members who had voiced criticism of some government policies on economic and other issues were not renominated, even though each of them received a very polite—even sentimental—letter of thanks with a request for continued advice in the future. This gesture did not surprise or disappoint us too much. It became more and more obvious that with time, Yeltsin, like most other political leaders, lost the ability to tolerate dissent.

Nor do I understand why, as he was making his decision on economic reform in October 1991, he did not even discuss Gaidar's "shock therapy" with prominent Russian economists such as Nikolai Petrakov, Grigori Yavlinsky, or Oleg Bogomolov. Nor why he discusses military reform only with generals. Nor why the problems of Russia's relations with the other former Soviet republics—our top foreign-policy priority—have been neglected for over a year. One could list many more such issues.

Boris Yeltsin initially impressed me with his willingness to tolerate other opinions and criticisms longer than any other leader I have worked with. But though he tolerated criticism, his ability to consider any of it seriously remained very limited. For instance, after his winter 1992 visit to the United States, where he made what I regarded as ill-considered proposals for retargeting nuclear missiles and for Russian participation in a global antimissile defense system, I gave a critical interview to the newspaper *Izvestia*. A few days after his return from the United States, Yeltsin met with me. He said, "I have read your interview and would like to explain something to you." I interrupted him, "As I understand our relations, Boris Nikolayevich, membership in the Presidential Consultative Council does not deprive me of a right to have my own opinion on any question and even to voice it publicly—in proper form, of course." "No doubt," Yeltsin replied. "We have had it up to here with uniformity of thought," he said, gesturing with his hand across his throat. But though he also tolerated criticism of Gaidar's economic policy from me and some of my colleagues, he nevertheless continued to support the policy with a stubbornness I could not comprehend. And he did not respond to criticism of mistakes in foreign and internal policy, including his lack of a strong anticrime and anticorruption program. I realized that tolerance of criticism alone did not give any guarantees against serious mistakes.

My observations and experience suggest it is a rule without exceptions that, sooner or later, powerholders become less willing to accept criticism (especially if things go badly). Power also changes a leader's character. The grave responsibility that comes with power has its effect, as well as the powerful feeling of invincibility augmented by the blind obedience and toadyism of many in the entourage. A leader is increasingly walled off by his staff, which is forever trying to monopolize influence by controlling not only the access of outsiders but the general flow of information. This is a very important lever in the decision-making mechanisms, especially in "post-revolutionary" governments. When democratic, constitutional procedures are not yet strong enough, and even simple order is often lacking, information is leaked and papers disappear, and documents are proffered for signing without adequate preparation and discussion much more often than in established democracies.

I'd like to turn now to the policy decisions of the past year. I shall start with diplomacy.

When Presidents Bush and Yeltsin signed the START II treaty on January 3, 1993, providing for a two-thirds reduction in the two countries' strategic nuclear arsenals, no lofty word was spared to praise the treaty, and I joined the chorus wholeheartedly. In fact, all the citizens of the Earth should be congratulated on this great achievement.

What did surprise me was that the leaders of both countries spoke of this landmark in disarmament as if it came from their efforts alone, as if it had not been preceded by years of tremendous effort, as if the end of the Cold War had not enabled the two superpowers to assess how much nuclear and conventional weaponry their arsenals actually needed.

The Cold War came to an end through the hard work and courageous struggles of millions of men and women. Forty years ago, great scientists like Albert Einstein and Bertrand Russell first sounded warnings about the nuclear danger. Throngs of ordinary people marched against the bomb, year in, year out, in London, New York, Bonn, and hundreds of other cities. While the Cold War was still on, prominent citizens risked their positions to join direct, uncompromising battles with the generals and the military-industrial complex. Groups of specialists like the Palme Commission and Physicians for Nuclear Disarmament and Peace dared spread the truth about nuclear weapons among both the public and the politicians. And, last but not least, there were the political leaders who labored hard at the summit conferences in Geneva, Reykjavik, Washington, Malta and elsewhere and were able to effect radical changes in the world's political climate. Mikhail Gorbachev, so prominent among them, fully deserved his Nobel Peace Prize.

It is important to remember the history that preceded the victory on January 3, 1993, not only to give each and every one his due, but also because we must learn to treat the past honestly. In order for future policies to be successful, it is very important for citizens to know how and at what cost great changes are achieved. Was it that innocent of the Bush administration to claim that it had defeated the USSR in the Cold War? Of course, that argument was clearly designed to help George Bush in his presidential race. But it was not the whole story. Whether he liked it or not, he was implying for the future that militray force remains an effective tool of foreign policy.

It is just as important to understand accurately why Communism collapsed. Some Americans argue that it happened because the West had stepped up the arms race, which undermined the Soviet economy. In fact, the arms race undermined both the Soviet and American economies and served to strengthen the positions of the Soviet military elite and the military-industrial complex, to boost the influence of militarism and Communist orthodoxy. By creating a hostile external environment, it frustrated the growth of internal contradictions, inherent in the system, as well as the courageous efforts of thousands and thousands of people who strove to free themselves from the totalitarian yoke.

These considerations, of course, do not diminish the importance of the START-II Treaty—in fact, in human terms I understand President Bush's desire, after his defeat at the polls, to crown his political career with a dazzling foreign-policy success. And indeed, it was a triumph for Russian foreign policy as well. But sadly it was about the only one we had in 1992. In the other spheres of Russian public policy, especially the economy, things went from bad to worse.

In the fall of 1991, many, including myself, thought that our historical opportunity for a renaissance could be effective only if we started with the country's economic crisis. Almost everyone regarded the economy as the number one priority, but in retrospect that seems to me to have been a major strategic mistake. Especially because the best and brightest of our economists and politicians understood that our economic crisis could not be cured by a quick shock therapy, that this task demanded many years of serious work, not haste and improvisation. Shock therapy deformed the whole process of economic and social development. It launched profound and nearly irreversible changes in the economy, the social sphere, and politics. Most of the population suffered serious and rationally unexplainable hardships, and so became disappointed and even desperate. This, in turn, fostered a danger that many people could become easy prey for demagoguery, thus seriously increasing the threat of authoritarianism and even fascism in Russia.

Culture, science, education, and health have inevitably become the first victims of Gaidar's Social Darwinism. But the costs of the shock therapy go beyond the impoverishment of the Russian people, hyperinflation, economic, social, and cultural degradation.

Throughout 1991 and 1992, debates raged over the Gaidar reforms. They were attacked by both those who wished to preserve the old system and those who, like me, thought that the "reforms," far from creating a market economy in Russia, would severely undermine our economy and social relations and create serious political dangers. We viewed them as variations on the "structural adjustment" model borrowed from the IMF. That model was designed for Third World countries specifically to squeeze debt payments out of them—and it had had negative results wherever it had been applied.

Today, a year and a half later, Gaidar has long since resigned. I, as one who has subjected the Gaidar reforms to harsh public criticism, should feel somewhat vindicated. But I feel sorrow at the lost opportunities, and I have remaining doubts and some guilt. Not because I am any less certain of my position, but I wonder whether our debates and polemics with Gaidar did not distract us from defining the major priorities. The victory over the August putsch created unique conditions for a political, not economic, reform. Economic problems needed to be addressed in the very first days, but there should have been a well-thought-out program of evolutionary changes rather than an ill-designed "big bang" of a policy.

It was of the highest importance to build a durable, stable political system based on a democratic constitution, one with real political parties, elections, a parliament, a presidency, a reliable civil service staffed with responsible officials, reformed army and security forces, a modern court system, human rights guarantees, and, of course, a free press. Democracy should have been institutionalized. Above all, it should have been a system based on the rule of law, capable both of protecting citizens' rights and of effectively combating crime and corruption. And, in a country like ours where the totalitarian legacy, the poverty of democratic traditions, and the weakness of legal institutions are all compounded by the myriad nationalities and religions and the age-old ethnic conflicts, there is an acute need for a sound ethnic and national policy.

Ethnic disputes are pregnant with danger even in their milder forms, such as those in Quebec or conflicts between small minorities. But we also have the bleeding wound of Ulster, and now, overshadowing all others, is the monstrous story of Yugoslavia's collapse. Simmering conditions in the former Soviet Union and in Russian territory, which encompasses a huge part of Europe and Asia, have the potential to produce a crisis on a global scale.

We in Russia have no right to avoid our responsibility for the events that are unfolding here. But we have a right to count on the support and if necessary, assistance of other countries. There must be no place for a revival of totalitarianism—be it communist red or fascist brown—no place for nationalism or ethnic and social extremism.

With such a formidable array of political problems, we placed an ill-conceived economic program at the top of the agenda and in doing so, I believe, we missed a rare opportunity to spur the country's revival. I do hope though, that Russia may soon redirect its efforts and institute far-reaching democratic and political changes, even this year. Then, perhaps, all other problems, including the economy, will become more manageable. The sad fact is we squandered a real chance immediately after the defeat of the coup, when the democratic forces were riding high and their opponents were in full disarray. Alas, it did not happen. And the situation began to deteriorate quite seriously.

By the fall of 1992, the failure of Gaidar's economic policy had become evident. In January 1992, the government promised that the economy would turn up in four to six months. In May, the promise was of improvement by the year's end. The failure of those calculations should have been obvious, at least to anyone who was not totally blind or deaf or had a personal stake in the chaos reigning the country's economic life. (It was chaos, which always breeds crime and corruption, that gave quite a few people a chance for quick personal enrichment.)

It is my impression that the Russian President was one of the few people who failed to assess the situation, and a major reason for his failure was the continued Western support for Gaidar's policy.

The country's economic crisis had disastrous political consequences; above all, it inspired a growing confrontation between the executive and legislative branches, which on the surface often looked like a personal conflict between President Yeltsin and Parliamentary Speaker Khasbulatov. It was an unfortunate image, for it prevented many Russians and an even greater number of Westerners from seeing the essence of the problem, which was the failure of economic policy and the unwillingness of either the legislative or executive branch to take the responsibility for it.

I believe the President's inner circle played a fateful role. Yegor Gaidar and some others (I will mention only one of them, Gennady Burbulis, who introduced Gaidar to the President and apparently was so eloquent in persuading the President of the virtues of shock therapy that the latter is said to have signed an order making Gaidar Vice Premier even before meeting him in person) were very scared that the expiration of the President's emergency powers on December 1, 1992, would allow the Parliament to call them to account and relieve them of their duties. To avoid such a turn of events, they started pushing the President toward a confrontation with the parliament.

In effect, it meant putting aside even the most pressing economic tasks, like a search for an exit from the government-triggered economic depression, and concentrating fully on political struggle against "the enemy"—and if such did not exist, one had to be created, fast.

So, the Parliament (the Supreme Soviet and the Congress of People's Deputies) was made Enemy No. 1, on the grounds that 25–30 percent of its cast were real reactionaries—either hard-line Communists or extreme Russian nationalists and even fascists.

The very fact that the parliament's proceedings are broadcast on TV, unlike meetings of the presidential administration and the government, worked against the legislative branch. It was quite an unattractive display, especially since extremist MPs were the most visible, although I do not think the other branches of government would have looked much better. Thus, the very parliament that elected Yeltsin its chairman in 1990 and gave him emergency powers in 1991 to enact reforms now looked as if it were a bulwark of Reds and Browns.

Eighty-seven percent of its members are former Communists. But there is an even higher percentage of them in the executive branch, including the presidential administration. All of them are made of the same dough, as the Russian saying goes, but you can meet people of widely varying views in both groups. And yet, a stereotype has been created—both in Russia and to an even greater degree in the West.

Be that as it may, by fall the country found itself distracted from constructive work and once again drawn into heavy political fighting. Society was becoming increasingly polarized; the center was eroding; moderates were losing ground. The press lost some of its freedom, as electronic media were under government administrative control and print media with a democratic orientation, fell into growing economic dependence on governmental subsidies. I consider these dangerous developments, especially for a country like Russia, which was for decades raised in the Bolshevist spirit of implacability and intolerance and in the traditions of struggle against foreign and domestic "enemies." We saw once again that the system was refusing to go quietly, showing a remarkable viability and capacity to adapt.

In May 1993, I turned 70. I will hardly continue in politics much longer. At this age, one inevitably tends to think more of one's reputation and one's soul, as it were, and least of all about swimming with the tide.

That is why I cannot be silent on what I disagree with, including some of the President's policies. In November 1992, both in a personal conversation with Yeltsin and later at a meeting of the Consultative Council, I firmly opposed the emerging trend toward political confrontation and defended the ideas of compromise and coalition-building. Alas, December brought a new period of acute political fighting, which continued into 1993 up to the April 25 referendum. Though the President won an indisputable victory, the battle is unlikely to abate. It began to rage first over the new constitution and later over the elections. Combined with the deteriorating economy, such a situation can have unforeseen consequences—like the threat of a new dictatorship. Apparently it will take a full change of political personalities and institutions to end it. I hope that the costs will not be too high. Nevertheless, it should be noted that we in Moscow, plus the majority of foreign observers, overestimate the importance of our political battles. Most of the country is too busy fighting for its survival to care about them too much. The success stories that we're beginning to see in these regions and communities may be the light at the end of the tunnel.

I agree with our well-known economist Grigori Yavlinsky, who recently concluded that the period of reforms from "above" has come to an end and a period of grassroots change has begun. After all, the country must overcome the crisis and survive. Destroying the totalitarian system is not enough: we must build a democratic state on its ruins. It is only as a full-blown democratic state that Russia can achieve progress and stability and enhance international security. And I am puzzled and angered by the talk by some of our homegrown "democrats," not to mention Western observers, that we should follow the examples of Pinochet, Marcos, and the Shah of Iran—they may not have been democrats, you see, but they were committed anticommunists!

In conclusion, I would like to address a few words to the West. Europe and America understand how important it is that reforms in Russia and the other republics be successful. But they still have no clear idea of how best to promote those reforms, and this fuzzy-mindedness played a very negative role in 1992.

I have wondered many times how we could have accepted the concept of the Gaidar reforms at face value. How could the country's generally cautious leadership have so easily trusted an unknown group of economists, unimpressive as theoreticians and totally lacking in practical experience.

I think this happened mainly because the leadership accepted the notion that Gaidar's group based its proposals on the best theories of world economics and the experience of the most prosperous countries. For one thing, there was a high regard for the IMF and its experts. No less importantly, Moscow interpreted the positions taken by some Western leaders including those of the U.S. as unequivocal approval of the ideas of the Gaidar cabinet. I am not sure whether there were grounds for such an interpretation, but the West encouraged Russians to think so. Perhaps Western leaders saw a reform that would make Russia's quick transformation to capitalism the top priority. This view was especially characteristic of American and British Conservatives—(Yegor Gaidar is also a conservative on economic issues) His program was a sort of Russian Reaganomics. The ideological considerations and excessive self-confidence on the part of some Western experts played a dominant role, though their knowledge and understanding of Russia were questionable. But I do reject the notion held and actively publicized by some of my countrymen that the West was intentionally giving us the kind of advice meant to destroy the Russian economy and deindustrialize the country: after all, most Western politicians are aware of the dangerous international ramifications of a Russian collapse.

Now the West finds itself faced with an option: What is more important for Russia, democracy or reform? I am convinced that such an option does not exist. Without democracy Russia will never have a developed, contemporary market economy which could insure social and political stability. It is especially urgent since the wrongheaded economic policy that has been embraced has already undermined the democratic forces in Russia, has to some degree even discredited the notion of democracy, of market economics, of Western policy toward Russia, and, though I wouldn't overestimate this threat, the increased danger of fascism.

If more and more Russians come to believe that the failures of democracy, market economics and reforms were the result of Western advice, that can undermine Russian trust toward those whom we only recently stopped perceiving as our adversaries and would now like to see as our friends. I would like to see us avoid such a scenario at all costs.

In the spring of 1985, I was a Communist—doubting and disappointed, but still a sincere Communist. Why? How could I keep the faith in socialism, Marxism, and even the Party? I had seen some of the things hidden from the public eye, I was knowledgeable and experienced, I had seen the world, and I could not take our propaganda seriously.

Let me clarify that when I speak of the Party, I mean not its power structure, the apparatus, and the leadership—my faith in those had long ago evaporated—but a general political notion of something fair and just. A religious person may remain loyal to his church despite disappointments in the clergy. The same applies to Marxism—not the crude stereotypes or quotation books, but some of the theoretical principles. I keep my faith in socialism, too, associating it not with my country's current reality or with its propaganda, but with the ideals of social justice that had existed for centuries.

My faith was not blind. As late as 1987–1988, I still believed in the possibility of the Party's renewal, which would help to reform the system. In 1990, there was almost nothing left of those hopes. And in 1991, I became convinced that the CPSU had become a force irrevocably hostile to the public interest.

I had seen the light and my political views and behavior had changed. Before Stalin's death I believed in much of what we were taught, even though I was neither a fanatic nor a cynic. After Stalin's death, and especially after the Twentieth Party Congress, I began the transformation from a subject to a citizen, trying to think for myself. And during some of the leadership's policy decisions I found myself at first in moderate opposition, calling for the reform, rather than the destruction, of the system.

During my work with the leadership, I had opportunities, however modest, to try to influence government policy. Often the chances were illusory; but I took seriously those opportunities that presented themselves. I tend to think now that I exaggerated what was actually possible but I tried to make the best use of the chances I had.

The small victories that my associates' and my own work sometimes gained were a cause for satisfaction. And in the first years of perestroika, when almost everything suddenly seemed possible, we became more and more convinced that we were doing the right thing.

It is natural that in such circumstances I would give most of my time and effort to work for the leadership, trying to help Gorbachev as best I could. While things were going well, the role of adviser, even an unofficial one, suited me. Especially since I so strongly believed in Gorbachev and in his absolute commitment to bold democratic reforms.

But the very logic of those reforms, as well as the political struggles, which were getting more and more acute, were forcing everyone to take a political stand, however modest. I started by participation in debates in the press, at Central Committee plenums and the Party Conference, at the discussions on economic and political matters Gorbachev was convening.

Gradually I decided to run for the Russian parliament in the country's first free (actually, semi-free) elections in the spring of 1988. My first attempt failed, when I was opposed by anti-Semitic reactionary groups tied to the notorious Pamyat society. Against the advice of many of my friends, who were concerned about my health and wanted to spare me the rigors of a new campaign, I made another attempt, this time running for one of the seats allocated to the Academy of Sciences. It was a tough, challenging race. I am proud that I did win and became a people's deputy of the U.S.S.R. from the Academy of Sciences, along with Andrei Sakharov and a number of other well-known Soviet scientists.

In parliament, I was quite busy. As a member of the commission formed to investigate the 1939 Molotov-Ribbentrop pact, I participated in establishing the truth about secret protocols to the treaty, whose very existence had long been denied by Soviet officials. That was a significant step in bringing to light Stalin's criminal policies on the eve of World

War II. I took part in the work of another commission, which was to give a political assessment of the decision to invade Afghanistan.

In December 1989, I took the next step, which put me into the ranks of radicals. Speaking at the Second Congress of People's Deputies, I advocated a deep reduction in military spending and substantive changes in our overall national security policy, which turned out to have been almost untouched by perestroika.

In recalling all of this, I do not want to be self-serving, but this subject has been dear to me for many years. I came of age during wartime and I have never forgotten the awesome carnage of war and the terrible impact of militarism on society. One of my first articles, published in 1955, set out to prove that militarism was historically doomed, and that was also one of the major themes of my doctoral dissertation and of my first book.*

Post-1985 changes in Soviet policies gave me opportunities to use my knowledge and experience in policy-making. In particular, I argued with the leadership for the earliest possible end to the war in Afghanistan and for a unilateral moratorium on nuclear testing. I urged the leaders to stop the buildup of SS-20 missiles in Europe and elsewhere, and to seek a rapid solution to the problem of deadlocked negotiations concerning conventional arms and forces in Europe, which could not proceed without our major unilateral cuts, given our superiority there. I objected to our being drawn into the ABM race, especially in regard to SDI and to the naval buildup.

I was happy that many of those ideas made their way into official policy, even though I am far from ascribing those successes only to my own efforts—those ideas were shared by many and they were ripe, some even overripe. But still, beginning in late 1988 and especially in 1989, I sensed a growing concern that our policy was losing its momentum. Despite the country's worsening economy, we were not taking advantage of the opportunities we had won to concentrate means and resources on domestic problems. It was getting increasingly clear that the main danger to the country was its internal crisis, rather than any external threats.

At the time, I interpreted Gorbachev's position in this way: he under-

*The subject has stayed with me through my scholarly and political work. Perhaps that was the reason I was invited to join the Palme Commission. Work there served to strengthen my anti-militarist convictions and add to my knowledge and experience.

stands that we must move forward on demilitarization, but faces strong resistance from the generals and the military-industrial complex, and thus needs help and support. I was trying to provide him with that.

In November 1989 I sent letters to the Presidium of the U.S.S.R. Supreme Soviet, then headed by Gorbachev, and the Central Committee—Gorbachev was its general secretary—proposing a radical reduction in military spending. The immediate reason for writing the letter was the news that the navy had just received two new aircraft carriers, while work on the third had begun. But I posed larger questions about serious changes concerning our military posture.

In December 1989 at the Malta summit, I had a rather harsh exchange with Admiral Chernavin in the presence of Gorbachev, Yakovlev, Shevardnadze, Akhromeyev, and others. Chernavin promised to respond to all the questions I had raised in my letters at a Supreme Soviet session. The response never came.

It was then that I decided to criticize our defense policy and exorbitant defense spending from the rostrum of the Congress of People's Deputies. I said in my speech that one of the opportunities that had developed as a result of international changes was "to substantially reduce military expenditures. We need it badly. One of the worst manifestations and products of stagnation was that the military and defense industry got a free hand. They launched numerous costly and often unjustified military programs, some of which would even violate existing treaties (the Krasnoyarsk radar station is an example). Now they are a heavy burden on the national economy.

"Our economy," I said, "has been literally eviscerated by military spending."

My remarks were met with applause, but a counterattack began immediately. Some of the statements contained lies and slander. I responded with a short retort. Gorbachev called me later that day to say that he liked my speech but thought I should not have answered my critics.

That was the start of my debate with the generals and the military-industrial complex, which continued until the putsch of August 1991. I am happy that I started the argument. After all, it was about the central issue of reforms—the departure from Stalinism. From an economic point of view, we will never be able to achieve any kind of prosperity in the country without radical demilitarization. It is the only way we will be able to build a civil society and establish the rule of law and a state based on democratic principles; in foreign-policy terms, it is the only way to build a durable peace.

This debate with the generals touched off the first ever public discussion of Soviet defense policy and military spending. Most important, I was able to draw my opponents out into an open discussion in which they lost their main traditional advantage—mysterious silence, justified by national security. Open discussions made it easier to ask our generals some very uncomfortable questions that they had studiously avoided answering in the past. I consider it a victory, though the forces were unequal. In the course of those debates, I published three articles in *Ogonyok* and two in *Izvestia,* and twice I appeared on TV. My opponents published several dozen articles. Many of them went beyond the bounds of civilized discussion and were more like a Stalinist informer's report, full of invective and slander.* The weightiest of them were written by Marshal Sergei Akhromeyev, who committed suicide after the putsch—I think because he understood that by joining the conspirators, he, an adviser to President Gorbachev, had committed treason.

But the struggle against our militarists earned me more than denunciations. Having found myself in the radical opposition, I also gained the support of many people, including honest military officers.

As I mentioned, the failed coup meant the end of evolutionary development, the end of the Communist political regime, and the end of the Soviet Union as a state.

I am sure that practically none of those who started and supported perestroika expected such consequences. These results may be welcomed abroad and by some people at home, but in the minds of my compatriots they also raise questions because together with the destruction of quite a few remnants of totalitarianism, the collapse of the whole political structure introduced serious uncertainties and problems.

I repeatedly asked myself: Was all of it—especially the negative events—inevitable? Accepting what has happened as a fact of life, I

---

*In particular, I was charged with attempts "to undermine the military doctrine and defense capability" of the country, a desire to destroy "defense consciousness" and assure "the death of the Russian state." Authors were advancing guesses that "agents of the American CIA or the Israeli Mossad were ensconced in the institute, headed for a quarter of a century by Academician G. A. Arbatov," calling me a "U.S. *Gauleiter,*" and so on.

must at the same time express my sincere belief that the course of events could have been different. The System had to go. It had to die, though maybe not by committing suicide. I do not mean the falling apart of totalitarianism—this of course was a welcome inevitability. I mean unnecessary and rather costly "by-products" of such a development. The most obvious casualty of the post-coup chaos was that the economic crisis became much more acute. Another, more complicated side effect was the collapse of the Party. Of course, the Communist Party was one of the main instruments of totalitarian rule. But its sudden collapse left a power vacuum and a completely disorganized political process. Could it have happened differently? I think so. Had the policy of our leaders been more farsighted, the Party would have split into two or three parts, including a strong social-democratic faction. And that might have laid the foundation for a multiparty system, an absolutely crucial element in a truly democratic society.

I know for a fact that several years ago such a scenario was discussed within a narrow circle of Soviet leaders. But Gorbachev rejected it and soon capitulated to the reactionary majority of the Party leadership, virtually betraying the reform wing. A renewal of the Party was possible in principle, but only with a more resolute leadership prepared to take unorthodox steps.

The so-called real socialism under which we allegedly lived before perestroika was far removed from the original ideals. And our first and foremost task was to solve the most pressing problems—food, housing, social security, protection of human rights, and so on—in short, to become a normal society. I think it was well within our capabilities. We did not have to destroy the economy first to build a market on its ruins. After all, the old economy did work—admittedly poorly—but the people were fed and its performance was certainly better than during five to six years of perestroika. What prevented us from proceeding with reform was the country's disastrous economic management and the ideological timidity of the leadership, including Gorbachev. Up to his last day in office he did not dare utter the words "private ownership of land." As a result, even in a country as rich in natural and intellectual resources as ours, the task of assuring decent lives for our people is even more difficult than before.

Despite the current state of the country I cannot agree with the opinion that our failures have killed the socialist idea itself. It was born at the dawn of civilization and had, and still has, many adherents and a real viability. To some extent, it has already been implemented in the world. It encompasses social justice, care about the common people, opportunity, peace, a right to participate in decision-making.

It is a great paradox of history that, having brought so many sacrifices to socialism's altar, the Soviet people have achieved so few socialist gains. What's worse, we have thoroughly compromised the very notion of socialism. But our sacrifices have helped other countries make their societies more decent and, in many cases, quite prosperous. Franklin D. Roosevelt's New Deal was the most prominent example. It borrowed something from the socialist ideal and even something from the Soviet experience, which pioneered large-scale social programs and economic planning. Ironically, the sheer fact of the Soviet Union's existence and the perceived threat of communism and bolshevism made even the more conservative opponents of President Roosevelt more willing to accept liberal reforms (from above) in order to avoid a revolution (from below). In this sense we pressured Roosevelt (and other Western leaders) into saving capitalism. It became a new capitalism, one with a human face and one very different from the society argued against by Marx, Engels, and Lenin.

Must we ignore these pages of history now that we have acknowledged our mistakes and miscalculations? Should we attempt now, as some of the economist disciples of Friedrich von Hayek, Milton Friedman, and Jeffrey Sachs are urging, to "build" nineteenth-century capitalism at the threshold of the twenty-first century? I am deeply convinced that such a capitalism today would be rejected by the United States and other advanced Western countries, but many in my country, burdened as they are with their own failures, have forgotten about capitalism's darker side and inglorious ancestry.

We need not take this path. But I am not sure that we will be wise enough to heed the world's experience and our own, and refrain from overreacting to our unhappy past. There is a real danger of this, and it is intensified by the fact that we were not only too slow and indecisive at the start of perestroika but have also made huge blunders in managing the economy.

I for one have not lost my faith in the core of the socialist ideal, which is much closer to the social-democratic, rather than Bolshevik, variety. Nor can I fully renounce Marxism despite all the new experiences of my

country. I have never been a Marxist fanatic; nor have I been very dili-
gent in my study of works by the founders, even as a student. Some
elements of Marxism seemed to me obsolete, dull, or irrelevant to real
life, but I do respect quite a few Marxist works and ideas. I include not
only the "founding fathers" of Marxism but also outstanding leaders of
the Socialist International, as well as people like Antonio Gramsci, Gy-
örgy Lukács, Ernst Bloch, and Herbert Marcuse.

Of course, Marxism cannot be held responsible for the political follies
perpetrated in its name or for the fact that it was turned into an official
state ideology and even a state religion.

Law-and-order advocates see perestroika as the source of the suffering that accompanies the death throes of the old society and the birth of
a new one. They maintain that the reforms should not have been started
at all. But whatever they may say, the totalitarian system carried within
it the seeds of its own downfall. It was not a viable system to begin with,
at least not for the long term. It was not viable economically or politically because it did not provide real economic incentives and destroyed
or removed capable people from leadership positions, leading to erosion
of the country's intellectual potential, especially at the elite level. It was
not viable socially because oppression of nationalities and trampling
upon human rights and freedoms were creating internal strains that
were destined to break out into the open. But it was (and, to a degree,
still is) within the power of the political leadership either to make the
process of the system's disintegration less painful and destructive or to
exacerbate its chaotic and calamitous potential.

We lost, perhaps inevitably, our first chance to influence this process
constructively and in a humane way in the late 1950s and early 1960s.
Perestroika gave us another chance to reduce the destructive potential of
our systemic disintegration: to move more steadily toward democracy
and satisfaction of the republics' national aspirations, toward implemen-
tation of gradual economic and political reforms. Unfortunately, that
opportunity was largely lost, and Gorbachev, despite all his past merits,
bears a large share of responsibility. Of course he had to maneuver, to
play complicated tactical games, because the reforms were confronted by
very strong opposition. But it is Gorbachev's fault that, having become
general secretary, having inherited awesome power that thrived on the
fear ingrained in most of us since the horrors of Stalinism, he did not use
this power for the public good. But here, to be fair, we must acknowl-

edge not only Gorbachev's responsibility but that of his democratic allies—people like Alexander Yakovlev, Eduard Shevardnadze, as well as those at lower levels, like me.

Despite all the sporadic and sometimes courageous acts of resistance we have not been effective enough in the practical work of organizing a strong democratic movement that could have served as the basis of reform. We have spent too much time and energy arguing among ourselves instead of fighting jointly against our common enemies.

In conclusion I would like to return to the question raised in the beginning of the postscript: Will we still be able to salvage whatever remains of this second chance, a chance not only to destroy the vestiges of the totalitarian past but also to build a society that can become prosperous, ensure the well-being of its people, and contribute scientific, technological, cultural, and rational solutions to the world's problems?

At the moment the answer to this critical question seems to lie in our ability to pull ourselves out of the present economic crisis. We can do it if we do not stubbornly pursue false policies and are able to draw the proper lessons from our recent experience. As it is being written, our economic policy remains disappointing. It has already become a real Achilles heel during this first stage of our post-Communist development. The failure of the economic reforms may bring about the restoration of authoritarian or even totalitarian rule.

Even a moderate success with the economy would help us to resolve other major problems and secure the future of the Commonwealth. If we avoid the dangers of nationalism (the bigger the state that falls into this trap, the more devastating the consequences can be) and if all the former republics become independent and do not fear the imperial ambitions of their neighbors, there will be more room for the national interests of all the states to play their role. These interests, as we have seen in Western Europe, would eventually push the countries toward integration—at first economically, then politically.

In a proper international environment all of these steps may lead us to a decent future. The former Soviet Union is at a very complex and unpredictable point in its history. The totalitarian empire is gone—most likely, forever. It is not clear how the transformation of its successor states will go—smoothly or convulsively, at what cost and pain. But Russia and all the other independent states that constituted the Soviet

Union simply cannot disappear from the map and world history. Their renaissance is just a matter of time and human effort. It is in the interest of my country and the whole world community that both the time and the cost be minimal.

INDEX